Lecture Notes in
Computer Scien

Edited by G. Goos

217

Programs as Data Obj

Proceedings of a Workshop
Copenhagen, Denmark, October 198

Edited by H. Ganzinger and N.D. Jones

Springer-Verla
Berlin Heidelberg New York T

Lecture Notes in Computer Science

Vol. 117: Fundamentals of Computation Theory. Proceedings, 1981. Edited by F. Gécseg. XI, 471 pages. 1981.

Vol. 118: Mathematical Foundations of Computer Science 1981. Proceedings, 1981. Edited by J. Gruska and M. Chytil. XI, 589 pages. 1981.

Vol. 119: G. Hirst, Anaphora in Natural Language Understanding: A Survey. XIII, 128 pages. 1981.

Vol. 120: L. B. Rall, Automatic Differentiation: Techniques and Applications. VIII, 165 pages. 1981.

Vol. 121: Z. Zlatev, J. Wasniewski, and K. Schaumburg, Y12M Solution of Large and Sparse Systems of Linear Algebraic Equations. IX, 128 pages. 1981.

Vol. 122: Algorithms in Modern Mathematics and Computer Science. Proceedings, 1979. Edited by A. P. Ershov and D. E. Knuth. XI, 487 pages. 1981.

Vol. 123: Trends in Information Processing Systems. Proceedings, 1981. Edited by A. J. W. Duijvestijn and P. C. Lockemann. XI, 349 pages. 1981.

Vol. 124: W. Polak, Compiler Specification and Verification. XIII, 269 pages. 1981.

Vol. 125: Logic of Programs. Proceedings, 1979. Edited by E. Engeler. V, 245 pages. 1981.

Vol. 126: Microcomputer System Design. Proceedings, 1981. Edited by M. J. Flynn, N. R. Harris, and D. P. McCarthy. VII, 397 pages. 1982.

Voll. 127: Y.Wallach, Alternating Sequential/Parallel Processing. X, 329 pages. 1982.

Vol. 128: P. Branquart, G. Louis, P. Wodon, An Analytical Description of CHILL, the CCITT High Level Language. VI, 277 pages. 1982.

Vol. 129: B. T. Hailpern, Verifying Concurrent Processes Using Temporal Logic. VIII, 208 pages. 1982.

Vol. 130: R. Goldblatt, Axiomatising the Logic of Computer Programming. XI, 304 pages. 1982.

Vol. 131: Logics of Programs. Proceedings, 1981. Edited by D. Kozen. VI, 429 pages. 1982.

Vol. 132: Data Base Design Techniques I: Requirements and Logical Structures. Proceedings, 1978. Edited by S.B. Yao, S.B. Navathe, J.L. Weldon, and T.L. Kunii. V, 227 pages. 1982.

Vol. 133: Data Base Design Techniques II: Proceedings, 1979. Edited by S.B. Yao and T.L. Kunii. V, 229–399 pages. 1982.

Vol. 134: Program Specification. Proceedings, 1981. Edited by J. Staunstrup. IV, 426 pages. 1982.

Vol. 135: R.L. Constable, S.D. Johnson, and C.D. Eichenlaub, An Introduction to the PL/CV2 Programming Logic. X, 292 pages. 1982.

Vol. 136: Ch. M. Hoffmann, Group-Theoretic Algorithms and Graph Isomorphism. VIII, 311 pages. 1982.

Vol. 137: International Symposium on Programming. Proceedings, 1982. Edited by M. Dezani-Ciancaglini and M. Montanari. VI, 406 pages. 1982.

Vol. 138: 6th Conference on Automated Deduction. Proceedings, 1982. Edited by D.W. Loveland. VII, 389 pages. 1982.

Vol. 139: J. Uhl, S. Drossopoulou, G. Persch, G. Goos, M. Dausmann, G. Winterstein, W. Kirchgässner, An Attribute Grammar for the Semantic Analysis of Ada. IX, 511 pages. 1982.

Vol. 140: Automata, Languages and programming. Edited by M. Nielsen and E.M. Schmidt. VII, 614 pages. 1982.

Vol. 141: U. Kastens, B. Hutt, E. Zimmermann, GAG: A Practical Compiler Generator. IV, 156 pages. 1982.

Vol. 142: Problems and Methodologies in Mathematical Software Production. Proceedings, 1980. Edited by P.C. Messina and A. Murli. VII, 271 pages. 1982.

Vol. 143: Operating Systems Engineering. Proceedings, 1980. Edited by M. Maekawa and L.A. Belady. VII, 465 pages. 1982.

Vol. 144: Computer Algebra. Proceedings, 1982. Edited by J. Calmet. XIV, 301 pages. 1982.

Vol. 145: Theoretical Computer Science. Proceedings, 1983. Edited by A.B. Cremers and H.P. Kriegel. X, 367 pages. 1982.

Vol. 146: Research and Development in Information Retrieval. Proceedings, 1982. Edited by G. Salton and H.-J. Schneider. IX, 311 pages. 1983.

Vol. 147: RIMS Symposia on Software Science and Engineering. Proceedings, 1982. Edited by E. Goto, I. Nakata, K. Furukawa, R. Nakajima, and A. Yonezawa. V. 232 pages. 1983.

Vol. 148: Logics of Programs and Their Applications. Proceedings, 1980. Edited by A. Salwicki. VI, 324 pages. 1983.

Vol. 149: Cryptography. Proceedings, 1982. Edited by T. Beth. VIII, 402 pages. 1983.

Vol. 150: Enduser Systems and Their Human Factors. Proceedings, 1983. Edited by A. Blaser and M. Zoeppritz. III, 138 pages. 1983.

Vol. 151: R. Piloty, M. Barbacci, D. Borrione, D. Dietmeyer, F. Hill, and P. Skelly, CONLAN Report. XII, 174 pages. 1983.

Vol. 152: Specification and Design of Software Systems. Proceedings, 1982. Edited by E. Knuth and E. J. Neuhold. V, 152 pages. 1983.

Vol. 153: Graph-Grammars and Their Application to Computer Science. Proceedings, 1982. Edited by H. Ehrig, M. Nagl, and G. Rozenberg. VII, 452 pages. 1983.

Vol. 154: Automata, Languages and Programming. Proceedings, 1983. Edited by J. Díaz. VIII, 734 pages. 1983.

Vol. 155: The Programming Language Ada. Reference Manual. Approved 17 February 1983. American National Standards Institute, Inc. ANSI/MIL-STD-1815A-1983. IX, 331 pages. 1983.

Vol. 156: M.H. Overmars, The Design of Dynamic Data Structures. VII, 181 pages. 1983.

Vol. 157: O. Østerby, Z. Zlatev, Direct Methods for Sparse Matrices. VIII, 127 pages. 1983.

Vol. 158: Foundations of Computation Theory. Proceedings, 1983. Edited by M. Karpinski, XI, 517 pages. 1983.

Vol. 159: CAAP'83. Proceedings, 1983. Edited by G. Ausiello and M. Protasi. VI, 416 pages. 1983.

Vol. 160: The IOTA Programming System. Edited by R. Nakajima and T. Yuasa. VII, 217 pages. 1983.

Vol. 161: DIANA, An Intermediate Language for Ada. Edited by G. Goos, W.A. Wulf, A. Evans, Jr. and K.J. Butler. VII, 201 pages. 1983.

Vol. 162: Computer Algebra. Proceedings, 1983. Edited by J.A. van Hulzen. XIII, 305 pages. 1983.

Vol. 163: VLSI Engineering. Proceedings. Edited by T.L. Kunii. VIII, 308 pages. 1984.

Vol. 164: Logics of Programs. Proceedings, 1983. Edited by E. Clarke and D. Kozen. VI, 528 pages. 1984.

Vol. 165: T.F. Coleman, Large Sparse Numerical Optimization. V, 105 pages. 1984.

Vol. 166: STACS 84. Symposium of Theoretical Aspects of Computer Science. Proceedings, 1984. Edited by M. Fontet and K. Mehlhorn. VI, 338 pages. 1984.

Lecture Notes in Computer Science

Edited by G. Goos and J. Hartmanis

217

Programs as Data Objects

Proceedings of a Workshop
Copenhagen, Denmark, October 17–19, 1985

Edited by H. Ganzinger and N. D. Jones

Springer-Verlag
Berlin Heidelberg New York Tokyo

Editors

Harald Ganzinger
Fachbereich Informatik, Universität Dortmund
Postfach 500500, D-4600 Dortmund 50

Neil D. Jones
DIKU
Universitets Parken 1, DK-2100 Copenhagen Ø

The Workshop was organized by Neil D. Jones

CR Subject Classifications (1985): D.3.1, D.3.4, F.3, I.2.2

ISBN 3-540-16446-4 Springer-Verlag Berlin Heidelberg New York Tokyo
ISBN 0-387-16446-4 Springer-Verlag New York Heidelberg Berlin Tokyo

Printing and binding: Beltz Offsetdruck, Hemsbach/Bergstr.
2145/3140-543210

PREFACE

There has been a nearly explosive growth in the usage of computers over the past twenty years, especially in the last decade due to the advent of microcomputers. On the other hand, the increase in the number of qualified computer scientists has been much less. The result has been the now well-known "software crisis".

An obvious solution, but one which is still somewhat in advance of the state of the art, is to use the computer itself as a tool, to produce and maintain software on a large scale with minimal human intervention. In particular, we need to be able to treat programs *en masse* - as members of collections rather than as individuals (similar changes of viewpoint had to occur with the introduction of both agriculture and mass production).

Unfortunately, programming as now practiced is at best a well-developed handcraft. In the last decade we have learned some techniques which allow faster development of more reliable and user-friendly programs than could be done before, but program development is still far from an assembly line process. Aside from compilers, text editors and file systems, there are in fact very few computer-based tools to facilitate program construction and maintenance.

What is needed is a wide range of flexible tools which can be used to manipulate programs - tools which treat programs as *data objects,* which can be executed, analyzed, synthesized, transformed, verified and optimized. Treatment of programs as data is far from trivial, though, since programs are objects which carry *meanings*. Program meanings are rather complex, and can only be discussed in relation to the *semantics* of the programming language in which they are written.

Consequently, development of truly powerful program manipulation tools will require a deeper understanding of semantics and its relation to possible principles for systematic and automatic program construction. This new understanding is analogous to the new insights in physics and engineering that had to be developed before the first automobile factories based on the assembly line and mass production could be built.

The theme of this workshop was "Programs as Data Objects", and it will be seen that all the papers in this proceedings are concerned with the problems just mentioned. Some address the development of methods for automatic construction, transformation and analysis of programs, others introduce new programming constructs which it is hoped will aid the construction and manipulation of large-scale, high-level programs, and others formulate and solve mathematical questions which are directly relevant to treating programs as data.

Most of the papers are concerned with functional programming languages. Only a few years ago a book with the same title would have exclusively been concerned with compiler-writing systems oriented around more traditional imperative languages and compiler-writing systems (based on, for example, parser generators and attribute grammar evaluators). It has become clear in practice, though, that one needs more than tools for syntax analysis and computation and management of the values used during compilation (although these are indispensible, and their successful automation has been a very big step forward).

One needs as well a precise understanding of the semantics of the programming languages involved in order to construct program manipulation systems such as compilers, verifiers, intelligent editors and program synthesizers. It is here that functional languages have significant advantages, for they have shown themselves to be more tractable and in general easier to transform and analyze, due to their relatively simple semantics in comparison with the more traditional imperative languages.

The papers in this collection fall into several natural groups. Two papers, those by Bellegarde and Wadler, are concerned with program transformation with the aim of more efficient implementation. Bellegarde addresses the problem of transforming programs written in John Backus' FP language into equivalent ones which use less intermediate storage. She shows that this may be done by using algorithms from the theory and practice of term rewriting systems to rewrite programs. Wadler showed (in an earlier article) how to transform programs written in a lazy functional language into much more efficient *listless* ones resembling finite automata, using Turchin's "driving" algorithm. In the current paper he shows that a large class of listless programs may be constructed from basic ones by symbolic composition, and shows how to integrate execution of listless programs with the usual graph reduction implementation techniques.

The papers by Ganzinger and Giegerich address the question of how one may develop formal specifications of compilers and interpreters by means of small, relatively independent and loosely coupled modules (in contrast with the large, monolithic, unstructured language specifications all too often seen in practice). Further, they show how logic programming may be used to develop prototype implementations directly from the specifications. The papers differ in their choice of problem areas, and in the prototyping techniques they use.

Christiansen describes parsing and compilation techniques for "generative languages", a class of extensible languages with powerful abstraction mechanisms and a wide range of binding times which generalize some aspects of denotational semantics and attribute grammars.

Nordström shows that the multilevel arrays which have been used in the VDL and VDM projects may be generalized to allow *multilevel functions*, and that this rather general class may be formalized within the framework of Martin-Löf's highly constructive type theory. He then shows that a number of familiar data structures and algorithms may be naturally expressed in terms of multilevel functions.

Program flow analysis is a well-established technique for program analysis, which has its roots in methods developed for highly optimizing compilers for imperative languages. It is largely based on *abstract interpretation, i.e.* the execution of programs over nonstandard domains of data values which describe the sets of data on which the program may be run. Nielson's paper is concerned with making a rather general framework he developed earlier more usable for practical applications. He shows that "safe" data flow analysis may be done by using any of several *expected forms;* these are more natural and easily computable than the more precise "induced" flow analyses which come out of his general framework.

Burn, Hankin and Abramsky develop a mathematically elegant and very general framework for the flow analysis of the typed lambda calculus, using categories and power domains, and show that strictness analysis (discussed below) is in fact a very natural abstract interpretation over finite lattice structures. One outcome is a surprisingly simple and efficient algorithm for strictness analysis.

Mycroft and Jones show that a wide variety of flow analyses of the lambda calculus (not necessarily typed) may be naturally regarded as *interpretations* within a common semantic framework, and show how one may use relations to compare one interpretation with another. As an application, they show that soundness of the polymorphic type system of Milner, Damas and others may be established by showing that it abstracts the standard call-by-name interpretation.

In all, four papers are concerned with the problem of determining whether a given argument of a given defined function is *strict*, meaning that undefinedness of the argument will imply undefinedness of the function's value. One reason for doing strictness analysis is for efficient implementation of functional languages: a strict argument may be evaluated prior to calling the given function, thus avoiding the often significant overhead involved in sending arguments "by name" or "by need". Further, the results obtained in these papers have wider implications than may be apparent from the problem description. An important reason is that strictness analysis is the simplest natural nontrivial flow analysis of lazy higher order functional languages (a class whose popularity is growing rapidly). As such, it points the way to further, more sophisticated flow analyses which could aid materially in implementing these powerful and concise languages with high efficiency.

The paper by Maurer extends earlier results by Mycroft. It presents a method using abstract interpretation of the lambda calculus over a domain of "need expressions", and gives algorithms for constructing safe approximations to a lambda expression's strictness properties. Burn, Hankin and Abramsky develop (as mentioned above) a framework for strictness analysis of the typed lambda calculus.

Hughes extends the strictness question to structured data, and derives *evaluation contexts* from a first-order program; expressions which describe those substructures of a structured data object which actually must be available in order to evaluate a given program. This is particularly relevant to programs that manipulate conceptually infinite data structures, *e.g.* communication streams within an operating system.

Finally, Abramsky shows a very elegant result: that nearly any program property of computational interest is *polymorphically invariant.* One consequence is that many familiar program analysis algorithms which have been developed to handle the monomorphic case can be carried over to polymorphic programs. In particular, the techniques of Burns, Hankin and Abramsky can be applied, essentially without change, to the polymorphic lambda calculus.

The last group of papers can be described as steps towards semantics-directed compiler generation. Nielson and Nielson show how machine code may be generated for semantic definitions written using the two-level metalanguage they developed in previous papers. This indicates the possibility of using data flow information in automatic compiler generation from denotational semantics.

Sestoft describes the techniques used by MIX, a *partial evaluation* system which can been used for compilation. MIX has also been self-applied to achieve compiler generation and even compiler generator generation (the last was done by using MIX to partially evaluate the MIX program, when run on itself as known input!).

Turchin's work centers about the concept of *metasystem transition,* in which one program performs an analysis of the behavior of another program written in the same language. This leads to the possibility of self-application. Turchin was the first to understand that triple self-application can, in principle, yield a compiler generator, and MIX was its first realization on the computer. The paper here is concerned with *supercompilation,* a powerful program transformation technique capable of partial evaluation, compilation, data structure analysis and other operations on programs.

Schmidt outlines a strategy for converting a "direct" denotational semantics into a compiler from the language it defines into stack code. Particular attention is paid to the question of serializing the store, to attain reasonable efficiency on traditional Von Neuman architectures. Wand addresses similar problems using a continuation-based semantics, and describes a systematic way to transform a language definition in the form of an interpreter written in an applicative language into a compiler producing efficient code using the familiar stack-offset addressing of data.

The workshop "Programs as Data Objects" was held October 17-19, 1985. It was made possible by two Danish grants, one from the Natural Science Research Council and one from the the Ministry of Education's "Pool for International Contacts in Computer Science" (Statens naturvidenskabelige Forskningsråd og DVUs "pulje for internationale kontakter i datalogi"). The workshop was conceived in a conversation with Harald Ganzinger; it was planned and organized by the undersigned, and editing of the papers was done jointly with Harald Ganzinger. The University of Dortmund printed preliminary conference proceedings for the participants, and DIKU (the department of Computer Science at the University of Copenhagen) provided reproduction facilities and secretarial help. Local arrangements were handled by Gunvor Howard (thanks for an outstanding job, Gunvor!). The contributions of a number of individuals are warmly acknowledged, including: Nils Andersen, Klaus Grue, Peter Sestoft and Harald Søndergaard.

Neil D. Jones
November 1985
Copenhagen, Denmark

Contents

Strictness Analysis And Polymorphic Invariance
(EXTENDED ABSTRACT)

Samson Abramsky

Imperial College of Science and Technology
180 Queen's Gate, London SW7 2BZ

1. Introduction

Consider a programming language L in which we can form expressions which denote functions. Recall that a function is said to be *strict* if its result is undefined whenever its argument is undefined. Suppose we had a test which we could apply to functional expressions to determine if they denote strict functions. There is a clear conflict between two desiderata on such a test, namely accuracy and effectiveness. No test for strictness which yields exact answers can be a recursive predicate on expressions, by standard results of computability theory. On the other hand, if we are to *use* such a test in practice, e.g. for compile-time optimisation, then effectiveness is essential. A satisfactory compromise is obtained by relaxing our correctness requirement on the test to *soundness* or *safety*; we ask that whenever an expression satisfies the test, the function it denotes is indeed strict, but accept that the test may be *incomplete*, in the sense that it does not detect some cases of strictness. *Strictness analysis* then refers to any safe, computable analysis of this form. The value of strictness analysis in providing information which may lead to important optimisations in both sequential and parallel implementations of functional languages is by now quite well established - see e.g. [CPJ]. The original work on strictness analysis was done by Mycroft [Myc]. The programming language he considered was that of first-order recursion equations over flat domains. Subsequently, strictness analysis has been extended to higher-order functions in [BHA], where a detailed treatment of the mathematical foundations, and a proof of soundness is given. In the present paper, we are concerned with an important extension to the work of [BHA]. The programming language considered there was the typed λ-calculus, e.g. expressions such as

$$\lambda f^{A \to A}.\lambda x^{A}.f(f(x))$$

In this language, every expression is rigidly typed, and the types are *finite*, built up from given base types by constructions such as → (function types). This finiteness of types was important in [BHA], since it ensured the finiteness of the abstract domains used in the strictness analysis developed there, and hence its effectiveness. The motivation for the present work arises from two limitations of [BHA]:

(1) The syntax of the typed λ-calculus is rather restrictive. Most current functional programming languages have some form of typing; however, this usually takes the form of the much more flexible *polymorphic* type discipline introduced by Milner [Mil].

(2) While the strictness analysis described in [BHA] is certainly computable, its feasibility is called into question because of the rate of growth of the size of the abstract domains as we go up the types.

We are led by these specific problems to introduce a rather general notion - what we call *polymorphic invariance*. As a consequence of the fact that strictness analysis is a polymorphic invariant, we obtain promising answers for (1) and (2) above. Firstly, we get a simple reduction of strictness analysis for polymorphic functions to strictness analysis for the typed λ-calculus. Secondly, by means of this reduction it should be possible in practice to confine applications of the strictness analysis algorithm to low-order types.

In the next section, we shall define the syntax of the λ-calculi we shall be dealing with, and introduce the notion of polymorphic invariance. In section 3, we prove that strictness analysis is a polymorphic invariant. Section 4 develops an approach to strictness analysis for polymorphic functions based on this result.

2. Polymorphic Invariance

2.1. Syntax Of Types

We assume a fixed countable set of *type variables* ranged over by α, β. We also assume given a set of *base types*, ranged over by A, B. Then the syntax of *type expressions*, ranged over by τ, υ, is:

$$\tau ::= \alpha \mid A \mid \tau \to \upsilon.$$

A *monotype* is a type expression in which no type variables occur. We use μ, ν to range over monotypes.

A *type substitution*

$$[\tau_1/\alpha_1, \ldots, \tau_n/\alpha_n] \ (n \geq 0)$$

(to be read "α_i is replaced by τ_i") is a mapping from type variables to type expressions. We use R, S, V to range over type substitutions, which may be extended canonically to maps from type expressions to type expressions. We write Id for the identity substitution, $S\tau$ for the application of S to τ, and RS for composition of substitutions. A *ground substitution* maps variables, and hence type expressions, to monotypes. We use G, H to range over ground substitutions.

We now assume a standard countable set of *(individual) variables* (disjoint from type variables), ranged over by x,y,z,f,g. A *type environment* or *assumption* Γ is a partial function, with finite domain of definition, from variables to type expressions. We write **dom** Γ for the domain of definition of Γ, and $\Gamma(x)$ for application of Γ to x ($x \in \mathbf{dom}\,\Gamma$). A useful operation on type assumptions is *extension*: $\Gamma,x{:}\upsilon$ defined by

$$\mathbf{dom}\ \Gamma,x{:}\upsilon = \mathbf{dom}\ \Gamma \cup \{x\}$$

$$\Gamma,x{:}\upsilon(x) = \upsilon$$

$$\Gamma,x{:}\upsilon(y) = \Gamma(y) \quad (y \in \mathbf{dom}\ \Gamma,\ y \neq x)$$

Thus type assumptions can be displayed as lists

$$x_1{:}\upsilon_1, \ldots, x_k{:}\upsilon_k \quad (k \geq 0).$$

2.2. Syntax Of Typed λ-Calculus

A *language* is given by the following data:

(i) A set of base types - this determines the set of type expressions as in (2.1).

(ii) A set of constants, ranged over by c.

(iii) A function π from constants to type expressions; $\pi(c)$ is the (polymorphic) type of c.

Example

(i) **int bool**

(ii) **Y succ pred cond 0 tt ff zero?**

(iii) $\pi(\mathbf{Y}) = (\alpha \rightarrow \alpha) \rightarrow \alpha$

$\pi(\mathbf{cond}) = \mathbf{bool} \rightarrow \alpha \rightarrow \alpha \rightarrow \alpha$

$\pi(\mathbf{succ}) = \pi(\mathbf{pred}) = \mathbf{int} \rightarrow \mathbf{int}$

$\pi(\mathbf{zero?}) = \mathbf{int} \rightarrow \mathbf{bool}$

$\pi(\mathbf{tt}) = \pi(\mathbf{ff}) = \mathbf{bool}$

We now give an inference system for assertions of the form $\Gamma \vdash_L t{:}\tau$, to be read: "t is a term of type τ (on assumptions Γ) over the language L". This system will implicitly define the well-formed typed terms, which are ranged over by t, u.

(VAR) $\Gamma \vdash_L x{:}\tau \quad (x \in \mathbf{dom}\ \Gamma,\ \Gamma(x)=\tau)$

(CON) $\Gamma \vdash_L c^{\tau}{:}\tau \quad (\exists S.\ \tau = S \circ \pi(c))$

$$\text{(ABS)}\quad \frac{\Gamma, x{:}\tau \vdash_L t{:}\upsilon}{\Gamma \vdash_L \lambda x^{\tau}.t{:}\tau \to \upsilon}$$

$$\text{(APP)}\quad \frac{\Gamma \vdash_L t{:}\upsilon \to \tau \quad \Gamma \vdash_L u{:}\upsilon}{\Gamma \vdash_L tu{:}\tau}$$

Definition

FV(t), the set of free variables occuring in t, is defined as usual:

$FV(x)=\{x\}$

$FV(c^{\tau})=\varnothing$

$FV(\lambda x^{\tau}.t)=FV(t)-\{x\}$

$FV(tu)=FV(t)\cup FV(u)$.

Fact

(i) Given Γ, t there is at most one τ such that $\Gamma \vdash_L t{:}\tau$.

(ii) $\Gamma \vdash_L t{:}\tau \Rightarrow FV(t) \subseteq \mathbf{dom}\,\Gamma$.

In the light of (ii), we shall say that Γ is *canonical* for t when $\Gamma \vdash_L t{:}\tau$ and $FV(t)=\mathbf{dom}\,\Gamma$.

We now define the *typed* (and *monotyped*) expressions over L:

$\Lambda_T(L) = \{(\Gamma)t \mid \exists\tau.\Gamma \vdash_L t{:}\tau\}$

$\Lambda_M(L) = \{(\Gamma)t \in \Lambda_T(L) \mid$ all types occuring in Γ or t are monotypes$\}$

Thus objects in $\Lambda_T(L)$ have the form

$(x_1{:}\upsilon_1, \ldots, x_k{:}\upsilon_k)t$

where $FV(t) \subseteq \{x_1, \ldots, x_k\}$. The overall type of such an object is uniquely determined according to (i) above.

A term t is *closed* if $FV(t)=\varnothing$. We write t rather than $()t$ for closed terms.

2.3. Untyped λ-calculus

We now define $\Lambda(L)$, the untyped λ-calculus over a language L. We use e to range over $\Lambda(L)$.

$e ::= x \mid c \mid \lambda x.e \mid ee'$

(Thus $\Lambda(L)$ depends only on the set of constants from L.)

We shall now take advantage of our formulation of the typed λ-calculus to express connections with the untyped calculus in a succinct fashion.

2.4. Definition

We define a map

$$\epsilon : \Lambda_T(L) \rightarrow \Lambda(L)$$

$$\epsilon((\Gamma)t) = (t)^*$$

where

$$(x)^* = x$$

$$(c^\tau)^* = c$$

$$(\lambda x^\tau.t)^* = \lambda x.(t)^*$$

$$(tt')^* = (t)^*(t')^*$$

Examples

(*i*) $\epsilon(\lambda x^A.x) = \lambda x.x$

(*ii*) $\epsilon((x{:}A \rightarrow A)\lambda y^B.x) = \lambda y.x$

2.5. Definition (The *typed instances* of an untyped expression):

$$TI : \Lambda(L) \rightarrow P(\Lambda_T(L))$$

$$TI(e) = \{(\Gamma)t \in \Lambda_T(L) \mid \epsilon((\Gamma)t) = e\}$$

and similarly the *monotype instances:*

$$MTI : \Lambda(L) \rightarrow P(\Lambda_M(L))$$

$$MTI(e) = \{(\Gamma)t \in \Lambda_M(L) \mid \epsilon((\Gamma)t) = e\}$$

We also define the typed instances of e relative to type assumptions Γ:

$$TI((\Gamma)e) = \{(S\Gamma)t \in \Lambda_T(L) \mid S \text{ a type substitution}, \epsilon((S\Gamma)t) = e\}$$

and similarly for $MTI((\Gamma)e)$.

From a naive point of view, we may think of a polymorphic function, described by an untyped expression e, as an ambiguous notation for the *set* of its monotyped instances. When we apply the function in an actual computation, the ultimate effect is that data of a determinate base type is produced, so we can regard each application as one of the monotype instances. This suggests that sets of typed terms of the form $MTI(e)$ for some (untyped) e are linked in a semantically natural fashion, and that nice properties of typed terms should be invariant over such sets.

2.6. Definition (Polymorphic Invariance)

Let P be a property of (mono-)typed terms over a language L, i.e. $P \subseteq \Lambda_M(L)$. P is a *polymorphic invariant* if

$$\forall e \in \Lambda(L).\, \forall t_1,t_2 \in MTI(e).\, t_1 \in P \Leftrightarrow t_2 \in P$$

or, equivalently

$$\forall e \in \Lambda(L).\, MTI(e) \subseteq P \vee MTI(e) \cap P = \emptyset.$$

This says that for any untyped expression e, P must hold either for *all* its monotyped instances, or for none. E.g. if strictness is a polymorphic invariant, all or no monotype instances of the identity function must denote strict functions (in fact, all do).

Polymorphic invariance is a very general notion. An example of a property which is *not* a polymorphic invariant is "... denotes a finite element". With the example language of 2.2 under the standard interpretation, $\lambda x^{\mathrm{bool}}.x$ satisifies this property, while $\lambda x^{\mathrm{int}}.x$ does not. Note that the polymorphic invariants, considered as a subclass of the powerset of typed terms, are stable under the Boolean operations, and form an uncountable set with uncountable complement. We may pose the following problem:

> Give conditions on L and P which are necessary and/or sufficient for P to be a polymorphic invariant.

It remains to be seen if this problem is of any general theoretical interest. Some motivation for considering it will emerge in Section 4.

Our present concern is with the specific case of strictness analysis. In the next section, we shall formulate the strictness analysis test for typed λ-calculus, and prove that it is a polymorphic invariant.

3. Strictness Analysis Is A Polymorphic Invariant

First, some preliminary notation.

We assume standard notions of free and bound variables and substitution for the λ-calculus (typed and untyped) - see [Bar]. We write

$$t[t_1/x_1, \ldots, t_n/x_n] \quad (\text{resp. } e[e_1/x_1, \ldots, e_n/x_n])$$

for the result of performing substitution of t_i (resp. e_i) for x_i in t (resp. e), $i=1,\ldots,k$, with the standard provisos for avoiding variable capture by renaming.

Application associates to the left:

$$e_1e_2\cdots e_n \quad \text{means} \quad (\cdots(e_1e_2)\cdots e_n).$$

Function type construction associates to the right:

$$\tau_1\to\tau_2\to\cdots\to\tau_n \quad \text{means} \quad \tau_1\to(\tau_2\to\cdots(\tau_{n-1}\to\tau_n)\cdots).$$

Note that every monotype may be written in the form

$$\mu_1\to\cdots\mu_n\to A \quad (n\geq 0).$$

We recall Martin-Lof's notation for dependent types [ML]:
If A is a set and $\{B_a\}_{a\in A}$ an A-indexed family of sets, then:

$$(i)\ (\Pi x\in A)B(x) = \{f : A\to\cup_{a\in A}B_a \mid \forall a\in A. f(a)\in B_a\}.$$

$$(ii)\ (\Sigma x\in A)B(x) = \{\langle a,b\rangle \mid a\in A \ \&\ b\in B_a\}.$$

Now we shall define the non-standard semantics of the typed λ-calculus on which strictness analysis is based. We assume familiarity with elementary domain theory and denotational semantics, as in e.g. [Sto].

(1) Firstly, we have a language, L_{SA}, as follows:

- there is a single base type A
- the constants in L_{SA} are **and**, **or**, Y, 1, 0
- $\pi(\mathbf{and}) = \pi(\mathbf{or}) = A\to A\to A$
  $\pi(0) = \pi(1) = \alpha$
  $\pi(Y) = (\alpha\to\alpha)\to\alpha$

Thus we have constants 0^μ, 1^μ, $Y^{(\mu\to\mu)\to\mu}$ for each μ.

(2) Next, we define a domain B_μ for each monotype μ.

$$B_A = 2 \quad (=\{0,1\},\ 0\leq 1)$$

$$B_{\mu\to\nu} = B_\mu\to B_\nu.$$

Fact

Each B_μ is a finite complete lattice, with bottom element $\perp_\mu$ and top element $\top_\mu$.

(3) We define an interpretation $K(c^\mu)\in B_\mu$ for each constant in L_{SA}.

K(**and**) and K(**or**) are the standard truth-table definitions over 2:

$$K(\mathbf{and})00 = K(\mathbf{and})10 = K(\mathbf{and})01 = 0$$

$\mathbf{K}(\mathbf{and})11 = 1$

$\mathbf{K}(\mathbf{or})00 = 0$

$\mathbf{K}(\mathbf{or})10 = \mathbf{K}(\mathbf{or})01 = \mathbf{K}(\mathbf{or})11 = 1$

$\mathbf{K}(1^{\mu}) = \top_{\mu}$, $\mathbf{K}(0^{\mu}) = \bot_{\mu}$, each μ

$\mathbf{K}(\mathbf{Y}^{(\mu\to\mu)\to\mu})$ is the least fixpoint operator over $B_{\mu}\to B_{\mu}$:

$$\mathbf{K}(\mathbf{Y}^{(\mu\to\mu)\to\mu})(f) = \bigsqcup_{n=0}^{\infty} f^{(n)}(\bot_{\mu}).$$

(4) We now extend $\mathbf{K}$ to an interpretation for all terms in $\Lambda_M(L_{SA})$. Let MTA be the set of all type assumptions Γ such that $\Gamma(x)$ is a monotype for each $x \in \mathbf{dom}\,\Gamma$.

$$Env \equiv (\Pi\Gamma \in MTA)(\Pi x \in \mathbf{dom}\,\Gamma) B_{\Gamma(x)}$$

Thus $\rho \in Env(\Gamma)$ maps each $x \in \mathbf{dom}\,\Gamma$ to an element of $B_{\Gamma(x)}$.

We need the operation of *updating* an environment. If $\rho \in Env(\Gamma)$, $d \in B_{\mu}$, then

$$\rho[x \mapsto d] \in Env(\Gamma, x{:}\mu)$$

where

$$\rho[x \mapsto d]x = d$$

$$\rho[x \mapsto d]y = \rho y \quad (y \in \mathbf{dom}\,\Gamma,\ y \neq x).$$

Now we define:

$$tabs : (\Pi(\Gamma) t{:}\mu \in \Lambda_M(L_{SA}))(\Pi\rho \in Env(\Gamma)) B_{\mu}$$

$$tabs[\![x]\!]\rho = \rho x$$

$$tabs[\![c^{\mu}]\!]\rho = \mathbf{K}(c^{\mu})$$

$$tabs[\![\lambda x^{\mu}.t]\!]\rho = \lambda\xi \in B_{\mu}.tabs[\![t]\!]\rho[x \mapsto \xi]$$

$$tabs[\![tt']\!]\rho = (tabs[\![t]\!]\rho)(tabs[\![t']\!]\rho)$$

Note that there is a unique type assumption $\Gamma_{\varnothing}$ with $\mathbf{dom}\,\Gamma_{\varnothing} = \varnothing$. Correspondingly, there is a unique environment Ω in $Env(\Gamma_{\varnothing})$. Closed terms can always be evaluated relative to Ω.

We now describe how to use $\Lambda_M(L_{SA})$ to do strictness analysis. Suppose we are given a language L, and a standard semantics for $\Lambda_M(L)$. We assume that each constant of L can be "safely represented" by a term in $\Lambda_M(L_{SA})$. This is made precise in [BHA], where a number of cases are dealt with explicitly. In particular, we have:

(i) Every strict first-order function

$$f : A_1 \to \cdots \to A_n \to B$$

$$f\, a_1 \cdots a_n = \perp_B \text{ if } \exists i{:}1 \leq i \leq n.\, a_i = \perp_{A_i}$$

can be safely represented by

$$\lambda x_1^A. \cdots \lambda x_n^A.\mathbf{and}\, x_1 (\mathbf{and}\, x_2 \cdots (\mathbf{and}\, x_{n-1} x_n) \cdots)$$

where each base type of L is represented by the single base type A of L_{SA}.

(ii) A conditional

$$cond : Bool \to B \to B \to B$$

is represented by

$$\lambda x^A.\lambda y^A.\lambda z^A.\mathbf{and}\, x\, (\mathbf{or}\, y\, z).$$

(iii) $\mathbf{Y}^{(\mu \to \mu) \to \mu}$ is represented by $\mathbf{Y}^{(\mu' \to \mu') \to \mu'}$, where μ' is the result of replacing all base types in μ by A.

We can add various other constants, e.g.

(iv) "parallel or" [Plo] is represented by **or**.

In this way, we can replace a term t in $\Lambda_M(L)$ by a term u in $\Lambda_M(L_{SA})$ by replacing all base types in t by A, and replacing each constant in t by its representing term. We then use u as the input for strictness analysis. The basis for doing strictness analysis is the following result from [BHA]: if $tabs[\![u]\!]$ is strict, then t is strict in the standard semantics. Thus our task reduces to testing u for strictness under $tabs$. If $u : \mu_1 \to \cdots \to \mu_n \to A$ is closed, we must test

$$tabs[\![u]\!]\Omega \perp_{\mu_1} = \perp_{\mu_2 \to \cdots \to \mu_n \to A}$$

$$\text{i.e. } \forall a_2 \in B_{\mu_2}.tabs[\![u]\!]\Omega \perp_{\mu_1} a_2 = \perp_{\mu_3 \to \cdots \mu_n \to A}$$

$$\vdots$$

$$\text{i.e. } \forall a_2 \in B_{\mu_2}, \ldots, a_n \in B_{\mu_n}.tabs[\![u]\!]\Omega \perp_{\mu_1} a_2 \cdots a_n = \perp_A = 0.$$

But by monotonicity, this will hold if and only if

$$tabs[\![u]\!]\Omega \perp_{\mu_1} \top_{\mu_2} \cdots \top_{\mu_n} = 0$$

i.e. iff

$$tabs[\![u 0^{\mu_1} 1^{\mu_2} \cdots 1^{\mu_n}]\!]\Omega = 0.$$

Now consider an arbitrary term

$$(x_1{:}\nu_1, \ldots, x_k{:}\nu_k)u{:}\mu_1 \to \cdots \mu_n \to A.$$

We say that u is strict if all its closed instances are strict. Once again, by monotonicity it is sufficient to ask if $u[1^{\nu_1}/x_1, \ldots, 1^{\nu_k}/x_k]$ is strict. Thus the test for strictness of a term

$$(x_1{:}\nu_1, \ldots, x_k{:}\nu_k)u : \mu_1 \to \cdots \mu_n \to A$$

in $\Lambda_M(L_{SA})$ is :

$$tabs[\![u[1^{\nu_1}/x_1, \ldots, 1^{\nu_k}/x_k]0^{\mu_1}1^{\mu_2} \cdots 1^{\mu_n}]\!]\Omega = 0.$$

Having defined strictness analysis, we now turn to the task of proving that it is a polymorphic invariant. Our strategy is to go via an *operational* semantics, despite the fact that so far the problem is formulated purely denotationally. The reason for this is that the common structure shared by elements of $MTI(e)$ is, in the first instance, syntactic; and use of the operational semantics allows us to capitalise on the intuition that the types on a term play no part in how we compute with it.

A *program* is a closed term of ground type. We shall now give an operational semantics for programs via a reduction relation $\twoheadrightarrow$ on closed terms, which is defined to be the least relation satisfying the following axioms and rules.

$(T1)$ $(\lambda x^{\mu}.t)u \twoheadrightarrow t[u/x]$

$(T2)$ $1^{\mu\to\nu}t \twoheadrightarrow 1^{\nu}$

$(T3)$ $0^{\mu} \twoheadrightarrow 0^{\mu}$

$(T4)$ $\mathbf{Y}^{(\mu\to\mu)\to\mu}t \twoheadrightarrow t(Y^{(\mu\to\mu)\to\mu}t)$

$(T5)$ $\dfrac{t_1 \twoheadrightarrow t_1'}{\mathbf{and}\,t_1 t_2 \twoheadrightarrow \mathbf{and}\,t_1' t_2}$

$(T6)$ $\mathbf{and}\,1^{A} t_2 \twoheadrightarrow t_2$

$(T7)$ $\dfrac{t_1 \twoheadrightarrow t_1' \quad t_2 \twoheadrightarrow t_2'}{\mathbf{or}\,t_1 t_2 \twoheadrightarrow \mathbf{or}\,t_1' t_2'}$

$(T8)$ $\mathbf{or}\,1^{A} t_2 \twoheadrightarrow 1^{A}$

$(T9)$ $\mathbf{or}\,t_1 1^{A} \twoheadrightarrow 1^{A}$

$(T10)$ $\dfrac{t_1 \twoheadrightarrow t_1'}{t_1 t_2 \twoheadrightarrow t_1' t_2}$

Fact

The relation $\twoheadrightarrow$ is a partial function on closed terms. The only *program* not in the domain of $\twoheadrightarrow$ is 1^A. If a term t is not in the domain of $\twoheadrightarrow$, we write $t \not\twoheadrightarrow$.

A consequence of this fact is that for each program t, exactly one of the following two possibilities obtains:

(i) There is a sequence of programs $\{t_n\}$ such that $t=t_0$ and $\forall n. t_n \twoheadrightarrow t_{n+1}$. In this case we write $t\uparrow$ (to be read "t diverges").

(ii) $t \twoheadrightarrow^* 1^A$, where $\twoheadrightarrow^*$ is the reflexive transitive closure of $\twoheadrightarrow$.

We shall now show that this operational semantics corresponds exactly to the denotational semantics via *tabs*. Our proof is modelled closely on that in [Plo].

Our aim is to prove the following

3.1. Theorem

For any program t in $\Lambda_M(L_{SA})$,

$tabs[\![t]\!]\Omega = 1 \Leftrightarrow t \twoheadrightarrow^* 1^A$.

Corollary

$tabs[\![t]\!]\Omega = 0 \Leftrightarrow t\uparrow$.

One half of the theorem is easy to prove. We note that

3.2. Fact

$t \twoheadrightarrow t' \Rightarrow tabs[\![t]\!]\Omega = tabs[\![t']\!]\Omega$

and then

$t \twoheadrightarrow^* 1^A \Rightarrow tabs[\![t]\!]\Omega = tabs[\![1^A]\!]\Omega = 1.$

In order to prove the converse, we define predicates $Comp_\mu$ on terms of type μ by induction on μ. Firstly, for *closed* terms t:

(1) $Comp_A(t) \equiv tabs[\![t]\!]\Omega = 1 \Rightarrow t \twoheadrightarrow^* 1^A$

(2) $Comp_{\mu\to\nu}(t) \equiv \forall closed\ u{:}\mu. Comp_\mu(u) \Rightarrow Comp_\nu(tu)$.

Now, for $(x_1{:}\nu_1, \ldots, x_k{:}\nu_k)t{:}\mu$

(3) $Comp_\mu(t) \equiv \forall closed\ u_1{:}\nu_1, \ldots, u_k{:}\nu_k. \bigwedge_{i=1}^{n} Comp_{\nu_i}(u_i) \Rightarrow Comp_\mu(t[u_1/x_1, \ldots, u_k/x_k])$.

We say that $(\Gamma)t{:}\mu$ is *computable* if $Comp_\mu((\Gamma)t)$. Note that $(\Gamma)t{:}\mu_1\rightarrow\cdots\mu_n\rightarrow A$ is computable iff, for all $\underline{t}$ such that $\underline{t}$ is a closed instantiation of $(\Gamma)t$ by computable terms, and closed computable $u_1{:}\mu_1,\ldots,u_n{:}\mu_n$:

$$Comp_A(\underline{t}u_1\cdots u_n).$$

Now to prove the Theorem, it clearly suffices to show

3.3. Lemma

Every term is computable.

Before proving 3.3, we need an auxiliary result about the recursion combinators.

Definition

We define $Y_{(n)}^{(\mu\rightarrow\mu)\rightarrow\mu}$, $(n\geq 0)$ by:

$$Y_{(0)}^{(\mu\rightarrow\mu)\rightarrow\mu} = 0^{(\mu\rightarrow\mu)\rightarrow\mu}$$

$$Y_{(k+1)}^{(\mu\rightarrow\mu)\rightarrow\mu} = \lambda x^{\mu\rightarrow\mu}.x(Y_{(k)}^{(\mu\rightarrow\mu)\rightarrow\mu}x)$$

Now we have

3.4. Fact

$$tabs[\![Y^{(\mu\rightarrow\mu)\rightarrow\mu}]\!]\Omega = \bigsqcup_{i=0}^{\infty} tabs[\![Y_{(k)}^{(\mu\rightarrow\mu)\rightarrow\mu}]\!]\Omega.$$

We define a relation $\ll$ between terms as the least satisfying

(1) $0^\mu \ll t$, *all* $t{:}\mu$

(2) $t \ll 1^\mu$, *all* $t{:}\mu$

(3) $Y_{(k)}^{(\mu\rightarrow\mu)\rightarrow\mu} \ll Y^{(\mu\rightarrow\mu)\rightarrow\mu}$, *all* $k\geq 0$

(4) $t \ll t$

(5) $t \ll t' \Rightarrow \lambda x^\mu.t \ll \lambda x^\mu.t'$

(6) $t \ll t', u \ll u' \Rightarrow tu \ll t'u'$

3.5. Lemma

$t_1 \ll t_2, u_1 \ll u_2 \Rightarrow t_1[u_1/x] \ll t_2[u_2/x]$

Proof

By induction on t_1, and cases on why $t_1 \ll t_2$. □

3.6. Lemma

If $t \ll u$ and $t \twoheadrightarrow t'$, then

(*i*) $u \twoheadrightarrow u' \Rightarrow t' \ll u'$

(*ii*) $u \not\twoheadrightarrow \Rightarrow t' \ll u$

Proof

By induction on t, and cases on why $t \twoheadrightarrow t'$ and $t \ll u$. The case for $(T1)$ uses Lemma 3.5. □

Corollary

$t \twoheadrightarrow^* 1^A \ \& \ t \ll u \Rightarrow u \twoheadrightarrow^* 1^A$.

Remark

The reader may have wondered why we introduced the constants 0^μ, when we could have *defined*

$$0^\mu = Y^{(\mu\to\mu)\to\mu}\lambda x^\mu.x.$$

The reason is that with this definition, 3.6 is false! Indeed, let $\mu = A\to A$. Then

$$0^\mu \ll \lambda x^A.0^A,$$

and

$$0^\mu \twoheadrightarrow (\lambda x^\mu.x)(Y^{(\mu\to\mu)\to\mu}\lambda x^\mu.x)$$

but $\lambda x^A.0^A \not\twoheadrightarrow$, and it is not the case that

$$(\lambda x^\mu.x)(Y^{(\mu\to\mu)\to\mu}\lambda x^\mu.x) \ll \lambda x^A.0^A.$$

(For similar reasons, Lemma 3.2 in [Plo] and Lemma 4.1.5 in [HA] are incorrect as stated; they can be repaired by introducing constants for $\perp_\mu$.)

Lemma 3.3 can now be proved by induction on terms.

We now consider computation in the *untyped* λ-calculus. Our aim is to make precise the intuition that the type information on a term does not affect how we compute with it.

We begin by defining a reduction relation over closed, untyped terms in $\Lambda(L_{SA})$.

$(U1)$ $(\lambda x.e)e' \twoheadrightarrow e[e'/x]$

$(U2)$ $\mathbf{1}e \twoheadrightarrow \mathbf{1}$

$(U3)$ $\mathbf{0} \twoheadrightarrow \mathbf{0}$

$(U4)$ $\mathbf{Y}e \twoheadrightarrow e(\mathbf{Y}e)$

$(U5)$ $\dfrac{e_1 \twoheadrightarrow e_1'}{\mathbf{and}\, e_1 e_2 \twoheadrightarrow \mathbf{and}\, e_1' e_2}$

$(U6)$ $\mathbf{and}\,\mathbf{1}\, e_2 \twoheadrightarrow e_2$

$(U7)$ $\dfrac{e_1 \twoheadrightarrow e_1' \quad e_2 \twoheadrightarrow e_2'}{\mathbf{or}\, e_1 e_2 \twoheadrightarrow \mathbf{or}\, e_1' e_2'}$

$(U8)$ $\mathbf{or}\,\mathbf{1}\, e_2 \twoheadrightarrow \mathbf{1}$

$(U9)$ $\mathbf{or}\, e_1 \mathbf{1} \twoheadrightarrow \mathbf{1}$

$(U10)$ $\dfrac{e_1 \twoheadrightarrow e_1'}{e_1 e_2 \twoheadrightarrow e_1' e_2}$

Thus each rule (Ui) is obtained from the typed version (Ti) above by applying ϵ to the premises and conclusion. We write $e\uparrow$ with the same meaning as for typed terms.

3.7. Lemma

For any program t:

(i) $t \twoheadrightarrow t' \Rightarrow \epsilon(t) \twoheadrightarrow \epsilon(t')$

(ii) $\epsilon(t) \twoheadrightarrow e \Rightarrow \exists! t'. t \twoheadrightarrow t' \;\&\; \epsilon(t') = e.$

Corollary

For all programs t, $t\uparrow \Leftrightarrow \epsilon(t)\uparrow$.

We note the additional, simple

3.8. Fact

(*i*) $e_1 \twoheadrightarrow * 1 \Rightarrow e_1 \cdots e_n \twoheadrightarrow * 1 \;\; (n \geq 1)$

(*ii*) $e_1 \uparrow \Rightarrow e_1 \cdots e_n \uparrow \;\; (n \geq 1)$

We are now ready to prove our main result.

3.9. Theorem

Strictness analysis is a polymorphic invariant.

Proof

Let

$$(x_1:\nu_1, \ldots, x_k:\nu_k) t_1:\mu_1 \to \cdots \mu_n \to A,$$

$$(x_1:\nu_1', \ldots, x_k:\nu_k') t_2:\mu_1' \to \cdots \mu_m' \to A$$

be in $MTI(e)$ for some untyped e.

Now let

$$u_1 = t_1[1^{\nu_1}/x_1, \ldots, 1^{\nu_k}/x_k] 0^{\mu_1} 1^{\mu_2} \cdots 1^{\mu_n}$$

$$u_2 = t_2[1^{\nu_1'}/x_1, \ldots, 1^{\nu_k'}/x_k] 0^{\mu_1'} 1^{\mu_2'} \cdots 1^{\mu_m'}$$

and let $e_1 = \epsilon(u_1)$, $e_2 = \epsilon(u_2)$.

Now for $i = 1,2$:

t_i satisfies the strictness analysis test

$\Leftrightarrow$ $tabs[\![u_i]\!]\Omega = 0$

$\Leftrightarrow$ $u_i \uparrow$ by the Corollary to Theorem 3.1

$\Leftrightarrow$ $e_i \uparrow$ by the Corollary to 3.7.

So we have to show that $e_1 \uparrow \Leftrightarrow e_2 \uparrow$.

We consider two cases:

Case (1): $n \leq m$. In this case, note that $e_2 = e_1 s_{n+1} \cdots s_m$ where

$$s_0 = 0, \;\; s_{k+1} = 1 \;\; (0 \leq k < m).$$

Now if $e_1 \uparrow$, then $e_2 \uparrow$ by 3.8(*ii*), while if $e_1 \twoheadrightarrow * 1$, then $e_2 \twoheadrightarrow * 1$ by 3.8(*i*). Thus $e_1 \uparrow \Leftrightarrow e_2 \uparrow$.

Case (2): $m \leq n$. Symmetrical to Case (1). □

4. Strictness Analysis For Polymorphic Functions

We now consider how to do strictness analysis for polymorphically typable terms of the untyped λ-calculus $\Lambda(L)$. We begin by recalling Milner's type-checking algorithm W [DM]. Given type assumptions Γ and an untyped expression e, $W((\Gamma)e)$ returns:

- either error, in which case e is not typable (on assumptions Γ)
- or (S,τ) where τ is the "most general" type of e under assumptions $S\Gamma$.

The algorithm W uses Robinson's unification algorithm [Rob], in the following form: a function U such that, given type expressions τ, υ, $U(\tau,\upsilon)$ returns:

- either error, if τ, υ are not unifiable
- or a substitution V which is the most general unifier of τ, υ.

We can then describe algorithm W as follows:

$$(W1)\quad W((\Gamma)x) = (Id, \Gamma(x)) \text{ if } x \in \mathrm{dom}\,\Gamma$$

$$(W2)\quad W((\Gamma)c) = (Id,\tau) \ \ \textit{where } \tau = \pi(c) \textit{ with new variables}$$

$$(W3)\quad W((\Gamma)\lambda x.e) = \textit{let } (S_1,\tau_1) = W((\Gamma, x{:}\beta)e),\ \beta \textit{ new}$$
$$\textit{in } (S_1, S_1\beta\to\tau_1)$$

$$(W4)\quad W((\Gamma)e_1e_2) = \textit{let } (S_1,\tau_1) = W((\Gamma)e_1)$$
$$(S_2,\tau 2) = W((S_1\Gamma)e_2)$$
$$V = U(S_2\tau_1, \tau_2\to\beta),\ \beta \textit{ new}$$
$$\textit{in } (VS_2S_1, V\beta)$$

The intention is that W returns error if the condition in $(W1)$ is not satisfied, or if calls to U or recursive calls to W return error.

Notation

We extend type substitutions to apply to typed terms:

$$Sx = x$$

$$Sc^{\tau} = c^{S\tau}$$

$$S(\lambda x^{\tau}.t) = \lambda x^{S\tau}.S(t)$$

$$S(tu) = (St)(Su)$$

Example

$$[A\to A/\alpha](\lambda x^{\alpha}.x) = \lambda x^{A\to A}.x$$

We shall now describe a modified algorithm W_1. $W_1((\Gamma)e)$ returns *three* things if successful: (S,t,τ), where S, τ are as for algorithm W, and t is a typed term. W_1 is defined as follows:

(W_1.1) $W_1((\Gamma)x) = (Id, x, \Gamma(x))$ if $x \in \mathrm{dom}\,\Gamma$

(W_1.2) $W_1((\Gamma)c) = (Id, c^{\tau}, \tau)$ *where* $\tau = \pi(c)$ *with new variables*

(W_1.3) $W_1((\Gamma)\lambda x.e) =$ *let* $(S_1, t, \tau_1) = W_1((\Gamma, x{:}\beta)e)$, β *new*

in $(S_1, \lambda x^{S_1\beta}.t, S_1\beta \rightarrow \tau_1)$

(W_1.4) $W_1((\Gamma)e_1e_2) =$ *let* $(S_1, t_1, \tau_1) = W_1((\Gamma)e_1)$

$(S_2, t_2, \tau_2) = W_1((S_1\Gamma)e_2)$

$V = U(S_2\tau_1, \tau_2 \rightarrow \beta)$, β *new*

in $(VS_2S_1, (VS_2t_1)(Vt_2), V\beta)$

We shall now investigate the main properties of W_1.

4.1. Fact

(i) $W((\Gamma)e) = (S,\tau) \iff \exists t. W_1((\Gamma)e) = (S,t,\tau)$

(ii) $W_1((\Gamma)e) = (S,t,\tau) \Rightarrow \epsilon((S\Gamma)t) = e$

Thus W_1 is compatible with W, and the typed term it returns if successful is an instance of its untyped argument. We now develop some results analogous to those in [DM].

4.2. Proposition (Soundness of W_1)

$W_1(\Gamma,e) = (S,t,\tau) \Rightarrow S\Gamma \vdash_L t{:}\tau$

4.2 is proved by a straightforward induction on e, using the following

4.3. Lemma

$\Gamma \vdash_L t{:}\tau \Rightarrow S\Gamma \vdash_L St{:}S\tau$

Proof

By induction on proofs in the type inference system. □

4.4. Theorem (Completeness of W_1)

$S\Upsilon \vdash_L u{:}\upsilon \ \&\ \epsilon((S\Upsilon)u) = e \ \Rightarrow$

(i) $W_1((\Gamma)e) = (S,t,\tau)$ for some S,t,τ

(ii) $\exists R.\, S\Upsilon = RS\Gamma \ \&\ Rt = u \ \&\ R\tau = \upsilon$

4.5. Corollary

(i) $W_1((\Gamma)e) = (S,t,\tau) \Rightarrow MTI((\Gamma)e) = \{(GS\Gamma)(Gt) \mid G \text{ ground}\}$

(ii) $W_1((\Gamma)e) = \textbf{error} \Rightarrow MTI((\Gamma)e) = \emptyset.$

The Corollary relates polymorphic type checking to the idea of monotype instances we introduced in Section 2.

We can now formulate our strictness analysis algorithm for untyped λ-expressions e, under type assumptions Γ.

4.6. Algorithm

Input: $(\Gamma)e$.

Step 1.

Form $W_1((\Gamma)e)$. If this returns **error**, $(\Gamma)e$ is not polymorphically typable, by 4.1(i). Otherwise, let $W_1((\Gamma)e) = (S,t,\tau)$.

Step 2.

Let G be a *simplest* ground substitution, i.e. $G = \lambda\alpha.A$, where A is any base type. Let $u = (GS\Gamma)(Gt)$.

Step 3.

Now $u \in \Lambda_M(L)$. Apply the strictness analysis algorithm for monotyped terms described in Section 3 to u. The result of this is the overall result of the algorithm. □

4.7. Theorem (Soundness Of Strictness Analysis For Polymorphic Functions).

If algorithm 4.6 returns **true** for $(\Gamma)e$, then each $(S\Gamma)t$ in $MTI((\Gamma)e)$ is strict in the standard semantics. Moreover, the algorithm returns **true** iff the algorithm for typed terms returns **true** on *all* terms in $MTI((\Gamma)e)$, iff it returns **true** for *any* term in $MTI((\Gamma)e)$.

Proof

Directly from Corollary 4.5, Theorem 3.9 and the Soundness Theorem for strictness analysis of typed λ-calculus of [BHA]. □

From this theorem we see that showing strictness *analysis* to be a polymorphic invariant is a more useful result for our purposes than showing that *strictness* (i.e. being strict under the standard semantics) is a polymorphic invariant. The latter result would leave open the possibility, in the case that our strictness analysis returned **false** for some monotype instance of e, that some other instance could be detected as strict. The fact that strictness analysis is a polymorphic invariant precludes this possibility.

Examples

(1) $W_1(()\lambda x.x) = (S, \lambda x^{\alpha}.x, \alpha\to\alpha)$

$tabs[\![\lambda x^{A}.x\,0^{A}]\!]\Omega = 0$

Conclude that $()\lambda x.x$ *is strict.*

(2) $W_1(()\lambda f.\lambda x.f\,x) = (S, \lambda f^{\alpha\to\beta}.\lambda x^{\alpha}.f\,x, (\alpha\to\beta)\to(\alpha\to\beta))$

$tabs[\![\lambda f^{A\to A}.\lambda x^{A}.f\,x\,0^{A\to A}1^{A}]\!]\Omega = 0$

Conclude that $()\lambda f.\lambda x.f\,x$ *is strict.*

(3) $W_1((x{:}\alpha\to A)\lambda y.x(xy)) = (S[A/\alpha], \lambda y^{A}.x(xy), A\to A)$

$tabs[\![(\lambda y^{A}.1'^{A\to A}(1^{A\to A}y))0^{A}]\!]\Omega = 1$

We cannot conclude that $(x{:}\alpha\to A)\lambda y.x(xy)$ *is strict.*

Important Remark

It should be noted that algorithm 4.6 is by no means specific to strictness analysis. If we have *any* safe computable analysis for typed λ-terms, then we may extend it to polymorphically typable terms of the untyped λ-calculus in identical fashion. *Provided* that our property is a polymorphic invariant, the Soundness Theorem 4.7 carries through unchanged. This supplies some motivation for studying the concept of polymorphic invariance in greater depth and generality than we have attempted here.

Type Schemes and Generic Polymorphism

We must now confront an important point which so far we have glossed over. Milner's theory of type polymorphism is in one important respect more general than what we have described. He considers not just types but *type schemes*, ranged over by σ, the syntax of which is

$$\sigma ::= \tau \mid \forall\alpha.\sigma$$

Thus type expressions are special cases of type schemes. The role of the type quantifier, which is only applied at the outermost level in Milner's system, is to allow for *generic* polymorphism, that is, for different instantiations of a polymorphic object within a single context. In fact, our treatment of constants has been a special case of generic polymorphism, which we can illustrate by

$$\mathbf{Y}^{((A\to A)\to(A\to A))\to(A\to A)}(\lambda f^{A\to A}.\lambda x^{A}.\mathbf{Y}^{(A\to A)\to A} f\,).$$

Here there are two different instantiations of $\mathbf{Y}^{(\alpha\to\alpha)\to\alpha}$. Think of $\mathbf{Y}$ and the other constants of the language as being "declared" in a global environment of type assumptions. In this environment, $\mathbf{Y}$ is declared to have the type *scheme* $\forall\alpha.(\alpha\to\alpha)\to\alpha$, rather than the type $(\alpha\to\alpha)\to\alpha$. The choice of different substitutions for α then becomes a particular case of the standard notion of universal instantiation. The syntactical vehicle which Milner uses for setting up such environments for generically polymorphic objects is Landin's *let* construction [Lan]:

$$e ::= \cdots \mid let\ x = e\ in\ e'$$

Type assumptions Γ are generalised to maps from variables to type schemes. Algorithm W is then modified by replacing ($W1$) by

$$(W1')\quad W((\Gamma)x) = (Id,\tau')$$

where

$$x \in \mathbf{dom}\,\Gamma,\ \Gamma(x) = \forall\alpha_1,\ldots,\alpha_n.\tau,$$

$$\text{and } \tau' = [\beta_1/\alpha_1,\ldots,\beta_n/\alpha_n]\tau,\ \beta_1,\ldots,\beta_n\ new.$$

and adding an additional clause:

$$(W5)\quad W((\Gamma)let\ x = e_1\ in\ e_2) = let\ (S_1,\tau_1) = W((\Gamma)e_1)$$
$$(S_2,\tau_2) = W((S_1\Gamma, x{:}\overline{S_1\Gamma}(\tau_1))e_2)$$
$$in\ (S_2S_1,\tau_2)$$

where $\overline{S_1\Gamma}(\tau) = \forall\alpha_1,\ldots,\alpha_n.\tau$, where $\alpha_1,\ldots,\alpha_n$ are the type variables occurring free in τ but not in $S_1\Gamma(x)$ for any $x \in \mathbf{dom}\,\Gamma$. Note that, if we treat constants as variables and take

$$W((\Gamma, c_1{:}\sigma_1,\ldots,c_n{:}\sigma_n)e)$$

where $c_1,\ldots,c_n$ are the constants appearing in e, and σ_i is the universal closure of $\pi(c_i)$, then this will yield exactly the same result as

$$W((\Gamma)e)$$

according to our original definition of W, with the modified rule ($W1'$) replacing uses of ($W2$).

How are we to treat generic polymorphism in our framework? The problem is that we can no longer resolve a polymorphic expression into its typed instances as before. In particular, note that the familiar equivalence which is valid in the standard semantics

$$(*)\ let\ x = e_1\ in\ e_2 \equiv (\lambda x.e_2)e_1$$

does not hold for the non-standard semantics defined by W, in the sense that in general

$$W((\Gamma)let\ x = e_1\ in\ e_2) \neq W((\Gamma)(\lambda x.e_2)e_1).$$

For example,

$$W(()let\ I = \lambda x.x\ in\ I(I)) = (Id, \alpha \to \alpha)$$

$$W(()(\lambda I.I(I))\lambda x.x) = \text{error}.$$

However, we do have

4.8. Fact

$$W((\Gamma)e_1) = (S_1, \tau_1) \Rightarrow W((\Gamma)let\ x = e_1\ in\ e_2) \equiv W((S_1\Gamma)e_2[e_1/x]).$$

In other words, we restore (*) to a valid equivalence under the non-standard semantics W by performing one step of β-reduction. In this way, we can eliminate all occurrences of *let* from an untyped expression without affecting its polymorphic typing, and then apply our strictness analysis algorithm as before. This is semantically sound; from the point of view of pragmatics, however, it is not completely satisfactory, for two reasons. Firstly, we must do some expensive compile-time copying corresponding to the β-reductions. Secondly, if we are developing definitions incrementally

$$\begin{aligned} def\ f_1 &= e_1 \\ &\vdots \\ f_n &= e_n \end{aligned}$$

then to perform strictness analysis for e_{n+1}, the process of expanding out the definitions of $f_1, \ldots, f_n$ means that we may have to recompute $tabs[\![u_i]\!]$, $tabs[\![u_i']\!]$, $tabs[\![u_i'']\!]$ etc. for different monotype instances of some e_i, in the course of doing strictness analysis for e_{n+1}.

Thus there is considerable scope for improvement as regards efficiency. I hope that some of the issues raised by these remarks can be addressed by extensions to the basic theory developed in this paper.

Acknowledgements

The stimulus for the work reported in this paper came from my continuing collaboration with Chris Hankin and Geoffrey Burn on Abstract Interpretation for functional programming languages. Iain Phillips and Axel Poigne listened patiently to my ideas about polymorphic invariance. Chris, Geoffrey and Iain made a number of helpful comments on a draft of this paper.

References

[Bar]

Barendregt, H. *The Lambda Calculus: Syntax and Semantics 2nd. ed.*, North Holland, Amsterdam, 1984.

[BHA]

Burn, G. Hankin, C. and Abramsky, S. "Strictness Analysis For Higher Order Functions", to appear in *Science Of Computer Programming*, also Imperial College Department Of Computing Research Report DOC 85/6, 1985.

[CPJ]

Clack, C. and Peyton Jones, S. "Generating Parallelism from Strictness Analysis", to appear in *Proc. IFIP International Conference On Functional Languages and Computer Architectures*, Springer LNCS, 1985.

[DM]

Damas, L. and Milner, R. "Principal Type Schemes for Functional Programs", in *Proc. 9th ACM Symposium On Principles Of Programming Languages*, 1982.

[HA]

Hennessy, M. C. B. and Ashcroft, E. A. "A Mathematical Semantics For A Nondeterministic Typed λ-Calculus", *Theoretical Computer Science 11 (1980) pp. 227-245*, 1980.

[Lan]

Landin, P.J. "The Next 700 Programming Languages", in *Communications of the ACM, 9, pp. 157-166*, 1966.

[ML]

Martin-Löf, P. *Intuitionistic Type Theory*, Bibliopolis, Naples, 1984.

[Mil]

Milner, R. "A Theory Of Type Polymorphism In Programming", *Journal Of Computer And Systems Sciences, 17,3 pp. 348-375,* 1978.

[Myc]

Mycroft, A. *Abstract Interpretation And Optimising Transformations For Applicative Programs,* Ph.D. Thesis, Edinburgh University, 1981.

[Plo]

Plotkin, G. "LCF Considered As A Programming Language", *Theoretical Computer Science 5, pp. 223-255,* 1977.

[Rob]

Robinson, J. A. "A Machine-Oriented logic based on the resolution principle", *Journal of the ACM 12,1 pp. 23-41,* 1965.

[Sto]

Stoy, J. *Denotational Semantics: The Scott-Strachey Approach To Programming Language Theory,* MIT Press, Cambridge Mass. 1977.

Convergent Term Rewriting Systems Can be Used for Program Transformation.

Françoise BELLEGARDE

CRIN CENTRE DE RECHERCHE EN INFORMATIQUE DE NANCY
F-54506 VANDOEUVRE LES NANCY CEDEX, FRANCE

Structured programming methods [10] make programs easier to understand and to prove correct. However, these programs are often inefficient. This motivates the development of program transformation systems that derive an efficient program from an inefficient one. For obvious reason, the source program and the target program are supposed to be written in the same language. By the way, the optimization process is more easily understood. This approach has raised a lot of interest in the recent years.

However, most researchers (for example [9,27,17]) were rather interested in the transformation of recursive functional programs into iterative ones. Here we are mostly concerned with the transformation of iterative programs.

At the very beginning, we have considered iterative source programs developed by a particular style of programming [14] called MEDEE. This style of progamming uses sequences defined using recurrence relations mixed with a stepwise refinement methodology [28]. Since the language is FP-like, we decided to state the problem in FP.

So doing, non expert progammers naturally define too many sequences. For example, if they want to obtain a program which computes the scalar product of two given sequences $\langle x_1,x_2,\ldots,x_n\rangle$ and $\langle y_1,y_2,\ldots,y_n\rangle$, they sometimes define a sequence

$S_1 = \langle x_1y_1, x_2y_2, \ldots, x_ny_n \rangle$,

then define a sequence

$S_2 = \langle 0, x_1y_1, x_1y_1 + x_2y_2, \ldots, x_1y_1 + x_2y_2 + \ldots + x_ny_n \rangle$

and the last term of S_2 is the scalar product. A sequence such as S_1 will be called an intermediate sequence. The programmer could also define the sequence S_2 without using the sequence S_1 as an intermediate sequence. We say that S_1 is useless. Our purpose is to improve this kind of program by decreasing the number of intermediate sequences. The programs are supposed to run on a Von Neumann machine. A similar idea can be found in [26].

Use of these transformations requires reasoning about programs. For that, we use a term rewriting system to transform programs. This leads us to describe the source program as a functional expression.

1. The functional expression of a program

has mathematical properties which are useful to find the intermediate sequences computed by the program.

For example, the result r of the computation of the program with the data d is the result of the application of a function p with the argument d.

$r = p(d)$.

If x is an intermediate result, there exist a function pl such that

$x = pl(d)$

and a function p2 such that

$r = p2(x)$.

Thus p is the result of the composition between p1 and p2. If the composition between two functions is written "o", the expression for p is

$$p = p2 \text{ o } p1.$$

If x is useless, there exists another expression for p without this occurrence of "o". We know how many intermediate results are present by looking at the occurrences of "o".

Thus, the source program is written as a functional expression. That is an expression without variables. In other words, it uses neither x, nor r, nor d and the transformation rules come from an algebra of functions. Such a simple algebra of functional programs was introduced by John Backus in [5,4,3].

Iterations are just appropriate functional forms. Recall that a functional form is a map which returns a function when applied to functions. For instance "o" and "ALL" are functional forms. "o" is the composition of functions. "ALL" is similar to "MAPCAR" in LISP. Let f be a function, "ALL f" is another function and when "ALL f" is applied to the sequence $\langle x_1,x_2,\ldots,x_n\rangle$, the result is the sequence $\langle f(x_1),f(x_2),\ldots,f(x_n)\rangle$. "ALL f" expresses one kind of iteration.

We use some functional forms which are not defined in FP, they are similar to those defined by [24]. The choice of our functional forms is discussed in [8]. We only want to get a simple but rich algebra. For example, a function "*f" expresses the sequence of computations of a recurrent iteration. Let x_0 be an initial value. When "*f" is applied to x_0 and a sequence $\langle x_1,x_2,x_3\rangle$, the result is the sequence $\langle x_0$, $f(x_0,x_1)$, $f(f(x_0,x_1)x_2)$, $f(f(f(x_0,x_1),x_2),x_3)\rangle$. This allows us to compose a function "*f" with all functions which have a sequence in argument and thus to get a rich algebra. We use also a kind of while: "WH(p,f) [8]. "WH(p,f) needs the same arguments as "*f", an initial value and a sequence. A predicate p allows the iteration to terminate. In all cases, it is bounded by the length of the sequence in argument. Thus, we only describe iterative programs that terminates.

For example, let us code in FP a program which computes 2^n/n! and use a lot of intermediate sequences.

- S_0= <1,2,...,n> is the result of the primitive function "iota".

- 2^- is the constant function 2. The sequence

  S_1= <2,2,...,2> is the result of the function "ALL 2^-" being applied to S0.

- "*" may be applied to the primitive function mult. Let us apply the function "*mult" to 1 and S_1 thus we get S_2

  S_2= <1,2,4,...,2^n>.

- In the same way, we get

  S_3= <1,1!,2!,...,n!> when we apply "*mult" to 1 and S_0.

- The primitive function "trans" is applied to S_2 and S_3 and the result is

  S_4= <[1,1],[2,1!],[4,2!],...,[2^n,n!]>

- Now, "ALL div" is applied to S_4, we get

  S_5= <1/1,2/1!,4/2!,...,2^n/n!>

and the last term is "2^n/n!".

When [f,g] is applied to x, it returns the pair [f(x),g(x)]. Thus the FP expression is

```
e0 = last o (ALL div o (trans o [*mult o [1¯,ALL 2¯ o iota],
                                  *mult o [1¯,iota]]
```

that computes **five intermediate sequences** on a Von Neumann machine.

Fortunately, there exist other programs that compute fewer sequences, for instance

```
e1= div o (last o (trans o [*mult o [1¯,ALL 2¯ o iota],
                             *mult o [1¯,iota]]))
```

that computes **four intermediate sequences** (S_1, S_2, S_3 and S_4), or the following expression (?1 and ?2 are the two selectors in a pair):

```
e2= div o (last o (trans o [*(mult o [?1,2¯]) o [1¯,iota],
                             *mult o [1¯,iota]]))
```

that computes **three intermediate sequences** (S_2, S_3 and S_4). or

```
e3= div o [last o (*(mult o [?1,2¯]) o [1¯,iota]),
           last o (*mult o [1¯,iota])]
```

that computes **two intermediate sequences** (S_2 and S_3). or

```
e4= div o (last o ( *[ mult o [?1o?1,2¯],
                       mult o [?2o?1,?2] ] o [ [1¯,1¯],iota] )
```

that computes only **one intermediate sequence** (S_4).

e_0, e_1, e_2, e_3 and eventually e_4 are transformed into e_4. We expect e_4 to be a normal-form.

We would like transformation rules to be rewriting rules in the FP-algebra. Furthermore we consider a functional expression as a term of the FP-algebra.

2. The FP-algebra

FP-expressions are terms (we say FP-terms) of a free algebra whose functional symbols are functional forms. Constant symbols are the primitive functions and the constant functions.

Two functional expressions are equal if they express two programs which return the same result when applied to the same data. The equality we want to describe is known as extensional equality

f = g if and only if f(x) = g(x) for all x.

This equality allows us to validate a set of equations A of the FP-algebra. In A, we find for instance

- the axiom of the associativity of "o"

(a) (f o g) o h = f o (g o h),

and of the distributivity of "o" with respect to "[_,_]"

(b) [f,g] o h = [f o h,g o h]

- axioms on "ALL" and "*" such as

(c) ALL f o ALL g = ALL(f o g),

(d) trans o [ALL f,ALL g] = ALL[f,g],

(e) (*f o [x,ALL g]) = *(f o [?1,g o ?2]) o [x,id].

- and also axioms on primitive functions like

(f) last o (trans o [a,b]) = [last o a,last o b] (valid when "trans o [a,b]" is defined).

Most of the axioms in A (about 90 axioms) are in [4].

The set A allows us to define an A-equality. Two FP-terms are proved to be A-equal by substituting equals for equals. This way, we easily prove that the expressions e_0, e_1, e_2, e_3 and e_4 in the example above are A-equal.

A includes all ways to compose functions that produce sequences (i.e. that have a sequence in their arguments) with functions that consume sequences (i.e. that have a sequence as a result). Let us consider the axioms we cited above. In the left-hand side of the axiom (c), the function "ALL f" is composed with "ALL g". The intermediate sequence, generated by "ALL g" and consumed by "ALL f", in the left-hand side is not in the right-hand side. In the same way, we can see that the left-hand side expressions of the axioms (d), (e) and (f) compute fewer sequences than the right-hand side expressions.

Each class of A-equivalence has, at least, one term which generates a fewest number of intermediate sequence, let us call it a best term. For example, e_4 is an improved term in the class which includes e_0, e_1, e_2, e_3 and e_4.

Our purpose is to automatize the transformation from a term to a best term. Thus, we want to find automatically one of the best terms in each A-equivalence class and thus, the result of the rewriting process (i.e. a normal-form) need to be a best term and moreover need to be unique.

3. Term rewriting systems

Most of the transformation systems involve a set of rules which are expressed as schemas, containing patterns and templates [6,1]. J. S. GIVLER and B. KIEBURTZ [12] have the same approach but for FP-expressions.

We simply use term rewriting systems. We orient axioms into rules such that their right-hand side computes fewer sequences than their left-hand side. For example, we shall have the rules

(c) ALL f o ALL g => ALL(f o g),

(d) trans o [ALL f,ALL g] => ALL[f,g],

(e) *f o [x,ALL g] => *(f o [?1,g o ?2]) o [x,id] and

(f) last o (trans o [a,b]) => [last o a,last o b].

We orient the equations in rules such that, rewriting a term, one of these rules removes at least one sequence of computations. Thus, the normal-form of an FP-term, if it exists, is a best term. To get automatic transformations, each term need to have one, and only one, normal form. Thus, the term rewriting system must be locally confluent and noetherian [15] (we also say convergent).

If we apply the Knuth-Bendix procedure [20] to a set A of equations, then it provides us with an equivalent convergent rewriting system. "equivalent" means that two A-equivalent terms have the same normal-form.

According to a well-founded ordering on terms, the procedure orients equations in rules in order to get a noetherian term rewriting system and adds equational consequences (derived from critical pairs) in order to get a locally confluent term rewriting system. If the procedure does not fail (to orient an equation) and does not loop (it loops when it generates infinitely many new equations), then, it returns a convergent rewriting system.

We defined a set A of equations of the FP-algebra which includes all ways to compose functional forms that express iterations. For this purpose, we used the REVE [22,11] implementation of the Knuth-Bendix procedure. We got some interesting results but many problems still remain open.

4. The results

We consider about 90 axioms of the FP-algebra. We found increasing convergent rewriting systems R which are equivalent to increasing subsets of the set of axioms of the FP-algebra. Using the biggest of these systems (let us name it R) REVE provides us the normal form $t{\downarrow}_R$ of a FP-term t. $t{\downarrow}_R$ is an improvement of t. We can say that the REVE rewriting procedure is able, using R, to remove the intermediate sequences generated by all the ways to compose functions which describes iterations.

For example, if we give to REVE one of the expressions e_0, e_1, e_2 and e_4 above, then they are rewritten automatically to e_4.

However, we have not yet found the best (if it exists) rewriting system for our purpose. For example the expression e_3 is irreducible, with the system R, because we were not able to put all the axioms we wanted in R.

5. The problems

In R, we cannot put the axiom

(f) last o (trans o [a,b]) = [last o a,last o b].

This is indeed a classical problem with the Knuth-Bendix procedure since it loops when generating infinitely many new rules. Let us look at the loop of the procedure. In R, we have the following important rule

(g) trans o [*f o [x,a] , *g o [y,b]]

=> *[f o [?1o?1,?2] , g o [?2o?1,?2]] o [[x,y] , a]

The sequence S (result of "trans") of the pairs which are produced by two recurrent iterations ("*f" and "*g") when they are applied to the same sequence (result of a), is also the direct result of one recurrent iteration I ("*[f o [?1o?1,?2] , g o [?2o?1,?2]]"). I computes pairs when it is also applied to the sequence (result of a).

The Knuth-Bendix procedure finds a critical pair

(h) [last o (*f o [x,a]),last o (*g o [y,a])]

= last o (*[f o [?1o?1,?2] , g o [?2o?1,?2]] o [[x,y] , a])

and orients it, from left to right, in a new rule (h). But, in R, the knuth-Bendix procedure has the following rule

(i) ?1 o [f,g] => f (valid if g is defined),

thus it finds a critical pair with (h) and then it creates the new rule

```
(1) ?1 o (last o (*[ f o [?1o?1,?2] , g o [?2o?1,?2] ] o [ [x,y] , a ]))

     => last o (*f o [x,a])
```

But now, with the rule (a) of the associativity of "o", the Knuth-Bendix procedure generates infinitely many rules such that

```
(2) ?1 o (last o (*[f1o(f2 o [?1o?1,?2]),
                    g1o(g2 o [?2o?1,?2])] o [ [x,y] , a ]))

     => last o (*(f1of2) o [x,a])

(3) ?1 o (last o (*[f1o(f2o(f3 o [?1o?1,?2])),
                    g1o(g2o(g3 o [?2o?1,?2])) ] o [ [x,y] , a ]))

     => last o (*(f1o(f2of3)) o [x,a]) .....
```

5.1. Loops in the Knuth-Bendix procedure,

theoretically, are not a problem, because the proof of the Knuth-Bendix procedure remains valid with an infinity of rules. For example, if we interrupt the procedure after it has found the rule (h), and give e_3 as a data for rewriting, then the Knuth-Bendix procedure gives the normal-form e_4. Thus, we have a semi-decision procedure which is able to give us the normal-form for the whole axioms. However this is not realistic.

The practical problem is to find a way to synthesize an infinity of rules.

H. KIRCHNER [19] proposes a solution to extend the Knuth-Bendix procedure to a meta-completion procedure. The set of equations includes meta-rules. Meta-rules are schemas for an infinity of rules. For example, the family of rules (1), (2), (3), ...

above is synthesized into the meta-rule

(M) ?1 o (last o (*[F o [?1o?1,?2] , G o [?2o?1,?2]] o [[x,y] , a]))

=> last o (*F o [x,a])

(M) proceeds as if F and G are substituted by the infinite family of terms

x_0, x_0 o x_1, x_0 o (x_1 o x_2), ...

owing to the rule of the associativity of "o".

Some useful axioms in the FP-algebra produce loops during the Knuth-Bendix process. In each case, we are able to schematize the infinity of rules by a meta-rule, using the notations proposed by H. Kirchner.

Thus, it will be possible to improve our results. Another problem comes from the ordering which is included in the Knuth-Bendix procedure.

5.2. Termination proofs

The ordering implemented in REVE (the recursive decomposition ordering) [23] , is not always the one that we need. It does not always orient the equation such that the rule removes the useless intermediate sequences. For example, let us consider the two axioms

- associativity of "o"

  (a) (f o g) o h = f o (g o h),

- and endomorphism

(c) ALL f o ALL g = ALL(f o g),

They are oriented from left to right, in two rules (any other orientation of (a) makes the procedure to loop). However, there is a critical pair

ALL f o (ALL g o h) = ALL(f o g) o h

and the procedure orients it in a rule from right to left and loops. Moreover, it is just the reverse which eliminates the intermediate sequence provided by "ALL g",

Thus, we inhibit REVE's orientation of the equations in rules and do it by ourselves. But we have to prove ourselves the finite termination property of the term rewriting systems. We use methods derived from [21] and we get successfully through our first results but it is difficult to go further without computing aids. Some researchers [2] have begun to study these kind of termination problems in a more general way which includes the problem of proving the termination of a set of rules modulo a set of equations (for example associativity and commutativity). Before long, we may hope that [13] may solve the general problem of proving termination modulo a set of equations and the problem of proving simple termination (which includes for example the possibility of proof for associativity and endomorphism) in a unique formalism.

However, other problems still remain.

5.3. The FP-algebra includes permutative axioms

such as

x + y = y + x

and also

(j) p->(q->x;y);(q->u;v) = q->(p->x;u);(q->y;v)

To process these kind of axioms we have to use an implementation of the Knuth-Bendix procedure modulo an equational theory which includes these permutative axioms. The next version of REVE will do that.

However, there still remains a problem. We have to find unification algorithms for an equational theory which includes the axiom (j). S. GIVLER presents a matching algorithm, but we need a unifier. C. Kirchner expects to use general results from [18] to do that in a near future.

5.4. Conclusion

Our current results [7,8] and the coming development of efficient tools in REVE comfort us in using a term rewriting system provided the problems we pointed out are solved. Moreover, other problems still remain because the procedure did not take into account specific properties of the functions such as the domain where they are defined. For example,

(d) last o (trans o [a,b]) = [last o a,last o b]

is valid as "trans o [a,b]" is defined. Thus it will be necessary to combine a kind of type evaluator with the procedure. Type evaluation is enough to know if a function is defined because we only consider functions that terminate. Future work will explore integration of type evaluation facilities in a Knuth-Bendix procedure.

We also would like to find and take into account rules on particular theories (for example an operation f which is associative and commutative like "+" which generates rules for "ALL f" or "*f" and accordingly for "ALL +" and "*+"). A solution for these kind of rules is to add premisses. These premisses allows us to take equalities or equations into account. They are also conditional rules. But theory and tools for such term rewriting systems are not yet ready though much work is done in this direction [25,16].

References

1. J. Arsac, La construction de programmes structures, Dunod, Paris, 1977.

2. L. Bachmair and D. Plaisted, "Associative Path Orderings," in Proc. 1st Conference on Rewriting Techniques and Applications, Lecture Notes in Computer Science, vol. 202, pp. 241-254, Springer Verlag, Dijon (France), 1985.

3. John Backus, "Function Level Programs As Mathematical Objects," Proceedings of the Conference on Functional Programming Languages And Computer Architecture, Portmouth, New Hampssire, pp. 1-10, Oct. 1981.

4. John Backus, "The Algebra of Functional Programs: Function Level Reasoning, Linear Equations, And Extended Definitions," Proceedings International Colloquium on the Formalization of Programming Concepts, Peniscola, Spain, vol. 107, pp. 1-43, Springer-Verlag, April 1981.

5. J. Backus, "Can Programming Be Liberated From the Von Neumann Style? A Functional Style And Its Algebra of Programs," Comm. of ACM, vol. 21, no. 8, pp. 613-641, 1978.

6. F. L. Bauer, M. Broy, N. Partsh, P. Pepper, and H. Wossner, Systematics Transformation Rules, Lecture Notes in Computer Science, 69, Springer-Verlag, 1979.

7. F. Bellegarde, "Rewriting Systems on FP Expressions that Reduce the Number of Sequences they yield," in Symposium on LISP and Functional Programming, ACM, Austin, USA, 1984.

8. F. Bellegarde, "Utilisation des Systèmes de Réécriture d'Expressions Fonctionnelles comme outils de Transformation de Programmes Itératifs," Thèse de doctorat d'Etat, Université de Nancy I, 1985.

9. R.M. Burstall and J. Darlington, "A Transformation System for Developping Recursive Programs," J of ACM, vol. 24, pp. 44-67, 1977.

10. E. W. Dijkstra, A Discipline of Programming, Prentice-Hall, 1976.

11. R. Forgaard and J.V. Guttag, "REVE: A Term Rewriting System Generator with Failure-Resistant Knuth-Bendix," MIT-LCS, 1984.

12. J. S. Givler and R. B. Kieburz, "Schema Recognition for Program Transformations," ACM Symposium on Lisp and Functional Programming, pp. 74-84, Austin, 1984.

13. I. Gnaedig and P. Lescanne, "Rewriting Systems for proving termination of rewriting systems," a paraitre, 1985.

14. J. Guyard and J. P. Jacquot, "MAIDAY : An environment for Guided Programming with a definitional language," Conf. Genie Logiciel, Orlando, 1984.

15. G. Huet, "Confluent reductions: abstract properties and applications to term rewriting systems," J. of ACM, vol. 27, no. 4, pp. 797-821, Oct. 1980.

16. S. Kaplan, "Fair Conditional Term Rewriting Systems: Unification, Termination and Confluence," Laboratoire de Recherche en Informatique, Universite d'Orsay

(France), Orsay, 1984.

17. Richard B. Kieburtz, "Transformations of FP Program Schemes," Proceedings of the Conference on Functional Programming Languages And Computer Architecture, Portmouth, New Hampshire, pp. 41-48, Oct. 1981.

18. C. Kirchner, "Méthodes et outils de conception systématique d'algorithmes d'unification dans les théories équationnelles," Thèse de doctorat d'Etat, Université de Nancy I, 1985.

19. H. Kirchner, "Preuves par complétion dans les variétés d'algèbres," Thèse de doctorat d'Etat, Université de Nancy I, 1985.

20. D. Knuth and P. Bendix, "Simple Word Problems in Universal Algebras," Computational Problems in Abstract Algebra Ed. Leech J., Pergamon Press, pp. 263-297, 1970.

21. D.S. Lankford, "On Proving Term Rewriting Systems Are Noetherian," Report Mtp-3, Math. Dept., Louisiana Tech University, May 1979.

22. P. Lescanne, "Computer Experiments with the REVE Term Rewriting System Generator," in 10th ACM Conf. on Principles of Programming Languages, pp. 99-108, Austin Texas, January 1983.

23. P. Lescanne, "Uniform termination of term rewriting systems - Recursive decomposition ordering with status," Proceedings 9th Colloque les Arbres en Algebre et en Programmation, pp. 182-194, Cambridge University Press, Bordeaux (France), 1984.

24. U. S. Reddy, "Programming with Sequences," ACM Southest Regional Conf., 1982.

25. J.L. Remy and H. Zhang, "REVEUR 4: a System for Validating Conditional Algebraic Specifications of Abstract Data Types," Proceedings of the 5th ECAI, Pisa, 1984.

26. P. Wadler, "Applicative Style Programming, Program Transformation, And List Operators," Proceedings of the Conference on Functional Programming Languages And Computer Architecture, Portmouth, New Hampshire, pp. 25-32, Oct. 1981.

27. B. Wegbreit, "Goal Directed Program Transformation," IEEE Trans. on Software Engineering, vol. 2, pp. 69-80, 1976.

28. N. Wirth, Algorithms + Data Structures = Programs, Prentice-Hall series in Automatic Computation, 1973.

The Theory of Strictness Analysis for Higher Order Functions

G L Burn(†)
GEC Hirst Research Centre, East Lane, Wembley, Middx. HA9 7PP, England.

C L Hankin and S Abramsky
Department of Computing, Imperial College of Science and Technology, 180 Queen's Gate, London, SW7 2BZ, England.

ABSTRACT

Abstract interpretation is a compile-time technique which is used to gain information about a program that may then be used to optimise the execution of the program. A particular use of abstract interpretation is in strictness analysis of functional programs. This provides the key to the exploitation of parallelism in the evaluation of programs written in functional languages. In a language that has lazy semantics, the main potential for parallelism arises in the evaluation of operands of strict operators. A function is strict in an argument if its value is undefined whenever the argument is undefined. If we can use strictness analysis to detect which arguments a function is strict in, we then know that these arguments can be safely evaluated in parallel because this will not affect the lazy semantics. Experimental results suggest that this leads to significant speed-ups.

Mycroft was the first person to apply abstract interpretation to the strictness analysis of functional programs. His framework only applies to first-order functions on flat domains. Several workers have proposed practical approaches to strictness analysis of higher-order functions over flat base domains but their work has not been accompanied by extensions to Mycroft's theoretical framework. In this paper we give sound mathematical foundations for this work and discuss some of the practical issues involved. The practical approach is proved correct in relation to the theoretical framework.

Keywords: Abstract interpretation, Strictness analysis, Functional programming, Parallel Processing, Power domains

†This author was partially supported by ESPRIT project 415 : Parallel Architectures and Languages for AIP - A VLSI Directed Approach.

1. Introduction

Abstract Interpretation is a compile-time technique that may be used to infer certain properties of a program that may then be used to optimise the performance of the program. A particular form of abstract interpretation is Strictness Analysis which allows us to infer the strictness properties of a program. This analysis was first applied to applicative programs by Mycroft [Mycroft 1981] whose work was restricted to first-order functions on flat domains. If the approach is to be of practical use it must be extended to higher-order functions on non-flat domains and this paper represents a step in that direction by presenting a theoretical framework for the strictness analysis of higher-order functions on flat domains.

A function is strict in an argument if the result of an application of the function is undefined whenever the argument is. This information may be used to control the evaluation mechanism because arguments that a function is strict in may be passed by value without affecting the termination properties of the program. In a sequential setting, the expense of building closures for strict parameters is thus avoided; in a parallel system, the strictness information may be used to control the "eagerness" of the evaluation.

What sort of information do we expect to obtain from a strictness analyser? Consider the two example functions:

$$g = \lambda w.w*2$$

$$h = \lambda x.\lambda y.\lambda f.x + f(g(y))$$

In the first case, the body of the function is a strict primitive operator and so we expect that g will be strict in its single argument. In the second case, h is a higher-order function whose body contains a strict primitive operator and from this we can infer that h is strict in both x and f but we do not have any information about y. However, for a particular application such as :

*h exp*1 *exp*2 *g*

we can see that y can also be passed by value. We require that our strictness analyser should provide us with adequate information for this analysis. In order to achieve this, the strictness analyser will need to annotate not only formal parameters to the function but also applications. (Application is a binary operation with a function and an argument as its two operands; an expression such as $x+y$ therefore involves two applications, viz. *apply* (*apply* + x) y.) This issue arises because of the higher-order parameter to h and does not arise if we restrict ourselves to first-order functions.

Abstract Interpretation involves compile-time interpretation of a program using finite domains of values that represent the properties of interest. In the case of strictness analysis for first-order functions the domain 2 (= $\{0, 1\}$ with $0 \leqslant 1$ and 0 representing non-termination and 1 representing possible termination) is a suitable candidate. The primitive operations of the language are interpreted as boolean expressions, for example the result of any strict primitive operation will be undefined if either of its operands is. Thus the required input/output behaviour is

0 *op* 0 => 0
0 *op* 1 => 0
1 *op* 0 => 0
1 *op* 1 => 1

which implies that we should interpret all strict primitive operators by :

$\lambda x.\lambda y.x$ **and** y

Applying this analysis to g, noting that the evaluation of constants always terminates, gives us

$g^{\#} = \lambda x.x$ **and** 1 $\quad (= \lambda x.x)$

as the abstract interpretation. We can then see that g needs its parameter since when we apply the abstract version to 0 we find that the result is also 0. In general, for a first-order function of n arguments, we test the strictness of the function in each argument in turn by setting the particular argument to 0 and all others to 1; if the result is 0 then we can infer that the function is strict in the selected argument. In order to perform strictness analysis for higher-order functions, we need a much richer set of values in our abstract domain; we also need type information as for each finite type there are only a finite number of possible abstract functions, and thus the process of strictness analysis becomes effective. The domain used in this new setting is defined in the next section and we solve the second problem by restricting ourselves to the typed lambda-calculus. This restriction is slightly unsatisfactory because it prohibits the definition of functions such as h which are polymorphic; however it is shown in a companion paper [Abramsky 1985] that our framework extends naturally to polymorphic functions.

Returning to the first-order case, an abstract interpretation of the conditional is :

$\lambda x.\lambda y.\lambda z.x$ **and** (y **or** z)

indicating that the condition and either the then or the else branch must be defined for the overall result to be defined. This introduces a source of inaccuracy into the analysis because if one branch of the conditional always terminates (e.g. is a constant) then we will get no information about any parameters that are only used in the other branch. An important property of abstract interpretation, that defines the sort of inaccuracy that is acceptable, is the notion of safety. If the strictness analysis indicates that a function is strict in a particular argument then we can be sure that it is; however there may be some arguments that the function is strict in which will not be detected, for example the analysis of :

$$f = \lambda x.\lambda y.\text{if } y = y \textit{ then } x+2 \textit{ else } 0$$

gives us no information about x although f is clearly strict in x. (In [Mycroft 1981] a second abstract interpretation is introduced which overcomes this particular problem. However our main point here is that we can never hope for completely accurate information from any particular abstract interpretation for strictness).

We now turn to a detailed consideration of strictness analysis for the typed lambda-calculus. First we present the abstract syntax that we shall be using:

Exp = c^α	- constants (such as 4, +, etc.)
| x^α	- variables of type α
| λx^α **Exp**	- function of type $\alpha \to \beta$ if **Exp** : β
| (**Exp**$_1$ **Exp**$_2$)	- function application, result of type β if **Exp**$_1$: $\alpha \to \beta$ and **Exp**$_2$: α
| *fix* **Exp**	- fixed point definition, result of type α if **Exp** of type $\alpha \to \alpha$

If we let Env denote the set of type-respecting mappings from variables to elements in some suitable semantic domain D (to be defined in the next section) then the standard semantics of this language are given by:

$$sem : \textbf{Exp} \to \text{Env} \to D$$

$$sem\,[[c]]\,\sigma = \mathbf{K}([[c]]) \textit{ where } \mathbf{K} : constants \to D$$

$$sem\,[[x]]\,\sigma = \sigma([[x]])$$

$$sem\,[[\lambda x^\alpha.e]]\,\sigma = \lambda y^{D_\alpha}.sem\,[[e]]\,\sigma[y/x^\alpha] \qquad (\dagger)$$

$$sem\,[[(e_1 e_2)]]\,\sigma = (sem\,[[e_1]]\,\sigma)(sem\,[[e_2]]\,\sigma)$$

$$sem\,([[fix\ e]])\,\sigma = fix(sem\,[[e]]\,\sigma)$$

where

† where D_α is the subdomain of D containing all the elements of type α.

$\sigma[y/x]$

is the environment that is the same as sigma except at x where its value is y.

Strictness analysis can be defined as a non-standard semantics using a simplified semantic domain B:

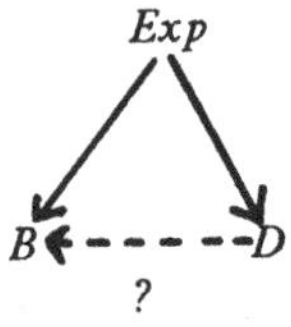

In order to satisfy ourselves that the non-standard semantics is correct (i.e. gives safe information) we will require some relationship between B and D. This relationship is defined by an abstraction map *abs* which is constructed in the next section and is used explicitly in the non-standard semantics of constants. Letting Env' denote the set of type-respecting mappings from variables to elements of B, we can define the non-standard semantics as:

$$tabs : \mathbf{Exp} \rightarrow \text{Env}' \rightarrow B$$

$$tabs\ [[c]]\ \rho = abs(\mathbf{K}([[c]]))$$

$$tabs\ [[x^\alpha]]\ \rho = \rho([[x^\alpha]])$$

$$tabs\ [[\lambda x^\alpha.e]]\ \rho = \lambda y^{B_\alpha}.tabs\ [[e]]\ \rho[y/x^\alpha]$$

$$tabs\ [[(e_1 e_2)]]\ \rho = (tabs\ [[e_1]]\ \rho)(tabs\ [[e_2]]\ \rho)$$

$$tabs\ [[fix\ e]]\ \rho = fix(tabs\ [[e]]\ \rho)$$

The main result of this paper, the Soundness Theorem for Strictness Analysis, shows that *tabs* is correct - in other words if the strictness test indicates that a particular function in B is strict in one of its arguments then the corresponding function in D will also be strict.

In the next section we define constructions for D and B, define *abs* and prove the Soundness Theorem. Because of lack of space the proofs of all but the most important results are omitted; a detailed treatment of this material may be found in [Burn, Hankin and Abramsky 1985].

2. Abstraction of Semantic Domains

We start this section by defining the domains in which our concrete functions and our abstracted functions exist, and then define a hierarchy of abstraction maps between them. A notion of *safety* is introduced, where we say that calculation in the abstract domain, in some sense, correctly models computation in the concrete domain, and our abstraction maps are shown to satisfy this criterion.

It must be noted that we are working with *semantic* objects here. For example, the textual expressions "+ 5", "$\lambda x^A .x+5$" and "$\lambda x^A .2\times 2+x+1$" all denote the same semantic object (under a normal interpretation) - the function of one argument which adds 5 to any argument. To obtain these semantic objects, we can just take a denotational semantics of the program text.

We are working with the typed λ-calculus with a single ground type, A. The syntax of type expressions, ranged over by α, β is then given by

$$\alpha ::= A \mid \alpha \rightarrow \beta .$$

Now let D_A be a flat domain containing, amongst other things, the integers and the booleans.† Then we can recursively define the domains at higher types by $D_{\alpha\rightarrow\beta} = D_\alpha \rightarrow D_\beta$. Then the domain of the typed λ-calculus is

$$D = +\{D_\alpha \mid \alpha \text{ is a type expression}\}$$

where '+' is the separated sum functor. Instead of this we could have defined the domain $D = A + D \rightarrow D$ and then interpreted correctly typed expressions in suitable retracts of D. However, we have chosen the first method of forming D because it more closely mirrors the way we wish to proceed with the theoretical development.

In the same manner, we can define $B_A = 2$ and $B_{\alpha\rightarrow\beta} = B_\alpha \rightarrow B_\beta$. We can then say

$$B = +\{B_\alpha \mid \alpha \text{ is a type expression}\}$$

where again '+' is the separated sum functor.

The idea is that B is to be our domain of abstract interpretations of elements of D. We will not define an abstraction map

$$D \xrightarrow{abs} B$$

† At the expense of decreased clarity, we could construct D_A as a sum of its various components, with injection and projection functions so that arguments to operators like '+' and 'if' would be correctly typed. We prefer not to worry about such details here.

directly, but will define maps which mirror the structure of the domains, as shown in the following diagram :

$$\begin{array}{ccccccccc} D = & D_A & + & D_{A\to A} & + & D_{A\to(A\to A)} & + & D_{(A\to A)\to A} & + \cdots \\ & \Big\downarrow abs_A & & \Big\downarrow abs_{A\to A} & & \Big\downarrow abs_{A\to(A\to A)} & & \Big\downarrow abs_{(A\to A)\to A} & \\ B = & B_A & + & B_{A\to A} & + & B_{A\to(A\to A)} & + & B_{(A\to A)\to A} & + \cdots \end{array}$$

To make notation easier, we will write typed λ-expressions in the following form :

$\lambda x^{\alpha}.e$ for $\lambda x^{D_\alpha}.e$
$\lambda x^{\bar{\alpha}}.e$ for $\lambda x^{B_\alpha}.e$

and we similarly use $\lambda x^{\mathbf{P}\alpha}.e$ and $\lambda x^{\mathbf{P}\bar{\alpha}}.e$. Also we write $\lambda x^{2}.e$ rather than $\lambda x^{\bar{A}}.e$, with obvious extensions to other "barred types", and we subscript $\perp$ by the type rather than the domain, thus using $\perp_\alpha$ for $\perp_{D_\alpha}$ and $\perp_{\bar{\alpha}}$ for $\perp_{B_\alpha}$.

Before we go on to define the abstraction maps, it is useful to have a look at the structure of B. It has some extremely important properties. In particular, each summand of B is a complete lattice, as is clear from the construction and is illustrated in the figure below.

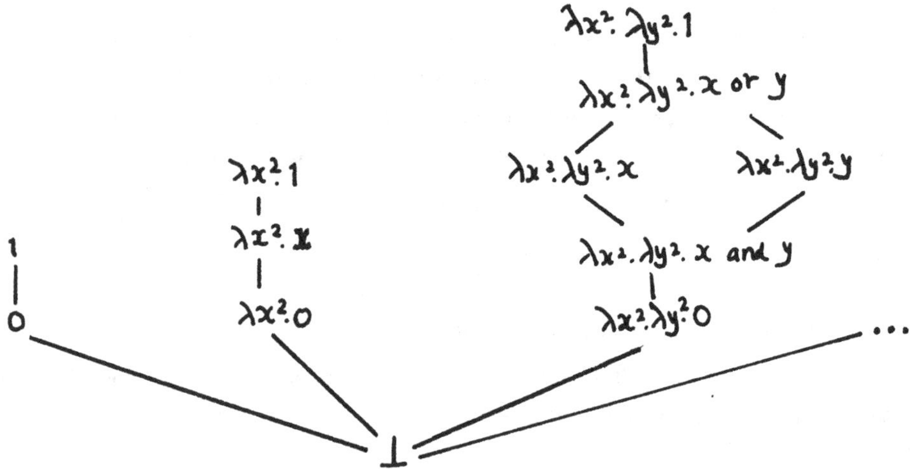

This means that the test for strictness of a function

$f : \alpha_1 \to \alpha_2 \to \cdots \to \alpha_n \to A$

reduces to testing whether

$$(abs_{\alpha_1 \to \alpha_2 \to \cdots \to \alpha_n \to A}(f)) \perp_{\overline{\alpha_1}} \top_{\overline{\alpha_2}} \cdots \top_{\overline{\alpha_n}} = 0$$

(where $\top_{\overline{\alpha_i}}$ is the top element of B_{α_i}), for if this holds then, by monotonicity, we have for any arguments $\overline{a_i} \in B_{\alpha_i}$

$$(abs_{\alpha_1 \to \alpha_2 \to \cdots \to \alpha_n \to A}(f)) \perp_{\overline{\alpha_1}} \overline{a_2} \cdots \overline{a_n} = 0$$

and so indeed, $(abs_{\alpha_1 \to \alpha_2 \to \cdots \to \alpha_n \to A}(f))\,(\perp_{\overline{\alpha_1}})$ is the bottom element of $B_{\alpha_2 \to \cdots \to \alpha_n \to A}$.

Furthermore, all the domains B_α are finite, which means we are guaranteed to be able to find fixed points and do any other calculations we may be required to do in a finite amount of time.

We shall now develop the basic definitions and facts from domain theory which we will be using throughout the rest of the paper. We shall employ some terminology from elementary category theory (see [Arbib and Manes 1975]), but this is not essential for understanding what we do. The proofs of the basic facts cited below are either directly in the literature, or obtainable by minor modifications therefrom; see [Plotkin 1976], [Hennessy and Plotkin 1979].

We shall be working over the category of domains described in [Scott 1981, 1982]. The objects of this category are the bounded-complete ω-algebraic cpo's, and the morphisms are the continuous functions between domains. The composition of morphisms $f: D \to E$, $g: E \to F$ is written thus :

$$g \circ f : D \to F.$$

The identity morphism on D is written id_D. Given domains D and E, the domain $D \to E$ is formed by taking all continuous functions from D to E, with the pointwise ordering :

$$f \leqslant g \text{ iff for all } x \in D,\ f(x) \leqslant g(x)$$

Given a domain D, then $\mathbf{P}D$, the *Hoare* (*lower* or *partial correctness*) *power domain* is formed by taking as elements all non-empty Scott-closed† subsets of D, ordered by subset inclusion. A subset $X \subseteq D$ is *Scott-closed* if

† This terminology is due to the fact that these are the closed sets with respect to the Scott topology (c.f. for example [Gierz et. al. 1980]).

(*i*) If $Y \subseteq X$ and Y is directed, then $\bigsqcup Y \in X$.

(*ii*) If $y \leqslant x \in X$ then $y \in X$.

The least Scott-closed set containing X is written X^*.

Another useful concept is that of *left-closure*; a set $X \subseteq D$ is left-closed if it satisfies (*ii*) above. The left closure of a set X is written $\mathbf{LC}(X) = \{y \mid \text{there exists } x \in X,\ y \leqslant x\}$.

Note that for elements of the Hoare power domain, the subset inclusion ordering is equivalent to the well known *Egli-Milner* ordering :

$$X \subseteq Y \text{ iff for all } x \in X, \text{ there exists } y \in Y,\ x \leqslant y$$

$$\text{and for all } y \in Y, \text{ there exists } x \in X,\ x \leqslant y$$

We shall also apply $\mathbf{P}$ to morphisms. If $f{:}D \rightarrow E$, then $\mathbf{P}f{:}\mathbf{P}D \rightarrow \mathbf{P}E$ is defined thus:

$$(\mathbf{P}f)(X) = \{f(x) \mid x \in X\}^*$$

The main properties of $\mathbf{P}$ are :

(P1) If D is a domain, $\mathbf{P}D$ is a domain.
(P2) If $f{:}D \rightarrow E$, $\mathbf{P}f{:}\mathbf{P}D \rightarrow \mathbf{P}E$ is a continuous function.
(P3) $\mathbf{P}(f \circ g) = (\mathbf{P}f) \circ (\mathbf{P}g)$
(P4) $\mathbf{P}\, id_D = id_{\mathbf{P}D}$.

This says that $\mathbf{P}$ is a *functor* from the category of domains to itself. A further property of $\mathbf{P}$ is that it is *locally monotonic* and *continuous*. This means that if $\{f_i\}$ is a chain of functions in $A \rightarrow B$, then for all i, $\mathbf{P}f_i \leqslant \mathbf{P}f_{i+1}$, and $\mathbf{P}(\bigsqcup f_i) = \bigsqcup \mathbf{P}f_i$.

Why are we using the Hoare powerdomain construction? Previous work on the theory of strictness analysis, e.g. [Mycroft 1981, Mycroft and Nielson 1983], has either used the Plotkin powerdomain, or modifications thereof. However, that work was concerned with *two* kinds of abstract interpretation; strictness analysis - definitely will *not* terminate - and also information that a computation definitely *will* terminate. The latter kind of analysis requires the Plotkin powerdomain. However, as already mentioned, we are only interested in strictness analysis. The Hoare powerdomain is well suited to this purpose, since for example at a flat domain F, $\mathbf{P}F$ contains the sets $\{\bot\}$ and F, the first of which corresponds to definite non-termination, the second to possible termination. The Hoare powerdomain is also pleasant to work with from a technical point of view.

We shall need to use some additional constructions associated with the powerdomain functor. Firstly, for each domain D we have a map

$$\{\!|.|\!\}_D : D \to \mathbf{P}D$$

defined by :

$$\{\!|d|\!\}_D = \mathrm{LC}(\{d\}).$$

This satisfies the following properties :

(P5) $\{\!|.|\!\}_D$ is continuous.

(P6) For $f{:}D \to E$, $\mathbf{P}f \circ \{\!|.|\!\}_D = \{\!|.|\!\}_E \circ f$.

This says that $\{\!|.|\!\}$ is a *natural transformation* from $\mathbf{I}$, the identity functor on the category of domains, to $\mathbf{P}$.

Secondly, for each domain D we define

$$\biguplus_D : \mathbf{PP}D \to \mathbf{P}D$$

by

$$\biguplus_D(\Theta) = \{x \mid \text{for some } X \in \Theta,\ x \in X\} = \bigcup \Theta.$$

This satisfies :

(P7) $\biguplus_D$ is continuous.

(P8) for $f{:}D \to E$, $\biguplus_E \circ \mathbf{PP}f = \mathbf{P}f \circ \biguplus_D$.

This says that $\biguplus$ is a natural transformation from $\mathbf{P}^2$ to $\mathbf{P}$.

Now $(\mathbf{P}, \{\!|.|\!\}, \biguplus)$ forms a *monad* or *triple*. We shall not use this fact, but we will use the following, additional observation. Suppose D is a domain which is a complete lattice. Then the least upper bound operation, viewed as a function

$$\bigsqcup : \mathbf{P}D \to D$$

satisfies :

(P9) $\bigsqcup$ is continuous

(P10) $\bigsqcup \circ \{\!|.|\!\}_D = id_D$

(P11) $\bigsqcup \circ \mathbf{P}(\bigsqcup) = \bigsqcup \circ \biguplus_D$.

This says that $\biguplus : \mathbf{P}D \to D$ is an *algebra* of the monad $(\mathbf{P}, \{\!|.|\!\}, \biguplus)$. We will use (P9) and (P10) in the sequel.

Henceforth, we shall omit the subscripts from instances of $\{\!|.|\!\}$, $\biguplus$ where they are clear from the context. The facts we shall be assuming about the constructions introduced above are summarised in (P1) - (P11).

We now turn to the crux of this paper, namely the definitions of the abstraction maps. This provides the basis for the entire theory subsequently developed. Recall that our task is to define, for each type α, a map

$$abs_{\alpha} : D_{\alpha} \to B_{\alpha}$$

We proceed by induction over types. At each type α, we will in fact define *three* maps :

$abs_{\alpha} : D_{\alpha} \to B_{\alpha}$ (pronounced 'little abs')

$Abs_{\alpha} : \mathbf{P}D_{\alpha} \to \mathbf{P}B_{\alpha}$ (pronounced 'big abs')

$Conc_{\alpha} : \mathbf{P}B_{\alpha} \to \mathbf{P}D_{\alpha}$

The crucial part of the definition is abs_{α}. Once we have defined abs_{α}, the other definitions follow directly :

$$Abs_{\alpha} = \mathbf{P}abs_{\alpha}$$

$$Conc_{\alpha}(S) = \biguplus\{T \mid Abs_{\alpha}(T) \leqslant S\}.$$

Moreover, the base case for the definition of abs, that is abs_A, is straightforward - it is exactly the same as Mycroft's definition of HALT in [Mycroft 1981] :

$$abs_A(a) = 1 \quad (a \neq \bot_A)$$

$$abs_A(\bot_A) = 0.$$

(Note that we then have

$$Conc_A(\{0\}) = \{\bot_A\}$$

$$Conc_A(\{0, 1\}) = D_A$$

as expected.)

Thus what remains to be done is the inductive step in the definition of abs, i.e. to define $abs_{\alpha \to \beta}$, assuming we have already defined abs_{α}, Abs_{α} and $Conc_{\alpha}$, and abs_{β}, Abs_{β}

and $Conc_\beta$. A diagram is helpful here :

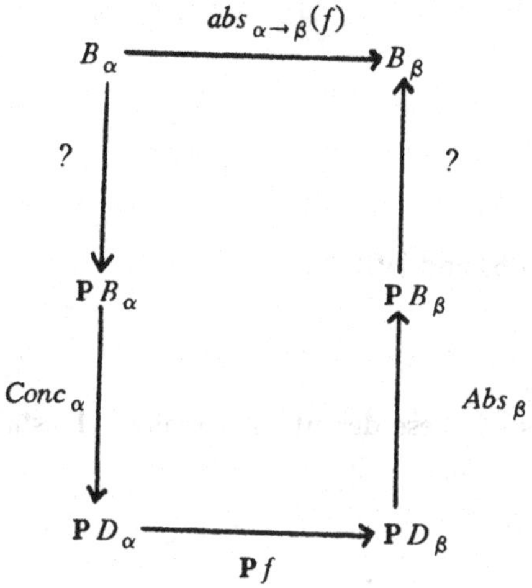

Given $f{:}D_\alpha \to D_\beta$, we want to define $abs_{\alpha\to\beta}(f)$. Starting with an argument b in B_α, a diagram chase using the functions already defined will give us a result in B_β, *provided* we can :

(i) embed b in $\mathbf{P}B_\alpha$

(ii) collapse the set of abstractions of possible results in $\mathbf{P}B_\beta$ into a *single* abstract value in B_β.

Clearly, we have a ready-made solution to (i) in the form of $\{\!|\,.\,|\!\}$, whose purpose is precisely to embed a domain in its powerdomain. For (ii), we use the function $\bigsqcup{:}\mathbf{P}B_\beta \to B_\beta$. The intuitive motivation for this is that in performing (ii) we must ensure that any possibility of termination in the actual computation is recorded, in order to preserve the safety of our abstract interpretation. This is done by taking the least upper bound, as the minimal safe representative.

We can also justify the choice of $\bigsqcup$ formally, by noting that it gives an algebra for the powerdomain monad, and indeed is the unique function from $\mathbf{P}B_\beta$ to B_β which does so. In particular, the identity (P10) will be important in the sequel.

Thus our definition of $abs_{\alpha\to\beta}$ is :

$$abs_{\alpha\to\beta}(f) \;=\; \bigsqcup \circ Abs_\beta \circ \mathbf{P}f \circ Conc_\alpha \circ \{\!|\,.\,|\!\}.$$

If we define

$$\Psi : (\mathbf{P}B_\alpha \to \mathbf{P}B_\beta) \to (B_\alpha \to B_\beta)$$

by

$$\Psi(g) = \bigsqcup \circ g \circ \{.\}$$

then obviously we have

$$abs_{\alpha\rightarrow\beta}(f) = \Psi(Abs_{\beta} \circ \mathbf{P}f \circ Conc_{\alpha}).$$

A useful property of Ψ, which follows from (P6) and (P10), is :

(P12) $\Psi(\mathbf{P}f) = f$.

We now consider some of the properties of these definitions. Lemma 1 establishes that the definitions are well-founded.

Lemma 1:

For all types α we have the following :

(*i*) abs_{α} and Abs_{α} are continuous.

(*ii*) There is a continuous function $abs_{\alpha}^{-1} : B_{\alpha} \rightarrow D_{\alpha}$ which is a right inverse of abs_{α}. i.e. $abs_{\alpha} \circ abs_{\alpha}^{-1} = id_{B_{\alpha}}$.

(*iii*) abs_{α} and Abs_{α} are onto.

(*iv*) $Abs_{\alpha} \circ Conc_{\alpha} = id_{\mathbf{P}B_{\alpha}}$

(*v*) $Conc_{\alpha}$ is well-defined and continuous.

Proof:

By induction over the type α.

□

Having defined our abstraction and concretisation maps, we must define what is an appropriate notion of safety. A criterion must be established which says when calculations in the abstract domain :

$$B_{\alpha} \xrightarrow{abs_{\alpha\rightarrow\beta}(f)} B_{\beta}$$

correctly mirror calculations in the concrete domain :

$$D_{\alpha} \xrightarrow{f} D_{\beta}$$

The following diagram expresses what we will mean by *safety*. It is essentially a generalisation of diagrams appearing elsewhere (for example [Cousot and Cousot 1979],

[Mycroft 1981], [Mycroft and Nielson 1983]).

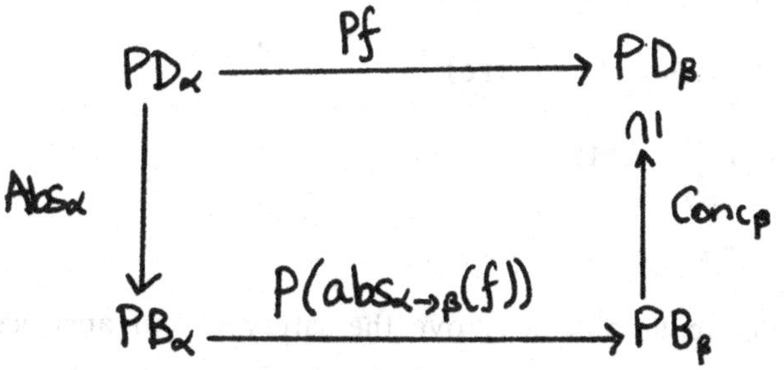

In words this diagram says that if we abstract the argument (set) to the function, apply the abstracted function (pointwise) and concretise the result, then we will obtain more results than if we had applied the function (pointwise) to the argument (set). For instance, when doing strictness analysis, this means that if the calculation along the first route gives the set with only $\perp_\beta$ in it when applied to $\{\perp_\alpha\}$, then the route along the top must also have given $\{\perp_\beta\}$, and so the function must have been strict in its argument.

That the abstraction and concretisation maps we have defined satisfy the safety criterion is Proposition 2, and we will proceed by introducing a preliminary lemma and a proposition. Proposition 1 is well worth taking special note of, as it is used repeatedly throughout the rest of the paper. It says that abstraction is a semi-homomorphism of function application.

Lemma 2:

$$Conc_\alpha \circ Abs_\alpha \geqslant id_{\mathbf{P}\,D_\alpha}$$

□

Proposition 1:

If $f \in D_{\alpha\to\beta}$ then $abs_{\alpha\to\beta}(f) \circ abs_\alpha \geqslant abs_\beta \circ f$ (or in terms of elements, if $s \in D_\alpha$, then $abs_{\alpha\to\beta}(f)(abs_\alpha(s)) \geqslant abs_\beta(f(s))$).

Proof:

$$abs_{\alpha\to\beta}(f) \circ abs_\alpha = \biguplus \circ Abs_\beta \circ \mathbf{P}f \circ Conc_\alpha \circ \{\!|.|\!\} \circ abs_\alpha$$

$$= \biguplus \circ Abs_\beta \circ \mathbf{P}f \circ Conc_\alpha \circ Abs_\alpha \circ \{\!|.|\!\} \qquad \text{(P6)}$$

$$\geqslant \biguplus \circ Abs_\beta \circ \mathbf{P}f \circ \{\!|.|\!\} \qquad \text{Lemma 2}$$

$$= \biguplus \circ \mathbf{P}\, abs_{\beta} \circ \mathbf{P} f \circ \{.\}$$

$$= \biguplus \circ \mathbf{P}(abs_{\beta} \circ f) \circ \{.\} \qquad \text{(P3)}$$

$$= \biguplus \circ \{.\} \circ abs_{\beta} \circ f \qquad \text{(P6)}$$

$$= abs_{\beta} \circ f \qquad \text{(P10)}$$

□

We are now in a position to be able to prove the safety of our abstraction and concretisation maps.

Proposition 2:

The abstraction and concretisation maps satisfy the safety criterion. That is,

$$\mathbf{P} f \subseteq Conc_{\beta} \circ \mathbf{P}(abs_{\alpha \to \beta}(f)) \circ Abs_{\alpha}$$

Proof:

$$\mathbf{P}(abs_{\alpha \to \beta}(f)) \circ Abs_{\alpha} = \mathbf{P}(abs_{\alpha \to \beta}(f)) \circ \mathbf{P}\, abs_{\alpha}$$

$$= \mathbf{P}(abs_{\alpha \to \beta}(f) \circ abs_{\alpha}) \qquad \text{(P3)}$$

$$\geqslant \mathbf{P}(abs_{\beta} \circ f)$$

Proposition 1 and **P** is locally monotone

$$= \mathbf{P}\, abs_{\beta} \circ \mathbf{P} f \qquad \text{(P3)}$$

$$= Abs_{\beta} \circ \mathbf{P} f$$

Now we can take $Conc_{\beta}$ of both sides and write $\geqslant$ as $\supseteq$ to obtain

$$Conc_{\beta} \circ \mathbf{P}(abs_{\alpha \to \beta}(f)) \circ Abs_{\alpha} \supseteq Conc_{\beta} \circ Abs_{\beta} \circ \mathbf{P} f$$

$$\supseteq \mathbf{P} f \qquad \text{Lemma 2}$$

□

The next two lemmata allow us to see what happens when we abstract and concretise the least element of various types.

Lemma 3:

(*i*) $abs_\alpha(\perp_\alpha) = \perp_{\bar\alpha}$ and $Abs_\alpha(\{\perp_\alpha\}) = \{\perp_{\bar\alpha}\}$.

(*ii*) If $f \in D_\alpha$, $f \neq \perp_\alpha$, then $abs_\alpha(f) \neq \perp_{\bar\alpha}$ and $Abs_\alpha(\{\!|f|\!\}) \neq \{\perp_{\bar\alpha}\}$.

□

Lemma 4:

$Conc_\alpha(\{\perp_{\bar\alpha}\}) = \{\perp_\alpha\}$.

□

The following proposition shows that $abs_{\alpha\to\beta}$ is completely accurate as regards strictness information. Use of this proposition simplifies the ensuing development. It was suggested to us by Simon Peyton Jones.

Proposition 3:

$(abs_{\alpha\to\beta}(f))\perp_{\bar\alpha} = \perp_{\bar\beta}$ if and only if $f(\perp_\alpha) = \perp_\beta$.

Proof:

(only if) $\perp_{\bar\beta} = abs_{\alpha\to\beta}(f)\,(\perp_{\bar\alpha})$

$= abs_{\alpha\to\beta}(f)\,(abs_\alpha(\perp_\alpha))$ Lemma 3

$\geqslant abs_\beta(f(\perp_\alpha))$ Proposition 1

So $abs_\beta(f(\perp_\alpha)) = \perp_{\bar\beta}$ and thus, by Lemma 3, $f(\perp_\alpha) = \perp_\beta$.

(if) $(abs_{\alpha\to\beta}(f))\,(\perp_{\bar\alpha}) = \biguplus Abs_\beta(\mathbf{P}\,f(Conc_\alpha(\{\!|\perp_{\bar\alpha}|\!\})))$

$= \biguplus Abs_\beta(\mathbf{P}\,f(\{\!|\perp_\alpha|\!\}))$ Lemma 4

$= \biguplus Abs_\beta(\{\!|f(\perp_\alpha)|\!\})$ (P6)

$= \biguplus Abs_\beta(\{\!|\perp_\beta|\!\})$ since $f(\perp_\alpha) = \perp_\beta$

$= \biguplus \{\!|\perp_{\bar\beta}|\!\}$ Lemma 3

$= \perp_{\bar\beta}$ (P10)

□

We are now in the position where we can work out what the abstract interpretations of the predefined functions are.

Lemma 5:

Denoting A by A^1 and $A \rightarrow A^n$ by A^{n+1}, if $f : A^{n+1}$, $f \neq \bot_{A^{n+1}}$, f strict in all its arguments, then $abs_{A^{n+1}}(f) = \lambda x_1^2 \cdots \lambda x_n^2 . x_1 \textbf{ and } \cdots \textbf{ and } x_n$.

□

We see this means that functions such as '+' and '×' have abstract interpretation $\lambda x^2 . \lambda y^2 . x \textbf{ and } y$ which is the same as in [Mycroft 1981], except that we regard the functions as being curried.

For each type α we have the conditional if_α of type $if_\alpha : A \rightarrow \alpha \rightarrow \alpha \rightarrow \alpha$.

Lemma 6:

$abs_{A \rightarrow \alpha \rightarrow \alpha \rightarrow \alpha}(if_\alpha) = \lambda x^2 . \lambda y^{\overline{\alpha}} . \lambda z^{\overline{\alpha}} . x \textbf{ and}_{\overline{\alpha}} \bigsqcup\{y, z\}$ where $\textbf{and}_{\overline{\alpha}} : 2 \rightarrow B_\alpha \rightarrow B_\alpha$ is defined by :

$$0 \textbf{ and}_{\overline{\alpha}}\, e = \bot_{\overline{\alpha}}$$

$$1 \textbf{ and}_{\overline{\alpha}}\, e = e$$

□

This is the natural extension of the interpretation of the conditional over $A \rightarrow A \rightarrow A \rightarrow A$, for in this case $\textbf{and}_{\overline{\alpha}}$ is just the ordinary **and** function, and $\bigsqcup$ is just the **or** function. For objects y and z of higher type, $\bigsqcup\{y, z\}$ is computed pointwise.

Before proving the main result, the Soundness Theorem for Strictness Analysis, we need two technical lemmata. The first states a semi-homomorphic relationship between fixed points and abstraction. This is used in the proof of the second, which states that if the environments ρ and σ stand in the relationship $\rho \geqslant abs \circ \sigma$, then the *tabs* of an expression in the environment ρ is at least as defined as the abstraction of the semantics of the expression in the environment σ.

Lemma 7:

$$fix(abs_{\alpha \rightarrow \alpha}(f)) \geqslant abs_\alpha(fix(f))$$

□

Lemma 8:

If $\rho \geqslant abs \circ \sigma$ and $e : \alpha$, then $tabs\ [[e]]\ \rho \geqslant abs_{\alpha}(sem\ [[e]]\ \sigma)$.

□

Theorem (Soundness Theorem for Strictness Analysis):

If $f : \alpha \rightarrow \beta$ and $\rho \geqslant abs \circ \sigma$, then $(tabs\ [[f]]\ \rho)(\perp_{\bar{\alpha}}) = \perp_{\bar{\beta}}$ implies $(sem\ [[f]]\ \sigma)(\perp_{\alpha}) = \perp_{\beta}$.

Proof:

Suppose $f : \alpha \rightarrow \beta$.

$(tabs\ [[f]]\ \rho)(\perp_{\bar{\alpha}}) = \perp_{\bar{\beta}}$

=> $abs_{\alpha \rightarrow \beta}(sem\ [[f]]\ \sigma)\ (\perp_{\bar{\alpha}}) = \perp_{\bar{\beta}}$ Lemma 8

=> $(sem\ [[f]]\ \sigma)(\perp_{\alpha}) = \perp_{\beta}$ Proposition 3

□

Thus if $(tabs\ [[f]]\ \rho)(\perp_{\bar{\alpha}}) = \perp_{\bar{\beta}}$ then we can safely deduce that f needs its argument.

3. Conclusions

We have exhibited a method for strictness analysis of a typed language incorporating higher order functions over flat base domains, which has a sound theoretical foundation. This is an expression based interpretation, which works on program texts, allowing us to decide at each apply node whether an argument is definitely needed or not. The pragmatics of implementing the textual abstraction map in a compiler are currently being investigated by the authors. Some work on the implementation of strictness analysis has been reported in [Clack and Peyton Jones 1985].

Much of the material is independent of the interpretation of the base domains, so it should be fairly easy to extend the framework to handle other abstract interpretations. For example, if we were to define strictness analysis for non-flat base domains, then we may be able to extend this to higher order functions by using the structure presented in this paper. (The trivial approach of setting the abstract interpretation of *cons* to $\lambda x.\lambda y.1$ is already supported here.)

Another, highly desirable extension is to a language allowing polymorphic functions ([Milner 1978]). This topic is treated in a forthcoming paper by one of the authors

[Abramsky 1985].

Acknowledgements

A number of people have assisted in the development of the ideas presented in this paper. The first author had many useful discussions with David Bevan during the early development of this work. We thank Pete Harrison and Simon Peyton Jones for their careful reading of this paper, and for their helpful comments. Simon in particular made many excellent suggestions and constructive criticisms which have materially improved the presentation.

Geoffrey Burn is partly funded by ESPRIT project 415 : Parallel Architectures and Languages for AIP - A VLSI Directed Approach.

References

[Abramsky 1985]

Abramsky, S., Strictness Analysis and Polymorphic Invariance, *Workshop on Programs as Data Objects*, DIKU, Denmark, 17-19 October, 1985.

[Arbib and Manes 1975]

Arbib, M.A., and Manes, E.G., *Arrows, Structures and Functors : The Categorical Imperative*, Academic Press, New York and London, 1975.

[Burn, Hankin and Abramsky 1985]

Burn, G.L., Hankin, C.L., and Abramsky, S., Strictness Analysis for Higher-Order Functions, To appear in *Science of Computer Programming*. Also *Imperial College of Science and Technology, Deprartment of Computing, Research Report DoC 85/6, April 1985*,

[Clack and Peyton Jones 1985]

Clack, C., and Peyton Jones, S.L., Generating Parallelism From Strictness Analysis, *Department of Computer Science, University College London, Internal Note 1679*, February, 1985.

[Cousot and Cousot 1979]

Cousot, P., and Cousot, R., Systematic Design of Program Analysis Frameworks, *Conference Record of the 6th ACM Symposium on Principles of Programming Languages*, pp. 269-282, 1979.

[Gierz et. al. 1980]

Gierz, G., Hofmann, K.H., Keimel, K., Lawson, J.D., Mislove, M. and Scott, D.S., *A Compendium of Continuous Lattices*, Springer-Verlag, 1980.

[Hennessy and Plotkin 1979]

Hennessy, M., and Plotkin, G.D., Full Abstraction for a Simple Parallel Programming Language, Proceedings MFCS '79, Becvar, J. (ed.), *Springer Verlag LNCS 74*, 1979.

[Milner 1978]

Milner, R., A Theory of Type Polymorphism in Programming, *Journal of Computer and System Sciences 17*, 348-375, 1978.

[Mycroft 1981]

Mycroft, A., *Abstract Interpretation and Optimising Transformations for Applicative Programs*, PhD. Thesis, University of Edinburgh, 1981.

[Mycroft and Nielson 1983]

Mycroft, A., and Nielson, F., Strong Abstract Interpretation Using Power Domains (Extended Abstract) *Proc. 10th International Colloquium on Automata, Languages and Programming : Springer Verlag LNCS 154*, Diaz, J. (ed.), Barcelona, Spain, 18th-22nd July, 1983, 536-547.

[Plotkin 1976]

Plotkin, G.D., A Powerdomain Construction, *SIAM J. Comput. 5* 3 (Sept 1976) 452-487.

[Plotkin 1982]

Plotkin, G.D., A Power Domain For Countable Non-Determinism (Extended Abstract), *Proc. 9th International Colloquium on Automata, Languages and Programming : Springer Verlag LNCS 140*, Nielson, M, and Schmidt, E.M. (eds.), 1982, 418-428.

[Scott 1981]

Scott, D., *Lectures on a Mathematical Theory of Computation*, Tech. Monograph PRG-19, Oxford Univ. Computing Lab., Programming Research Group, 1981.

[Scott 1982]

Scott, D., Domains for Denotational Semantics, *Automata, Languages and Programming*, Proceedings of the 10th International Colloquium, Nielsen M, and Schmidt, E.M., (eds.), Springer-Verlag Lecture Notes in Computer Science, vol. 140, 1982, 577-613.

[Stoy 1977]

Stoy, J.E., *Denotational Semantics: The Scott-Strachey Approach to Programming Language Theory*, MIT Press, Cambridge Massachusetts, 1977.

[Wadsworth 1971]

Wadsworth, C.P., *Semantics and Pragmatics of the Lambda Calculus (Chapter 4)*, PhD Thesis, University of Oxford, 1971.

Recognition of generative languages

Henning Christiansen
Roskilde University Centre
Post Box 260, DK-4000 Roskilde, Denmark

Generative languages are a comprehensive class which includes so-called extensible programming languages. Our formal descriptions of syntax and semantics of these languages differ from traditional approaches in that any kind of declaration is viewed as a language extension. As a consequence, the concept of types in programming languages is handled in a simple and conceptually satisfactory fashion. In this paper we show how recursive-descent parsing can be adapted for generative languages.

New powerful languages may be described this way and implementations of traditional languages can be improved.

1 Introduction

What is a generative language?

The term 'extensible language' has been used with different meanings — most often to describe a traditional programming language equipped with some kind of macro pre-processor (Solntseff, Yezerski, 1974, Layzell, 1985, Triance, Layzell, 1985). It is inherent in the design of most of these 'extensible languages' that their creators have not recognized the close analogy between such 'extensions' and usual abstraction mechanisms. For example, the following declaration in a Pascal program

procedure P;
begin . . . **end**

can be thought of as an extension of Pascal. A brand new kind of statement has been created and new algorithms such as P; P; P can be written.

In another paper, (Christiansen, 1985), we have developed the concept of generative language descriptions by which one can describe languages with extremely powerful abstraction mechanisms, such as declaration of new control structures. Further, generative language descriptions provide a conceptually more satisfactory treatment of context-sensitive aspects of programming languages: Any type, predefined or declared by the user, has its own nonterminal in the grammar and any declaration gives birth to new syntactic and semantic rules. Consequently type-checking disappears.

When we use the term 'generative language' we emphasize that the language has some capability for introducing new linguistic concepts — and we focus on that property. Examples of generative languages are compiler generators (with dedicated languages to express syntax and semantics), Pascal, (constants, variables, types, procedures, and functions), and so-called 4th generation tools for development of user interfaces.

The achievements of this paper

This paper presents a set of concepts and tools for designers and implementors of generative programming languages. We develop general top-down parsing techniques for such languages and give suggestions for multi-pass parsing of recursive grammars.

Our generative language descriptions are generalizations of attribute grammars (Knuth, 1968, Watt, Madsen, 1979) and denotational semantics (Milne, Strachey, 1976, Mosses, 1983). A full account of generative language descriptions can be found in (Christiansen, 1985). Parsing techniques are 'adaptive' versions of traditional recursive-descent (or predictive) parsers (Aho, Ullman, 1977).

Our definition of parsers and their correctness is made on a formal algebraic basis. However, the parsers that appear in this paper are written in a hypothetical, algorithmic language. Correctness can be demonstrated for the most part through common sense based upon the readers intuition and experience with such languages. No formal semantics of this language needs to be involved.

Compilers for generative languages can be derived from these parsers using well-known techniques for compiler generation (Mosses, 1980, Christiansen, Jones, 1983). This subject is elaborated in the report (Christiansen, 1986).

Generative language descriptions together with the suggested implementation techniques open a way towards new powerful programming languages with a high capability of abstraction and extensibility. Our techniques may also be used in the development and improvement of incremental programming environments. For example, it would be natural for a syntax-directed editor, given a procedure identifier, to set up a template showing the types of the actual parameters or, given a variable indicating the head of an assignment statement, the editor would cause a template involving the type of that variable to appear.

Outline

Section 2 gives an informal introduction to generative language descriptions. Necessary mathematical tools and notation are introduced in section 3 whereas section 4 gives precise definitions of our grammars and language descriptions.

In section 5 we introduce the concept of interpretations: A language description may be interpreted as a 'rewriting system' which generates all possible programs in the language; or alternatively, as an algorithm, each rule describing a sequence of actions to be taken by some parser or compiler.

Section 6 is concerned with the actual parsing techniques. In section 7 we summarize the different techniques and give directions for necessary or related future research.

2 An informal introduction to generative language descriptions

Precise definitions of generative grammars and language descriptions are given in section 4. In the present section we give a gentle introduction with examples to the concepts. More comprehensive examples may be found in (Christiansen, 1985).

Our first example language consists of simple integer expressions with local constant declarations. An example of a program is

1 + **const** two = 2 **in** two + 3 **end**

whose semantics or meaning is a computation which yields the result 6. The constellation

1 + two

is not a program in the language.

A traditional description of this language will include a number of context-free rules, including the following.

⟨exp⟩::= **const** ⟨identifier⟩ = ⟨integer⟩ **in** ⟨exp⟩ **end**

⟨integer⟩::= ⟨identifier⟩

The latter rule, however, is too general so a clever system of predicates must be added to exclude nonsense like '1 + two' as programs. A denotational semantic description of the language must — by nature — express the meaning of an application of that rule as a function which looks up the current value of a constant in a table of some sort.

This kind of description is conceptually unsatisfactory: The programmers purpose of writing

const two = 2 **in** . . . **end**

is to make a new linguistic concept, namely an integer constant with the name 'two', available. Further, the programmers conception of the *meaning* of 'two' is not some mysterious function, but simply the number 2.

In our approach, this discrepancy is remedied as follows. The declaration above is considered to be a creation of a new syntactic rule

⟨integer⟩::= two

with an associated semantic rule which directly states the value 2.

This view of programming languages is formally expressed in our descriptive tools, generative grammars and generative language descriptions, the latter expressing both syntax and semantics. A generative grammar is a variant of attribute grammars enhanced with a context-sensitive derivation relation: The possible derivations from a nonterminal is determined by the grammar found in a specialized inherited attribute of that nonterminal. For example, a generative grammar rule for the **const-in-end** construct may be sketched as follows. The notation is taken over from the extended attribute grammars of (Watt, Madsen, 1979).

⟨exp↓grammar⟩::=
  const ⟨identifier↓grammar↑id⟩ = ⟨integer↓grammar⟩
  in ⟨exp↓grammar extended with a rule for the new constant⟩ **end**

Hence we need no equivalent to the general context-free rule

⟨exp⟩::= ⟨identifier⟩.

A specialized version of that rule is created whenever a new constant is declared.

Example 2.1. The following rules constitute a generative grammar for the example language.

⟨program↓g⟩::= ⟨exp↓g⟩
⟨exp↓g⟩::= ⟨integer↓g⟩
⟨exp↓g⟩::= ⟨exp↓g⟩ + ⟨exp↓g⟩
⟨exp↓g⟩::=
  const ⟨identifier↓g↑id⟩ = ⟨integer↓g⟩
  in ⟨exp↓g & generate-const(id)⟩ **end**
where generate-const(*id*) is the rule
  ⟨integer↓g⟩::= *id*
for any identifier *id*.
⟨identifier↓g⟩::= A
  . . .
⟨integer↓g⟩::= 0
  . . .

The variable 'g' represents the set of generative grammars. The operator '&' adds a rule to a grammar; if the rule is already present, the grammar is unchanged.
□

A generative language description is a generative grammar in which the synthesized attributes are used to convey the meanings of language constructs. As in a denotational semantics, the dependencies of semantic expressions are constrained such that the meaning of a phrase depends only on the meanings of its subphrases. For the example language considered above we have chosen to express meanings in terms of a language which represents an abstract stack machine. In this semantic language '•' is a sequencing operator, '***plus***' adds the two top elements on the stack, and '***answer***' returns the value on top of the stack. For example, the rule

⟨exp↓g↑$\boldsymbol{a_1}$•$\boldsymbol{a_2}$•***plus***⟩::= ⟨exp↓g↑$\boldsymbol{a_1}$⟩ + ⟨exp↓g↑$\boldsymbol{a_2}$⟩

expresses that the meaning of the compound expression is a computation which consists of the computations for the subexpression (denoted by $\boldsymbol{a_1}$ and $\boldsymbol{a_2}$) followed by the '***plus***' operator.

Example 2.2. A generative language description for the example language is as follows.

⟨program↓g↑*answer(a)*⟩::= ⟨exp↓g↑*a*⟩

⟨exp↓g↑*n*⟩::= ⟨integer↓g↑*n*⟩

⟨exp↓g↑a_1•a_2•*plus*⟩::= ⟨exp↓g↑a_1⟩ + ⟨exp↓g↑a_2⟩

⟨exp↓g↑*a*⟩::=
  const ⟨identifier↓g↑id⟩ = ⟨integer↓g↑*n*⟩
  in ⟨exp↓g & generate-const(id, *n*)↑*a*⟩ **end**

where generate-const(*id*, *n*) is the rule
  ⟨integer↓g↑*n*⟩::= *id*
for any identifier *id* and integer *n*.

⟨identifier↓g↑A⟩::= A

. . .

⟨integer↓g↑*0*⟩::= 0

. . .

The operator '&' adds a rule to a language description; if there is already a rule with the same right-hand side it is removed.

□

For example, for the program

1 + **const** two = 2 **in** two + 3 **end**

the language description in example 1.2 prescribes the following semantic term.

answer(1•(2•3•plus)•plus).

In section 4 a language description for a simple imperative language with mutually recursive procedures is given. Examples describing declarations of types, modules, control-structures, etc. may be found in (Christiansen, 1985). For example, when a new type is declared new rules are created for

- construction and selection of values,
- declarations of variables of that type,
- the use of the type in other declarations.

3 Tools and notation

Here we introduce the necessary mathematical tools and notation. Without further definition we use the following concepts from many-sorted algebra. For an introduction to this subject, see (Goguen, Thatcher, Wagner, 1979).

- signatures, Σ, consisting of sorts s, . . . and operations op: $s_1\ s_2 \ldots s_n \rightarrow s$, . . .
- for given signature Σ, Σ-algebras A with carriers A^s, . . ., and operations op_A, . . .
- for given signature Σ, subsignatures $\Sigma' \subseteq \Sigma$,
- for given algebra A, subalgebras $A' \subseteq A$,
- for given signature Σ and Σ-algebras A and B, Σ-homomorphisms: A → B
- for given signature Σ, the term algebra Σ-TERM,
- for given signatures Σ_1 and Σ_2, signature morphisms $\sigma: \Sigma_1 \rightarrow \Sigma_2$ which map sorts of Σ_1 to sorts of Σ_2 and operators of Σ_1 to suitable terms over Σ_2 (extended with variables),
- for given signature morphism $\sigma: \Sigma_1 \rightarrow \Sigma_2$ and Σ_2-algebra A, the derived algebra σ(A); the canonical homomorphism Σ_1-TERM → σ(A) is (ambiguously) denoted σ.

The following definition is meant to set up a general signature and algebra which is expected to include any mathematical notion we might need.

Definition 3.1. Let D be a particular signature, **D** a particular D-algebra.

□

In the sequel we often require[1] that some signature is a subsignature of D or some algebra is a subalgebra of **D**. The symbol **D** is also used to denote carriers in **D** when no further specification is needed.

Definition 3.2. If S is some set, then Set-of(S) denotes the set of subsets of S. Further, S^* denotes the set of finite and possibly empty strings of elements of S.
□

The set Token defined below is identical to terminal symbols in grammars and input symbols for parsers.

Definition 3.3. Let Token be a particular sort in D and corresponding carrier in **D**. A *language* is an element of Set-of(Token*). A translation is an element of Set-of(Token* × **D**).
□

If a translation includes $\langle abc, 3\rangle$ this should be understood: The string 'abc' is translated into the number 3.

The following definition introduces convenient notation.

Definition 3.4. If f is a function A → B, f is (ambiguously) extended to sets and translations as follows.

$$f\colon \text{Set-of}(A) \to \text{Set-of}(B)$$
$$\equiv \lambda A'.\{f(a) \mid a \in A'\}$$
$$f\colon \text{Set-of}(\text{Token}^* \times A) \to \text{Set-of}(\text{Token}^* \times B)$$
$$\equiv \lambda \text{trans}.\{\langle \text{token}^*, f(a)\rangle \mid \langle \text{token}^*, a\rangle \in \text{trans}\}$$

□

The following definition states a general purpose algorithmic language, GALGOL. The content of GALGOL is not specified further, but we expect the language to include recursive procedures, a variety of data types, and, in fact, any feature we might desire. As indicated by the definition, GALGOL is expected to include nondeterminism, i.e. the ability to produce a *set* of results for given input.

Definition 3.5. Let GALGOL denote a particular subsignature of D and the corresponding subalgebra of **D**. Let further *program* be a particular sort of GALGOL whose carrier is

Token* → Set-of(**D**).

□

4 Syntax and semantics

Compared with the definitions of (Christiansen, 1985) we have made some technical restrictions of which the most important are

- only one synthesized and one inherited attribute can be associated with a nonterminal,
- it is required that each variable in a rule appears in exactly one defining position (Watt, Madsen, 1979).

This, however, does not limit on the expressive power of the formalism, but it is made comparatively easier to describe general parsing algorithms.

4.1 Grammars

It is assumed that **D** (definition 3.1) includes facilities to write typed (or 'sorted') expressions which include typed (or 'sorted') variables. Further, we use the concepts

- assignment of values to variables, and
- evaluation under given assignment

with their usual meaning — not specified further.

1. Sometimes implicitly!

Notation. The letter 'v' with possible subscripts and primes will denote variables of some type. The constellation

$$\exp(v_1 \ldots v_n)$$

(with possible subscripts and primes) denotes an expression whose variables are chosen among $v_1, \ldots, v_n$. The notation 'exp' (with possible . . .) denotes expressions regardless of which variables they might include.

□

Definition 4.1. A *vocabulary* V is a set of *grammar symbols* divided into two disjoint sets V_N and V_T of *nonterminal* and *terminal* symbols, respectively, and $V_T \subseteq$ Token.

To each nonterminal is associated two *attribute positions*, one classified as *inherited*, the other as *synthesized*. To each attribute position is associated a sort in D. For inherited attribute positions this sort always represents the set of all generative grammars.

□

Definition 4.2. For given vocabulary, V, nonterminal, N, in V with attribute positions whose sorts are s_1 and s_2 (inherited and synthesized, respectively), values $a_1 \in \mathbf{D}^{s1}$, $a_2 \in \mathbf{D}^{s2}$, and expresssions $\exp_1$ and $\exp_2$ of sort s_1 and s_2,

$$\langle N{\downarrow}a_1{\uparrow}a_2\rangle$$

is an *attributed nonterminal*, and

$$\langle N{\downarrow}\exp_1{\uparrow}\exp_2\rangle$$

is an *attributed nonterminal form*.

The values a_1 and a_2 are called *attributes*, $\exp_1$ and $\exp_2$ *attribute expressions*.

□

Definition 4.3. For given vocabulary V, a *production rule form* (or simply *rule*) has the form

$$F_0 ::= \alpha_0 F_1 \alpha_1 \ldots \alpha_{n-1} F_n \alpha_n$$

where $n \geqslant 0$, $F_0, F_1, \ldots, F_n$ are attributed nonterminal forms, $\alpha_0, \ldots, \alpha_n \in V_T^*$.

Further, it is required that

$$F_0 = \langle N_0{\downarrow}v_0{\uparrow}\exp_0(v_0 \ldots v_n)\rangle$$
$$F_i = \langle N_i{\downarrow}\exp_i(v_0 \ldots v_n){\uparrow}v_i\rangle, \; i=1 \ldots n$$

where $v_0, \ldots, v_n$ are distinct variables.

□

Definition 4.4. A *production rule* has the form

$$A_0 ::= \alpha_0 A_1 \alpha_1 \ldots \alpha_{n-1} A_n \alpha_n$$

where $n \geqslant 0$, $A_0, A_1, \ldots, A_n$ are attributed symbols.

The production rules *induced* by a production rule form $F_0 ::= \alpha_0 F_1 \alpha_1 \ldots \alpha_{n-1} F_n \alpha_n$ denoted $[F_0 ::= \alpha_0 F_1 \alpha_1 \ldots \alpha_{n-1} F_n \alpha_n]$ is defined as the set of production rules found as follows.

1. select an assignment of values to variables used in $F_0, F_1, \ldots, F_n$,
2. evaluate attribute expressions in $F_0, F_1, \ldots, F_n$ to get $A_0, A_1, \ldots, A_n$.

□

Definition 4.5. A *generative grammar* G = (V, S, R) consists of

V – a vocabulary,
S – a nonterminal called the *start symbol*,
R – a set of production rule forms.

Let further *grammar* be a sort in D which represents the set of all generative grammars.

□

Definition 4.6. The derivation relation $\Rightarrow$ is defined as follows. Let **a, b, c** be sequences in (**A** + Token)*, where **A** is the set of attributed nonterminals, and A an attributed nonterminal ⟨N↓G↑d⟩, then

$$\mathbf{a}\ A\ \mathbf{c} \Rightarrow \mathbf{a}\ \mathbf{b}\ \mathbf{c}$$

if G has a production rule form r such that

$$A ::= \mathbf{b} \in [r].$$

The relation $\Rightarrow^*$ is the transitive, reflexive closure of $\Rightarrow$.

□

Definition 4.7. The language *generated* by a generative grammar G = (V, S, R) is

$$\{\text{token}^* \mid \exists d: \langle S{\downarrow}G{\uparrow}d\rangle \Rightarrow^* \text{token}^*\}.$$

The translation *specified* by G is

$$\{\langle \text{token}^*, d\rangle \mid \langle S{\downarrow}G{\uparrow}d\rangle \Rightarrow^* \text{token}^*\}.$$

□

4.2 Language descriptions

Generative language descriptions are special cases of our generative grammars in which distinguished semantic terms are passed through the synthesized attributes and combined in a 'denotational' fashion.

In the parsing algorithms, however, language descriptions are handled like any other grammar — so readers whose main interest is on parsing may as well skip the rest of section 4.

Definition 4.8. Let SEM be a particular sub-signature of D and **SEM** the corresponding subalgebra of **D**. SEM and **SEM** are called the *semantic language*. Let further *semantic-program* be a particular sort in SEM.

□

It is not necessary in this treatise to make any further assumptions about the semantic language. The sort *semantic-program* represents meanings of entire programs, cf. the domain 'Answer' in classical denotational descriptions (Milne, Strachey, 1976).

Candidates for SEM could be the λ-calculus (Church, 1951, Milne, Strachey, 1976) or the abstract semantic algebras of (Mosses, 1983) — or any other formalism well-suited to express semantics of programming languages.

Definition 4.9. A *generative language description* is a generative grammar, such that

- the inherited attribute of each nonterminal is restricted to those generative grammars that are generative language descriptions,
- the sort of the synthesized attribute of each nonterminal represents a product of sorts, one of which may be distinguished as the *semantic component* for that nonterminal. The sort of a semantic component represents a carrier in SEM-TERM,
- the sort of the synthesized attribute of the start symbol consists of the semantic component only, and its sort represents $\text{SEM-TERM}^{\textit{semantic-program}}$,
- in each rule, the semantic components of the synthesized attribute position of the left-hand side depends only on the semantic components on the right-hand side.

□

Example 4.1. In this example we show a language description for a simple imperative language with mutually recursive, parameter-less procedures. The semantic description models procedures by 'macros'. The meaning of a procedure call is a semantic term generated from the procedure body. In example 4.2 we give an alternative (and more conventional) semantics in which semantic terms for procedure bodies are saved in a dynamic environment. In both examples we use a semantic language inspired by the abstract semantic algebras of (Mosses, 1983); a definition may be found in (Christiansen, 1985).

⟨program↓g↑***answer(a)***⟩ ::= ⟨stm-seq↓g↑***a***⟩

⟨stm-seq↓g↑$\boldsymbol{a_1}$***;*** $\boldsymbol{a_2}$⟩ ::= ⟨stm↓g↑$\boldsymbol{a_1}$⟩; ⟨stm-seq↓g↑$\boldsymbol{a_2}$⟩

⟨stm-seq↓g↑***null***⟩ ::= .

⟨stm↓g↑***a***⟩ ::=
  let ⟨dcl-seq↓g & g_1↑g_1⟩
  in ⟨stm-seq↓g & g_1↑***a***⟩ **end**

. . . a number of primitive statements

⟨dcl-seq↓g↑g_1 & g_2⟩ ::= ⟨dcl↓g↑g_1⟩; ⟨dcl-seq↓g↑g_2⟩

⟨dcl-seq↓g↑empty-grammar⟩ ::= .

⟨dcl↓g↑generate-proc(id, ***a***)⟩ ::=
  proc ⟨identifier↓g↑id⟩ **is** ⟨stm↓g↑***a***⟩ **end**
where generate-proc(*id*, *a*) is a grammar which has one rule
    ⟨stm↓g↑***a***⟩ ::= *id*

⟨identifier↓g↑A⟩ ::= A

. . .

The operator '&' joins the rules in two language descriptions. Given two language descriptions, g_1 and g_2, and rules $r_1 \in g_1$ and $r_2 \in g_2$, such that the right hand sides of r_1 and r_2 consist of the same terminal symbol, then r_2 'overwrites' r_1 in 'g_1 & g_2', i.e. r_1 disappears. For realistic languages the semantic term for procedure calls should also set up (and remove) a dynamic environment to handle references to local and global variables.

This example language displays a subtle property of our formalism. Consider the following declaration.

proc P **is** P **end**

The language description specifies that *any* semantic term can result from calling P. Our formalism has no means for chosing a 'least' — and intuitively correct — semantic term. If, however, the semantic macro is not just a simple copy the problem will never occur: An infinite (but well-defined) semantic term which represents 'infinite loop' will be generated.

□

Example 4.2. Here we give another language description for the language of example 4.1. Each procedure declaration generates a semantic action which saves the meaning of the procedure body in a dynamic environment. The semantic action for a procedure call will find this 'meaning' and execute it. The semantic expression '***forget*** $\boldsymbol{a_1}$ ***after doing*** $\boldsymbol{a_2}$' in the rule for statement blocks below takes care that the effects of $\boldsymbol{a_1}$ on the dynamic environment are only visible in $\boldsymbol{a_2}$.

We only show the rules which have been changed essentially compared with example 4.1.

⟨stm↓g↑***forget*** $\boldsymbol{a_1}$ ***after doing*** $\boldsymbol{a_2}$⟩ ::=
  let ⟨dcl-seq↓g & g_1↑⟨g_1, $\boldsymbol{a_1}$⟩⟩
  in ⟨stm-seq↓g & g_1↑$\boldsymbol{a_2}$⟩ **end**

⟨dcl↓g↑⟨generate-proc(id), (id***); enclose(a) ! bind***⟩⟩ ::=
  proc ⟨identifier↓g↑id⟩ **is** ⟨stm-seq↓g↑***a***⟩ **end**
where generate-proc(*id*) is a grammar which has one rule
    ⟨stm↓g↑***(id) ! lookup ! execute***⟩ ::= *id*.

The synthesized attributes for the nonterminals 'dcl' and 'dcl-seq' has two components, one which represents a language description and one, the semantic component, which is a semantic action. In order to avoid extensive use of selector functions we allow patterns like '⟨g_1, $\boldsymbol{a_1}$⟩' as attribute variables when used in a consistent manner.

We return to this language description in section 6.5 when considering multi-pass techniques.

□

4.3 Classification

Different classes of grammars may require different parsing strategies. For that purpose we define the following classifications for rules and grammars.

Definition 4.10. A rule is a *copy-rule* if it has the form

$$\langle N_0 \downarrow v_0 \uparrow exp(v_0 \ldots v_n)\rangle ::= \alpha_0 \langle N_1 \downarrow v_0 \uparrow v_1\rangle \alpha_1 \langle N_2 \downarrow v_0 \uparrow v_2\rangle \alpha_2 \ldots \alpha_{n-1} \langle N_n \downarrow v_0 \uparrow v_n\rangle \alpha_n$$

□

A language description in which each rule is a copy-rule is equivalent to a context-free grammar with associated denotational semantics.

Definition 4.11. A language description rule is said to be *left-to-right* if it has the form

$$F_0 ::= \alpha_0 F_1 \alpha_1 \ldots \alpha_{n-1} F_n \alpha_n, \quad n \geqslant 0$$

where

$$F_0 = \langle N_0 \downarrow v_0 \uparrow exp_0(v_0 \ldots v_n)\rangle$$
$$F_1 = \langle N_1 \downarrow exp_1(v_0) \uparrow v_1\rangle$$
$$F_2 = \langle N_2 \downarrow exp_2(v_0\ v_1) \uparrow v_2\rangle$$
$$\ldots$$
$$F_n = \langle N_n \downarrow exp_n(v_0 \ldots v_{n-1}) \uparrow v_n\rangle$$

A grammar or language description is *left-to-right* if every rule is left-to-right.

□

Definition 4.12. A rule is said to be *left-to-right recursive* if it has the form

$$F_0 ::= \alpha_0 F_1 \alpha_1 \ldots \alpha_{n-1} F_n \alpha_n, \quad n \geqslant 0$$

where

$$F_0 = \langle N_0 \downarrow v_0 \uparrow exp_0(v_0 \ldots v_n)\rangle$$
$$F_1 = \langle N_1 \downarrow exp_1(v_0\ v_1) \uparrow v_1\rangle$$
$$F_2 = \langle N_2 \downarrow exp_2(v_0\ v_1\ v_2) \uparrow v_2\rangle$$
$$\ldots$$
$$F_n = \langle N_n \downarrow exp_n(v_0 \ldots v_{n-1}\ v_n) \uparrow v_n\rangle$$

A grammar or language description is *left-to-right recursive* if each rule is left-to-right recursive. Rules, grammars, and language descriptions that are not left-to-right recursive is said to be *generally recursive*.

□

Example 4.3. The following rule is an example of a left-to-right rule.

$\langle block \downarrow g\rangle ::=$ **let** $\langle dcl \downarrow g \uparrow g_1\rangle$ **in** $\langle body \downarrow g\ \&\ g_1\rangle$

A left-to-right recursive rule:

$\langle block \downarrow g\rangle ::=$ **let** $\langle dcl \downarrow g\ \&\ g_1 \uparrow g_1\rangle$ **in** $\langle body \downarrow g\ \&\ g_1\rangle$

The following rules are generally recursive.

$\langle module \downarrow g \uparrow g_1\rangle ::=$
  export $\langle dcl \downarrow g\ \&\ g_2\ \&\ g_1 \uparrow g_1\rangle$
  private $\langle dcl \downarrow g\ \&\ g_1\ \&\ g_2 \uparrow g_2\rangle$
$\langle where\text{-}construct \downarrow g\rangle ::= \langle body \downarrow g\ \&\ g_1\rangle$ **where** $\langle dcl \downarrow g \uparrow g_1\rangle$

□

A parsing strategy often depends on certain assumptions about the grammar. The following definition may be used to ensure that no extension or modification of the grammar will obstruct such assumptions.

Definition 4.13. A grammar $G = (V, S, R)$ which satisfies a property $P(G)$ is said to *preserve* that property if, for any attributed nonterminal $A = \langle N{\downarrow}G'{\uparrow}d' \rangle$ such that for some d

$$\langle S{\downarrow}G{\uparrow}d \rangle \Rightarrow^* \ldots A \ldots,$$

$P(G')$ holds.

□

Example 4.4. The grammar for the language of simple integer expressions given in example 2.1 preserves the property:

An identifier represents at most one integer constant.

The language descriptions in examples 4.1 and 4.2 preserve the property:

If all attribute expressions are removed from the rules, the remaining context-free grammar is LL(1).

□

5 Interpretations

The most obvious way to understand or interpret a grammar or language description is as a 'rewriting system' which generates the set of all programs in a language. A grammar may also be interpreted as a table which directs the actions of a general parsing algorithm. Semantic terms in a language description might further be interpreted as commands to the code generation module of a compiler. We define a precise concept of interpretations below which is the central point in our formal correctness considerations. (For the use of D and **D**, see the remarks to definition 3.1).

Definition 5.1. An *interpretation*, I, consists of
- a D-algebra I(D),
- a sort *envelope* in D and function envelope_I: $I(D)^{grammar} \rightarrow \mathbf{D}^{envelope}$,
- an *abstraction morphism* which is a homomorphism abstract_I such that the following diagram commutes:

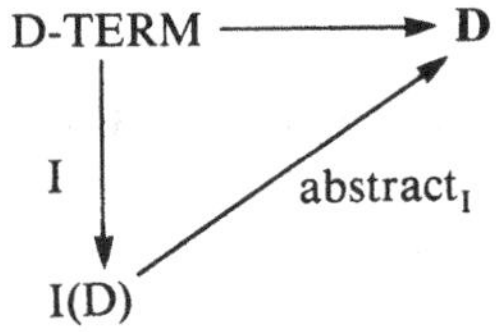

The canonical homorphism D-TERM → I(D) is denoted I.

□

For an interpretation I, I(D) defines a representation of grammars and the functions which appear in attribute expressions. The function envelope_I sets up the context for interpreting this representation. Due to the existence of an abstraction morphism, a grammar or a particular rule can always be 'reconstructed' for further processing — no information has been lost.

As an example, I(D) may represent grammars as suitable data structures in GALGOL and envelope_I is an algorithm referring to these.

The definition below states the canonical interpretation of a grammar as a rewriting system: In a given string of nonterminal and terminal symbols, nonterminals are successively replaced by other such strings according to the derivation relation. The standard reference on rewriting systems is (Knuth, Bendix, 1970). However, we can do here with the following vague concept of a rewriting system.

Definition 5.2. The interpretation rewrite is defined as follows.

rewrite(D) = **D**

$\text{envelope}_{\text{rewrite}}$, supplies the definition of ⇒ *

$\text{abstract}_{\text{rewrite}} = \text{Id}_{\mathbf{D}}$

□

The notions of the language generated by and the translation specified by a grammar viewed as a rewriting system is taken over from section 4.

In the following section we define a special class of interpretations to represent parsers.

6 Parsing

In this section we define what is understood by a parsing strategy and its correctness relative to a class of grammars. A general, non-deterministic parser which is trivially correct for all grammars will be defined. For certain classes of grammars, however, this parser can be transformed into an equivalent, deterministic one.

Evaluation of attribute values can take place in a straight-forward manner for left-to-right grammars (definition 4.11). For recursive grammars there does not seem to exist any general strategy. For left-to-right recursive grammars we suggest a class of multi-pass techniques.

Our parsing algorithms are all based on a central, recursive procedure which takes an entire grammar as an argument. In a naive implementation, e.g. using call-by-value, this would lead to an extremely poor storage utilization. However, a large number of well-known programming techniques can be used to minimize the amount of copying and hence this subject will not be discussed further.

6.1 Parsing strategies

Definition 6.1. A *parsing strategy* is an interpretation, parser, such that

- parser(D) is an algebra whose carriers are in GALGOL and whose operations are derived from those of GALGOL,
- $\text{envelope}_{\text{parser}}: \text{parser}(\mathbf{D})^{\mathit{grammar}} \rightarrow \text{GALGOL}^{\mathit{program}}$.

□

A parsing strategy might represent grammars as parsing tables and manipulation of grammars as manipulation of parsing tables. The function $\text{envelope}_{\text{parser}}$ can then put a parsing table into a program which includes a general parsing algorithm. Another example is a parsing strategy which maps rules to certain functions in LISP, and $\text{envelope}_{\text{parser}}$ sets up a LISP program which is able to control creation and deletion of such functions.

Definition 6.2. For given parsing strategy, parser, and grammar, G, we define the language *recognized by* parser from G to be

$$\{\text{token}^* \mid \text{envelope}_{\text{parser}}(\text{parser } G)\ \text{token}^* \neq \emptyset\}$$

and the translation *performed by* parser from G as

$$\{\langle \text{token}^*, d\rangle \mid \text{envelope}_{\text{parser}}(\text{parser } G)\ \text{token}^* \ni d\}.$$

□

Definition 6.3. A parsing strategy, parser, is *correct* for a subset **G** of all grammars if the following diagram commutes.

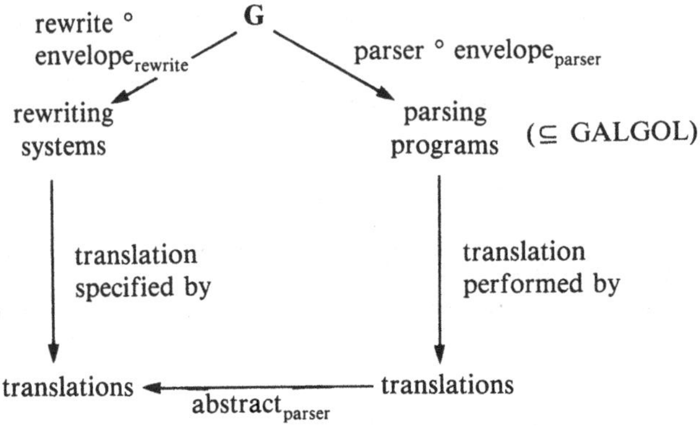

□

In other words, a parsing strategy is correct if it performs exactly the same translations (the abstraction morphism in account) as those generated by corresponding rewriting systems.

6.2 The general top-down parser

Our hypothetical, general top-down parser (and all other parsers derived from it) works basically the same way as traditional recursive-descent or predictive parsers (Aho, Ullman, 1977). Right hand sides of syntax rules are matched with the input-stream: Terminal symbols appearing in a rule must be identical to those read from the input-stream. A nonterminal is replaced by the right hand side of some rule selected by the parser — and this right hand side is recursively processed the same way.

In our parsers this algorithm is realized as a recursive procedure: Rules are selected in a grammar given to the procedure as an argument. This way we are able to simulate the 'flow' in the inherited attributes and the context-sensitive derivation relation.

In the following we describe the general parsing algorithm or, more precisely, the envelope of the general parsing strategy. Its correctness is regardless of which representation is prescribed for grammars and rules (provided the required abstraction morphism exists, of course).

The central part of the parser is the procedure 'nonterminal' which takes a nonterminal (to be matched) and a grammar (in which to select an appropriate rule) as arguments. The procedure returns a value which represents the synthesized attribute of the nonterminal.

procedure nonterminal(**in** N_0, G);
  select a rule r in G such that
    $r = F_0 ::= \alpha_0 F_1 \alpha_1 \ldots \alpha_{n-1} F_n \alpha_n$,
    $F_0 = \langle N_0 \downarrow v_0 \uparrow exp_0 \rangle$
    $F_i = \langle N_i \downarrow exp_i \uparrow v_i \rangle$, $i = 1 \ldots n$;
  select values for $v_1, \ldots, v_n$, let $v_0 = G$ and
  evaluate attribute expressions to get
    $A_0 ::= \alpha_0 A_1 \alpha_1 \ldots \alpha_{n-1} A_n \alpha_n$,
    $A_i = \langle N_i \downarrow inh_i \uparrow syn_i \rangle$, $i = 0 \ldots n$;
  terminals(α_0);
  for i:= 1 **to** n **do**
    s_i:= nonterminal(N_i, inh_i);
    check($s_i = syn_i$);
    terminals(α_i);
  return syn_0

Note that some of our notational freedom has to do with the existence of an abstraction morphism. All assignments in the procedure are expected to be local.

The procedure 'terminals' simply skips a sequence of terminal symbols. The calls of procedure 'check' ensure that delusive selections of rules and attribute values do not give rise to any output.

```
procedure terminals(in α);
    check(α is a prefix of the input-stream);
    remove α from the input-stream
procedure check(in condition);
    if ¬condition then crash
```

The main program calls 'nonterminal' with the given start symbol and grammar and prints out the returned value.

For the general top-down parsing strategy to work, it is necessary to assume an extremely powerful, nondeterministic semantics of GALGOL: The result of running the parser on a given input-stream is the set of all outputs which could result from a combination of selections of rules and attribute values.

Theorem 6.1. The general top-down parsing strategy described above is correct for all grammars.
□

We only give the sketch of a proof. The main ideas in the parser and the proof are illustrated in a following example.

Proof. Assume the parser has given some output for a certain input-stream. Further, assume that a history of procedure calls and returns has been recorded. This history includes values of parameters and the rules and values for attribute variables selected in the nonterminal procedure. From this history a derivation of the input-stream can be constructed.

On the other hand: Any derivation leading to a string of terminal symbols has an equivalent derivation in which always the leftmost nonterminal is expanded. It is easy to prove that this derivation corresponds to a possible history of the parsers activity as above.
□

Example 6.1. Consider the following derivation made from the language description given in example 1.2.

⟨program↓L↑*answer(0•1•plus)*⟩ ⇒ . . .
⇒ **const** A = 0 **in** ⟨integer↓L'↑*0*⟩ + ⟨exp↓L'↑*1*⟩
⇒ **const** A = 0 **in** A + ⟨exp↓L'↑*1*⟩ ⇒ . . .
⇒ **const** A = 0 **in** A + 1

L is the original language description and L' is L enhanced with the rule ⟨integer↓g↑*0*⟩::= A. The derivation step in which ⟨integer↓L'↑*0*⟩ is replaced by A corresponds to the following part of a parsers history.

- 'nonterminal' is called with 'integer' and L' as parameters,
- the rule ⟨integer↓g↑*0*⟩::= A in L' is selected,
- 'terminals' is called with 'A' as parameter,
- 'terminals' removes 'A' from the input-stream and returns to the activation of 'nonterminal' above,
- 'nonterminal' returns the semantic term '*0*' to where it was called from.

□

6.3 Deterministic selection of rules

Various techniques may be suggested to get rid of the nondeterminism involved in the general parser's selection of syntactic rules.

At a first glance it seems rather obvious to apply well-known techniques for parsing of context-free LL(1)-grammars (Aho, Ullman, 1977). However, a short investigation will show that the LL(1)-property cannot be generalized without the following restriction.

Definition 6.4. A *prefix-stable* grammar is one in which the right-hand side of any rule which is not a copy-rule starts with a terminal-symbol.

□

Example 6.2. The required terminal symbol in definition 6.4 is probably one of the following: **let**, **declare**, **begin**, **with**.

□

The definition of LL(1)-grammars given by (Aho, Ullman, 1977) can immediately be generalized for generative grammars that are prefix-stable. As in the context-free case, rules may be selected on the basis of the next input symbol to be read.

Example 6.3. The language description in example 4.1 for the language with parameter-less procedures is prefix-stable and LL(1). In this case grammars are represented conveniently as parsing tables for predictive parsers (Aho, Ullman, 1977) and selection of rules is a matter of looking up in a tabel.

□

To escape from the straitjacket of LL(1) (or LL(k) for that matter) other techniques such as bottom-up parsing[1)] for LR-grammars and various back-tracking schemes may be suggested. These approaches have not yet been tried; their possible failure or success can only be judged in future experiments.

A promising direction seems to be a generalization of definite clause grammars (see Pereira, Warren, 1980): Syntactic rules are formulated as clauses in Prolog — which directly constitute an executable parser.

6.4 Evaluation of attributes

A parser for an ordinary attribute grammar can in principle build a syntax tree according to the underlying context-free grammar and then process this tree to yield the values of the attributes (see e.g. Bochmann, 1976, or Watt, Madsen, 1979). In our case, evaluation of attributes is far more intricate. On one hand, the grammar according to which the parser is going to recognize the input is given by the attribute values — on the other, these values result from the recognition of that input. Consider, for example, a language in which mutually recursive declarations of control structures are allowed. Unless some special conventions are made the parser has no idea of how to read a series of declarations before having read them!

For left-to-right grammars attributes can be evaluated in a straight-forward manner. For left-to-right recursive grammars we suggest a class of multi-pass techniques. However, such techniques does not exist in general — for each application a new multi-pass technique has to be developed and proved correct.

Left-to-right grammars

When the attributes in each rule depend on each other in a simple left-to-right fashion (definition 4.11) their values can be evaluated sequentially while the parser is scanning the input. We can express this in the following derivative of the general top-down parser. The nonterminal procedure is changed as follows.

1. Since the parsing process is directed by inherited attributes (which hold the grammar!) the use of bottom-up parsing makes sense only in regions of a program where the grammer is stable. Hence a mixture of bottom-up and top-down techniques is necessary.

procedure nonterminal(**in** N_0, G);
  select a rule r in G such that
    $r = F_0 ::= \alpha_0 F_1 \alpha_1 \ldots \alpha_{n-1} F_n \alpha_n$
    $F_0 = \langle N_0 \downarrow v_0 \uparrow exp_0(v_0 \ldots v_n) \rangle$
    $F_i = \langle N_i \downarrow exp_i(v_0 \ldots v_{i-1}) \uparrow v_i \rangle, \; i = 1 \ldots n;$
  bind v_0 locally to G;
  terminals(α_0);
  for i: = 1 **to** n **do**
    bind v_i locally to the return value of
      nonterminal(N_i, the value of $exp_i(v_0 \ldots v_{i-1})$
        wrt. local bindings);
    terminals(α_i);
  return the value of $exp_0(v_0 \ldots v_n)$ wrt. local bindings

The values of attribute variables are bound locally in each activation of the procedure.

It is easy to show that the indicated parsing strategy is correct. In each activation of the procedure, the values bound to attribute variables correspond to the only 'successful' selection of values made by the general top-down parser. Hence:

Theorem 6.2. The parsing strategy for left-to-right grammars which preserve that property is correct.
□

It is also clear that this parser is deterministic if selection of rules is deterministic.

Left-to-right recursive grammars

It does not seem possible to find a general deterministic strategy which is correct for all recursive grammars. However, we suggest a class of multi-pass techniques for left-to-right recursive grammars: If each left-to-right recursive rule can be replaced by a well-defined multi-pass rule (to be defined), then a correct parser can be constructed.

Our definition of multi-passing is given in purely linguistic terms. Hence the development and proof of new multi-pass techniques is comparatively easier than if new parsing algorithms should be constructed.

Our multi-pass techniques are slightly more complicated than multi-pass techniques for evaluation of attributes in traditional attribute grammars (Bochmann, 1976): We cannot expect a well-defined syntax tree to be given when the attributes are evaluated.

To keep the notation simple we restrict ourselves to two-pass techniques for grammars involving rules of the form

$$F_0 ::= \alpha_0 F_1 \alpha_1 F_2 \alpha_2$$

where F_1 gives occasion to left-to-right recursion. However, our results are easily generalized to *n*-pass techniques for any kind of left-to-right recursive rules. Further, the rules we consider include the most common use of recursion — a block construct involving mutually recursive declarations.

Before giving the precise definition of two-pass replacement rules we give an informal discussion of the concept. Consider the rule

$F_0 ::=$ **let** F_1 **in** F_2 **end**

where F_1 describes a sequence of mutually recursive declarations.

A two-pass parser will scan the string generated by F_1 twice. This can be described linguistically by a new rule, a so-called multi-pass rule:

$F_0 ::=$ **let** F_1^1 **in** F_1^2 **in** F_2 **end**

If programmers are forced to write the string generated by F_1 twice (cf. forward declarations in Pascal), F_1^1 may describe the task of the first pass: to reveal some of the required information which in turn is given to F_1^2 which is now able to determin the final result. The duplication of the symbol '**in**' provides suitable stop-markers for the parser.

The intuition behind the multi-pass techniques described in this paper is the following. Each recursive rule is replaced by a multi-pass rule which contains no recursion — and the parser is instructed to do appropriate rewinding of the input-stream. (Hence the parsing algorithm 'cheats' the modified grammar instead of requiring programmers to write their declarations twice!)

Definition 6.5. Assume r is a rule

$$F_0 ::= \alpha_0 F_1 \alpha_1 F_2 \alpha_2$$

where

$$F_0 = \langle N_0 \downarrow v_0 \uparrow exp_0(v_0 v_1 v_2)\rangle$$
$$F_1 = \langle N_1 \downarrow exp_1(v_0 v_1) \uparrow v_1\rangle$$
$$F_2 = \langle N_2 \downarrow exp_2(v_0 v_1) \uparrow v_2\rangle$$

α_0, α_1, and α_2 are nonempty sequences of terminal symbols.

A *two-pass replacement* for r valid for a class of grammars **G** is a left-to-right rule

$$F_0 = \alpha_0 F_1^1 \alpha_1 F_1^2 \alpha_1 F_2 \alpha_2$$

where

$$F_1^1 = \langle N_1^1 \downarrow exp_1^1(v_0) \uparrow v_1^1\rangle$$
$$F_1^2 = \langle N_1^2 \downarrow exp_1^2(v_0 v_1^1) \uparrow v_1\rangle$$

such that for all assignments of values to v_0 and v_1, where the value of v_0 belongs to **G** and F_1 evaluates to A_1, the following holds: $A_1 \Rightarrow^* \beta_1$ if and only if there exist a value for v_1^1 such that F_1^1, F_1^2 evaluates to A_1^1, A_1^2 and $A_1^1 \Rightarrow^* \beta_1$, $A_1^2 \Rightarrow^* \beta_1$ where β_1 is a sequence of terminal symbols.

Further, the two-pass replacement is *well-defined* if, for any assignment as above, the following holds: Whenever, for some sequences of terminal symbols β_1 and β_2,

$$\alpha_0 A_1 \alpha_1 A_2 \alpha_2 \Rightarrow^* \alpha_0 \beta_1 \alpha_1 A_2 \alpha_2 \Rightarrow^* \alpha_0 \beta_1 \alpha_1 \beta_2 \alpha_2$$

any left-most derivation

$$\alpha_0 A_1^1 \alpha_1 A_1^2 \alpha_1 A_2 \alpha_2 \Rightarrow^* \alpha_0 \beta_1 \alpha_1 \beta_1 \alpha_1 \beta_2 \alpha_2$$

must go through the following steps

$$\alpha_0 A_1^1 \alpha_1 A_1^2 \alpha_1 A_2 \alpha_2 \Rightarrow^*$$
$$\alpha_0 \beta_1 \alpha_1 A_1^2 \alpha_1 A_2 \alpha_2 \Rightarrow^*$$
$$\alpha_0 \beta_1 \alpha_1 \beta_1 \alpha_1 A_2 \alpha_2 \Rightarrow^*$$
$$\alpha_0 \beta_1 \alpha_1 \beta_1 \alpha_1 \beta_2 \alpha_2$$

□

The definition of well-definedness makes sure that the occurrences of α_0, α_1, and α_2 constitute a bracketing structure — which makes it possible for the parser to navigate through the linguistic darkness of the (yet) unstructured input-stream.

Strictly speaking, the requirement that α_0, α_1, and α_2 be non-empty is not necessary, but it makes it comparatively easier to prove well-definedness.

Example 6.4. The language description in example 4.2 has one recursive rule, namely:

⟨stm↓g↑***forget*** $\boldsymbol{a_1}$ ***after doing*** $\boldsymbol{a_2}$⟩::=
  let ⟨dcl-seq↓g & g_1↑⟨g_1, $\boldsymbol{a_1}$⟩⟩
  in ⟨stm-seq↓g & g_1↑$\boldsymbol{a_2}$⟩ **end**

A two-pass replacement rule for this rule is as follows.

⟨stm↓g↑***forget*** $\boldsymbol{a_1}$ ***after doing*** $\boldsymbol{a_2}$⟩::=
  let ⟨dcl-seq↓g & general-stm↑⟨g_1^1, $\boldsymbol{a_1^1}$⟩⟩
  in ⟨dcl-seq↓g & g_1^1↑⟨g_1, $\boldsymbol{a_1}$⟩⟩
  in ⟨stm↓g & g_1↑$\boldsymbol{a_2}$⟩ **end**

where general-stm is a grammar which has one rule, namely

$\langle \mathrm{stm}{\downarrow}g{\uparrow}\textbf{\textit{null}}\rangle ::= \langle \mathrm{identifier}{\downarrow}g{\uparrow}\mathrm{id}\rangle$

i.e. a rule which syntactically generalizes all possible procedure calls. The semantic action, ***null***, is arbitrary and is thrown away (as a_1^1).

If, in a clever implementation, the construction of the useless a_1^1 and of g_1 (which is equal to g_1^1) is avoided the rule describes the traditional approach for implementing recursive procedures: pass one generates rules for calling procedures, pass two compiles their bodies. The replacement rule is well-defined since **let**, **in**, and **end** are special symbols not used in any other rule, and they cannot be generated as identifiers, thus being smuggled into the grammar (special symbols are written in bold-face, identifiers are not).

If a language features declarations of new control structures with a more or less arbitrary syntax the same technique may be used. In that case, the general or 'dummy' grammar used in the first pass may specify that a statement can be any sequence of non-bold symbols.
□

The general multi-pass parser

Let **G** be a class of grammars satisfying
- the property '∈ **G**' is preserved,
- all rules are either left-to-right or of the form required by definition 6.6 above,
- for any recursive rule, a well-defined two-pass rule valid for **G** exists and can be computed.

For example, the last requirement is satisfied if there is only one recursive rule and its replacement rule has been constructed by hand.

For classes of grammars which satisfy the conditions above we present the following general multi-pass strategy. Each recursive rule is represented by (a representation of) its replacement rule, which further is augmented with instructions to the parser[1] (indicated by square brackets). With the notation of definition 6.6 the augmented replacement rule is as follows.

$$F_0 ::= \alpha_0[\text{save input}]F_1^1\alpha_1[\text{reset input}]F_1^2\alpha_1 F_2\alpha_2$$

The parsing algorithm is the same as the one used for left-to-right grammars, except that the nonterminal procedure is instructed to interpret these instructions when appropriate. The nonterminal procedure becomes as follows.

procedure nonterminal(**in** N_0, G);
  select a rule r in G such that
    $r = F_0 ::= \alpha_0[\text{inst}_1]F_1\alpha_1[\text{inst}_2]F_2\alpha_2 \ldots \alpha_{n-1}[\text{inst}_n]F_n\alpha_n$
    $F_0 = \langle N_0{\downarrow}v_0{\uparrow}\text{exp}_0(v_0 \ldots v_n)\rangle$
    $F_i = \langle N_i{\downarrow}\text{exp}_i(v_0 \ldots v_{i-1}){\uparrow}v_i\rangle$, $i = 1 \ldots n$;
  bind v_0 locally to G;
  terminals(α_0);
  for i:= 1 **to** n **do**
    execute [inst_i];
    bind v_i locally to the return value of
      nonterminal(N_i, the value of $\text{exp}_i(v_0 \ldots v_{i-1})$
        wrt. local bindings);
    terminals(α_i);
  return the value of $\text{exp}_0(v_0 \ldots v_n)$ wrt. local bindings

The meaning the instructions found in rules is given as follows.

[save input]
  the current input-stream is saved in a variable local to the nonterminal procedure,

[reset input]
  the input-stream is (globally) set to the one saved by the corresponding [save input].

1. For this nontrivial representation to fit into the algebraic framework of interpretations we assume powerful representation functions to be programmed in GALGOL as part of the 'envelope.'

Note that the parsing algorithm can be used, not only for two-pass replacement rules, but also with any kind of multi-pass technique resulting from appropriate generalizations of definition 6.6.

Theorem 6.3. The general multi-pass parsing strategy is correct for classes of grammars satisfying the conditions above.

□

A correctness proof can be set up as for the left-to-right parser. The multi-pass parser (with the modified grammar) will go through exactly the same steps as the nondeterministic parser (with the original, recursive grammar). It is routine symbol manipulation to show from the well-definedness condition that the two nonterminals replacing a 'recursive' nonterminal are matched with the correct portion of the input.

7 Summary

In this paper we have described top-down techniques for recognition of generative languages which is a comprehensive class of languages with a bias towards abstraction and extensibility. Our syntactic and semantic descriptions generalize context-free grammars with associated denotational semantics: Language descriptions are made context-sensitive in the sense that language constructs (e.g. declarations) are allowed to change the syntax and semantics of the language. Correspondingly, our approach to parsing generalize traditional recursive-descent parsing.

Our general parsing technique is presented as a nondeterministic algorithm which, under certain conditions, can be made deterministic. The sources of nondeterminism in our parsers are selection of rules (to match the 'next' portion of the input) and evaluation of attributes. Selection of rules is deterministic for grammars which satisfy an LL(1)-like property and also other techniques may be suggested for this purpose. Evaluation of attributes is straight-forward for non-recursive grammars. For grammars whose attributes depend on each other in a left-to-right recursive manner we suggest a class of multi-pass techniques, whereas there does not seem to exist a strategy which apply to all recursive grammars.

The future

In this paper, however, we have not given any details on how generative grammars actually are represented in parsers. Our toy experiments (not described in the paper) have indicated that the choice of representation has a crucial influence on efficiency — so with respect to practical use of our techniques, this subject should be investigated more closely.

Further, LL(1)-like grammars are undesirable from a linguistic point of view: A number of irrelevant nonterminals has to be introduced and 'natural' rules must be split into a number of rules which convey very little intuition of the language being defined. In their paper, 'Deterministic parsing of ambiguous grammars', Aho, Johnson, and Ullman (1975) advocate (in a very convincing manner!) the use of ambiguous grammars supplied with so-called disambiguating rules. They give both top-down and bottom-up parsing techniques for such syntactic descriptions. Since our approach is related to languages in which programmers are manipulating (more or less explicitly) the language syntax 'generative' versions of these techniques should be tried out also.

Finally, we do not believe that powerful generative languages will be implemented by parsers and compilers in the traditional sense. From a methodological (and practical!) point of view such languages should be rather be realized as interactive and incremental programming environments. In this paper we have investigated parsers and compilers in isolation and we plan to investigate and experiment with incremental versions of our techniques — combined with other techniques for syntax-directed editing.

References

Aho, A.V., Johnson, S.C., and Ullman, J.D., Deterministic Parsing of Ambiguous Grammars, *Communications of the ACM* 8, pp. 441-452 (1975).

Aho, A.V. and Ullman, J.D., *Principles of Compiler Design,* Addison-Wesley, Reading, Massachusetts (1977).

Christiansen, H. Syntax, semantics, and implementation strategies for programming languages with powerful abstraction mechanisms, *Proc. 18th Hawaii International Conference on System Sciences*, pp. 57-66 (1985).

Christiansen, H., *Parsing and compilation of generative languages*, Datalogiske skrifter 3, Roskilde University Centre (1986).

Christiansen, H. and Jones, N.D., Control Flow Treatment in a Simple Semantics-Directed Compiler Generator, *Proc. Formal Description of Programming Concepts II*, pp. 73-97, North-Holland, Amsterdam (1983).

Church, A., The Calculi of Lambda-Conversions, *Annals of Mathematical Studies* 6, Princeton Univ. Press, Princeton, N.J. (1951).

Goguen, J.A., Thatcher, J.W., and Wagner, E.G., An initial algebra approach to the specification, correctness, and implementation of abstract data types, *Current Trends in Programming Methodology*, vol. IV, ed. R.T. Yeh, Prentice-Hall (1979).

Knuth, D.E., Semantics of context-free languages, *Mathematical Systems Theory* 2, pp. 127-145 (1968).

Knuth, D.E. and Bendix, P.B., Simple Word Problems in Universal Algebras, *Computational Problems in Abstract Algebra*, ed. J .Leech, pp. 263-297, Pergamon Press (1970).

Layzell, P.J., The History of Macro Processors in Programming Language Extensibility, *The Computer Journal*, vol. 28, pp. 29-33 (1985).

Milne, R. and Strachey, C., *A Theory of Programming Language Semantics*, Chapman and Hall, London (1976).

Mosses, P.D., A constructive approach to compiler correctness, *Lecture Notes in Computer Science* 85, pp. 449-469, Springer-Verlag, Berlin, Heidelberg (1980).

Mosses, P.D., Abstract semantic algebras! *Proc. Formal Description of Programming Concepts II*, pp. 45-70, North-Holland, Amsterdam, 1983.

Pereira, F.C.N. and Warren, D.H.D., Definite Clause Grammars for Language Analysis — A Survey of the Formalism and a Comparison with Augmented Transition Networks, *Artificial Intelligence* 13, pp. 231-278 (1980).

Solntseff, N. and Yezerski, A., A Survey of Extensible Programming Languages, *Annual Rewiev in Automatic Programming* vol. 7, pp. 267-307 (1974).

Triance, J.M. and Layzell, P.J., Macro Processors for Enhancing High-Level Languages — Some Design Principles, *The Computer Journal*, vol. 28, pp. 34-43, 1985.

Watt, D.A., and Madsen, O.L., *Extended attribute grammars*, DAIMI PB-105, Computer Science Department, Aarhus University (1979).

Modular First-Order Specifications of Operational Semantics

Harald Ganzinger

FB Informatik
Universität Dortmund
D-4600 Dortmund 50
W. Germany
e-mail: hg@unido.uucp

Abstract

This paper is about modular specification of operational semantics and the execution of such specifications. It gives a first-order specification of the semantics of a simple applicative programming language. This specification is modular in the sense that binding rules are specified independently of the concrete syntax of the language and that expression evaluation needs not consider any concept of names. We then propose a simple lemma generation technique that achieves the effect of partial evaluation to implement such specifications in Prolog.

1. Introduction

The work reported on this paper is concerned with modular specifications of operational aspects of programming languages. Our goals are to achieve a higher degree of modularity in such specifications, in particular we think that semantic equations should not directly refer to all details of the semantic domains. Rather, we propose the introduction of additional intermediate abstraction levels that correspond to fundamental concepts (called *facets*) of languages and operational interpretation techniques. The specifications should be completely formal, in particular the combination of specifications out of the more primitive specifications for the various facets should be formal, too. A second goal of this work is the development of techniques for the execution of such specifications. In particular we are interested in using Prolog for these purposes as more advanced systems for testing specifications are at the moment still of rather experimental nature.

Our work is is related to many approaches that have been reported in the literature. Following the paper by Wand about first-order identities as a defining language [Wan79], Goguen and Parsaye-Ghomi [GP81] give a specification of a compiler for a simple imperative language as a hierarchical abstract data type using the specification language OBJ1 [GT79]. Mosses in a series of papers (e.g. [Mos83]) advocates for making denotational semantics less concrete and more modular. He axiomatically specifies "semantic algebras" to formally capture fundamental properties of various "facets" of programming languages. His approach, however, at the moment lacks a (published) formal way of combining the algebras into complete semantics definitions for conrete languages. Ganzinger [Gan83] uses algebraic structures that consist of functions and relations to modularly specify compilers. The theoretical basis is a modelling of parameterized abstract data types in the spirit of [Lip82]. Technical vehicle for the prototyping of such specifications is a generalization of attribute grammars that can be transliterated into Prolog-programs [GH85]. Operational semantics has regained popularity through the work of Plotkin (e.g. [Plo83]). In fact there is quite some similarity between his inference rules or the inference rules in [Clé85] and our way of defining semantic values to program constructs in syntactic contexts.

In this paper we propose a method for language specifications by which, as in [Gan83], syntactic constructs are distinguished according to their occurrence in a program. A program is considered as a set of relations among such occurrences. As language definitions thus refer to relations, the use of Prolog for testing such specification comes into mind. We will indicate how to implement the proposed kind of specifications in Prolog. The programs that are obtained by these techniques are very inefficient. Therefore we will propose an optimization technique that achieves effects similar to what is achieved by partial evaluation in the sense of Ershov [Ers77]. (For recent achievements in the area of partial evaluation cf. [JSS85].) The optimized programs are sufficiently efficient for prototyping purposes.

2. Programs as Conjunctions of Facts

In language definitions, syntax is usually represented by a set of operators, where each operator constructs a more complex expression out of simpler ones. The syntactic structure of a program such as

begin var x:int; x:=1, x:=1 end.

might, perhaps, be represented by the term

prog(scope(seq(decl(x,int),seq(assign(x,const(1)),assign(x,const(1)))))).

Such a term algebraically abstracts from a tree structure like

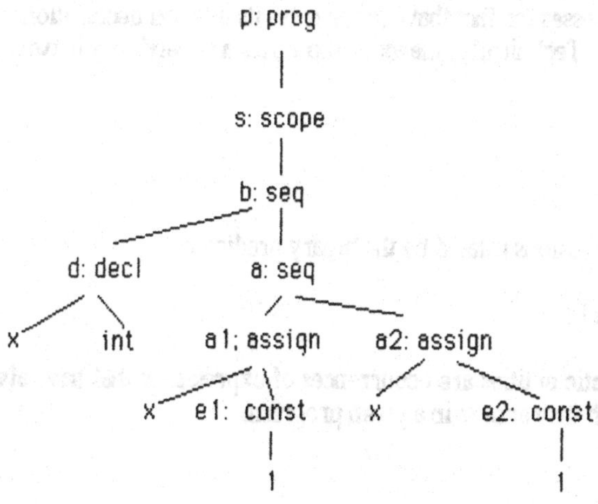

by forgetting about the (names of the) nodes $p,s,b,d,a,a1,a2,e1$ and $e2$. Our way of representing such a syntactic situation retains these names. Rather than writing a term we write a conjunction of facts

prog(p,s)∧ scope(s,b)∧ seq(b,d,a)∧ decl(d,x,int)∧ seq(a,a1,a2)∧
  assign(a1,x,e1)∧ assign(a2,x,e2)∧ const(e1,1)∧ const(e2,1)

built from relation symbols rather than operators. Thereby, the occurrences of constructs in a program are explicitly distinguished by names. Whereas in the term case *assign(x,const(1))* represents both the first and the second assignment, in our representation we have the explicit names *a1* and *a2* to distinguish between them. As the names stand not only for the construct but also for its occurrence we will often able to represent context-dependent semantic values by first-order objects where in usual denotational semantics one needs to introduce functions such as environment transformations. This property (which our approach shares with the inference rules of [Plo83] and [Clé85]) and the fact that we can associate semantic values with occurrences (as is done in attribute grammars) will be crucial for being able to pass semantic values between semantics modules.

In this paper we will not discuss the problem of specifying syntactic analysis. We simply assume that programs are given as such conjunctions of facts. Readers interested in the subject of algebraic specification of syntactic analysis and construction of program representations are referred to [BHP85].

Semantic properties of a program can now be given by conditional axioms where conditions may refer to syntactic facts. As an example, consider visibility of declarations in a block-structured language. The binding rules can be presented by a definition of a function *visibleAt* which gives for any occurrence of an expression *E* (of sort *ExpB*) and any identifier *X* information about the declaration of *X* that is visible at *E*. An axiom for *visibleAt* using an auxiliary function *visibleLeftOf* that returns the visible declaration to the left of an expression *E* might be

scope(Scope,Body) ⇒ visibleAt(Scope,X) = visibleLeftOf(Scope,X) .

We can read this axiom as follows: If *Scope* is a scope with a body *Body*, then, for any identifier *X*, its visible declaration outside the scope is the same as the one that is visible immediately to the left of it. Such an axiom formally expresses the fact that a scope hides its internal declarations such that they are invisible from the outside. Technically, the axiom specifies a dependency between the two functions

visibleAt	: Exp, Id -> Decl
visibleLeftOf	: Exp, Id -> Decl

in cases of any two occurrences of expressions related by the binary predicate

scope	: Exp, Exp -> Bool.

It only makes sense because the syntactic entities are occurrences of expressions that have always implicitly attached the context in which they appear in a given program.

3. Abstract Views of Programs

We want to achieve modularity of specifications where the modules correspond to fundamental operational concepts of languages. We propose to introduce for each module a specific abstract view of the concrete program. As an example consider again the specification of binding rules in the presence of hierarchical scopes. In order to associate an applied occurrence of an identifier to the declaration that is visible at that occurrence one only has to consider the scope structure, the declarations and the sequential order of constructs in the programs. The remaining structure of the program is completely irrelevant. A specification of binding rules should, therefore, be independent of the concrete syntax of the language and instead be based on a small set of primitives for expressing syntactic relations between scopes and defining and applied occurrences of identifiers. Hence, the following set of relations (written as boolean functions) among occurrences of expressions appears to be sufficient:

mainScope	: Exp	$\rightarrow$ Bool
scope	: Exp, Exp	$\rightarrow$ Bool
definingOcc	: Exp, Id, Decl	$\rightarrow$ Bool
appliedOcc	: Id	$\rightarrow$ Bool
seq	: Exp, Exp, Exp	$\rightarrow$ Bool
empty	: Exp	$\rightarrow$ Bool.

Then,

mainScope(p) $\wedge$ seq(p,d,a) $\wedge$ definingOcc(d,x,int) $\wedge$ appliedOcc(a,x)

expresses that *a* is an applied occurrence of *x* which is preceded by a defining occurrence *d* for *x* and that both constructs are immediately enclosed by the main scope of the program *p*. This information is sufficient to conclude that

visibleAt(a,x) = int

or that

visibleAt(a,y) = undeclared, for all x $\neq$ y.

To put it differently, the definition of the function *visibleAt* can completely be given in terms of these elementary predicates.

For different language concepts, different abstract views of a program are usually appropriate. This means that a different set of basic predicates must be introduced.

In the following we will give a specification of a lazy functional language which consists of three modules for handling binding rules, expression evaluation and λ-expressions. In section 5 we will, then, indicate techniques to run such specifications using Prolog.

4. Specification of an Interpreter

We want to demonstrate the use of abstract views with a simple yet nontrivial example. We have chosen to specify an interpreter for a Lisp-like language. Our intention is to separate the treatment of binding rules for variables from the expression evaluation proper. For that purpose we use two abstract views of Lisp programs. What concerns binding rules we will adopt the view that is formally represented by the above predicates. This view is independent of the concrete constructs which the language offers for the computation of values. Expression evaluation itself will be defined for nameless expressions similar to the ones used by de Bruijn [Bru72]. This means that at this level we need not be concerned about the naming of objects. Rather, variable names are replaced by numbers so that one can directly speak about the i-th bound variable or the j-th free variable of a λ-expression. Furthermore, at this level of abstraction, all λ-expressions will be closed, i.e. have explicitly associated with them the list of free variables that are referenced inside the expression. As an example, let us look at the λ–expression

$$\lambda f, x . \lambda y . f(x,y) .$$

Its abstraction with respect to binding rules will be represented as the conjunction of facts

```
mainScope(s1)∧
  scope(s1,b1)∧
    seq(b1,d,s2)∧ seq(d,d1,d2)∧ definingOcc(d1,f,0)∧ definingOcc(d2,x,1)∧
  scope(s2,b2)∧
    seq(b2,d4,s4)∧ definingOcc(d4,y,0)∧ seq(s4,a1,s5)∧
          appliedOcc(a1,f)∧ seq(s5,a2,a3)∧ appliedOcc(a2,x)∧ appliedOcc(a3,y).
```

Declaration information is in this case the position of the variable in the list of declarations of the scope. The formula expresses the fact that the λ-expression contains sequences of altogether three defining and three applied occurrences of variables in two different scopes.

For the evaluation proper we want to abstract from the problems that arise from names and therefore expect that no more explicit bindings and names occur in an expression. Instead we expect occurrences of indexes which, from an operational point of view, represent information of how to access a variable during evaluation. Expression evaluation will, therefore, be specified for expressions which for the above given concrete expression would be

```
exp(l1)∧
   lambda(l1,2,(),l2)∧
     lambda(l2,1,(bound(0),bound(1)),e)∧
       apply(e,e1,e2)∧
            var(e1,free(0))∧
            seq(e2,e3,e6)∧seq(e3,e4,e5)∧var(e5,free(1))∧var(e6,bound(0))∧empty(e4).
```

Here, *lambda(l,N,(V1,..., Vk),B)* represents the occurrence *l* of a λ-expression with *N* parameters, a body *B* and occurrences of *k* free variables. *V1,..., Vk* are the indexes of these free variables with respect to the surrounding λ-expression. Here, as in the *var*-construct, *bound(i)* denotes the *(i+1)*-th bound variable, i.e. the *i*-th parameter of the enclosing λ-expression. *free(j)* refers to the *(j+1)*-th free variable in the list of free variables of the enclosing λ-expression. In the example, *l1* has no free variables in its body and *l2* has two free variables which are both bound in the enclosing λ-expression *l1*. Similarly, *var(e5,free(1))*, representing the applied occurrence of *x* in the inner λ-expression, refers to the second free variable of *l2*. In the corresponding list one finds *bound(1)* as entry, saying that it is the second bound variable of the expression *l1* enclosing *l2*.

It is then the task of the combining module to pass address information such as *free(i)* or *bound(j)* from the binding rules module to the expression evaluation module.

4.1 Binding Rules

The binding rules are given by specifying the function *visibleAt* which returns for any occurrence *E* (of sort *ExpB*) of an expression and for any identifier *X* the declaration of *X* that is visible at *E*. *visibleLeftOf* is an auxiliary function, giving the visible declaration to the left of an expression *E*. Declaration information is a pair consisting of the scope which contains a declaration and the declaration itself. What a declaration and what an identifier is, is irrelevant. Thus the sorts *Decl* and *Id* are parameters of the specification. Another parameter is the predicate *isBuiltin* on identifiers which gives the set of names of globally known builtin objects. Additionally, we specify a function *freeVars* which returns for a scope the list of free variables in that scope, i.e. the variables which are referenced but not defined in that scope. For that purpose, auxiliary functions *refVars* and *defVars* will be defined.

The axioms written below will all be in the form of univerally quantified positive Horn clauses with equations. We will use a polymorphic *if_then_else_*-operator (not to be mixed up with the binary ⇒ which stands for implication in Horn clauses) based on a pregiven specification of Booleans with the usual properties. Furthermore, a polymorhic equality predicate *==* is used which is true for two terms *t1* and *t2* of the same sort iff *t1=t2* holds in the initial algebra model of the specification. This means that we use a meta-language that has the expressive power of OBJ2 [Fut85]. The subsorting facilities of OBJ2, although very useful, will not be employed here. Also we will not introduce any notation for expressing module hierarchies, parameterization and parameter passing. We only remark that the constructs which OBJ2 offers for these issues would be quite useful and satisfactory. For constructing lists we assume that a type constructor * may be applied to any sort *s* to give the sort of sequences over *s*. In connection with this constructor we use the usual polymorphic operators (_,...,_), _∘_ and _[_] to represent sequences, concatenation and list elements, respectively. ∪ and - denote union and difference of sets represented by sequences.

```
module BindingRules
sort ExpB DeclInfo
op          % syntactic relations among occurrences of expressions
    mainScope       : ExpB                  → Bool
    scope           : ExpB, ExpB            → Bool
    definingOcc     : ExpB, Id, Decl        → Bool
    appliedOcc      : ExpB, Id              → Bool
    seq             : ExpB, ExpB, ExpB      → Bool
    empty           : ExpB                  → Bool.
            % constructors for declaration information
    (_,_)           : ExpB, Decl            → DeclInfo
    undeclared      :                       → DeclInfo
    builtin         : Id                    → DeclInfo
            % exported functions
    visibleAt       : ExpB, Id              → DeclInfo
    visibleLeftOf   : ExpB, Id              → DeclInfo
    enclScope       : ExpB                  → ExpB
    refVars         : ExpB                  → Id*
    defVars         : ExpB                  → Id*
    freeVars        : ExpB                  → Id*
vars
```

```
    E E1 E2 E′ : ExpB
    X Y : Id
    D : Decl
axioms
              % visibility rules
    mainScope(E)  ⇒
        visibleLeftOf(E,X) = if isBuiltin(X) then builtin(X) else undeclared .
    seq(E,E1,E2)  ⇒
        visibleLeftOf(E1,X) = visibleLeftOf(E,X) ∧
        visibleLeftOf(E2,X) = visibleAt(E1,X) ∧
        visibleAt(E,X)      = visibleAt(E2,X) .
    scope(E,E′)   ⇒
        visibleLeftOf(E′,X) = visibleLeftOf(E,X) ∧
        visibleAt(E,X)      = visibleLeftOf(E,X) .
    definingOcc(E,X,D)  ⇒
        visibleAt(E,X) = if X==Y then (enclScope(E),D) else visibleLeftOf(E,X) .
    appliedOcc(E,X) ∨ empty(E) ⇒  visibleAt(E,X) = visibleLeftOf(E,X) .
              % enclosing scope function
    mainScope(E) ∨ scope(E′,E) ⇒ enclScope(E)=E.
    seq(E,E1,E2) ⇒ enclScope(E1) = enclScope(E) ∧ enclScope(E2) = enclScope(E) .
              % free variables in an expression
    seq(E,E1,E2) ⇒ refVars(E) = refVars(E1) ∪ refVars(E2) .
    appliedOcc(E,X) ⇒ refVars(E)=if visibleAt(E,X)=builtin(X) then () else (X) .
    definingOcc(E,X,D) ∨ empty(E) ⇒ refVars(E) = () .
    scope(E,E′)    ⇒   refVars(E) = freeVars(E′) .
    seq(E,E1,E2)   ⇒   defVars(E) = defVars(E1) ∪ defVars(E2) .
    appliedOcc(E,X) ∨ scope(E,E′) ∨ empty(E)  ⇒  defVars(E) = () .
    definingOcc(E,X,D)                        ⇒  defVars(E)=(X) .
    freeVars(S) = refVars(S) - defVars(S).
```

4.2 Expression Evaluation

We now specify expression evaluation. Expressions here may be constants, variables, function applications, if-expressions and λ–expressions. Variables are represented by indexes. Indexes may have the three forms *builtIn(I)*, *free(I)*, *bound(I)*, depending on the kind of the variable. All λ–expressions are closed, i.e. have associated with them the list of free variables that occur in the body of the expression. Values may either be elementary or closures consisting of expressions and the values of the free variables. Expressions are evaluated with respect to an environment of values for the bound and the free variables. The evaluation of a constant yields the value represented by the constant. The evaluation of a variable accesses its current value in the environment. (The evaluation of builtin objects is not further specified here.) λ–expressions are evaluated to yield a closure consisting of the body of the expression and the values of its free variables. Application of functions to arguments is lazy.

The module for expression evaluation is parameterized with the elementary values *ElemValue* and the evaluation of builtin objects *builtinVal*. (Of course, Booleans are such elementary values.) It is furthermore based on a suitable specification for natural numbers and integers.

```
module ExpressionEvaluation
sort      Value Index Env ExpE ExpListE ElemValue
op        % syntactic predicates
    exp        : ExpE                              → Bool
    const      : ExpE, ElemValue                   → Bool
    var        : ExpE, Index                       → Bool
    ifExp      : ExpE, ExpE, ExpE, ExpE            → Bool
    lambda     : ExpE, Nat, Index*, ExpE           → Bool
    apply      : ExpE, ExpE, ExpListE              → Bool
    empty      : ExpListE                          → Bool
    seq        : ExpListE, Exp, ExpListE           → Bool
          % constructors for values
    closure    : ExpE, Value*                      → Value
    _          : ElemValue                         → Value
          % constructors for variable indexes
    bound      : Nat                               → Index
    free       : Nat                               → Index
    builtin    : Id                                → Index
          % constructor for environments
    (_,_)      : Value*, Value*                    → Env
          % auxiliary functions for expression evaluation
    access     : Env, Index                        → Value
    access     : Env, Index*                       → Value*
    apply      : Env, Value, Value*                → Value
          % expression evaluation
    eval       : ExpE, Env                         → Value
vars
    E E' E1 E2 E3 F Body            : ExpE
    EL                              : ExpListE
    S                               : Env
    C                               : ElemValue
    I                               : Index
    FreeVarIndexes  Is              : Index*
    BoundVars FreeVars  VL          : Value*
    N Arity                         : Nat

axioms
          % variable access
    access((BoundVars,FreeVars),bound(N))     = BoundVars[N].
    access((BoundVars,FreeVars),free(N))      = FreeVars[N].
    access((BoundVars,FreeVars),builtin(X))   = builtinVal(X).
    access(S,())        = ().
    access(S,Is ∘ (I)) = access(S,Is) ∘ (access(S,I)).
          % function application
    apply(S,builtin(F),VL)                 = builtinVal(F,VL).
    apply(S,closure(Body,FreeVars),VL) = eval(Body,(VL,FreeVars)).
          % for expression evaluation
    const(E,C)        ⇒      eval(E,S) = C .
```

```
var(E,I)             ⇒    eval(E,S) = access(S,I) .
ifExp(E,E1,E2,E3) ⇒  eval(E,S) = if eval(E1,S) then eval(E2,S) else eval(E3,S) .
apply(E,F,EL)     ⇒    eval(E,S) = apply(S,eval(F,S),eval(EL,S)) .
lambda(E,Arity,FreeVarIndexes,Body) ⇒
                       eval(E,S) = closure(Body,access(S,FreeVarIndexes)) .
seq(EL,EL1,E)     ⇒    eval(EL,S) = eval(EL1,S) ∘ (eval(E,S)) .
empty(EL)         ⇒    eval(EL,S) = () .
```

4.3. Combining the Modules

The interpreter for the concrete language is determined by specifying two abstraction functions

b : Exp -> ExpB   and   e : Exp -> ExpE

from the concrete expression language *Exp* to the abstractions *ExpB* and *ExpE*. It will be the case that some of the concrete expressions give rise to more than one abstract B- or E-expression. In such cases, more than one abstraction function must be used. We will use indexes to *b* or *e* to denote those. The parameter Decl of the binding rules specification is instantiated by Nat, for reasons indicated in the beginning of chapter 2.

The main technical problem to be solved here is the specification of how the indexes for variables are to be calculated. For that purpose we define a function *index(X,B)*, for identifiers X in binding contexts *B* (of sort *ExpB*). If the scope containing the visible declaration for *X* is at the same time the directly enclosing scope, *X* is a bound variable and its index is obtained through *visibleAt*. Otherwise, and if it is not a built-in value, *X* is a free variable and we take as its index its position in the list of free variables of the current scope. By *index* we also denote the extension of *index* to lists of identifiers, yielding lists of indexes. The obvious axioms for *nmbElems* and *positionIn* are left out.

```
module LazyMiniLisp
sort Exp ExpList Idlist
op  % syntax
    exp        : Exp                        → Bool
    const      : Exp, ElemValue             → Bool
    var        : Exp, Id                    → Bool
    if         : Exp, Exp, Exp, Exp         → Bool
    apply      : Exp, Exp, ExpList          → Bool
    seq        : ExpList, ExpList, Exp      → Bool
    empty      : ExpList                    → Bool
    lambda     : Exp, IdList, Exp           → Bool
    seq        : IdList, IdList, Id         → Bool
    empty      : Idlist                     → Bool
          % abstraction functions
    e          : Exp                        → ExpE
    b, b1      : Exp                        → ExpB
          % auxiliary functions
    nmbElems : IdList                       → Nat
    index      : Id, ExpB                   → Index
    index      : Id*, ExpB                  → Index*
```

```
    positionIn : Id*, Id                        → Nat
vars
    E E1 E2 E3 F Body                 : Exp
    EL                                : ExpList
    IdL IdL1                          : IdList
    EV                                : ElemValue
    DeclaringScope EnclScope B        : ExpB
    N                                 : Nat
    X                                 : Id
    Xs                                : Id*
axioms
    visibleAt(B,X) = (DeclaringScope,N) ∧ EnclScope=enclScope(B)
        ⇒ index(X,B) = if DeclaringScope == EnclScope then bound(N)
                       else free(positionIn(freeVars(EnclScope),X)) .
    visibleAt(B,X) = builtin(X) ⇒ index(X,B) = builtin(X) .
    index((),B) = () .
    index(Xs∘(X),B) = index(Xs,B)∘(index(X,B)) .
    exp(E)          ⇒ exp(e(E))          ∧ mainScope(b(E)) .
    const(E,EV)     ⇒ const(e(E),EV)     ∧ empty(b(E)) .
    var(E,X) ∧ visibleAt(b(E),X) = (DeclaringScope,Index)  ⇒ appliedOcc(b(E),X) .
    var(E,X)        ⇒ var(e(E),index(X,b(E))) .
    seq(IdL,IdL1,X)⇒
        seq(b(IdL),b(IdL1),b1(IdL)) ∧ definingOcc(b1(IdL),X,nmbElems(IdL1)) .
    lambda(E,IdL,E1) ⇒
        scope(b(E),B) ∧ seq(B,b(IdL),b(E1) ∧
        lambda(e(E), nmbElems(IdL), index(freeVars(b(E1)),b(E)), e(E1)).
    apply(E,F,EL) ⇒ seq(b(E),b(F),b(EL)) ∧ apply(e(E),e(F),e(EL)) .
    if(E,E1,E2,E3) ⇒
        seq(b(E),b(E1),B) ∧ seq(B,b(E2),b(E3))  ∧ if(e(E),e(E1),e(E2),e(E3)) .
```

We have specified that the evaluation abstraction of a constant is a constant and that its binding abstraction is an empty expression. Variables are transformed into indexes of the evaluation facet. If its not a built-in object, it is at the same time an applied occurrence in the binding rules facet. Sequences of identifiers (in lambda expressions) have no meaning at evaluation time. However at binding time they are the defining occurrences of variables and bind names to their indexes in the identifier list. λ-expressions are scopes wrt. binding and λ-expressions wrt. evaluation.

The axiom for variables defines a direct interaction between our two basic semantics modules. First, for identifiers *X* in a context represented by its occurrence *E* in an expression the visible declaration is looked up. This is achieved by calling *visibleAt* (from binding rules semantics) for *X* and binding abstraction context *b(E)*. Its result is used to calculate an index which then becomes the abstraction of the variable in the evaluation abstraction context *e(E)*. It is important to observe that this passing of semantic information between modules crucially depends on the fact that *b(E)* and *e(E)* are abstractions *of one and the same occurrence E* of the identifier *X* in the given program. It is exactly this situation which accounts for our motivation to base semantics on relations between occurrences of expressions.

5. Execution of Specifications Using Prolog

This section summarizes some experiments in using Prolog as implementation language for specifications of the above kind.

5.1. Translating Axioms into Prolog-Clauses

The following examples of the Prolog-versions of some of our axioms illustrate the massaging that has to be done due to the lack of functions and equality in Prolog. One of the axioms for visibility would in Prolog read as

```
visibleAt(E1,X,D):- seqB(E,E1,E2), visibleAt(E,X,D).
```

There is no problem with boolean functions such as *seq* which we use to denote syntactic relations. These can be represented by Prolog-predicates. Other functions such as *visibleAt* have to be represented by their graphs. At the same time, equalities have to be directed into head and body, making explicit the actual calculation process. With that our axioms become rather similar to the inference rules used by Plotkin [Plo83] or Clément et al [Clé85]. As, in the absence of typing, overloading is not available to the needed extent, functions must be renamed, e.g. *seq* becomes *seqB* or *seqE*. The abstraction functions from concrete syntax to the abstract views, e.g. *e, b, b1, b2,* are in fact constructors, and hence can be implemented by functors in Prolog. (In fact we do not know how to represent them otherwise.) Some further examples of Prolog-versions of axioms are

```
varE(e(E),I) :-
      var(E,X), index(X,b(E),I).

index(X,B,I) :-
      visibleAt(b(E),X,D),
      (D=builtin(X) -> I=D;
       D=(DeclaringScope,Index) ->
            enclScope(b(E),EnclScope),
            (EnclScope=DeclaringScope -> I=bound(Index);
                  freeVars(EnclScope,FreeVars),
                  positionIn(FreeVars,X,Offset), I=free(Offset))).
```

Finally, since equations must not occur as heads of Prolog-clauses, we need to introduce explicit equality relations on abstract syntactic objects of sorts such as *ExpB* and *ExpE*.

One principal problem remains. A function (e.g. eval) which is specified by a system of equations in general requires a leftmost-outermost reduction strategy for its evaluation, if classical first-order logic is assumed. Thus, what we have specified in section 4.2 is a lazy functional language. Translating the axiom

$$\text{apply}(E,F,EL) \Rightarrow \text{eval}(E,S) = \text{apply}(S,\text{eval}(F,S),\text{eval}(EL,S))$$

into the Prolog clause

```
eval(E,S,V) :- applyE(E,F,EL), eval(F,S,FV), eval(EL,S,VL), apply(S,FV,VL,V)
```

would make the evaluation become eager. Hence, the translation scheme for a term

$$T = f(t_1,...,t_k)$$

into the Prolog conjuction

$t_1(\ldots,T_1),\ldots,t_k(\ldots,T_k),f(T_1,\ldots,T_k,T)$

is correct only for total functions *f* . *eval*, of course, is not a total function. There are two solutions to this problem. Either one uses a more powerful prototyping approach, e.g. based on term rewriting, or one starts out from a continuation semantics specification which involves first-order representations of continuations. In the latter case, the application order of the Prolog goals does becomes independent of the application order of the defined language [Rey72]. As we discuss in this paper Prolog as implementation language for our specifications, it would have been more appropriate to give a continuation-style specification in the examples. However, in order to have small examples that illustrate the modulary which we have in mind, we have decided otherwise.

5.2. Optimization of the Prolog-Programs

Apart from the mentioned problems with termination, equivalent Prolog-programs can be obtained rather systematically from the original axioms. These programs are, however, very inefficient. In fact we cannot really execute them on any reasonable input. As any real interpreter, syntactic and semantic analysis is repeated whenever control is transferred to a point in the program. In our case this means that the abstraction functions from concrete to abstract views are also recomputed over and over again. In addition to that, we have chosen to specify the visibilty rules rather directly, without making use of implementation concepts such as symbol tables. Therefore, whenever a variable occurs in a source program, the interpreter recomputes the B-abstraction and searches it right-to-left until the declaration is found. Then, it starts to recompute the relevant declaration information, which usually is static anyway, i.e. independent of the input to the source program.

Fortunately, a rather simple technique which somewhat resembles partial evaluation removes a major portion of this overhead. The idea is to memoize computations and record source program-specific lemmas that have been derived during interpretation. Logically, this process is based on the observation that if

(1) $Th[L] \quad \vdash q(X) \wedge r(X,Y) \Rightarrow p(X,Y).$

can be derived in a theory *Th[L]* and if

(2) $Th[L]+Th[p] \vdash q(X0).$

can be derived in an enriched theory *Th[L]+Th[p]* for some instance *X0* of *X*, then,

(3) $Th[L]+Th[p] \vdash r(X0,Y) \Rightarrow p(X0,Y).$

is also derivable in the enriched theory. Our application of this is as follows. *Th[L]* is the set of axioms for the interpreter specification for a language *L*. Starting an interpreter on a source program p requires to first enrich *Th[L]* by the set of facts *Th[p]* by which the program is represented. *q(X0)* now stands for a program-specific property that had to be proved during applying the interpreter axiom (1). Therefore, if (1) needs to be computed a second time one might as well try to apply (3) first, which, if successful, saves the recomputation of *q(X0)*. This effect is obtained in a Prolog-program, if one uses *asserta* to enter (3) into the data base after having succeeded with (2) in the call of (1). More exactly, a clause such as

(4) p(X,Y) :- q(X), asserta((p(X,Y0) :- r(X,Y0)), r(X,Y).

exactly achieves this effect. (Note that due to the functioning of *asserta*, the variable *Y* must be renamed to not enter its instantiated value into the data base.) If one, moreover, shortcuts long chains caused by rules of type *P:-Q*, one obtains an even better Prolog-program.

Now, in theory it does not matter in which cases one decides to enter a lemma. In practice, however, entering too many lemmas means to blow up the data base, whereas entering to few lemmas means to slow down the resolution process. Neither situation is desirable. In our examples which we have run so far, we have left this decision to the interpreter specifyer. We have written a little preprocessor in Prolog which reads clauses such as

```
    visibleAt(E1,X,D):- seqB(E,E1,E2), ^ visibleAt(E,X,D).
```

where the hat "^" annotates literals for which no lemma generation should be made, and transforms them into the Prolog-clause

```
    visibleAt(E1,X,D):-
                seqB(E,E1,E2),
                asserta((visibleAt(E1,X0,D0):- visibleAt(E,X0,D0))),
                visibleAt(E,X,D).
```

This example demonstrates how, during interpretation, lemma generation produces a functional representation of the symbol table for the concrete source program. In cases where *r(X, Y)* is trivial, i.e. empty, the generated lemma is a fact which can be considered to represent a semantic attribute of the program which is only calculated once and then stored for further use. Clauses which are obtained by preprocessing the annotated axioms for expression evaluation, e.g.

```
    eval(E,S,V):-
        applyE(E,F,EL),
            asserta((eval(E,S0,V0):-
                    eval(F,S0,FV0), eval(A,S0,AV0), apply(S,FV0,AV0,V0))),
        eval(F,S,FV), eval(EL,S,VL),apply(S,FV,VL,V).
```

during execution gradually translate a source program during interpretation into Prolog. This is an effect that is otherwise obtained by partially evaluating an interpreter.

To give an illustration for the effectiveness of this procedure, we present some figures about cpu times. Running an interpreter for a language similar to the one specified in this paper on the standard definition for a function that reverses lists, including the definition for an auxiliary *append*-function, takes 90 sec. to reverse the list *(3, 4)*. Restarting the evaluation function, then, executes the compiled program, which takes in this case on the same input "only" 4 seconds of runtime. (The figures are taken on a 68000-based micro running C-Prolog.) These 4 seconds are still quite long so that one might want a somewhat more elaborated optimization scheme. However, even with the simple scheme explained above, one can conduct nontrivial experiments even on a not really sophisticated Prolog-system.

6. Conclusions

We have shown that modular first-order specifications of operational semantics are made possible if one uses predicates to characterize the syntactic relations between occurrences of subexpressions in a program, and if one chooses module-specific abstractions of the concrete language on which to base the specifications of a semantics module. The examples which we have given in this paper include binding rules and expression evaluation. We have achieved that binding rules could be specified independent of the concrete expression syntax. Expression evaluation, on the other hand, did not need to be concerned with searching names in name lists, but could be based on a rather simple (and at the same time more efficient) indexing scheme for variables. The price which we pay for this increase in modularity is that semantics specifications are no longer compositional. As programs are not terms here, semantics cannot be a homomorphism into a semantic algebra. One may argue that this is too high a price which our approach shares with the operational semantics definitions à la Plotkin and Kahn. On the other hand, what we gain are completely formal specifications of the combination of languages from semantics modules. (This is something which is still missing in the work of Mosses.) The use of context relations on program constructs allows to associate semantic values with constructs in their context in a program and, more importantly, for passing such values between the various abstractions of the construct.

We have also given a proposal for an optimized implementation of such specifications using Prolog. A lemma generation technique serves to avoid recomputation of static semantic properties. The specification technique, together with this implementation technique, can hence also be considered as a technique for modular design and logic programming of interpreters.

References

[BHK85] Bergstra, J.A., Heering, J., Klint, P.: Algebraic definition of a simple programming language. CWI, Dept. of Comp. Sci., Report CS-R8504, Amsterdam, 1985.

[Bru72] De Bruijn, N.G.: Lambda calculus notation with nameless dummies, a tool for automatic formula manipulation. Indag. Math. 34, (1972), pp. 381-392.

[Clé85] Clément, D., Despeyroux, J., Despeyroux, Th., Hascoet, L., Kahn, G.: Natural semantics on the computer. RR 416, INRIA, Sophia Antipolis, June 1985.

[Ers77] Ershov, A,: On the partial evaluation principle. Inf. Proc. Letters 6,2 (1977), 38-41.

[Fut85] Futatsugi, K., Goguen, J.A., Jouannaud, J.-P., Meseguer, P.: Principles of OBJ2. Proc. POPL 1985.

[Gan83] Ganzinger, H.: Increasing modularity and language- independency in automatically generated compilers. SCP 3 (1983), 223-287.

[GH85] Ganzinger, H., Hanus, M.: Modular logic programming of compilers. Proc. IEEE Symp. on Logic Programming, Boston, 1985.

[GP81] Goguen, J.A., Parsaye-Ghomi, K.: Algebraic denotational semantics using parameterized abstract modules. LNCS 107, 1981.

[GT79] Goguen, J.A., Tardo, J.J.: An introduction to OBJ: A language for writing and testing formal algebraic specifications. Proc. IEEE Conf on Spec. of Reliable Software, Cambridge, Mass. 1979.

[Hen80] Henderson, P.: Functional Programming: Application and Implementation. Prentice Hall, 1980.

[JSS85] Jones, N.D., Sestoft, P., Søndergaard, H.: An experiment in partial evaluation: the generation of a compiler generator. Copenhagen, 1985, to be published.

[Lip82] Lipeck, U.: An algebraic calculus for structured design of data abstractions (in German). PhD- Thesis, U. Dortmund, 1982.

[Mos83] Mosses, P.: Abstract semantic algebras. In Bjørner, D. (ed.): Formal Description of Programming Concepts II, North-Holland, 1983, 45-70.

[Plo83] Plotkin, G.D.: An operational semantics for CSP. In Bjørner, D. (ed.): Formal Description of Programming Concepts II, North-Holland, 1983, 199-126.

[Rey72] Reynolds, J.C.: Definitional interpreters for higher-order programming languages. 25th ACM Annual Conf., Boston 1972, pp. 717-740.

[Wan79] Wand, M.: First-order identities as a defining language. TR No. 29, Comp. Sci. Dep´t, Indiana U., Bloomington, Indiana, May 1979.

Logic Specification of Code Generation Techniques

Robert Giegerich

FB Informatik
Universität Dortmund
D-4600 Dortmund 50
W.Germany

1. Introduction

1.1 The Problem

We are interested in techniques and tools for the implementation of code generators for target machines such as the MC68000 or the VAX. Difficulties of this task arise from two sources:

(a) While many techniques for particular subtasks of code generation are known (take Sethi-Ullman numbering [SeU70] as a famous example), there are no universal rules how these techniques are to be combined to obtain a code generator for a given target machine. The decisions taken by different subtasks can be mutually dependent (this was termed the "phase ordering problem" in [Wul75]), and so, the ultimate design is influenced by target machine properties as well as pragmatic decisions with respect to code generation effort and code quality.

(b) The techniques for particular subtasks themselves must be adapted to the peculiarities of a given instruction set. Sethi-Ullman numbering, for example, must be adapted to different sorts of registers available, to the presence or absence of 3-address instructions or complex addressing modes, and so on.

In order to be helpful with these sources of problems, a flexible code generation tool should have two properties:

(A) It must allow to separately describe various code generation subtasks (phases), but not prescribe a particular order in which they are applied. In other words, it should allow - even encourage - the implementor to experiment with different overall strategies of code generation.

(B) There should be a clear-cut descinction between (the description of) a general technique, and its application to a particular machine. Only so, we can carry over the trust we place in (or the proof we have given for) a technique to a particular code generator we devise.

While (A) and (B) clearly are desirable properties, it is not known to what extend they can be achieved. Can we design a code generation tool with these properties, which supports a significant number of code generation techniques, works for an interesting class of target machines, and produces acceptably efficient code generators? This question is yet to be answered. The current paper describes an experiment that was performed to investigate the feasibility of such a tool.

1.1 Informal Outline of the Approach

We restrict our attention to code generation for basic blocks. Let IL be the language of intermediate programs, as input to the code generator, let TM be a target machine, and let *ip* and *tp* be IL- and TM-programs, respectively. We shall specify the following predicates (loosely also called phases) over TM-programs:
tmProg(tp,ip) holds if *tp* is an encoding of *ip* in terms of TM-instructions. This encoding is abstract in the sense that it need not respect compatability rules for machine data types on TM, knows nothing about operand bindings, assumes an infinite number of temporary registers to be available, etc. Such aspects are defined separately by subsequent predicates.
wellTyped(tp) holds if *tp* observes TM's data type rules.
wellBound(tp) holds if *tp* observes TM's source/target operand bindings, as may arise from 2-address arithmetic instructions, for example.
wellOrd(tp) holds if an evaluation order can be chosen for *tp* (according to a Sethi- Ullman numbering scheme) such that the temporary register requirements of *tp* do not exceed a pregiven limit *k*.

Code generation for a given *ip* amounts to a constructive proof that there exists a *tp* that satisfies the conjunction of these predicates. To structure this proof in an incremental manner, we derive functions from the phase predicates with the following properties:

make_tmProg(ip) = tp such that *tmProg(tp,ip)*,
and for *phase* ∈{*wellTyped, wellBound, wellOrd*}
make_phase(tp) = tp' such that
$\forall$*ip: tmProg(tp,ip)* → *tmProg(tp',ip) & phase(tp')*.

In words: each *make_phase* function preserves the *tmProg* predicate, and establishes the *phase* predicate on *tp'*.
Note that we do not require phases to respect any other phases except *tmProg*. This is necessary when we want to describe phases separately. An optimal evaluation order as determined by *make_wellOrd* may conflict with operand bindings, establishing correct operand bindings may create new opportunities for peephole optimization,etc. In general, we cannot exclude that later application of some phase invalidates properties established earlier. Generally we allow that a phase be applied several times (as is also reported from PQCC generated compilers [WuN82]), and we ensure that they always can.
So, the code generator implementor decides on an overall strategy, which is a composition of phase applications, starting with *make_tmProg(ip)*, and followed by an arbitrary (but hopefully well-chosen) sequence of other phases. This sequence may be infinite (e.g. in the presence of peephole optimization phases), and in any case, the implementor must ensure that the sequence of the obtained *tp's* has a finite limit which satisfies the conjunction of all phase predicates. So much for property (A).

Property (B) is approached as follows: A phase predicate like *wellBound(tp)* is not specified directly as a predicate on TM-programs. Rather, it is defined for an abstract machine aBIND. In the case of aBIND, the abstract machine has one instruction for each conceivable form of operand binding - a 3-address instruction (no binding), a 2-address instruction binding the first source operand to the target, one binding the second,etc. We define *wellBound(ap)* on aBIND-programs, as the common base technique for all code generators we may develop. For a particular TM, we specify an abstraction mapping

absBIND: TM-programs → aBIND-programs

and define

wellBound(tp) = wellBound(absBIND(tp)).

This is how all phases except *tmProg* are defined. For *tmProg*, the appropriate abstract machine is the intermediate language IL, and *tmProg* is identical to *absIL*.

1.3 Related Work

The approach to code generation that we have in mind tries to bridge the gap between the elegance of the Graham-Glanville style approaches ([Gla77], [Gra80], [Gnp80], [Hen84]), and the flexibility in providing a multitude of machine specific analyses of the PQCC approach ([PQC80], [WuN82]). Our interest here concentrates on the conceptual aspects of such an approach. The idea of separate descriptions of different subtasks of code generation, using the method of describing abstract machines and mappings between them, was explicated in [Gie84], although in a more implementation oriented fashion. Here, the technique of [Gan86] is used for relating concrete machine descriptions to the abstract modules descibing the various code generation phases.

2. Machine Model and Program Representation

A target machine is described as a signature together with an associated set of axioms. Although there is some freedom in drawing this distinction, we may say that the signature defines the syntax of target machine programs, while the axioms add semantic constraints. Those are introduced both by the hardware and by compiler implementation decisions. Examples of the respective kinds are laws for instruction width and operand length consistency, or the rule that a certain number of temporary registers may not be exceeded.

2.1 Categories of the Basic Machine Model

In a target machine signature, sorts and operators are categorized according to the machine specific concepts they model. Among the sorts, we distinguish

- *constants*, such as register numbers, absolute addresses and constant data of various sizes, and also the (names of the) machine data types, such as *byte*, *word*, etc.
- *address modes*, modelling a particular machine cell (register or memory) according to the way in which it is addressed,
  - *address templates*, representing the result of a dynamic address calculation,
  - *operand classes*, representing sets of address modes allowed at some operand position in an instruction,
  - *result operand classes* and *result address modes*, modelling results of some computation which are to be placed into a machine cell accessed by a particular address mode belonging to a particular opernd class. It is important to think of a *result* as a calculated value calling for a machine cell to hold it, and not as that cell itself.

Among the operators, we distinguish

- *instructions*, mapping operand classes into result operand classes,
- (*result) operand class definers*, indicating membership of address modes in operand classes, and of result operand classes in result address modes,
- *cell constructors*, mapping either an address template, a result address mode and a machine data type, or else a constant, into the corresponding address mode,
- *address functions*, modelling the machine's capabilities for calculating dynamic addresses.

However, for reasons discussed below, operators of form $A_p,\dots,A_n \rightarrow B$ are written as predicates $B, A_p,\dots,A_n \rightarrow Bool$. A minimal example target machine is TM as shown below.

```
Target machine signature TM:
sort
   ConstW, ConstB, Regno, Types,        -- constants
   Reg,  Mbd,   Imm,                    -- address modes
   Reg_r, Mbd_r,                        -- result address modes
   All,  Alt,   Ea,                     -- operand classes
   Alt_r,                               -- result operand class
   Bd                                   -- address template
op         -- syntactic predicates
                                        -- cell constructors
    m_mbd: Mbd, Bd, Mbd_r,  Types       --> Bool
    m_imm: Imm, ConstW,     Types       --> Bool
  m_reg: Reg, Regno, Reg_r, Types       --> Bool
                                        -- operand class definers
   reginall: All, Reg                   --> Bool
  mbdinall: All, Mbd                    --> Bool
  imminall: All, Imm                    --> Bool
   bdinea: Ea, Bd                       --> Bool
                                        -- result opd. class definers
  altinreg: Reg_r, Alt_r                --> Bool
        ##: Reg_r                       --> Bool
  altinmbd: Mbd_r, Alt_r                --> Bool
        ##: Mbd_r                       --> Bool
                                        -- address function
     a_bd: Bd, Reg, ConstW              --> Bool
                                        -- instructions
     mov: Alt_r, All                    --> Bool
     mea: Alt_r, Ea                     --> Bool
    sext: Alt_r, All                    --> Bool
     add: Alt_r, All,  All              --> Bool
  tmProg: All                           --> Bool
            -- semantic functions
   word, byte:                          --> Types
```

A Remark on Result Arguments and Assignment

Note that in our machine signature there are no operators corresponding to an explicit assignment operator. Instead, assignment is expressed by using the value to be assigned (resp. its denotation) as a "result"-argument to the cell constructor forming the target cell. Where a cell is used as a source operand only, the "result"-argument of its constructor is *##*.

Let us ignore for the moment that target machine operators were written as predicates, and let us view them as functions (with the first argument sort of the predicate being the target sort of the function). Then, TM-programs are represented as terms, and a move-word instruction MOV.W 220(R0),R5 looks like

```
m_reg(5,
      altinreg(mov(mbdinall(m_mbd(a_bd(m_reg(0, ff, word),
                                         220),
                               ff,
                               word)))),
      word).
```

Note that the target register is not an argument to the *mov*-instruction, but vice versa.

This somewhat unusual treatment of assignment is rather essential for our subsequent development.

One advantage over using an explicit assignment operator is that inserting temporary locations - be they registers or arbitrarily addressed memory locations (the latter being a problematic point in the Graham-Glanville technique) - works very smoothly, without distorting the program representation.

Another advantage is that we can form larger units than single assignments for which our code selection techniques will work. An extra explicit assignment operator is used in [Gie84] to restrict evaluation ordering. For the rudimentary intermediate language we are introducing below, the evaluation order can be chosen arbitrarily.

As a third advantage, implicit assignments provide a definition-use chain of length one, and hence we can work with only a single representation of the address calculation for a cell which is used twice - first as a target operand of one, and thereafter as a source operand of some other instruction. This is why a term formed by an instruction does only represent its target operand class, but not its target address mode.

The Intermediate Language

The intermediate language IL from which we generate code is not chosen independently of the target machine. Rather, it is derived from TM as an abstraction in some respects, and an extension in others. With operands, IL only distinguishes whether they reside in a cell, or are an intermediate result with no machine cell associated to it. A single address mode corresponds to all TM modes addressing the same cell ckass. Operand classes and address functions disappear. For each TM instruction, IL has several variants, which may take machine cells as well as results as their operands.

Our code generator input language is machine specific to the extend of the implementation mapping, which the compiler writer defines when he chooses a representation of source program variables by machine cells, and maps source program operators onto those present in the target machine. (For example, IL-operators *plus* must have the same interpretation in the source language semantics, as *add* has in TM's instruction set semantics.) No other aspects of TM are represented in IL.

```
Intermediate Language Signature IL
sort
    ConstW, ConstB, Regno,
    E,                        -- operand occupying a cell
    R,                        -- computed result
op                            -- syntactic predicates
    cellRW: E, Regno, R       --> Bool
    cellRB: E, Regno, R       --> Bool
    cellMW: E, R, R           --> Bool
```

cellMB: E, R, R --> *Bool*
constWE: E, ConstW --> *Bool*
constBE: E, ConstB --> *Bool*
f: R --> *Bool*
mv: R, E --> *Bool*
plus: R, E, E --> *Bool*
plus: R, R, E --> *Bool*
plus: R, E, R --> *Bool*
plus: R, R, R --> *Bool*
ilprog: E --> *Bool*

Representation of TM- and IL-Programs

As in the compiler front end of [Gan86], programs are represented as conjunctions of facts, wherein different syntactic entities of the program are referred to by unique names. We shall speak of these conjunctions as "ensembles" of facts, to express that they must be complete with respect to facts about sub-entities.

TM-programs are much more refined than IL-programs. So, a particular entity in the IL-program gives rise to several TM-entities. We derive TM-names from an IL-name by applying abstraction functions. By convention, these are named after their target sort, using lower case letters.

Below we show what the move-instruction MOV.W 220(R0),R5 looks like both in the target machine and the intermediate language:

IL program	***TM program***
ilprog(r5)	*tmProg(all(r5)),*
	reginall(all(r5),reg(r5)),
cellRW(r5,5,m),	*m_reg(reg(r5),5,reg_r(m),word),*
	altinreg(reg_r(m),alt_r(m)),
mv(m,n),	*mov(alt_r(m),all(n)),*
	mbdinall(all(n),mbd(n)),
cellMW(n,o,q),	*m_mbd(mbd(n),bd(o),mbd_r(q),word),*
f(q),	*ff(mbd_r(q)),*
plus(o,r0,c),	*a_bd(bd(o),reg(r0),220),*
constWE(c,220),	
cellRW(r0,0,s),	*m_reg(reg(r0),0,reg_r(s),word),*
f(s).	*ff(reg_r(s)).*

3. Specifications of Code Generation Phases

3.1 Code Selection

Code selection is deriving TM-facts from IL-facts. The predicate *tmProg* is now specified by the following axioms (Only a subset of the axioms can be shown here, but the completion is straightforward):

TM -to-IL- Abstraction

-- *abstraction functions*

reg: E --> Reg

```
   all: E --> All                              -- etc.
   reg_r: R --> Reg_r
   alt_r: R --> Alt_r                          -- etc.
   ...
vars X,X1: E
     Y: R
     I: Regno
     T: Types
axioms
   tmProg(all(X))
             if    ilprog(X)
             and  (    mbdinall(all(X),mbd(X))
                    or  reginall(all(X),reg(X))       )
   reginall(all(X),reg(X))
             if    m_reg(reg(X),I,reg_r(Y),T)
   m_reg(reg(X),I,reg_r(Y),word)
             if    cellRW(X,I,Y)
             and   (altinreg(reg_r(Y),alt_r(Y)) or ff(reg_r(Y)) )
   . . .
   altinreg(reg_r(Y),alt_r(Y))
             if    (    mov(alt_r(Y),all(X))
                    or  add(alt_r(Y),all(X),all(X1))
                    or  mea(alt_r(Y),ea(Y))
                    or  sext(altr_r(Y),all(X))     )
   mov(alt_r(Y),all(X))
             if    mv(Y,X)
             and   (   reginall(all(X),reg(X))
                    or  mbdinall(all(X),mbd(X))
                    or  imminall(all(X),imm(X))    )
   add(alt_r(Y),all(X),all(X1))
             if    plus(Y,X,X1)
             and   (   reginall(all(X),reg(X)) or ...)
             and   (   reginall(all(X1),reg(X1)) or ...)
```

Given the representation of IL-program as an ensemble of facts, such as *ilprog(ip)*, the above specification allows us to proof *tmProg(all(ip))* in some cases. The TM-predicates proved in the course of this proof are an ensemble of facts representing a TM-program. However, the proof will work only in the trivial case, where no temporary allocation is required.
The need for temporary allocation is encountered when the proof for, say,

add(alt_r(Y),all(X),all(X₁)) fails because there is no IL-fact

plus(Y,X,X₁).

However, *plus(Y,X,Y₁)* may hold for some Y_1 of sort *R*. If we added a fact like *cellRW(X₁, tmp, Y₁)* to our representation of *ip*, the proof of *add* could proceed beyond this point. Rather than transforming the input program in this fashion, we add extra lemmas to the specification of TM-predicates, which ensure in another way that a temporary register can always be allocated. Logically, we are extending TM to an infinite register machine.
Below, we show the lemmas only for the other, slightly more sophisticated case where temporary

allocation may be required. They assure that an operand occupying a cell (say an *mbd(X)*) may always be placed in a register before being used.

Infinite Register Lemmas

```
            -- abstraction functions for new  unique names
  loc: E    --> E
  loc: E    --> R
            --   lemmas for operand that occupies a cell, but of the
            --  wrong kind, and hence needs  a temporary
  mbdinall(all(loc(X),mbd(X))
            if     m_mbd(mbd(X), bd(Y),mbd_r(Y1), T)
  reginall(all(loc(X),reg(X))
            if     m_reg(reg(X), I,reg_r(Y), T)
  imminall(all(loc(X)),imm(X))
            if     m_imm(X,X1, T)
            -- loading the temporary
  mov(alt_r(loc(X),all(loc(X)))
            if      (reginall(all(loc(X),reg(X)) or  mbdinall... )
  altinreg(reg_r(loc(X)),alt_r(loc(X)))
            if      mov(alt_r(loc(X)))
            -- allocating the temporary
  m_reg(reg(loc(X), I,reg_r(loc(X)), T)
            if      altinreg(reg_r(loc(X)),alt_r(loc(X)))
            -- a temporary reg is  used as a reg
  reginall(all(X),reg(loc(X))
            if      m_reg(reg(loc(X), I,reg_r(loc(X)), T)
            --  lemmas for result that needs a temporary
            -- omitted --
```

Thus, *reginall(all(X),...)* holds whenever (say) *m_mbd(mbd(X),....)* holds. Rather than specifying this implication directly, we do it via a chain of implications, ensuring that, as before, the set of clause instances proved constitutes an ensemble of TM facts.
This completes the specification of the predicate *tmProg*, and hence, the specification od a (preliminary) code selection phase. *tmProg* defines all encodings as a TM-program that can be given for an IL program according to the plain TM signature. Code selction is constructing an inverse to the abstraction mapping TM-programs to IL-programs. In phases specifications discussed subsequently, the concrete TM program is given, and mapped onto further abstractions in order to verify (or establish) its semantic properties.

3.2 Machine Data Type Consistency and Coercion

Data type laws specify constraints on the data types of the operands and the result of an instruction, address calculation, memory access, etc. It may or may not be possible to add a byte to a word.
In principle, machine data type rules can be expressed syntactically by suffixing the sorts and operators of the target machine signature. This is undesirable, since the size of the TM signature multiplies by the number of machine data types (the VAX has about 12). Moreover, such a syntactic description would be over-detailed, since different data types often follow the same rules with most instructions, and behave differently only for a few.
For IL we allow implicit coercion from byte to word data where required. Exact data type rules for IL can be specified the same way as done below for TM, but this will not be shown here.

Where IL is more permissive than TM (as in our example) in this respect, explicit coercion operations (using the *sext*-instruction) must be inserted in the target program.

Abstract machine data type laws specify whether an operand must be of a specific size, be of identical size as some other operand, or may have a coercion applied to it. Obviously, the number of sensible type laws is rather small, and all they need to talk about are typed objects and the arity of the constructs which form them. Thus they are be specified as a machine independent module:

```
Abstract Machine Data Type Laws
sort Typ_obj, Types, TM_Rules
op              -- syntactic predicates
        w: Typ_obj                                  --> Bool
      xxx: Typ_obj, Typ_obj, Typ_obj                --> Bool
     xwxx: Typ_obj, Typ_obj, Typ_obj, Types         --> Bool
   x_to_y: Typ_obj, Typ_obj, TM_Rule                --> Bool
      ...
                           -- semantic predicates
       isdt: Typ_obj, Types                         --> Bool
  wellTyped: Typ_obj                                --> Bool

vars  A, B, C: Typ_obj
      S, T: Types
      TM_Rule: TM_Rules

axioms
   wellTyped(A)    if  isdt(A, T)
   isdt(A, word)   if  w(A)

   isdt(A, T)  if  xxx(A,B,C)
                   and isdt(B, T)
                   and isdt(C, T)

   isdt(A, T)  if  xwxx(A,B,C,T)
                   and isdt(B, word)
                   and isdt(C, T)

   isdt(A, T)  if  x_to_y(A,B, TM_Rule)
                   and isdt(B,S)
                   and coerce(T,S, TM_Rule)
   ...
```

Predicate *isdt(A, T)* inductively defines when a program *A*, represented as facts over *xxx*, *xwxx* etc., is well typed, and that its result type is *T*. We use the following simple notational convention: the predicate name *xwxx*, for example, is used for the rule with four arguments, where the first, third and fourth arguments must have or be arbitrary, but identical types, while the second is required to be of type *word*.
In the last clause, a coercion from *S* to *T* is indicated. What the exact situation is, is machine specific knowledge passed as *TM_Rule* to *coerce*, which defines what a coercion is, and is also machine specific. The module of abstract data tpye rules needs to know nothing about either of them, except that it imports *coerce* and sort *TM_rules*.

The specification of concrete data type rules for TM is straightforward. Potential coercions have an exact place in our machine model: they are associated with operand class and result operand class definers.

Machine Data Type Abstraction

```
                      -- signature of TM, augmented by
    dt: All --> Typ_obj              -- abstraction functions
    dt: Mbd --> Typ_obj              -- etc.
vars All1 All2 : All
      Mbd: Mbd                       -- etc.
axioms
    v(dt(Const W)
    xxx(dt(Alt_r), dt(All1), dt(All2))
               if add(Alt_r, All1, All2)
    xvxx(dt(Mbd), dt(Bd), dt(Mbd_r), T)
               if m_mbd(Mbd, Bd, Mbd_r, T)
    x_to_y(dt(All), dt(Mbd), mbdinall(All, Mbd))
               if mbdinall(All, Mbd)
```

If we let *coerce* be constantly *false*, we have now defined the type consistency rules which are part of the constraints associated with our target machine signature. From the code generator's point of view, what is left to specify are the particular coercion laws for TM by supplying another *coerce*.

Of the interesting cases, we show the situation where a byte is about to be placed into a word-sized cell, which we allow by "inserting" a *sext*-instruction:

```
    coerce(word, word, R).
    coerce(word, byte, ioc(Am_r, alt_r(X))).

    ioc(Am_r, alt_r(coe(X)))
    and sext(alt_r(coe(X)), all(coe(X))
    and alloc(all(coe(X)))
    and altinreg(reg_r(coe(X), alt_r(X))
                        if coerce(word, byte, ioc(Am_r, alt_r(X)))
...
```

Herein, *ioc* and *Am_r* stand for a finite choice of result operand class definers, and their corresponding inverse address mode. *coe* provides another abstract view of *X*.

3.3 Operand Binding

The treatment of operand binding was sketched in section 1.2. Here is the abstract module describing operand bindings.

Absract Binding Rules *(Signature* aBIND)

```
sort O,M
op                      -- syntactic predicates
    b_root:O            --> Bool
    b_mode:O,O,O,M      --> Bool
    b_id:O,O            --> Bool
```

```
    b_addr:O,O,O      --> Bool
    b_firstOfTwo:O,O,O  --> Bool
    b_open: O,O       --> Bool
    b_end: O          --> Bool
                      -- semantic predicates
    wellBound: O      --> Bool
    bind: O,M         --> Bool
vars  O,O1,O2:O
      M,M1:M
axioms
    wellBound(O)   if b_root(O) and bind(O,M)
    bind(O,M)      if b_mode(O,O1,O2,M)
                   and bind(O1,M1)
                   and bind(O2,M)
    bind(O,M)      if b_id(O,O1) and bind(O1,M)
    bind(O,M)      if b_open(O,O1) and bind(O1,M1)
    bind(O,M)      if b_addr(O,O1,O2)
                   and bind(O1,M1)
                   and bind(O2,M2)
    bind(O,M)      if b_firstOfTwo(O,O1,O2)
                   and bind(O1,M1)
                   and (bind(O2,M2)
                   and if same(M, M1)  then true
                                       else setup(O,M,M1)
    bind(O,M)      if b_end(O)
```

(This time, the abstraction functions were chosen going from abstract into concrete sorts. As far as the logic specification is concerned, this appears to be a matter of convenience, but it does have an impact on the implementation.)
Here, parameters are sort *M*, for representing operands, *same*, which compares them, and *setup*, which will hold when a transformation has been specified which achieves well-binding.

```
Operand Binding Abstraction
sort  O, M,Regno,Const
      ...                              -- plus sorts of TM
op    b_mbd: Regno,Const --> M         -- address mode re-
      b_reg: Regno  --> M              -- presentation
      b_imm:        --> M
      reg:O         --> Reg            -- abstraction functions
      ...
vars          ...
axioms
      b_mode(O,O1,O2, b_reg(regno(O1)))
              if     m_reg(reg(O),regno(O1),reg_r(O2), T)
      b_open(O,O1)                     -- no bindings here
```

```
        if   mov(alt_r(O),all(O_1))
          or mea(alt_r(O), ea(O_1))
          or sext(alt_r(O),all(O_1))
b_firstOfTwo(O,O_1,O_2)              -- 2-address add
        if   add(alt_r(O),all(O_1),all(O_2))
...
```

The *setup(O,M,M₁)* - predicate is lengthy and not shown here. It provides alternative ways to establish *wellBound(O,M)*, depending on the address modes represented by *M* and M_1 and possibly also depending on the instruction predicate holding for *alt_r(O)*. In any case, a register will be allocated, either for the target, or for the bound source operand.

3.4 Register Allocation and Evaluation Ordering

The abstract view we employ for register allocation and evaluation ordering sees all TM-constructs as users of registers, for which there is to be determined the number of registers required for their evaluation, the number of registers occupied by the evaluated construct, and the evaluation order which miminizes register requirements. A predicate *available* is imported to ensure that the determined number of required registers does not exceed a certain limit, about which this module does not know.

The syntactic predicates in the abstract view are closely related to the categories of the machine model, except that temporary and dedicated registers are distinguished. The module specifies a generalization of the well-known Sethi-Ullman numbering technique [SeU70].

```
Abstract Sethi-Ullman Rules
sort Ureg, Direction, Requmts                 -- user of regs and
                                                 its requirements
op                                       -- syntactic predicates
       root: Ureg                        --> Bool
     empty: Ureg                         --> Bool
    c_mode: Ureg                         --> Bool      -- constants
   m_mode: Ureg, Ureg, Ureg              --> Bool      -- memory operands
      t_reg: Ureg, Ureg                  --> Bool      -- temporary regs
     d_reg: Ureg, Ureg                   --> Bool      -- dedicated regs
    id_req: Ureg, Ureg                   --> Bool      -- same requirements
  adr_tmp: Ureg, Ureg                    --> Bool      -- address template
      instr: Ureg, Ureg                  --> Bool      -- instructions
      instr: Ureg, Ureg, Ureg            --> Bool
                                         -- constructors for ordering info
   left_to_right: --> Direction
   right_to_left: --> Direction
   (_,_,_): Nat,Nat,Direction            --> Requmts
                                         -- semantic functions and predicates
   requ: Ureg --> Requmts
   available: Nat --> Bool               -- test for excessive requirements
vars
   Mode, Address, Value, Reg, Reg_r: Ureg
   Q, P, AQ, AP, VQ, VP, LR, RL, QR, PR: Nat
   D, DR: Direction
```

```
axioms
   wellOrd(Mode) if root(Mode) and requ(Mode) = (Q,P,D)
                                and available(Q)
   requ(Mode) = (Q,P,D)         -- (required regs, occupied regs,
                                -- evaluation direction)
       if m_mode(Mode, Address, Value)
       and requ(Address) = (AQ,P,AD)
       and requ(Value)  = (VQ, VP, VD)
       and LR=AP+VQ and RL=VP+AQ
       and if LR ≤ RL then D=left_to_right
                      else D=right_to_left
       and Q=min(LR,RL)
       and available(Q)

   requ(Mode) = (0,0,D)  if c_mode(Mode)

   requ(Reg) = (Q,1,D) if t_reg(Reg, Reg_r)
               and requ(Reg_r) = (QR,PR,DR)
               and Q=max(1,QR)
```

Only one nontrivial axiom - for memory address modes - is given above.
For the purpose of merely defining wellOrd, actually deriving values for D would be superflous, as long as we show that Q never exceeds the limit. The specification of D is included for implementation reasons.

The abstraction from TM to the register allocation view is specified by augmenting the target machine signature by

```
Register Allocation Abstraction
   all: Ureg --> All            -- abstraction functions
   mbd: Ureg --> Mbd            -- and so on for sorts of TM
vars
   U,U1,U2: Ureg                -- etc.
axioms
   m_mode(U,U1,U2)
      if m_mbd(mbd(U),bd(U1),mbd_r(U2), T)
   id_req(U,U1)
      if imminall(all(U),mbd(U1))
```

Again, with a definition of *available* like
available(Q) if $Q \le k$
the above specification defines all TM programs that do not need more than k temporary registers. As in the case of *coerce*, this *available* can be replaced by a more sophisticated predicate, which derives, in the case of $Q > k$, a TM-program without excessive register requirements. The program representation as a set of facts allows us to achieve this in a local fashion. This is not explicated here any further.

3.5 Cost Driven Code Selection

The code selection specified in section 3.1 defines all (syntactic) encodings of an IL-program as a TM-program. A cost driven code selector using the dynamic programming approach of [AhJ70] finds the cheapest of these encodings, given the elementary costs for addresses, instructions, etc. We view TM-constructs as items with which
(1) a fixed cost is associated, and which
(2) built up cumulated costs from their constituents.
While cost cumulating functions can be conveniently associated with abstract constructs corresponding to the categories of the machine model, a more fine-grained distinction must be retained if constructs within a category (say instructions *mov* and *mea*) differ with respect to their fixed costs.

Abstract Costs Calculation

```
sort C_item
op                                          -- syntactic predicates
   ...
   res_or_opd_class: C_item, C_item Nat --> Bool
   instr: C_item, C_item, Nat --> Bool
   instr: C_item, C_item, C_item, Nat --> Bool
   ...
           -- semantic functions
     cost:C_item --> Nat  -- cost for particular encoding
   mincost:C_item --> Nat  -- minimal cost

vars Item Item1 Item2: C_item
     C C1 FixedCost: Nat
axioms
   cost(Item) =  C+FixedCost
           if res_or_opd_class(Item,Item1,FixedCost)
           and mincost(Item1,C).
   cost(Item) =  C+FixedCost
         if instr(Item, Item1, FixedCost)
           and mincost(Item1,C)
   cost(Item) =  C+C1+FixedCost
         if instr(Item, Item1, Item2, FixedCost)
           and mincost(Item1,C)
           and mincost(Item2,C1)
   ...
```

In the mapping of concrete TM constructs to cost calculation categories, the appropriate fixed costs are specified, too:

Cost Calculation Abstraction

```
   cst: All --> C_item                 -- abstraction functions
   cst: Alt_r --> C_item               -- etc.
vars Res_Mode: Mbd_r
     Res_Class: Alt_r
     Class Class1: All
     Mode: Mbd
     Ea_Class: Ea
```

axioms

res_or_opd_class(cst(Res_Mode),cst(Res_Class),2)
if altinmbd(Res_Mode,Res_Class)
res_or_opd_class(cst(Class),cst(Mode),2)
if mbdinall(Class,Mode)
instr(cst(Res_Class),cst(Class),3)
if mov(Res_Class,Ea_Class)
instr(cst(Res_Class),cst(Class),4)
if mea(Res_Class,Ea_Class)
instr(cst(Res_Class),cst(Class),cst(class1),5)
if add(Res_Class,Class,Class)
...

Note that in general, the fixed cost (of 2) for addressing memory by the base-displacement addressing mode will be added to the cumulative costs twice each time this mode occurs. This is correct, since although represented once, it is used twice - as a target first and then as a source operand.

3.6 Combination of Phases

Our phase specifications allow to compose code generators of different strategies for a given machine from abstract specifications of variuos subtasks. Preliminary code selection may be used to produce a single encoding as well as a set of alternative encodings of the IL-Program. Using (single-alternative) code selection, data type coercion and operand binding yields a Graham-Glanville style code generator [Gra80], working for an infinite register machine model with fixed evaluation order. An added register allocation and evaluation ordering phase can produce substantially better code. Cost minimizing code selection can produce nearly optimal code [AhJ76], but is expensive. One worthwhile heuristic might be to run it prior to register allocation, such that the latter is done only for one of the alternative target programs.
At this point, the code generator designer is left alone. Formal techniques for proving properties of phases and their combinations - such as idempotence, commutativity, mutual insensitivity and eventually convergence must be the subject of future work.

4. Implementation in Prolog

An implementation of the above specifications in Prolog is straightforward. A modified version of the partial evaluator of [Gan86] is used in code selection to record derived TM-facts in the data base. Backtracking is used to find alternative encodings, and will use the facts already recorded. The number of alternatives is in principle infinite, since arbitrarily many (useless) registers can be allocated in the infinite register machine model used during code selection. We prohibit this by enforcing the *loc*-operator to be idempotent. In this way, a linear representation of an exponential number of alternative TM-programs can be derived efficiently, if desired.
Sorts of abstract modules (*E, R, O, Ureg,...*) are implemented by *Nat* abstraction functions as Prolog functors, e.g. *reg(_), all(_)*. Thus, their inverse is available via term decomposition. *cst* and *dt* were rewritten in this form.
The transforming predicates (*coerce, setup,...*) were written such that they retract the faulty TM-fact from the data base, and enter the facts representing the locally transformed program. All transformations are forced to be applicable at a given point only once. Each transformation recalls the phase-predicate that had failed and triggered the transformation for the transformed sub-program. This implementation technique assures dynamically the correctness of each application of a transformation. It cannot be a substitute for the formal techniques requested in

section 3.6, because besides being inefficient, it makes the whole code generator fail in case of an incorrect transformation.
Prolog backtracking is rather useless in cases more sophisticated than the one described above. It would be desirable, for example, where a semantic predicates fails, to call backtracking to derive an alternative preliminary encoding. However, backtracking starts from the last clause that completed the proof constructed up to the given point. From the kind of failure, one often has a good idea of which alternative should be tried - usually a close neighbour (in the proof tree) of the failure point. But there is no way to communicate this information, and innocent sub-sub-sub-programs will be recoded while the faulty clause is the last one to be reinspected.
Ordering of clauses is used in an attempt to generate a rather good solution without backtracking. This works fine with respect to register allocation, for example. The first solution constructed will be one using a minimal number of registers. However, where the cost trade-off is context-dependent, as with the competing *add* and *a_bd*, no good ordering of clauses exists.
Although the code generators obtained by immediately rewriting our logic specifications into prolog are not efficient enough for practical compilers, they appear to be quite suitable to demonstrate the different levels of object code quality that can be achieved by different code generation strategies for a given target machine.

References

[AhJ76] Aho, A.V., Johnson, S.C.: Optimal code generation for expression trees. JACM 23(3), 1976.

[Gan86] Ganzinger, H.: Modular first-order specifications of operational semantics. Lecture Notes, this Volume, 1986.

[Gie84] Giegerich, R.: Code generation phase models based on abstract machine descriptions. Report TUM-I8412, Technical University Munich, 1984.

[Gla77] Glanville, R.S.: A machine independent algorithm for code generation and its use in retargetable compilers. Technical report UCB-CS-78-01, University of California, Berkeley, 1977.

[Gnp80] Ganapathi, M.: Retargetable code generation and optimization using attribute grammars. Technical Report # 406, CS Department, University of Wisconsin - Madison, 1980.

[Gra80] Graham, S.L.: Table driven code generation. IEEE Computer 13(8), 1980.

[Hen84] Henry, R. R.: Graham-Glanville Code Generators. Report UCB/CSD84/184, University of California, Berkeley, 1984.

[SeU70] R. Sethi, Ullman, J.D.: The generation of optimal code for arithmetic expressions. JACM(17),4, 1970.

[Wul75] Wulf, W.A., Johnsson, R.K., Weinstock, C.B., Hobbs,S.O., Geschke, S.M.: The design of an optimizing compiler. American Elsevier, New York 1975.

[WuN82] Wulf, W.A., Nori, K.V.: Delayed binding in PQCC generated compilers. Report CMU-CS-82-138, Carnegie-Mellon University, Pittsburgh 1982.

Strictness Detection in Non-Flat Domains

John Hughes,
Institutionen før Informationsbehandling,
Chalmers Tekniska Høgskola,
41296 Gøteborg,
SWEDEN.

From January 1st 1986:
Department of Computer Science,
University of Glasgow,
University Avenue,
Glasgow,
UNITED KINGDOM.

Introduction

A function f is said to be *strict* if f $\bot=\bot$, that is, if whenever the evaluation of its argument fails to terminate then so does its result. Knowledge about strictness is of great practical importance in the implementation of functional languages, because of the freedom it gives to change the evaluation order. For example, the argument of a strict function can safely be evaluated before the call, avoiding the overhead normally associated with lazy evaluation. This is done in the Ponder compiler, where it appears to improve performance by a factor of between three and five[3]. Alternatively, the arguments of strict functions can be evaluated in parallel with the call, leading to better exploitation of parallel hardware[2].

In order to enjoy these benefits it is necessary to be able to identify strict functions automatically. The classic paper on this subject is Mycroft's[5]. Mycroft gives a method which can identify very many strict functions, but which has serious limitations - it is restricted to first order functions on flat domains. Since list processing and higher order functions are very common in functional languages the benefits of strictness analysis are much reduced. A Ponder implementation of Quicksort, for example, gains only 10% from strictness analysis. Recently Wray[6], Hudak[4] and Burn et al.[1] have extended Mycroft's method to deal with higher-order functions. In this paper we give a method which works for functions on non-flat domains.

The Source Language

The language we analyse is a very simple first order functional language. A program is a set of equations, each defining a function. For example, `append` and `reverse` are defined as follows:

```
append a b = case a:
                 nil → b
                 cons c d → cons c (append d b)

reverse a =  case a:
                 nil → nil
                 cons b c → append (reverse c) (cons b nil)
```

These examples use all the constructs of the language. There are three kinds of expressions: variables, function applications, and **case** expressions. Data structures are built using constructors such as cons and nil, and taken apart by **case** expressions. The patterns in a **case** expression consist of a constructor and variable names which are bound to the components. Since we are only interested in analysing the strictness of functions on data structures we have not included any "built-in" types such as integers or booleans. We call this language *FAD* (Functions and Data-structures).

The domain of *FAD* values, **V**, is the solution of the domain equation

$$\mathbf{V} = \mathbf{CON} \otimes \mathbf{V}*$$

where **CON** is a flat domain of constructors and $\otimes$ is the coalesced product. Every non-$\bot$ value has a non-$\bot$ constructor and a non-$\bot$ sequence of components, although any component may be $\bot$. (We ignore the arity of constructors in this equation). Given this domain, the denotational semantics of *FAD* is obvious and we will say no more about it.

Representing Lazy Closures

In any implementation of a lazy language values may be represented as *closures*. A closure contains all the information necessary to compute the associated value, and this is done when the value is actually required. In the standard semantics the distinction between closures and values is invisible. We introduce a domain **R** of representations, which can distinguish closures from the values they represent. We define **R** by

$$\mathbf{R} = \mathbf{2} \times (\mathbf{CON} \otimes \mathbf{R}^{\circ})$$

where **2** is the two-point domain $\{0 \sqsubseteq 1\}$ and $\mathbf{R}^{\circ}$ is the domain of sequences with non-$\bot$ elements. A closure is represented by a pair whose first component is 1, and a value is represented by a pair whose first component is 0. The function which evaluates a closure is eval, defined by

```
eval: R → R
eval <flag, v> = <0, v>
```

(note that the components of the result may still be closures). The intuition behind the definition of **R** is that a closure may represent $\bot$ while being perfectly well-defined itself. The closure which evaluates to $\bot$ is represented in **R** by $\langle 1, \bot \rangle$, which is indeed not $\bot$. Note that the components of data-structures may themselves be closures, and that any undefined component *must* be represented by a closure, otherwise the data-structure it is part of is also undefined.

V can be embedded in **R** by the function

```
embed: V → R
embed <con, <v_1, .., v_n>> = <1, <con, <embed v_1, .., embed v_n>>>
```

which sets all the "closure flags" to 1. Elements of **V** can be recovered using the function

```
value: R → V
value <flag, <con, <r_1, .., r_n>>> =
                    <con, <value r_1, .., value r_n>>
```

It is easy to show that

```
value ∘ embed = id
```

We can give an alternative denotational semantics for *FAD* using **R** as the semantic domain. We choose a semantics such that the alternative denotation of any expression is the result of applying embed to its standard denotation. (It follows that no expression denotes $\bot$ in **R**). The alternative semantics is straightforward and we do not give it here.

Since the result of embed is never $\bot$, we can replace all function applications in the alternative semantics by strict function applications, which we write using a colon. (f:x) is $\bot$ if x is $\bot$, and (f x) otherwise. This models the implementation closely, reflecting the fact that the closure of an argument is constructed before the function is called.

Now suppose that f is a strict function in *FAD* (i.e. that f $\langle 1, \bot \rangle = \bot$ in **R**). An argument to f can safely be evaluated before the call. We can model this by replacing calls such as f:x by f:(eval x). We can show that, for all closures x,

```
f:x = f:(eval x)
```

if f is strict, and so the transformation is correct.

Eval evaluates the top-level closure only. Depending on the properties of f, it might be possible to evaluate some components of the argument in the same way, to potentially unlimited depth. This more complicated pre-evaluation of arguments can be modelled by introducing a more complicated function than eval. Our approach to strictness analysis is to find functions that can be introduced in this way, without changing the meaning of the program. We call such functions *contexts*.

Contexts

What kind of function can serve as a context? Intuitively, a context should "do some evaluation", that is, it should map some 1s in its argument to 0s. A convenient way to state this is that a context c should be weaker than $\mathtt{id}:\mathbf{R}\rightarrow\mathbf{R}$. Also, if its argument is already sufficiently well evaluated, a context should have no effect. We may state this as

$$c \circ c = c$$

We define a context to be a function $c:\mathbf{R}\rightarrow\mathbf{R}$ with these two properties. Contexts form a domain, which allows us to use approximations and limits of contexts.

Let us introduce some simple contexts. One of the simplest is ABSENT, defined by

$$\mathrm{ABSENT}\ \langle \mathrm{flag},\ v\rangle = \langle \mathrm{flag},\ \bot\rangle$$

ABSENT can be introduced under the condition that for all closures x

$$\begin{aligned} f{:}x &= f{:}(\mathrm{ABSENT}\ x) \\ &= f{:}\langle 1, \bot\rangle \end{aligned}$$

That is, f must be a constant function. In other words, an argument's context is ABSENT if the value of the argument is not used by the function.

The ⊥ of the context domain can be interpreted as the "contradictory context". It can be introduced if

$$\begin{aligned} f{:}x &= f{:}(\bot\ x) \\ &= f{:}\bot \\ &= \bot \end{aligned}$$

that is, if f is never defined. Thus the value of an argument in a context ⊥ is irrelevant: the function applied to it will crash regardless.

Given an n-ary constructor CON and n contexts $c_1, .., c_n$, we can form a context c defined by

$$\begin{aligned} &c\ \langle \mathrm{flag},\ \langle \mathrm{CON}, \langle r_1, .., r_n\rangle\rangle\rangle = \langle 0,\ \langle \mathrm{CON}, \langle c_1\ r_1, .., c_n\ r_n\rangle\rangle\rangle \\ &c\ \langle \mathrm{flag},\ \langle \mathrm{CON'},\ ...\rangle\rangle = \bot \qquad \text{if } \mathrm{CON} \neq \mathrm{CON'} \end{aligned}$$

c evaluates its argument and returns ⊥, unless the argument is constructed by the constructor CON, in which case it evaluates the components with $c_1, .., c_n$. We write c as $(\mathrm{CON}\ c_1..c_n)$. This kind of context can be used when a function requires a particular kind of object as its argument. For example, head requires a cons as its argument, and

$$\mathrm{head}{:}x = \mathrm{head}{:}((\mathrm{cons}\ \mathrm{id}\ \mathrm{ABSENT})\ x)$$

Since contexts form a domain, we can also take the least upper bound of two contexts to get a context. We write the least upper bound operator as ⊔. For example,

```
nil ⊔ cons id id
```

is the context that maps values constructed with `nil` or `cons` to themselves, and all others to ⊥. This context could be used with a function which fails unless its argument is a list. As another example, the context

```
ABSENT ⊔ cons id id
```

returns a closure which evaluates to ⊥ unless its argument is a `cons`. This context could be used with a function which is not known to need its argument, but needs a `cons` if it does.

We will restrict our attention to contexts built from these four primitives: ABSENT, ⊥, constructors, and ⊔. Note that ⊔ distributes over constructors

$$\text{CON } a_1..a_n \sqcup \text{CON } b_1..b_n = \text{CON } (a_1 \sqcup b_1)..(a_n \sqcup b_n)$$

and that ⊥ is a unit for ⊔. We can therefore express every such context as an ⊔ of constructor contexts with distinct constructors, and possibly ABSENT. We say that a context expressed in this way is in *normal form* if all the component contexts are also in normal form. Normal forms (and other context expressions) may well be infinite: we can think of them as infinite trees. We are particularly interested in *finite* normal forms, which can be described by a finite set of equations. Such equations may be thought of as a (potentially cyclic) graph, and can represent rational infinite trees. Such equations are the usual way we describe contexts. Our strictness analyser expresses the contexts it finds as finite normal forms.

As an example of a context in finite normal form, consider `spine` defined by

```
spine = nil ⊔ cons ABSENT spine
```

`Spine` maps everything but finite lists to ⊥ (infinite lists are limits of partial lists, which `spine` maps to ⊥). All the list elements are ignored (mapped to <1, ⊥>) by ABSENT. As an example where `spine` can be used,

```
length:L = length:(spine L)
```

We say that a context is *strict* if it maps <1, ⊥> to <0, ⊥>. ABSENT is not strict; the other primitive contexts are. It follows that a context in normal form is strict unless it includes ABSENT at the top-level.

Normal forms can be used to guide compilation. An argument in a strict context can be evaluated before the call. An argument in a non-strict, non-ABSENT context must be compiled as a closure: it may or may not be evaluated. An argument in the context ABSENT need not be compiled at all! The code can pass a dummy value (<1, ⊥>) instead: it will never be used.

Strictness Functions

The condition for introducing a context that we gave above was that, for all closures x,

$$f:x = f:(c\ x)$$

In fact this is stronger than necessary, because it doesn't take into account the way that f's result is used. Suppose (f:x) is itself an argument of a function g, and suppose the context associated with g is c'. Then we only need to insist that

$$(c' \circ f):x = (c' \circ f):(c\ x)$$

Clearly c depends on c'. We express this dependence by introducing a *strictness function* F such that

$$c = F\ c'$$

satisfies the condition above. By convention we use capitalised versions of function names for the associated strictness functions.

We will show later how a definition of F can be derived from f's own definition, but we can already prove some theorems about strictness functions. For example, we can take F ABSENT = ABSENT for any function f. The condition that F ABSENT must satisfy is

$$(\mathrm{ABSENT} \circ f):x = (\mathrm{ABSENT} \circ f):((F\ \mathrm{ABSENT})\ x)$$

which is true provided ((F ABSENT) x) is never ⊥. The least context with this property is ABSENT.

So far we have discussed functions of one argument. However, *FAD* provides functions of several arguments. If f has n arguments, and a call is in context c', then the condition for using contexts $c_1, .., c_n$ to evaluate the arguments is

$$(c' \circ f):x_1:..:x_n = (c' \circ f):(c1\ x_1):..:(cn\ x_n)$$

(We take the composition of a unary and an n-ary function to be the function that applies the n-ary function to all the n arguments, and applies the unary function to the result). This is equivalent to

$$(c' \circ f):x_1:..:x_n = (c' \circ f):x_1:..:x_{i-1}:(c_i\ x_i):x_{i+1}:..:x_n$$

for each i separately. In this case we associate n different strictness functions with f, called $F_1, .., F_n$, such that

$$c_i = F_i \; c'$$

satisfies the condition above.

Operators on Contexts

We will need two other operators on contexts. The first is ⊓, which is used to express the "net context" of an argument that is used several times in different contexts. For example, suppose

```
f x = g x x
```

and for all closures u and v,

$$g{:}u{:}v = g{:}(c_1 \; u){:}v = g{:}u{:}(c_2 \; v)$$

Then $(c_1 \sqcap c_2)$ is a context c such that

```
g:x:x = g:(c x):(c x)
```

⊓ can be defined by

$$\bot \sqcap b = \bot$$
$$\text{ABSENT} \sqcap b = b$$
$$\text{CON } a_1..a_n \sqcap \text{CON } b_1..b_n = \text{CON } (a_1 \sqcap b_1)..(a_n \sqcap b_n)$$
$$\text{CON } a_1..a_n \sqcap \text{CON' } b_1..b_m = \bot \qquad \text{if CON} \neq \text{CON'}$$
$$(a_1 \sqcup a_2) \sqcap b = (a_1 \sqcap b) \sqcup (a_2 \sqcap b)$$

together with the commutative and associative laws.

Unfortunately this is the simplest way of characterising ⊓ we have found. The definition can be justified by showing that $(c_1 \sqcap c_2)$ satisfies

```
g:x:x= g:(c x):(c x)
```

in each case. It is tempting to believe that ⊓ is the greatest lower bound operator, but this is not the case. The reason is that, in general, ABSENT ⊓ b is not the greatest lower bound of ABSENT and b. In fact ⊓ and ⊔ do not form a Boolean algebra, despite the suggestive names. However, they are each idempotent, commutative and associative, and they satisfy both distributive laws. They fail to satisfy the cancellation laws

$$E \sqcup (E \sqcap F) = E$$
$$E \sqcap (E \sqcup F) = E$$

A counter-example to each of these is E=ABSENT, which satisfies

$$\text{ABSENT} \sqcap \text{F} = \text{F}$$

but

$$\text{ABSENT} \sqcup \text{F} \neq \text{ABSENT}$$

The other operator we will need is arrow →. We will introduce it by considering an example: the strictness function HEAD associated with head. Let c' be (HEAD c). Then c' must satisfy

$$(\text{c} \circ \text{head}):\text{x} = (\text{c} \circ \text{head}):(\text{c}' \text{ x})$$

It is tempting to take c' to be (cons c ABSENT), requiring x to be a cons, applying c to its head and throwing away its tail. However, this is wrong because (cons c ABSENT) is a strict context, and although head is a strict function, (c ∘ head) may not be. For example, if c is ABSENT then c' should also be ABSENT. We need to make the strictness of c' depend on the strictness of c, and this is what arrow does. We define

$$\text{HEAD c} = \text{c} \rightarrow \text{cons c ABSENT}$$

where

$$\text{ABSENT} \rightarrow \text{b} = \text{ABSENT}$$
$$\text{strict context} \rightarrow \text{b} = \text{b}$$
$$(a_1 \sqcup a_2) \rightarrow \text{b} = (a_1 \rightarrow \text{b}) \sqcup (a_2 \rightarrow \text{b})$$

and for completeness

$$\bot \rightarrow \text{b} = \bot$$

Deriving Definitions of Strictness Functions

Given a function definition

$$\text{f } a_1 \text{ .. } a_n = \text{E}$$

we want to derive definitions of the associated strictness functions $F_1,..,F_n$. With this aim we introduce a function D such that $D_x[\![\text{E}]\!]\text{c}$ is a context c' satisfying

$$(\text{c} \circ \lambda \text{x.E}):\text{u} = (\text{c} \circ \lambda \text{x.E}):(\text{c}' \text{ u})$$

for all closures u, and for all values of the free variables of E. Intuitively, c' is the net context applied to x when c is applied to E. The strictness functions can then be defined by

$$F_i \text{ c} = D_{a_i}[\![\text{E}]\!]\text{c}$$

D is defined by cases. Clearly, if x does not occur free in E then

$$D_x[\![E]\!]c = \text{ABSENT}$$

If E is the identifier x, then

$$D_x[\![x]\!]c = c$$

If E is a function application, then referring to the definition of ⊓ we deduce that

$$D_x[\![f\ E_1\ ..\ E_n]\!]c = D_x[\![E_1]\!](F_1\ c) \sqcap .. \sqcap D_x[\![E_n]\!](F_n\ c)$$

The hardest case is if E is a **case** expression:

case E_0:

$CON_1\ a_{11}\ a_{12}..\ \rightarrow E_1$
$CON_2\ a_{21}..\ \rightarrow E_2$
...
$CON_n\ a_{n1}..\ \rightarrow E_n$

where the CON_i are constructors. First suppose that x does not occur in E_0. Then the selection of one of the E_i is essentially arbitrary (depends on the values of the free variables), and the resulting context c' must be generous enough that whichever E_i is chosen,

$$(c \circ \lambda x.E_i):x = (c \circ \lambda x.E_i):(c'\ x)$$

We can ensure this by taking c' to be the upper bound of the contexts $D_x[\![E_i]\!]c$.

On the other hand, suppose x occurs only in E_0. We can assume that E_0 is precisely x (if not, we introduce $y{=}E_0$, find $c'{=}D_y[\![E]\!]c$, and then return $D_x[\![E_0]\!]c'$). Now let α_{ij} be $D_{a_{ij}}[\![E_i]\!]c$. Then the context

$$(CON_i\ \alpha_{i1}\ \alpha_{i2}\ \ldots)$$

evaluates x appropriately if E_i is the case selected. Since we don't know in advance which case will be selected, we take the upper bound of all these contexts. This upper bound is always a strict context, so we make its strictness depend on c using the arrow operator. The result in this case is

$$c \rightarrow (CON_1\ \alpha_{11}\ \alpha_{12}\ ..\ \sqcup\ CON_2\ \alpha_{21}\ ..\ \sqcup\ ..\ \sqcup\ CON_n\ \alpha_{n1}\ ..)$$

In the general case, where x may appear in E_0 and in the E_i we can treat the two kinds of occurrence independently, and then ⊓ the resulting contexts together. The final definition, then, is

D_x[**case** E_0:
    CON_1 a_{11} a_{12}.. → E_1
    CON_2 a_{21}.. → E_2
    ...
    CON_n a_{n1}.. → E_n] c =

(D_x[E_1]c ⊔ ... ⊔ D_x[E_n]c) ⊓
D_x[E_0]
    (c→CON_1 D_{a11}[E_1]c.. ⊔ ... ⊔ CON_n D_{an1}[E_n]c..)

As an example, when we apply these rules to the definitions of head and append, we get the following strictness functions (after a little simplification):

```
HEAD c = c → cons c ABSENT
APPEND1 c = c → nil ⊔ cons (CONS1 c) (APPEND1 (CONS2 c))
APPEND2 c = c ⊔ APPEND2 (CONS2 c)
```

Selectors

The method in the preceding section derives definitions of strictness functions from the definitions in the program. It cannot be used to derive definitions of strictness functions associated with predefined functions. In *FAD* the only predefined functions are constructors, and in this section we define the strictness functions associated with them. All such functions have the same form, which we will illustrate by considering $CONS_1$.

We define the strictness functions associated with constructors by showing how they act on contexts of various forms. The most interesting case is when the argument context is a matching constructor context, as in the example $CONS_1$ (cons a b). When the context (cons a b) is applied to the *FAD* expression (cons u v), then the function applied to u is, of course, a. Therefore we can take

$CONS_1$ (cons a b) = a

In the world of contexts, $CONS_1$ plays an analogous role to head. Similarly $CONS_2$ plays an analogous role to tail. Because of this analogy we call the strictness functions associated with constructors *selectors.*

The other cases of the definition are straightforward:

```
CONS1 ⊥ = ⊥
CONS1 ABSENT = ABSENT
CONS1 (CON a1 .. an) = ⊥                    if CON≠cons
CONS1 (a ⊔ b) = CONS1 a ⊔ CONS1 b
```

Selectors also satisfy

$$\text{CONS}_1\ (a \sqcap b) = \text{CONS}_1\ a \sqcap \text{CONS}_1\ b$$
$$\text{CONS}_1\ (a \rightarrow b) = a \rightarrow \text{CONS}_1\ b$$

Analysing Strictness

Now we know how to derive strictness functions, and how to simplify context expressions. We can use this to calculate the extent to which eager evaluation can be used. For example, consider the expression

```
head (append x y)
```

which is itself evaluated by a strict context c. To discover how eagerly x can be evaluated, we compute

$$
\begin{aligned}
D_x[\![\text{head(append x y)}]\!]c &= \text{APPEND}_1\ (\text{HEAD c}) \\
&= \text{APPEND}_1\ (\text{c} \rightarrow \text{cons c ABSENT}) \\
&= \text{APPEND}_1\ (\text{cons c ABSENT}) \qquad \text{because c is strict} \\
&= \text{cons c ABSENT} \rightarrow \text{nil} \sqcup \\
&\qquad \text{cons } (\text{CONS}_1\ (\text{cons c ABSENT})) \\
&\qquad\qquad (\text{APPEND}_1\ (\text{CONS}_2\ (\text{cons c ABSENT}))) \\
&= \text{nil} \sqcup \text{cons c } (\text{APPEND}_1\ \text{ABSENT}) \\
&\qquad \text{because (cons c ABSENT) is strict,} \\
&\qquad \text{CONS}_1\ (\text{cons c ABSENT}) = \text{c,} \\
&\qquad \text{and CONS}_2\ (\text{cons c ABSENT}) = \text{ABSENT} \\
&= \text{nil} \sqcup \text{cons c ABSENT} \\
&\qquad \text{because F ABSENT = ABSENT for all} \\
&\qquad \text{strictness functions F}
\end{aligned}
$$

which tells us that x can be computed eagerly, that it must yield a nil or a cons, and that if it yields a cons then the tail can be thrown away and the head evaluated by c. In the remainder of the paper we show how these calculations can be done automatically.

It is worth remarking that our approach is inherently less powerful than Mycroft's in the case of a flat domain. This is because we express the strictness of a function of several arguments as a combination of the strictness in each argument independently. Mycroft expresses the strictness of the function as a whole. To see the effect of this, consider the function if, defined by

```
if a b c = case a: true → b, false → c
```

Mycroft's method expresses the fact that (if a b c) evaluates a and b or c, whereas ours only expresses the fact that a is evaluated, and b or c might be. Mycroft's algorithm can therefore conclude that (if a x x) is certain to evaluate x, and ours cannot. Thanks to this

Mycroft can treat conditional as just another function, while a special treatment of the **case** construct is vital to our approach. The advantage of treating arguments independently is that it is simpler, and it is this simplification that has allowed us to extend the method to deal with data structures. In practice one can get the best of both worlds by running both strictness detection algorithms, one after another. It would be best to run Mycroft's algorithm second, as it can take advantage of information already found by our algorithm.

Calculating Contexts

We must now show how to calculate context expressions automatically. We start from a set of equations defining names for the context expressions to be evaluated. We aim to finish with finite normal forms for these variables - that is, another set of equations in a simpler form. We solve the equations in stages, eliminating one kind of operator at each stage, until a finite normal form remains. Note that "weaker" contexts provide more specific information, so it is the *least* solution of the equations that we want to find. However, often this least solution has no finite normal form, and so we look for an *upper bound* on the least solution instead. An upper bound can safely be used by the compiler instead of the least solution - it just carries less information. For example, if the compiler uses an upper bound (ABSENT OR c) instead of a strict context c, the only consequence is that a parameter will be passed as a closure that could have been passed in its evaluated form.

A trick we will use more than once is the *merging* of distinct variables or expressions. Suppose we have the equations

$$a = E_1$$
$$b = E_2$$
$$c = E_3$$
$$\ldots$$

where a, b, c.. are free in $E_1 .. E_n$. We merge a and b by changing the equations to

$$a = b = E_1 \sqcup E_2$$
$$c = E_3$$
$$\ldots$$

The reason for doing this is that the latter equations may be soluble, even if the former ones are not. For example, if we have an equation of the form

$$a = F\ (G\ a)$$

which we cannot solve, but we know how to solve

$$b = F\ b \sqcup G\ b$$

then we merge a and (G a) to transform the former into the latter.

Of course, this merging changes the solution of the equations in general. Before we use it we must prove that the least solution of the transformed equations is an upper bound for the least solution of the original ones. To see this, let us define G and H by

$$G(\langle a, b, c..\rangle) = \langle E_1, E_2, E_3, ..\rangle$$
$$H(\langle a, b, c..\rangle) = \langle E_1 \sqcup E_2,\ E_1 \sqcup E_2,\ E_3,\ E_4,\ ..\rangle$$

(where a, b, c.. are formal parameters and E_1, E_2,.. are the expressions involving a,b,c.. in the equations above. < and > are tuple brackets). The least solution of the original set of equations is **fix** G, and of the transformed equations is **fix** H. But for all x, G x ⊑ H x, and so G ⊑ H, from which it follows that **fix** G ⊑ **fix** H (here we use ⊑ to denote the domain approximation relation). Therefore the transformation is correct.

Eliminating Strictness Functions

The best way to eliminate calls of strictness functions other then selectors is to replace them with the function bodies, which are exactly equivalent. This is always possible with non-recursive functions, and sometimes possible even with recursive ones. A call of a recursive strictness function can be expanded in this way if there are only finitely many different arguments to all the recursive calls. For example, suppose F is defined by

```
F x = G (F (H x))
```

and H a = b, H b = a. Then c = F a can be expanded as follows:

```
c = F a
  = G (F (H a))
  = G (F b)
  = G (G (F (H b)))
  = G (G (F a))
  = G (G c))
```

Not all recursive functions can be expanded in this way, and in order to avoid trial and error we would like a sufficient condition for the expansion to be possible. Such a condition is that the argument be reduced to finite normal form before the call is expanded, and that the arguments of recursive calls be derived from the top-level argument by applying zero or more selectors. To see this, consider applying a selector to a finite normal form such as

```
spine = nil ⊔ cons ABSENT spine
```

For example, $CONS_2$ spine is

$$\begin{aligned} CONS_2\ spine &= CONS_2\ (nil \sqcup cons\ ABSENT\ spine) \\ &= CONS_2\ nil \sqcup CONS_2\ (cons\ ABSENT\ spine) \\ &\qquad \text{selectors distribute over } \sqcup \\ &= \bot \sqcup spine \\ &= spine \end{aligned}$$

After distributing the selector over ⊔, all but one of the resulting expressions must simplify to ⊥, since all the constructors ⊔ed together in a finite normal form are different. Since ⊥ is an identity for ⊔, all these expressions "drop out", leaving another part of the finite normal form as the result. Since a finite normal form only has a finite number of parts altogether, applying any number of selectors to a finite normal form can give only finitely many different results. If all the arguments to recursive calls of a strictness function are applications of selectors to a finite normal form, then we are certain to be able to perform a finite expansion. (This is a slight oversimplification. Expressions such as ABSENT ⊔ ... in the finite normal form may lead to selectors returning ABSENT ⊔ (an existing expression), but the argument still applies).

As an example, consider

$$\begin{aligned} &APPEND_1\ c = c \rightarrow nil \sqcup cons\ (CONS_1\ c)\ (APPEND_1\ (CONS_2\ c)) \\ &spine = nil \sqcup cons\ ABSENT\ spine \\ &ans = APPEND_1\ spine \end{aligned}$$

The sufficient condition is satisfied: spine is in finite normal form and the argument of the recursive call of $APPEND_1$ is $(CONS_2\ c)$ - an application of a selector to the top-level argument. In fact $CONS_2\ spine = spine$, and so the expansion gives

$$\begin{aligned} ans &= spine \rightarrow nil \sqcup cons\ (CONS_1\ spine)\ (APPEND_1\ spine) \\ &= spine \rightarrow nil \sqcup cons\ (CONS_1\ spine)\ ans \end{aligned}$$

This expansion is exactly equivalent to the original call. When such an expansion cannot be applied we approximate instead, by merging the top-level argument and the arguments of all recursive calls, allowing the results of all calls to be replaced by a single variable. In the case of $APPEND_1$, we start from

$$APPEND_1\ c = c \rightarrow nil \sqcup cons\ (CONS_1\ c)\ (APPEND_1\ (CONS_2\ c))$$

Let a be the argument of the top-level call, and b the argument of the recursive one. Then

$$\begin{aligned} &a = c \\ &b = CONS_2\ a \\ &APPEND_1\ a = a \rightarrow nil \sqcup cons\ (CONS_1\ a)\ (APPEND_1\ b) \end{aligned}$$

Merging a and b gives

$$a = b = c \sqcup CONS_2\ a$$

and now we can replace both calls of $APPEND_1$ by the same variable, g say, giving

$$a = b = c \sqcup CONS_2\ a$$
$$g = a \rightarrow nil \sqcup cons\ (CONS_1\ a)\ g$$

A similar transformation can be applied to mutually recursive functions.

Eliminating Selectors

The next stage is to eliminate selectors (such as $CONS_1$ and $CONS_2$) from the equations. This is by far the hardest part of the solution. Recursive equations such as

$$a = F\ (CONS_2\ a)$$

are often impossible to solve exactly (at least by our methods). In order to avoid too much approximation, and speed up the solution, we begin by splitting the equations into the smallest possible groups with no inter-group recursion (the strongly connected components of the variable dependency graph). We solve the groups one by one in a bottom up order (i.e. we don't solve a group until all groups it depends on have been solved). This guarantees that all the free variables of a group of equations are in finite normal form by the time the group is solved, which allows us to apply selectors to free variables with no difficulties.

We begin our explanation of selector elimination by noting that all selectors satisfy

$$S\ \bot = \bot$$
$$S\ ABSENT = ABSENT$$
$$S\ (a \sqcup b) = S\ a \sqcup S\ b$$
$$S\ (a \sqcap b) = S\ a \sqcap S\ b$$
$$S\ (a \rightarrow b) = a \rightarrow S\ b$$

Moreover, these laws are also satisfied by arbitrary compositions of selectors (including the identity function). We will refer to such compositions as *compound selectors*. The laws can be used to push selectors down through expressions towards the leaves, so that they are only applied to variables and constructions. Furthermore, applications of selectors to constructions can be simplified, giving one of the components of the construction if the selector and constructor match, and $\bot$ if they don't. Applications of selectors to free variables of the whole equation group can be simplified because the free variables are in finite normal form.

Now we take each equation in the group being solved and push the selectors down to the leaves. We introduce a new function F by abstracting out variables in the set being solved, together with any selectors applied to them. We can then express the equation as

$$a = F\ (S_1\ b_1)\ (S_2\ b_2)\ \ldots\ (S_n\ b_n)$$

where the b_i are variables and each S_i is a possibly compound selector (which could therefore be the identity function). F does not involve any selectors, and we can arrange that its parameters are used only once in its body (if a parameter were used twice we could just replace it by two parameters).

Now consider S(F x y z...) where S is a selector and the x, y.. are any expressions. S can be pushed through the body of F, giving

S (F x y z...) = F' x' y' z'...

where F' is another function not involving selectors and where x' is either x or a selector applied to x, y' is either y or a selector applied to y, and so on. (This selector is always S if S is a simple selector, but may be a "prefix" of S if S is compound). For example, if

F x y = x ⊔ y

then

S (F x y) = S (x ⊔ y) = S x ⊔ S y = F' (S x) (S y)

with F' actually equal to F. On the other hand, if

F x y = (cons ABSENT x) ⊔ y

then

$$
\begin{aligned}
\mathrm{CONS}_2\ (F\ x\ y) &= \mathrm{CONS}_2\ (\mathrm{cons\ ABSENT}\ x \sqcup y) \\
&= \mathrm{CONS}_2\ (\mathrm{cons\ ABSENT}\ x) \sqcup \mathrm{CONS}_2\ y \\
&= x \sqcup \mathrm{CONS}_2\ y \\
&= F'\ x\ (\mathrm{CONS}_2\ y)
\end{aligned}
$$

It is also possible that one of the parameters disappears completely, as in

$$
\begin{aligned}
\mathrm{CONS}_1\ (F\ x\ y) &= \mathrm{CONS}_1\ (\mathrm{cons\ ABSENT}\ x \sqcup y) \\
&= \mathrm{ABSENT} \sqcup \mathrm{CONS}_1\ y \\
&= F'\ (\mathrm{CONS}_1\ y)
\end{aligned}
$$

but this causes no complications so we ignore it.

We denote the new function F' by S^F. We can show that, for any function F, there are only finitely many different functions S^F, even when S may be any compound selector. The proof is by structural induction on the body of F. We will only sketch the proof here, as it is very easy. The only hard cases are variables. A free variable refers to a context in finite normal form, and we have shown above that applying arbitrary compound selectors to a finite normal form gives only finitely many different results. An application of a selector to a parameter, on the other hand, cannot be simplified, and so results in an expression (S x), which is then abstracted out when S^F is defined. Alpha conversions apart, the particular selector S makes no difference to the result.

Now let us express the equations to be solved as

$$a_1 = F_1\ (S_{11}\ b_{11})\ (S_{12}\ b_{12})\ldots$$
$$a_2 = F_2\ (S_{21}\ b_{21})\ \ldots$$
$$\ldots$$
$$a_n = F_n\ (S_{n1}\ b_{n1})\ \ldots$$

We have just shown that the set

$$\mathbf{F}^* = \{S\hat{}F \mid F \text{ is one of the } F_i,\ S \text{ is a compound selector}\}$$

is finite. We can therefore calculate it by forming the closure of $\{F_1, .., F_n\}$ under the simple selectors occuring in the equations being solved. Every selector S used in the equations induces a function from **F*** to **F***, which we call S^. S^ is a finite function, and we can calculate it for each selector.

Each variable a_i can be expressed as an infinite expression involving only the $F_1..F_n$ and selectors, just by expanding out the equations we gave above. But now the selectors can be propagated downwards through the tree, using the property

$$S\ (F\ x\ y\ z\ldots) = (S\hat{}F)\ x'\ y'\ z'\ldots$$

After propagating the selectors "infinitely far", we are left with an infinite expression which may involve any functions from **F***, but no others. Our task is to find a finite set of equations with the same solution. We begin by considering the special case in which all functions G in **F*** are *linear*, that is that for any selector S

$$S\ (G\ x\ y\ z\ldots) = (S\hat{}G)\ (S\ x)\ (S\ y)\ (S\ z)\ldots$$

This is not too unreasonable: we can easily show that if G is linear, so are all the S^G. It follows that all functions in **F*** are linear if and only if the original functions $F_1..F_n$ are.

The effect of a selector S on an expression involving only linear functions is particularly simple: every function G is replaced by S^G. That is, the effect of S on such an expression is completely determined by S^. But we showed above that there are only finitely many different S^. Since the a_i can be expressed as such an expression it follows that there are only finitely many different $(S\ a_i)$. Also, if S^ = T^ then we know that $(S\ a_i) = (T\ a_i)$. We can therefore introduce a new variable for each of the $(S\ a_i)$ we need, and express the solution in terms of these variables. We can derive an equation defining $(S\ a_i)$ by pushing S through the definition of a_i. For example, suppose we are solving a single equation

$$a = G\ (CONS_1\ a)$$

and we discover that $\mathbf{F}^* = \{G,\ H\}$ with $CONS_1\hat{} = \{G \mapsto H,\ H \mapsto H\}$. We see that

$$\mathtt{CONS_1\hat{}} \circ \mathtt{CONS_1\hat{}} = \mathtt{CONS_1\hat{}}$$

and so it follows that $(\mathtt{CONS_1}\ (\mathtt{CONS_1}\ a)) = (\mathtt{CONS_1}\ a)$. We introduce one new variable $b = \mathtt{CONS_1}\ a$, so $\mathtt{CONS_1}\ b = b$, and derive a definition for b:

$$\begin{aligned} b &= \mathtt{CONS_1}\ a = \mathtt{CONS_1}\ (G\ b) = H\ (\mathtt{CONS_1}\ b) \\ &= H\ b \end{aligned}$$

The results of selector elimination read

$$\begin{aligned} a &= G\ b \\ b &= H\ b \end{aligned}$$

In the case where all the F_i are linear, then, we can find an exact solution.

In the non-linear case we cannot find an exact solution, but we can use a similar method to help find an approximate solution that does not overestimate too grossly. We do this by introducing new variables to represent the different $(S\ a_i)$ exactly as in the linear case, but *merging* $S\ a$ and $T\ (S\ a)$ when $T\hat{} \circ S\hat{} = S\hat{}$. This leads to a finite set of selector-free equations as before. Thus we use knowledge about $S\hat{}$ to suggest terms that are "nearly equal", and can probably be merged without losing too much information. In practice most functions in $\mathbf{F}^*$ seem to be linear in most of their parameters, and this approximation seems to give fairly good results.

Eliminating Arrows

Once selectors are eliminated the lion's share of the work is done. The next step is to eliminate arrows, which we do via an abstract interpretation of contexts as subsets of $\{\mathtt{ABSENT}\} \cup \mathtt{constructors}$. The idea is that the abstract interpretation tells us whether each context is $(\mathtt{ABSENT} \sqcup \mathtt{something})$ or not, and its top-level constructors. The abstract interpretation (#) is defined by

$$\begin{aligned} \bot\# &= \{\} \\ \mathtt{ABSENT}\# &= \{\mathtt{ABSENT}\} \\ (\mathtt{CON}\ c_1..c_n)\# &= \{\mathtt{CON}\} \\ (a \sqcup b)\# &= a\# \cup b\# \end{aligned}$$

In order to compute the abstract values of all expressions we need abstract versions of $\sqcap$ and $\rightarrow$, which we can define by

$(a \sqcap b)\#$	$= a\# \cap b\#$	if neither $a\#$ nor $b\#$ contains ABSENT
	$= b\#$	if only $a\#$ contains ABSENT
	$= a\#$	if only $b\#$ contains ABSENT
	$= a\# \cup b\#$	if both contain ABSENT

$$
\begin{array}{llll}
(a \rightarrow b)\# & = \{\} & \text{if } a\# = \{\} \\
& = \{\text{ABSENT}\} & \text{if } a\# = \{\text{ABSENT}\} \\
& = b & \text{if } a\# \text{ contains a constructor,} \\
& & \text{but not ABSENT} \\
& = \{\text{ABSENT}\} \cup b & \text{if } a\# \text{ contains a constructor and ABSENT}
\end{array}
$$

The abstract values of each variable can now be calculated by an iteration, starting with all variables set to {}, and repeatedly calculating new abstract values for each variable until there is no change. These values can then be used to remove arrows, using the rules:

$$
\begin{array}{lll}
a \rightarrow b & = \bot & \text{if } a\# = \{\} \\
& = \text{ABSENT} & \text{if } a\# = \{\text{ABSENT}\} \\
& = b & \text{if } a\# \text{ contains only constructors} \\
& = \text{ABSENT} \sqcup b & \text{if } a\# \text{ contains constructors and ABSENT}
\end{array}
$$

Eliminating ⊓ and ⊔

Before eliminating ⊓s and as many ⊔s as possible it is convenient to introduce new variables for the components of all constructions. This results in equations whose right hand sides are built using ⊓ and ⊔ from variables, ABSENT, and constructions whose components are variables.

Now, as a first stage, we eliminate all top-level variables, so that each right-hand side is formed using ⊓ and ⊔ from ABSENT and constructions only. This is done by choosing any equation and expressing it in the form

$$a = E \sqcup (F \sqcap a)$$

where E and F do not contain a. We can find the least solution of this equation (regardless of the values of the other variables) by iteration. The first approximation is of course $\bot$, and the second is E since $\bot$ is a zero for ⊓ and an identity for ⊔. The third approximation is

$$E \sqcup (F \sqcap E)$$

and we can show that this is always the limit, because the fourth approximation is

$$
\begin{array}{ll}
E \sqcup (F \sqcap (E \sqcup (F \sqcap E))) & \\
\quad = E \sqcup (F \sqcap E) \sqcup (F \sqcap F \sqcap E) & \\
& (\sqcap \text{ distributes over } \sqcup) \\
\quad = E \sqcup (F \sqcap E) \sqcup (F \sqcap E) & \\
& (\sqcap \text{ is idempotent}) \\
\quad = E \sqcup (F \sqcap E) & \\
& (\sqcup \text{ is idempotent})
\end{array}
$$

We can use this solution to eliminate top level occurrences of a from the other equations.

Repeating the process for each equation, we can eliminate all top-level variables.

As a second stage, we take each equation in turn and push the $\sqcap$ and $\sqcup$ operations inside the constructors using the laws:

$$\mathrm{CON}\ a_1..a_n \sqcap \mathrm{CON}\ b_1..b_n = \mathrm{CON}\ (a_1 \sqcap b_1)..(a_n \sqcap b_n)$$
$$\mathrm{CON}\ a_1..a_n \sqcap \mathrm{CON'}\ b_1..b_m = \bot \qquad \text{if } \mathrm{CON} \neq \mathrm{CON'}$$
$$\mathrm{CON}\ a_1..a_n \sqcup \mathrm{CON}\ b_1..b_n = \mathrm{CON}\ (a_1 \sqcup b_1)..(a_n \sqcup b_n)$$

This results in a right hand side which is an $\sqcup$ of ABSENT and constructions with distinct constructors. The components of these constructions are "Boolean combinations" of variables. We replace each component by a new "derived" variable, which converts this equation into its final form. We must also add an equation defining each derived variable to the equations waiting to be processed. Each derived variable is defined to be equal to the expression it replaced, with the variables replaced by their values so that the new equation is in the same form as the other unprocessed ones (that is, built from ABSENT and constructors with variables as their components). Since each derived variable is a Boolean combination of older variables, each can also be expressed as a Boolean combination of *underived* variables. There are only finitely many different Boolean combinations of a finite set of variables, and so only finitely many derived variables need be introduced, and the process terminates if we include a check that prevents us introducing two derived variables to represent the same Boolean combination.

Practical Results

A slightly earlier version of the algorithm described here has been implemented in FranzLisp and used to analyse the strictness of simple list processing functions. It is perhaps surprising that, despite the approximations inherent in the method, quite useful results were obtained. Among the contexts calculated by the strictness analyser were

APPEND_1 spine = spine
APPEND_2 spine = spine
APPEND_1 (cons c ABSENT) = nil $\sqcup$ cons c ABSENT
APPEND_2 (cons c ABSENT) = ABSENT $\sqcup$ cons c ABSENT
LAST c = cons (ABSENT $\sqcup$ c) g
where g = nil $\sqcup$ cons (ABSENT $\sqcup$ c) g
REVERSE spine = spine

Each is the best possible result. These were its successes. It is instructive to consider one of its failures also. We attempted to calculate REVERSE (cons c ABSENT), expecting the result

g **where** g = nil $\sqcup$ cons (ABSENT $\sqcup$ c) g

Instead the strictness analyser found

$$\begin{aligned} &\mathrm{g}\ \textbf{where}\ \mathrm{g} = \mathrm{ABSENT} \sqcup \mathrm{nil} \sqcup \mathrm{cons\ h\ g} \\ &\qquad\qquad \mathrm{h} = \mathrm{c} \sqcup \mathrm{ABSENT} \sqcup \mathrm{nil} \sqcup \mathrm{cons\ h\ g} \end{aligned}$$

which is correct, of course, in that it is an overestimate of the best answer, but is a very gross overestimate indeed. There are two surprising things about this result. First, the strictness analyser appears to believe that the argument of reverse might be a list of lists (or even more deeply nested structure), because the context in which the elements of the argument appear (h) allows for nils and conses. Second, since g is not a strict context, it has failed to discover that reverse is strict in its argument, even though the very first thing reverse does is to evaluate that argument in a **case** expression! This example shows both the approximations in our algorithm at their worst.

The first problem is due to the approximation in selector elimination. Strangely, in this case ($\mathrm{CONS}_2 \circ \mathrm{CONS}_2$) and ($\mathrm{CONS}_1 \circ \mathrm{CONS}_2 \circ \mathrm{CONS}_2$) induce the same functions on $\mathbf{F}^*$, and so their results are merged, even though they have different types. It is this which led to a list context and element context being $\sqcup$ed together in the definition of h. The strictness analyser could avoid the problem by using information provided by the type-checker. Selector elimination would not merge terms of different types. Since there are only a finite number of types in any particular program this would not lead to non-termination.

The second problem is due to the approximation of recursive strictness functions by non-recursive ones. It is a little harder to understand, and can be corrected in two different ways, so we will consider it in some detail. The strictness functions involved in this example are

$$\begin{aligned} &\mathrm{REVERSE\ a} = \mathrm{a} \rightarrow \mathrm{nil} \sqcup \mathrm{cons}\ (\mathrm{CONS}_1\ (\mathrm{APPEND}_2\ \mathrm{a})) \\ &\qquad\qquad\qquad\qquad\qquad\qquad (\mathrm{REVERSE}\ (\mathrm{APPEND}_1\ \mathrm{a})) \\ &\mathrm{APPEND}_1\ \mathrm{b} = \mathrm{b} \rightarrow \mathrm{nil} \sqcup \mathrm{cons}\ (\mathrm{CONS}_1\ \mathrm{b})\ (\mathrm{APPEND}_1\ (\mathrm{CONS}_2\ \mathrm{b})) \end{aligned}$$

The strictness analyser attempts to expand (REVERSE (cons c ABSENT)) and observes that the recursive call of REVERSE does not have a selector applied to a as its argument, so it does not attempt to expand the recursion. Instead it merges the top-level and recursive arguments to give e, and approximates the call by d.

$$\begin{aligned} &\mathrm{e} = \mathrm{cons\ c\ ABSENT} \sqcup \mathrm{APPEND}_1\ \mathrm{e} \\ &\mathrm{d} = \mathrm{e} \rightarrow \mathrm{nil} \sqcup \mathrm{cons}\ (\mathrm{CONS}_1\ (\mathrm{APPEND}_2\ \mathrm{e}))\ \mathrm{d} \end{aligned}$$

But now the argument to APPEND_1 cannot be reduced to finite normal form before the call is expanded, and so APPEND_1 e is also approximated, by f where

$$\begin{aligned} &\mathrm{f} = \mathrm{g} \rightarrow \mathrm{nil} \sqcup \mathrm{cons}\ (\mathrm{CONS}_1\ \mathrm{g})\ \mathrm{f} \\ &\mathrm{g} = \mathrm{e} \sqcup \mathrm{CONS}_2\ \mathrm{g} \end{aligned}$$

Now the problem is unavoidable. $\mathrm{CONS}_2\ \mathrm{g} \sqsubseteq \mathrm{g}$, but $\mathrm{ABSENT} \sqsubseteq \mathrm{CONS}_2\ \mathrm{e} \sqsubseteq \mathrm{CONS}_2\ \mathrm{g}$. So $\mathrm{ABSENT} \sqsubseteq \mathrm{g}$, which implies $\mathrm{ABSENT} \sqsubseteq \mathrm{f}$ (because f is g→..), $\mathrm{ABSENT} \sqsubseteq \mathrm{e}$ (because e is .. $\sqcup$ f), and finally $\mathrm{ABSENT} \sqsubseteq \mathrm{d}$. d is the result of the analysis and cannot be a strict context. This is a general problem: whenever a recursive call occurs in a lazy context then our non-recursive approximation approximates the context of *all* calls by a lazy one, which prevents the analyser ever assigning a parameter a strict context. This is a serious limitation indeed.

One possible approach is to consider that the analyser was hasty in deciding to approximate the call of REVERSE non-recursively. In this example a little calculation shows that

$$\text{APPEND}_1\ (\text{cons c ABSENT}) = \text{nil} \sqcup \text{cons c ABSENT}$$
$$\text{APPEND}_1\ (\text{nil} \sqcup \text{cons c ABSENT}) = \text{nil} \sqcup \text{cons c ABSENT}$$

and so an exact expansion is indeed possible. The analyser could always attempt such an expansion, and give up only if it failed to find one after a few levels of recursion.

Alternatively, we could try to improve the non-recursive approximation so that it at least does not make this particular blunder. This can be done by replacing all recursive calls of strictness functions (F E) by the equivalent

$$\text{E} \rightarrow \text{F (STRICT E)}$$

before making the approximation. STRICT finds the strict part of a context, and satisfies

$$\text{STRICT ABSENT} = \bot$$
$$\text{STRICT (CON } c_1..c_n) = \text{CON } c_1..c_n$$
$$\text{STRICT (a} \sqcup \text{b)} = \text{STRICT a} \sqcup \text{STRICT b}$$

This ensures that the approximated context of all calls is a strict one, and so prevents the analyser making such an obvious mistake.

However, we cannot introduce a new operator on contexts without showing how to solve equations involving it. This is not so easy in the case of STRICT, because its properties are not very pleasant. In fact,

$$\text{STRICT (a} \rightarrow \text{b)} = \text{STRICT a} \rightarrow \text{STRICT b}$$
$$\text{STRICT (a} \sqcap \text{b)} = \text{(STRICT a} \sqcap \text{b)} \sqcup \text{(STRICT b} \sqcap \text{a)}$$

STRICT is in some ways similar to a selector, and we believe that it can be eliminated during selector elimination. In order to be sure that selector elimination still terminates, we need to convince ourselves that the set **F*** is still finite. We can do so by noting that, for any compound selector S,

$$\text{STRICT (S (STRICT a))} = \text{STRICT (S a)}$$

which allows us to restrict attention to compositions of selectors and STRICT involving STRICT at most once. **F*** can be calculated by forming the closure of $\{F_1..F_n\}$ under the selectors, adding all functions STRICT^F, and then forming the closure of the resulting set under the selectors.

Conclusion

We have shown that it is possible to compute useful strictness information about functions on non-flat domains in a first-order functional language, but there is much scope for further work. Our study of the operators on and properties of contexts seems a little complicated, and relies in places on informal reasoning. A proper treatment would be welcome. Our approach involves several approximations, and it may well be possible to find better approximations or even exact solutions. It is also a matter of urgency to extend the method to higher-order functions, since much manipulation of data-structures is done by higher-order functions in practical programs.

Can our method be applied in a real compiler? We must conclude that, at least in its present form, it cannot. Any method intended for practical use must be able to analyse one call in a relatively short time. Yet our method analyses a call by calling its strictness function, which in turn may call other strictness functions and so on to unlimited depth. Thus one call may take an arbitrarily long time to analyse, which is quite unacceptable in a real compiler. To alleviate this, the body of each strictness function must be simplified once and for all, so that it can be applied in a reasonably short time. This is essential, even if it involves further approximation.

Thus our work is a demonstration of possibility, and a potential basis for further work that may lead to practical strictness analysis of data-structures in the future.

Acknowledgements

I am grateful to Kent Karlsson and Mary Sheeran for studying my incomprehensible drafts with great care, to Lennart Augustsson, Peter Dybjer, Thomas Johnsson, Simon Peyton-Jones, and Phil Wadler for their helpful comments, to the Programming Methodology Group at Chalmers University for a stimulating environment, and to the UK Science and Engineering Research Council for their financial support in the form of a European Research Fellowship.

Addendum

During the workshop of which this is a Proceedings, Phil Wadler discovered a simple and elegant extension of the Mycroft approach to cope with non-flat domains. His work can easily be combined with Burn, Hankin and Abramsky's extension to higher-order functions. A slight disadvantage is that Wadler's approximation is cruder than ours, and so our method can sometimes discover more detailed information. Wadler will report his result in a forthcoming paper.

References

[1] G. L. Burn, C. Hankin, S. Abramsky, ***The Theory and Practice of Strictness Analysis for Higher-Order Functions***, **General Electric Company/Imperial College London 1985.**

[2] C. D. Clack, S. L. Peyton-Jones, ***Generating Parallelism from Strictness Analysis***, **Internal note 1679, University College London, February 1985.**

[3] J. Fairbairn, ***Removing Redundant Laziness from Super-combinators***, **in *Proceedings of the Workshop on Implementations of Functional Languages*, Aspenæs, Gøteborg, February 1985.**

[4] P. Hudak, J. Young, ***A Set-Theoretic Characterisation of Function Strictness in the Lambda Calculus***, **in *Proceedings of the Workshop on Implementations of Functional Languages*, Aspenæs, Gøteborg, February 1985.**

[5] A. Mycroft, ***The Theory and Practice of Transforming Call-by-Need into Call-by-Value***, **pp 269-281 in *Proceedings 4th International Symposium on Programming*, Lecture Notes in Computer Science, Vol. 83, Springer-Verlag, Paris, April 1980.**

[6] S. C. Wray, ***A New Strictness Detection Algorithm***, **in *Proceedings of the Workshop on Implementations of Functional Languages*, Aspenæs, Gøteborg, February 1985.**

Strictness Computation Using Special λ-Expressions

Dieter Maurer
Universität des Saarlandes
D-6600 Saarbrücken
maurer%sbsvax.uucp@germany.csnet

Abstract

In order to exploit implicit parallelism in demand driven functional programs the inference of information about the strictness of user defined functions is helpful. This article extends results of Mycroft [Myc80] about strictness detection in first order programs to higher order programs. Information about the strictness of higher order functions is represented by special λ-expressions, so called need expressions. A program over λ-expressions is translated into a program over need expressions by interpreting the constants as closed need expressions. After a suitable approximation – essentially a partial typing – expressions are computed by an iterative method allowing to derive strictness information for the functions defined in the original program.

1. Introduction

The interest in functional programming is growing because of its elegance and its promise to exploit implicit parallelism to a large extent. As John Hughes [Hug85] has pointed out, it gains its elegance among others from two features: lazy evaluation and higher order functions. But lazy evaluation hides some of the implicit parallelism. In an implementation that does not start possibly unneeded computations and thus avoids process garbage collection, only those actual parameters may be evaluated in parallel to the function body and to each other, in which the function is known to be strict in (for an alternative see [Bur84]). For user defined functions this information must be computed by a program analysis. It is well known [Myc80] that exact strictness information is uncomputable. The analysis can determine only an approximation to the exact information. In order not to invalidate the lazy semantics the approximation must be safe, i.e. if it states the strictness of a function, then this function must indeed be strict.

During his research on transforming call-by-need into call-by-value Mycroft [Myc80] developed an algorithm performing this analysis for first order programs. All expressions have a semantics as a function over a semantic domain $\mathcal{D}$, the least element of which, $\perp$, represents undefined. Then f is strict in its i-th parameter provided its semantics yields the value $\perp$ if its i-th argument is $\perp$. To analyse strictness in an effective way all non-$\perp$ elements of D are identified and the resulting class is called $\top$. The semantics of programs over the new domain $B = \left\{ \begin{smallmatrix} \top \\ \perp \end{smallmatrix} \right\}$ can be computed effectively because B is finite. This semantics expresses safe information about the strictness of the functions defined by a program.

In order to be applicable for a larger class of functional programs Mycroft's approach must be slightly extended. Functional programs usually use higher order functions and structured data objects often constructed by non-strict data constructors. The application of Mycroft's approach to programs of higher order is not elaborated and yields poor results for objects constructed by non-strict data constructors. In this paper an attempt is made to carry Mycroft's work over to higher order programs. The approach does not yield satisfactory results for non-flat domains.

After the presentation of some preliminaries in section 2, a semantic domain B is defined in section 3 corresponding to the domain B defined by Mycroft. Reflecting the higher order case, this domain not only contains the two values $\perp$ and $\top$ but also functions over these values and functions over such functions and so on. As with Mycroft's domain the semantics of a program when interpreted over B gives safe information about the strictness of the defined functions. But in contrast to the work by Mycroft, B does not satisfy the ascending chain condition, i.e. not every ascending sequence is finite. Therefore the meaning of a program cannot be effectively computed in general by the standard iteration algorithm. In section 4 a set N of *need expressions* is defined. Its elements are special λ-expressions. Need expressions can be interpreted to express strictness information. A part of this information can be obtained effectively. By means of a special interpretation of constants it is possible to associate a program π_N over N with the given program π to be analysed. π_N has a semantics over B, $I(\pi_N)$. An appropriate constant interpretation assumed, $I(\pi_N)$ gives safe information about the strictness of subexpressions of π. $I(\pi_N)$ is not computable in general. Therefore the concept of approximations is introduced. A closed need expression is said to approximate an element of B if its interpretation in B is at least as defined ($\geq$) as this element. Thus we might compute an approximation to $I(\pi_N)$. Section 5 gives computation rules for need expressions. Furthermore a preorder $\sqsubseteq$ is defined on typed need expressions such that the associated equivalence relation is decidable. On it section 6 bases an iterative method to compute an approximation to $I(\pi_N)$ for typed programs. Besides typing the method uses a cutting operation to limit the depth of the intermediate expressions thereby ensuring termination. The algorithm is summarized in section 7 and an example is presented. The paper concludes with a discussion of the presented approach and a comparison with related work in section 8.

Proofs and technical constructions are omitted in this paper. They can be found in a forthcoming paper [Mau86].

2. Preliminaries

In this section some terminology and notation on complete partial orders, continuous lattices, λ-expressions and their semantics are introduced. More details may be found in [Apt81] concerning partial orders, in [Sco72] concerning continuous lattices and in [Bar81] concerning λ-expressions. Furthermore the terms *program* and *strictness* (of an expression) are defined.

A *CPO* is a partially ordered set $(\mathcal{D}, \leq)$ with a least element, denoted by $\perp$, and where every directed subset D of $\mathcal{D}$ has a least upper bound, denoted by $\vee D$. A function f from a CPO $\mathcal{D}_1$ to a CPO $\mathcal{D}_2$ is said to be *continuous* if $f(\vee D) = \vee f(D)$ for every directed subset D of $\mathcal{D}_1$. If $\mathcal{D}_1, \ldots, \mathcal{D}_n$ are CPO's then the following structures are CPO's: 1). their *cartesian product* $\mathcal{D}_1 \times \cdots \times \mathcal{D}_n$, ordered componentwise, 2.) their *(coalesced) sum* $\mathcal{D}_1 + \cdots + \mathcal{D}_n$, i.e. $\{\perp\} \cup (\mathcal{D}_1 - \{\perp_1\}) \times \{1\} \cup \cdots \cup (\mathcal{D}_n - \{\perp_n\}) \times \{n\}$ ordered by defining $\perp$ as its least element and $(d, i) \leq (d', j) \Leftrightarrow i = j$ and $d \leq_i d'$, and 3.) the set $[\mathcal{D}_1 \rightarrow \mathcal{D}_2]$ of continuous functions from $\mathcal{D}_1$ to $\mathcal{D}_2$, ordered pointwise.

A *lattice* is a partial order $(L, \leq)$ in which every two elements x and y have a *least upper bound*, $x \vee y$, and a *greatest lower bound*, $x \wedge y$. A lattice is *complete*, if every subset S has a least upper bound, $\bigvee S$. Then it has also a greatest lower bound, $\bigwedge S$. Any complete lattice is also a CPO. A lattice is *distributive* if the distributivity laws are fulfilled $x \underset{\cup}{\cap} (y \underset{\cap}{\cup} z) = (x \underset{\cup}{\cap} y) \underset{\cap}{\cup} (x \underset{\cup}{\cap} z)$. A complete lattice is *continuous*, if every element x is the least upper bound of the elements which are well below it. An element y is said to be *well below* x, iff for every directed set C with $x \leq \bigvee C$ there is a $c \in C$ with $y \leq c$. In a continuous lattice the lattice operations are continuous. Define for continuous lattices L_1 and L_2 $Hom(L_1, L_2)$ as the set of continuous functions from L_1 to L_2. If we define (arbitrary) least upper bounds pointwise, $Hom(L_1, L_2)$ becomes a continuous lattice. In $Hom(L_1, L_2)$ the greatest lower bound of a finite subset is also given pointwise. (This is in general not true for infinite sets.)

Let $\mathcal{V}$ be a countably infinite set of variables and $\mathcal{K}$ a set of constants disjoint from $\mathcal{V}$. The abstract syntax of the set $\Lambda = \Lambda(\mathcal{V}, \mathcal{K})$ of *λ-expressions* (over the variables $\mathcal{V}$ and constants $\mathcal{K}$) is given by

$$\Lambda \quad = \quad \mathcal{V} \mid \mathcal{K} \mid \Lambda\Lambda \mid \lambda\mathcal{V}.\Lambda$$

An occurrence of a variable v in an expression E is said to be *bound* in E, if it occurs in $\lambda v.E'$ being a subexpression of E; otherwise it is said to be *free*. A variable with at least one bound occurrence in E is said to occur *bound* in E; a variable v with at least one free occurrence in E is said to occur *free* in E. In the latter case v is said to be a *free variable* of E. An expression is *closed* if it contains no free variables.
A binary relation R on Λ is said to be *compatible* if $\lambda v.E_1 \; R \; \lambda v.E_1'$, $E_1 E \; R \; E_1' E$ and $E\, E_1 \; R \; E E_1'$ for all λ-terms E_1, E_1', E with $E_1 \; R \; E_1'$.
The binary relation α on Λ is defined as the least compatible equivalence relation satisfying $\lambda v.E \; \alpha \; \lambda v'.E'$ if v' does not occur in E and E' is obtained from E by replacing all free occurrences of v by v'. Two λ-expressions E_1 and E_2 are said to be *α-convertible* iff $E_1 \; \alpha \; E_2$. We treat λ-expressions always modulo α-convertibility. Thus bound variables may be renamed whenever necessary(variable convention).

A *program* is a sequence $\pi = (f_1 = E_1, \ldots, f_n = E_n)$ of equations where the f_i are different variables and the E_i are λ-terms such that the set of free variables in $E_1, \ldots, E_n$ is a subset of $\{f_1, \cdots, f_n\}$. Without loss of generality we assume that none of the f_i occurs bound in an E_j. The set of programs satisfying these restrictions will be denoted by $\mathcal{P}$.

λ-terms and programs will be interpreted over semantic domains. This interpretation will be induced by an interpretation of constants.

A *semantic domain* $(\mathcal{D}, \uparrow, \downarrow)$ is a CPO $\mathcal{D}$, and continuous maps $\uparrow: \mathcal{D} \longrightarrow [\mathcal{D} \to \mathcal{D}]$ and $\downarrow: [\mathcal{D} \to \mathcal{D}] \longrightarrow \mathcal{D}$ with $\uparrow \circ \downarrow = id_{[\mathcal{D} \to \mathcal{D}]}$ and $\uparrow(\bot) = \bot_{[\mathcal{D} \to \mathcal{D}]}$. $\uparrow$ allows to interpret the elements of $\mathcal{D}$ as functions and $\downarrow$ transforms functions into objects. For convenience we define a binary operation $\cdot$ on $\mathcal{D}$ by $d_1 \cdot d_2 = (\uparrow(d_1))(d_2)$. $\cdot$ is treated as a left associative operator representing application.

A map $I_{\mathcal{K}}^{\mathcal{D}}$ from $\mathcal{K}$ into $\mathcal{D}$ is called an *interpretation of constants* (over $\mathcal{D}$). An interpretation of constants induces a *semantic function* $I = I(I_{\mathcal{K}}^{\mathcal{D}})$ associating an element of $\mathcal{D}$ with every λ-expression in a given environment $\rho \in (\mathcal{V} \to \mathcal{D})$. It is defined by:

$$I : (\mathcal{V} \to \mathcal{D}) \longrightarrow (\Lambda \to D); \quad I(\rho) = I_\rho;$$

$$I_\rho(E) \quad = \quad \begin{cases} I_{\mathcal{K}}^{\mathcal{D}}(k), & \text{if } E = k \in \mathcal{K}; \\ \rho(v), & \text{if } E = v \in \mathcal{V}; \\ I_\rho(E_1) \cdot I_\rho(E_2), & \text{if } E = E_1 E_2; \\ \downarrow (d \mapsto I_{\rho[v \leftarrow d]}(E')), & \text{if } E = \lambda v.E'. \end{cases}$$

I is extended to programs $\pi = (f_1 = E_1, \ldots, f_n = E_n)$ by defining $I(\pi)$ as the least solution in $\mathcal{D}^n$ of the equation system $d_1 = I_\rho(E_1), \ldots, d_n = I_\rho(E_n)$, where ρ maps f_i to d_i and all other variables to $\bot$.

The pair $(\mathcal{D}, I_{\mathcal{K}}^{\mathcal{D}})$ is called an interpretation, $I(\pi)$ is called the semantics or the meaning of π (under the interpretation $(\mathcal{D}, I_{\mathcal{K}}^{\mathcal{D}})$). We will now fix the semantic function I and interpret λ-expressions and programs by it. The interpretation giving programs the meaning intended by the programmer is called *standard interpretation*, the underlying domain *standard domain* and the image of a program π under the corresponding semantic function the *standard semantics* of π. Other interpretations, domains and semantics are called *nonstandard.*

Let $\mathcal{C}$ be a set of environments. An expression E is *strict in its i-th parameter, respectively the variable v, with respect to $\mathcal{C}$ and the interpretation I* if

$$I_\rho(E) \cdot d_1 \cdot \cdots \cdot d_{i-1} \cdot \bot = \bot$$

for every $\rho \in \mathcal{C}$ and for all $d_1, \ldots, d_{i-1}$, respectively $I_{\rho[v \leftarrow \bot]}(E) = \bot$ for every $\rho \in \mathcal{C}$.

A subexpression E of a program $\pi = (f_1 = E_1, \ldots, f_n = E_n)$ is said to be *strict* in its i-th parameter, respectively the variable v, if E is strict in its i-th parameter, respectively variable v, with respect to the set of environments ρ satisfying $(\rho(f_1), \ldots, \rho(f_n)) = I(\pi)$.

3. Termination Semantics

In this section a special non-standard semantics, called termination semantics, is developed. The termination semantics of a program expresses among other things the effect of an undefined/nonterminating parameter on the result of a function call. The underlying domain $\mathcal{B}$, called termination domain, corresponds to Mycroft's domain $\left\{ \begin{smallmatrix} \top \\ \bot \end{smallmatrix} \right\}$. Like there the termination semantics of a program allows to derive safe assertions about the strictness of the defined functions. We use the termination semantics because $\mathcal{B}$ can be given more structure then the standard domain $\mathcal{D}$.

In order for the approach of this paper to be applicable the standard domain must be of a special form. It is given in 3.1. In 3.2 $\mathcal{D}$ as well as $\mathcal{B}$ are explicitly constructed as (direct) limits of appropriate approximations. This construction allows to define a continuous map τ from $\mathcal{D}$ to $\mathcal{B}$ expressing 'termination/definedness properties' of elements of $\mathcal{D}$. Given two interpretations of constants $I_K^{\mathcal{D}}$ and $I_K^{\mathcal{B}}$ over $\mathcal{D}$ or $\mathcal{B}$, respectively, we define the correctness of $I_K^{\mathcal{B}}$ with respect to $I_K^{\mathcal{D}}$ in 3.3. It is then stated that this correctness can be proved by inspection of the values of $I_K^{\mathcal{B}}$ and $I_K^{\mathcal{D}}$. A correct interpretation $I_K^{\mathcal{B}}$ assumed, 3.4 states the strictness of an expression (in a variable or argument position) for $I^{\mathcal{D}}$, given the corresponding strictness for $I^{\mathcal{B}}$. 3.5 concludes by giving an example of a correct interpretation of constants.

3.1. Assumptions about the standard semantics

The standard domain $\mathcal{D}$ is assumed to be embeddable (as an approximation) in a special domain $\mathcal{D}'$ satisfying the following isomorphism

$$\mathcal{D}' \;\cong\; \mathcal{D}_0 + sep(\mathcal{D}' \times \mathcal{D}') + [\mathcal{D}' \to \mathcal{D}']$$

We consider the case $\mathcal{D} = \mathcal{D}'$, the other cases are obtained by restriction. In the above equation $\mathcal{D}_0$ denotes a CPO of 'atomic' values and *sep* adjoins a new least element to a CPO. $\downarrow$ and $\uparrow$ are defined as the injection of $[\mathcal{D} \to \mathcal{D}]$ into $\mathcal{D}$and as the identity on $[\mathcal{D} \to \mathcal{D}]$ and the constant $\perp$-function, respectively.

Note that '+' stands for coalesced sum. This leads to the identification of the constant $\perp$-function with $\perp$, i.e. the constant $\perp$-function is treated as an undefined/nonterminating value. This does not reflect the operational behaviour of many interpreters. It was nevertheless chosen because it simplifies the termination domain.

3.2. The standard and termination domains as limits of approximations

Like Mycroft we want to identify all non-$\perp$ values of $\mathcal{D}_0$. Thus our termination domain $\mathcal{B}$ contains the subcpo $\mathcal{B}_0 = \left\{ \begin{smallmatrix} \top \\ \perp \end{smallmatrix} \right\}$. Reflecting the higher order case it also contains functions over $\mathcal{B}_0$ and functions over such functions and so on. We choose $\mathcal{B}$ as a special continuous lattice with least element $\perp$ and greatest element $\top$ satisfying the isomorphism

$$\mathcal{B} \;\cong\; Hom(\mathcal{B}, \mathcal{B})$$

$\mathcal{B}$ is made into a domain by defining $\uparrow$ and $\downarrow$ as the respective isomorphisms between $\mathcal{B}$ and $Hom(\mathcal{B}, \mathcal{B})$.

Next a map τ from $\mathcal{D}$ into $\mathcal{B}$ is defined expressing termination properties of the elements of $\mathcal{D}$. τ maps the bottom element of $\mathcal{D}$ onto the bottom element of $\mathcal{B}$, the non-bottom elements of $\mathcal{D}_0$ and the elements of $\mathcal{D} \times \mathcal{D}$ are mapped onto the top element of $\mathcal{B}$. In order to define τ on $[\mathcal{D} \to \mathcal{D}]$ we give an explicit construction for both $\mathcal{D}$ and $\mathcal{B}$ as appropriate limits of sequences $(D_0, D_1, \ldots)$ and $(B_0, B_1, \ldots)$, respectively. (In fact this construction gives the definition of D and B.) Functions τ_n from D_n to B_n with the necessary properties can be defined inductively and τ on $[D \to D]$ is defined as an appropriate 'limit' of the τ_n.

The construction is now outlined. Define for $n \in \mathbf{N}$

$$\begin{aligned} D_{n+1} &:= D_0 + sep(D_n \times D_n) + [D_n \to D_n] \\ B_{n+1} &:= Hom(B_n, B_n) \end{aligned}$$

There are for $n \in \mathbf{N}$ function pairs (γ_n, α_n), with $\gamma_n \in [D_n \to D_{n+1}]$ and $\alpha_n \in [D_{n+1} \to D_n]$ that allow to view D_n as an approximation to D_{n+1}. D is the (direct) limit of the sequence $((D_0, (\gamma_0, \alpha_0)), (D_1, (\gamma_1, \alpha_1)), \ldots)$. For $n \in \mathbf{N}$ the function pairs $(\Phi_{n\infty}, \Phi_{\infty n})$ with $\Phi_{n\infty} \in [D_n \to D]$ and $\Phi_{\infty n} \in [D \to D_n]$ allows D_n to be viewed as an approximation to D. Analogous functions can be defined for B and analogous results are obtained.
This is the construction proposed by Scott [Sco72] to construct models for recursively defined types. We adapted this construction from [Bar81].
We use further that B is a distributive lattice and that in $Hom(B, B)$ (finite) meets and joins are given pointwise. (The former is a special property of B, the latter holds in all continuous lattices.)

Now a sequence $\tau_n : D_n \to B_n$ can be defined inductively by:

$$\tau_0(d) = \begin{cases} \bot, & \text{if } d = \bot; \\ \top, & \text{otherwise.} \end{cases}$$

$$\tau_{n+1}(d) = \begin{cases} \bot, & \text{if } d = \bot; \\ \top, & \text{if } (d \neq \bot \text{ and } d \in D_0) \text{ or } d \in D_n \times D_n; \\ \bigwedge\{g \in B_{n+1} : \tau_n \circ d \leq g \circ \tau_n\}, & \\ & \text{if } d \in [D_n \to D_n] - \{\bot\}. \end{cases}$$

The definition of $\tau_{n+1}(d)$ is interesting if d is a proper function. It should represent termination properties of d. Thus we claim that if $\tau_{n+1}(d)(y) = \bot$ for some $y \in B_n$, then $d(x) = \bot$ for all $x \in D_n$ with $\tau_n(x) = y$, i.e. for all x whose termination properties are represented by y. Because B_n is finite and therefore meets in $B_{n+1} = Hom(B_n, B_n)$ are pointwise, the definition of τ_{n+1} guarantees the stronger result $\tau_n \circ d \leq \tau_{n+1}(d) \circ \tau_n$.
In the inductive definition of τ_n a termination abstraction, τ_n, is lifted from D_n to D_{n+1}. The same lifting is done in [Bur85] using more advanced concepts such as powerdomains. They are applicable in a more general setting.

τ can now be defined as an appropriate limit of the τ_n ($\tau = \bigvee_{n \in \mathbf{N}} \Phi_{n\infty} \circ \tau_n \circ \Phi_{\infty n}$). It has the following properties.

Properties of τ

1. τ is continuous.
2. $\tau(d) = \bot \iff d = \bot$
3. $\tau(x \cdot y) \leq \tau(x) \cdot \tau(y)$ for all $x, y \in D$.
4. $\tau(\downarrow f) \leq \downarrow g$ for all $f \in [D \to D]$, $g \in Hom(B, B)$ with $\tau \circ f \leq g \circ \tau$.

Property 2 allows the test on $\perp$ to be performed in $\mathcal{B}$. Properties 2 and 3 state intuitively that for a function f over $\mathcal{D}$ its 'image under τ' is the least continuous function g satisfying $\tau \circ f \leq g \circ \tau$. Property 1 is used to relate fixpoint computations in $\mathcal{D}$ and $\mathcal{B}$.

3.3. *Correct interpretations of constants*

An interpretation of constants $I_{\mathcal{K}}^{\mathcal{B}}$ over $\mathcal{B}$ is said to be *correct* with respect to $I_{\mathcal{K}}^{\mathcal{D}}$, iff the induced semantics $I^{\mathcal{B}}$ and $I^{\mathcal{D}}$ satisfy $\tau \circ I^{\mathcal{D}} \leq I^{\mathcal{B}}$, i.e. $\tau(I_{\rho}^{\mathcal{D}}(E)) \leq I_{\tau\circ\rho}^{\mathcal{B}}(E)$ and $\tau(I^{\mathcal{D}}(\pi)) \leq I^{\mathcal{B}}(\pi)$ for each λ-term E and environment $\rho \in (\mathcal{V} \to \mathcal{D})$ and for each program $\pi \in \mathcal{P}$.

The properties of τ provide a simple local criterion for the correctness of $I_{\mathcal{K}}^{\mathcal{B}}$.

Lemma

A constant interpretation $I_{\mathcal{K}}^{\mathcal{B}}$ over $\mathcal{B}$ is correct with respect to $I_{\mathcal{K}}^{\mathcal{D}}$ iff $\tau \circ I_{\mathcal{K}}^{\mathcal{D}} \leq I_{\mathcal{K}}^{\mathcal{B}}$.

3.4. *Strictness properties over $\mathcal{D}$ and $\mathcal{B}$*

Theorem

Let $I_{\mathcal{K}}^{\mathcal{B}}$ be a correct interpretation of constants over $\mathcal{B}$ wrt. the standard interpretation $I_{\mathcal{K}}^{\mathcal{D}}$. Denote by $I^{\mathcal{B}}$ and $I^{\mathcal{D}}$ the respective induced semantic functions. Let $\pi = (f_1 = E_1, \ldots, f_n = E_n)$ be a program and E an expression in the program. If E is strict in its i-th parameter or in the variable v for $I^{\mathcal{B}}$, then it is likewise strict for $I^{\mathcal{D}}$.

This theorem states that safe approximations to the strictness properties of a λ-expression may be computed using $\mathcal{B}$, provided a correct constant interpretation is used. It is an easy consequence of the definition of correctness for constant interpretations, the properties of τ and the monotonicity of $\downarrow$ and $\cdot$ over $\mathcal{B}$.

3.5. *Example*

This section concludes with an example for a correct constant interpretation.

Assume that $\mathcal{D}_0$ contains the boolean values *true* and *false* and the natural numbers. Then the semantics of addition *add* and conditional *if* might be given by (with the isomorphism $[A \times B \to C] \cong [A \to [B \to C]]$):

$$I_{\mathcal{K}}^{\mathcal{D}}\, add(d_1, d_2) = \begin{cases} d_1 + d_2, & \text{if } d_1, d_2 \in \mathbf{N}; \\ \perp, & \text{otherwise.} \end{cases}$$

$$I_{\mathcal{K}}^{\mathcal{D}}\, if(d_1, d_2, d_3) = \begin{cases} d_2, & \text{if } d_1 = true; \\ d_3, & \text{if } d_1 = false; \\ \perp, & \text{otherwise.} \end{cases}$$

The following constant interpretation would be correct with respect to $I_K^{\mathcal{D}}$:

$$I_K^{\mathcal{B}}\, add(b_1, b_2) = \begin{cases} \bot, & \text{if } b_1 = \bot \text{ or } b_2 = \bot; \\ \top, & \text{otherwise.} \end{cases}$$

$$I_K^{\mathcal{B}}\, if(b_1, b_2, b_3) = \begin{cases} \bot, & \text{if } b_1 = \bot; \\ b_2 \vee b_3, & \text{otherwise.} \end{cases}$$

This constant interpretation is not the best possible, but it is one that may be described by the special λ-terms defined in the next section.

4. Need Expressions

In the last section it was shown that the interpretation of a λ-expression over $\mathcal{B}$, induced by a correct constant interpretation, gives safe information about the strictness of the expression. But $\mathcal{B}$ is inappropriate to compute this strictness information because $\mathcal{B}$ contains infinite chains and thus the usual iteration to compute a solution of an equation system does not terminate in general. This problem can be avoided by typing the programs. Then the computation can proceed in a finite lattice. But the lattice might nevertheless be large and complex and the question arises how to represent its elements (or at least approximations to them) and the operations application and functional abstraction. Chris Clack and Simon Peyton Jones [Cla85] seem to have a solution to this problem. They use a compact extensional representation of monotonic functions. The theory is provided by Burn et al. [Bur85]. In this paper an intensional representation of functions is explored. A subset of $\mathcal{B}$ is represented by special λ-terms called need expressions.

Need expressions are defined and related to $\mathcal{B}$ in 4.1. 4.2 defines programs and interpretations of constants over need expressions and shows how a program over need expressions can be obtained from a given program over Λ. 4.3 introduces the concept of approximations necessary to compute manageable expressions expressing strictness properties of the functions defined in a program.

4.1. Definition of need expressions

We want to express strictness properties as naturally as possible. For the first order case the following development is identical to [Ker84] and [Hud85]. The higher order case is handled differently.

In the first order case, an independent attribute method represents the strictness information for a function as a subset of its formal parameters. Therefore the set $\mathbf{N}(E)$ of arguments needed by an expression E can be related to those of its subexpressions by using the set operations $\cap$ and $\cup$. We have e.g.

$$\mathbf{N}(E_1 + E_2) = \mathbf{N}(E_1) \cup \mathbf{N}(E_2)$$
$$\mathbf{N}(\mathit{if}\ E_1\ \mathit{then}\ E_2\ \mathit{else}\ E_3) = \mathbf{N}(E_1) \cup (\mathbf{N}(E_2) \cap \mathbf{N}(E_3))$$
$$\mathbf{N}(1) = \emptyset$$

This is a natural way to represent strictness information and we would like to retain this kind of description. Fortunately, meets and joins are valid operations also on continuous functions between continuous lattices. Furthermore meet and join of such functions are given pointwise. Thus there should be a computation rule

$$(N_1 \overset{\cap}{\underset{\cup}{}} N_2)N \equiv (N_1 N) \overset{\cap}{\underset{\cup}{}} (N_2 N).$$

Furthermore it is natural to claim in the higher order case that

$$\mathbf{N}(EE') = \mathbf{N}(E)\mathbf{N}(E')$$

But then the above expression for the conditional leads into trouble. Obviously, $(\mathit{if}\ E_1\ \mathit{then}\ E_2\ \mathit{else}\ E_3)E$ and $\mathit{if}\ E_1\ \mathit{then}\ E_2 E\ \mathit{else}\ E_3 E$ are equivalent. Thus the associated need expressions should be equivalent. But the above rules give

$$\mathbf{N}(E_1)\mathbf{N}(E) \cup (\mathbf{N}(E_2)\mathbf{N}(E) \cap \mathbf{N}(E_3)\mathbf{N}(E)),$$

respectively

$$\mathbf{N}(E_1) \cup (\mathbf{N}(E_2)\mathbf{N}(E) \cap \mathbf{N}(E_3)\mathbf{N}(E)),$$

which are intuitively not equivalent. Therefore a special construct is introduced: ΦN. Intuitively, ΦN signals that it does not represent a genuine function but rather an atomic value, only viewed as a (self reproducing) function. We associate with Φ the following computation rules

$$(\Phi N)N' \equiv \Phi N \quad \text{and} \quad \Phi(\Phi N) \equiv \Phi N.$$

Semantically Φ is associated with the test function on $\bot$, yielding $\bot$ on $\bot$ and $\top$ otherwise. Using the Φ-construct $\mathbf{N}(\mathit{if})$ can be given as $\mathbf{N}(\mathit{if}) = \lambda b\,t\,e.\Phi b \cup (t \cap e)$.
As in the first order case the need expression is $\emptyset$ for atomic constants such as natural numbers. $\emptyset$ is associated with the $\top$ element of $\mathcal{B}$. Because we want to iterate on need expressions we need also an expression associated with the $\bot$ element of $\mathcal{B}$. This element is denoted by $\diamond$. In summary:

Definition need expressions, $\mathcal{N}$

The abstract syntax of *need expressions* is given by:

$$\mathcal{N} \to \mathcal{V} \mid \mathcal{N}\mathcal{N} \mid \lambda\mathcal{V}.\mathcal{N} \mid \diamond \mid \emptyset \mid \mathcal{N} \cup \mathcal{N} \mid \mathcal{N} \cap \mathcal{N} \mid \Phi\mathcal{N}.$$

Fritz Müller pointed out, that need expressions can be viewed as λ-expressions over the set of constants $\mathcal{K}_{\mathcal{N}} = \{\diamond, \emptyset, \cup, \cap, \Phi\}$, where the binary operations $\cup$ and $\cap$ are written infix. Therefore all definitions of section 2 for λ-expressions can be carried over to need expressions. Like λ-expressions, need expressions are treated modulo α-convertability. Furthermore an interpretation of $\mathcal{K}_{\mathcal{N}}$ induces a semantics on need expressions and programs over need expressions.

In the following we use $(\mathcal{B}, I)$ as interpretation of need expressions with $I(\diamond) = \bot$, $I(\emptyset) = \top$, $I(\cup)$ and $I(\cap)$ corresponding to the meet, respectively join in $\mathcal{B}$ and $I(\Phi)$ to the test function $\underline{\uparrow}$ on $\bot$ defined by $\underline{\uparrow}(b) = \bot$, if $b = \bot$, and $\top$, otherwise. Note that $\cup$ and $\cap$ are interpreted as meet and join (and not vice versa) because of the duality between termination and strictness properties.

By means of I the *strictness* of a need expression (in a variable or an argument ...) can now be defined as given in section 2.
This defines strictness by reference to the semantics in $\mathcal{B}$. But need expressions were specially designed to express (some of the) strictness properties directly, without reference to $\mathcal{B}$. Two predicates S_v and S_i perform a top-down traversal of a need expression N to obtain safe information about whether N is strict in the variable v, respectively its i-th argument. S_v is defined next, S_i can be defined similarly.

$$S_v(N) = \begin{cases} \mathit{true}, & \text{if } N = \diamond; \\ \mathit{true}, & \text{if } N = v; \\ S_v(N_1), & \text{if } N = N_1 N_2; \\ S_v(N_1) \text{ } \mathit{or} \text{ } S_v(N_2), & \text{if } N = N_1 \cup N_2; \\ S_v(N_1) \text{ } \mathit{and} \text{ } S_v(N_2), & \text{if } N = N_1 \cap N_2; \\ S_v(N_1), & \text{if } N = \Phi(N_1); \\ S_v(N_1), & \text{if } N = \lambda v'.N_1 \text{ and } v \neq v'; \\ \mathit{false}, & \text{otherwise.} \end{cases}$$

As a motivation for the definition of S_v we look at two examples: $N_1 \cup N_2$ is strict in v if N_1 or N_2 is, therefore $S_v(N_1 \cup N_2) = S_v(N_1)\, \mathit{or}\, S_v(N_2)$. If N_1 is strict in v, then also $N_1 N_2$, therefore $S_v(N_1 N_2)$ can be defined as $S_v(N_1)$. Thus S_v does not obtain the full strictness information expressed by an application. We could improve its result by defining $S_v(N_1 N_2) = S_v(N_1)\, \mathit{or}\, (S_1(N_1)\, \mathit{and}\, S_v(N_2))$. But this, too, could not detect that $((\lambda x.x)\mathit{successor})v$ is strict in v. In the next section a more general solution is given: if possible, applications are performed by β-reduction.

4.2. Programs over $\mathcal{N}$

It is our aim to derive strictness information about a subexpression of a program π over Λ. To this end a program $\pi_{\mathcal{N}}$ over $\mathcal{N}$ is associated with π. $\pi_{\mathcal{N}}$ is obtained from π by interpreting the constants in π as closed need expressions. Now the necessary terms are defined and some useful facts stated.

A *program* over $\mathcal{N}$ is a program $\pi_{\mathcal{N}} = (f_1 = N_1, \ldots, f_n = N_n)$ where the right hand sides are need expressions. An operator $\varphi = \varphi(\pi_{\mathcal{N}})$ from $\mathcal{N}^n$ to itself is associated with $\pi_{\mathcal{N}}$ by defining $\varphi_i(N_1, \ldots, N_n) = [N_1/f_1, \ldots, N_n/f_n]N_i$. By induction the semantics of $\pi_{\mathcal{N}}$, $I(\pi_{\mathcal{N}})$, is $\bigvee_{n \in \mathbf{N}} I(\varphi^n(\diamond, \ldots, \diamond))$.

A map $I_{\mathcal{K}}^{\mathcal{N}}$ from $\mathcal{K}$ into $\mathcal{N}$ is called an *interpretation of constants over* $\mathcal{N}$ if $I_{\mathcal{K}}^{\mathcal{N}}(k)$ is closed for every constant k. It induces a map $I^{\mathcal{N}}$ mapping λ-expressions onto need expressions and programs over Λ onto programs over $\mathcal{N}$ by replacing all constants by their image under $I_{\mathcal{K}}^{\mathcal{N}}$. $I_{\mathcal{K}}^{\mathcal{N}}$ is called *correct* with respect to an interpretation $I_{\mathcal{K}}^{\mathcal{B}}$ over $\mathcal{B}$, if $I \circ I^{\mathcal{N}} \geq I^{\mathcal{B}}$. As in the previous section there is a local correctness criterion: $I_{\mathcal{K}}^{\mathcal{N}}$ is correct iff $I \circ I_{\mathcal{K}}^{\mathcal{N}} \geq I_{\mathcal{K}}^{\mathcal{B}}$.

$I_K^{\mathcal{N}}$ is called correct with respect to the standard interpretation $I_K^{\mathcal{D}}$ or shortly correct, if $I_K^{\mathcal{N}}$ is correct with respect to $\tau \circ I_K^{\mathcal{D}}$.
The interpretations from the end of the previous section assumed, the following constant interpretation $I_K^{\mathcal{N}}$ is correct.

$$
\begin{aligned}
I_K^{\mathcal{N}}\, add &= \lambda xy.\Phi x \cup \Phi y \\
I_K^{\mathcal{N}}\, if &= \lambda xyz.\Phi x \cup (y \cap z)
\end{aligned}
$$

A correct constant interpretation assumed, $I(I^{\mathcal{N}}(\pi_{\mathcal{N}}))$ expresses safe information about the strictness of the functions defined in the program π over Λ. We would like to represent $I(I^{\mathcal{N}}(\pi_{\mathcal{N}}))$ by means of need expressions. In general, this is impossible, so we must be content with an 'approximate (but safe) representation'. The concept of approximation is introduced in the next subsection.

4.3. Approximations

Let $N_1, N_2 \in \mathcal{N}$. N_1 is said to be an *approximation* to N_2, ($N_1 \succ N_2$), if $I_\rho(N_1) \geq I_\rho(N_2)$ for every environment $\rho \in (\mathcal{V} \to \mathcal{B})$. An approximation N_1 to N_2 is said to be *closed* if N_1 is closed.
Intuitively $N_1 \succ N_2$ if strictness of N_1 implies the corresponding strictness of N_2.
$\succ$ is a compatible preorder. It is extended to $\mathcal{N}^n$ componentwise.

Let N be a closed need expression and $b \in \mathcal{B}$. N is said to *approximate* b ($N \succ b$), if $I(N) \geq b$.
$\succ$ is extended componentwise for tuples.

In section 6 approximations to the semantics of a program $\pi_{\mathcal{N}}$ are computed in an iterative way very similar to the usual computation of least fixed points. Usually this method does not process the program as a whole. Instead the mutually recursive definitions are collected into program components and the components processed one at a time in such an order that only the currently or previously processed components are referenced. The next lemma states that the same improvement can be used for the computation of approximations.

Lemma Component Lemma
Let $\pi = (\vec{f} = \vec{N}, \vec{g} = \vec{M})$ be a program over $\mathcal{N}$ such that the free variables of the N are among the f.
Then $\pi^{(1)} = (\vec{f} = \vec{N})$ is also a program. Let $\vec{N}'$ be an approximation to $I(\pi^{(1)})$.
Let $\pi^{(2)} = (\vec{g} = [\vec{N}/\vec{f}]\vec{M})$ and $\vec{M}'$ be an approximation to $I(\pi^{(2)})$.
Then $(\vec{N}', \vec{M}')$ is an approximation to $I(\pi)$.

The next lemma states that an approximation to $I(\pi')$ can be computed if an approximation to $I(\pi)$ is required, provided π' approximates π. This result is used when switching from arbitrary programs to typable programs, which is necessary to apply the results of section 6.

Lemma Approximating Programs
Let $\pi = (f_1 = N_1, \ldots, f_n = N_n)$ and $\pi' = (f_1 = N_1', \ldots, f_n = N_n')$ be programs over $\mathcal{N}$ such that $N_i' \succ N_i$ for $i = 1 \ldots n$. Then $I(\pi') \geq I(\pi)$.

The following theorem states that safe information about the strictness of an expression in a program π can be computed by means of S_v and S_i from an approximation to $I(I^{\mathcal{N}}(\pi))$. In the next section a transformation on $\mathcal{N}$ is introduced improving the strictness information obtainable by S_i and S_v without deteriorating the strictness information of an expression. In the section after next brute force is used to obtain the required approximation.

Theorem

Let $\pi = (\vec{f} = \vec{E})$ be a program over Λ and $I_K^{\mathcal{N}}$ be a correct interpretation of constants over $\mathcal{N}$. Let $(\vec{F})$ approximate $I(I^{\mathcal{N}}(\pi))$. Let E be an expression occurring in π, N an approximation to $[\vec{F}/\vec{f}]I^{\mathcal{N}}(E)$ and v a variable different from $f_1, \ldots, f_n$.
Then E is strict in its i-th argument, respectively the variable v, if $S_i(N) = \mathit{true}$, respectively $S_v(N) = \mathit{true}$.

5. Computation with Need Expressions

In 5.1 a set of computation rules is given which do not change the semantics of need expressions. They can be used to define a preorder on $\mathcal{N}$ with respect to which the operator associated with a program is monotonic. Unfortunately the associated equivalence is not decidable. 5.2 defines types, typed need expressions and typed programs. Computation rules similar to the one for the untyped case can be defined giving a similar preorder. There is a computable representation map for the associated equivalence. It can be chosen to transform a typed need expression into a multilevel disjunctive normal form. This is used in the next section to compute an approximation to $I(\pi_{\mathcal{N}})$.

5.1. Computation Rules

We give the computation rules as an equivalence $\equiv_u$ on $\mathcal{N}$.

Definition computation rules

Let $\equiv_u$ be the least compatible equivalence relation on $\mathcal{N}$ (modulo α-convertability) satisfying:

1. β-reduction: $(\lambda v.N_1)N_2 \equiv_u [N_2/v]N_1$
2. distributivity of application over $\overset{\cap}{\cup}$: $(N_1 \overset{\cap}{\cup} N_2)N \equiv_u N_1 N \overset{\cap}{\cup} N_2 N$
3. distributivity of λ-abstraction over $\overset{\cap}{\cup}$: $\lambda v.(N_1 \overset{\cap}{\cup} N_2) \equiv_u \lambda v.N_1 \overset{\cap}{\cup} \lambda v.N_2$
4. distributivity of Φ over $\overset{\cap}{\cup}$: $\Phi(N_1 \overset{\cap}{\cup} N_2) \equiv_u \Phi N_1 \overset{\cap}{\cup} \Phi N_2$
5. Φ as restriction to non-functional value:
   $(\Phi N_1)N_2 \equiv_u \Phi N_1$; $\Phi(\lambda v.N) \equiv_u \Phi([\emptyset/v]N)$
6. Φ as a projection: $\Phi(\Phi N) \equiv_u \Phi N$
7. $\overset{\diamond}{\emptyset}$-simplification: $\overset{\diamond}{\emptyset} N \equiv_u \overset{\diamond}{\emptyset}$; $\lambda v.\overset{\diamond}{\emptyset} \equiv_u \overset{\diamond}{\emptyset}$; $\Phi\overset{\diamond}{\emptyset} \equiv_u \overset{\diamond}{\emptyset}$
8. $\cup$ and $\cap$ as operations of a distributive lattice:

$$N_1 \substack{\cap \\ \cup} N_2 \equiv_u N_2 \substack{\cap \\ \cup} N_1; \quad N_1 \substack{\cap \\ \cup} (N_2 \substack{\cap \\ \cup} N_3) \equiv_u (N_1 \substack{\cap \\ \cup} N_2) \substack{\cap \\ \cup} N_3$$
$$N \substack{\cap \\ \cup} N \equiv_u N; \quad N_1 \substack{\cap \\ \cup} (N_1 \substack{\cup \\ \cap} N_2) \equiv_u N_1$$
$$N_1 \substack{\cap \\ \cup} (N_2 \substack{\cup \\ \cap} N_3) \equiv_u (N_1 \substack{\cap \\ \cup} N_2) \substack{\cup \\ \cap} (N_1 \substack{\cap \\ \cup} N_3)$$

9. $\diamond$ and $\emptyset$ as least and greatest element
$$\diamond \cap N \equiv_u N; \quad \diamond \cup N \equiv_u \diamond; \quad \emptyset \cap N \equiv_u \emptyset; \quad \emptyset \cup N \equiv_u N$$
10. ΦN-N rules: $\Phi N \cup N \equiv_u N; \quad \Phi N \cap N \equiv_u \Phi N$

Properties of $\equiv_u$

1. If $N_1 \equiv_u N_2$ then $I_\rho(N_1) = I_\rho(N_2)$ for any environment $\rho: \mathcal{V} \to \mathcal{B}$.
2. By rule 8 $\mathcal{N}/_{\equiv_u}$ is a distributive lattice with meet $\cup/_{\equiv_u}$ and join $\cap/_{\equiv_u}$. By rule 9 $\diamond$ and $\emptyset$ are its least, respectively greatest element.
   Let $\sqsubseteq_u$ be the preorder on $\mathcal{N}$, induced by the lattice order. By compatibility the operations application, λ-abstraction, meet, join and restriction are monotonic with respect to $\sqsubseteq_u$. It follows that the operator φ associated with a program is monotonic, too. Thus
$$\vec{\diamond} \sqsubseteq_u \varphi(\vec{\diamond}) \sqsubseteq_u \cdots \sqsubseteq_u \varphi^k(\vec{\diamond}) \sqsubseteq_u \cdots.$$

Unfortunately $\equiv_u$ is not computable. Thus property 2 can not be used to compute an approximation to $I(\pi_{\mathcal{N}})$ because we might be unable to detect that $\varphi^k(\vec{\diamond}) \equiv_u \varphi^{k+1}(\vec{\diamond})$. But an analogue on typed need expressions is computable.

5.2. *Typed Need Expressions*

Definition Types, typed need expressions

Following [Bar81] *Typ*, the set of types, and $\mathcal{N}_\sigma$, the set of need expressions of type σ, have the abstract syntax

$$Typ \longrightarrow \quad 0 \mid Typ \to Typ$$
$$\mathcal{N}_\sigma \longrightarrow \quad \mathcal{V}_\sigma \mid \mathcal{N}_{\sigma' \to \sigma}\mathcal{N}_{\sigma'} \mid \lambda \mathcal{V}_{\sigma'''}.\mathcal{N}_{\sigma''} \mid \diamond_\sigma \mid \emptyset_\sigma \mid \mathcal{N}_\sigma \substack{\cap \\ \cup} \mathcal{N}_\sigma \mid \Phi_{\sigma' \to \sigma}\mathcal{N}_{\sigma'}$$

where $\sigma''' \to \sigma'' = \sigma$ if $\sigma \neq 0$, otherwise the case is omitted.

Denote by $\mathcal{N}_\mathcal{T}$ the set of typed need expressions.

A *typed program* $\pi_{\mathcal{N}_\mathcal{T}}$ is a sequence $(f_1 = N_1, \ldots, f_n = N_n)$ where the f_i are different typed variables and the N_i are typed need expressions whose free variables are among the f_i.

Typed need expressions are treated modulo α-convertability. All definitions concerning the terms *free* and *bound* are inherited from need expressions.

Define an equivalence relation $\equiv$ as the least compatible equivalence relation on $\mathcal{N}_\mathcal{T}$ (modulo α-convertability) satisfying typed versions of rules 1 to 9. Note that rule 10 is not included.

As before $\mathcal{N}_\sigma/_\equiv$ is a distributive lattice with meet $\cup/_\equiv$ and join $\cap/_\equiv$. $\diamond_\sigma$ and $\emptyset_\sigma$ are its least and greatest element, respectively.
Let $\sqsubseteq$ be the preorder on $\mathcal{N}_\sigma$, induced by the lattice order. By compatibility the operations application, λ-abstraction, meet, join and restriction are monotonic with respect

to $\sqsubseteq$. It follows that the operator φ associated with a typed program is monotonic, too. Thus

$$\vec{\diamond} \sqsubseteq \varphi(\vec{\diamond}) \sqsubseteq \cdots \sqsubseteq \varphi^k(\vec{\diamond}) \sqsubseteq \cdots.$$

Theorem Existence of a computable representation map

There is a computable representation map $\xi : \mathcal{N}_\mathcal{T} \to \mathcal{N}_\mathcal{T}$ (i.e. $\xi^2 = \xi$ and $N_1 \equiv N_2 \iff \xi_1(N) = \xi(N_2)$).

ξ can be chosen that it transforms a typed need expression into a *multilevel disjunctive normal form*. More precisely, the range of ξ can be made to be $\mathcal{N}_\cup$ defined below.

$$\begin{aligned}
\mathcal{N}_\cup &\longrightarrow \mathcal{N}_\cap^{\{1\}} \cup \cdots \cup \mathcal{N}_\cap^{\{n\}}\\
\mathcal{N}_\cap &\longrightarrow \mathcal{N}_{\Phi\lambda\cdot}^{\{1\}} \cap \cdots \cap \mathcal{N}_{\Phi\lambda\cdot}^{\{n\}}\\
\mathcal{N}_\lambda &\longrightarrow \lambda\mathcal{V}.\mathcal{N}_{\Phi\lambda\cdot}\\
\mathcal{N}_\Phi &\longrightarrow \Phi\mathcal{N}.\\
\mathcal{N}. &\longrightarrow \mathcal{V}\mathcal{N}_\cup^{\{1\}} \cdots \mathcal{N}_\cup^{\{n\}}
\end{aligned}$$

where all expressions are typed, n represents natural numbers, including 0, $\mathcal{N}_{\Phi\lambda\cdot}$ represents the (disjoint) union of $\mathcal{N}_\Phi$, $\mathcal{N}_\lambda$ and $\mathcal{N}.$, the operators $\overset{\cap}{\cup}$ and application associate to the left, the operands of $\cup$ and $\cap$ are pairwise incomparable with respect to $\sqsubseteq$ and sorted by some order.

Intuitively, ξ uses rules 1 to 7 as reduction rules, directed from left to right. Every typed need expression has a unique normal form with respect to this reduction. Then rules 8 and 9 are used to transform this normal form into a multilevel disjunctive normal form. The details will be given in a forthcoming paper [Mau86].

6. Computing approximations to $I(\pi)$ for typed programs

In this section π is assumed to be a typed program over $\mathcal{N}$. The associated operator is denoted by φ. Then $(\varphi^k(\vec{\diamond}))_k$ is a sequence increasing with respect to $\sqsubseteq$. But it does not necessarily become eventually constant. As an example the Y combinator defined by $Y = \lambda f.f(Yf)$ has a nonterminating iteration sequence.

$$Y^{(0)} = \diamond,\ Y^{(1)} = \lambda f.f\diamond,\ Y^{(2)} = \lambda f.f(f\diamond),\ Y^{(3)} = \lambda f.f(f(f\diamond)), \ldots$$

A look at the sequence reveals that the application of f on $\diamond$ becomes nested deeper and deeper. To ensure termination of the iteration this deepening process must be broken. This can be done by a cutting operator *cut*. Controlled by a cutting parameter t, it limits the depth of nested applications by approximating subexpressions nested deeper then t by $\emptyset$. *cut* treats applications uncurried and is defined by:

$$
\begin{aligned}
&cut : \mathbf{N} \times \mathcal{N}_{\mathcal{T}} \to \mathcal{N}_{\mathcal{T}} \\
&cut(0, N) \quad = \emptyset_{\sigma}, \qquad \text{if } N \in \mathcal{N}_{\sigma}. \\
&cut(t+1, N) = \begin{cases} cut(t+1, N_1)cut(t, N_2), & \text{if } N = N_1 N_2; \\ cut(t+1, N_1) \mathbin{\substack{\cap \\ \cup}} cut(t+1, N_2), & \text{if } N = N_1 \mathbin{\substack{\cap \\ \cup}} N_2; \\ \Phi(cut(t+1, N')), & \text{if } N = \Phi N'; \\ \lambda v. cut(t+1, N'), & \text{if } N = \lambda v. N'; \\ N, & \text{otherwise.} \end{cases}
\end{aligned}
$$

$cut(t, \cdot)$ is monotonic wrt. $\sqsubseteq$ on $range(\xi)$ and $N \sqsubseteq cut(t, N)$ for all $t \in \mathbf{N}$ and $N \in \mathcal{N}_{\mathcal{T}}$.

For $N \in \mathcal{N}_{\mathcal{T}}$ its $\cdot$*-depth* is defined as the least t such that $cut(t, N) = N$. Then the following lemma holds.

Lemma

Let $\mathcal{V}_0$ be a finite set of variables, $\mathcal{T}_0$ be a finite set of types, $n \in \mathbf{N}$.
Then $range(\xi)$ contains only a finite number of elements whose free variables are from $\mathcal{V}_0$, whose subexpressions have types from $\mathcal{T}_0$ and whose $\cdot$-depth are bounded by n.

Now the theorem allowing to compute an approximation to $I(\pi)$ can be stated.

Theorem

Let $t \in \mathbf{N}$. Define $\Psi = \xi \circ cut(t, \cdot) \circ \xi \circ \varphi$.
Then the sequence $(x_k := \Psi^k(\vec{\emptyset}))_{k \in \mathbf{N}}$ becomes eventually constant and this constant approximates $I(\pi)$.

This result is not satisfactory. Nothing is said about the choice of t. Suppose t is large. Then the strictness information for Y would be the large expression

$$Y = \lambda f. \underbrace{f(f(\cdots(f\emptyset)\cdots)}_{t \text{ times}}$$

In many cases this would give the same information as $Y = \lambda f. f\emptyset$ which is much easier to work with. Thus for the Y combinator one would like to have $t = 1$ but for other definitions higher values of t might be useful. There is no problem to use different values of t for different components but it seems to be difficult to estimate a good value of t for a given definition.

Originally, I have looked for characteristics of programs leading probably to an infinite growth of the $\cdot$-depth. I found two classes. The Y-combinator is an example of the first class: a function is used as part of an application operand inside the program component it is defined in. An example of the second class is $f = \lambda x\,y. f\,x\,(xy) \cap y$ with the iteration sequence:

$$f^{(1)} = \lambda xy.y, \; f^{(2)} = \lambda xy.xy \cap y, \; f^{(3)} = \lambda xy.x(xy) \cap xy \cap y, \; \ldots$$

In this case the growth takes place by passing of the second parameter. The second parameter, y, appears in an actual second parameter on a "deepening position", i.e.

as part of an application operand. The second class can be classified by the existence of special cycles in a labeled directed graph associated with the program. Programs belonging to one of these classes can be approximated by programs not in these classes. The result would be $Y = \lambda f.f\emptyset$ and $f = \lambda x\,y.f\,x(x\emptyset) \cap y$ for our examples. The details are omitted here because of lack of space.

Unfortunately these two classes do not seem to cover all programs leading potentially to an infinite depth increase. Therefore the use of the *cut*-operation seems to be necessary beyond the application of the above heuristics.

7. Computation of strictness information

This section outlines how the tools developed in earlier sections are used to compute information about the strictness of an expression occurring in a given program. 7.1 gives a simplified version of the used algorithms, 7.2 presents an example.

7.1. Outline of the algorithm

We assume that a correct interpretation $I_K^{\mathcal{N}}$ of constants over $\mathcal{N}$ and a cutting parameter t are given.

Algorithm

INPUT: program $\pi = (f_1 = E_1, \ldots, f_n = E_n)$ over Λ.
expression E occurring in π.

OUTPUT: $((v_1, s_{v_1}), \ldots, (v_k, s_{v_k}))$
where $v_1, \ldots, v_k$ are the free variables in E different from $f_1, \ldots, f_n$ and the s_{v_i} are boolean values such that E is strict in v_i if $s_{v_i} = true$.
a list of boolean values $(s_1, \ldots, s_m)$
such that E is strict in its i-th parameter if $s_i = true$

1. Compute $\pi_{\mathcal{N}} = I^{\mathcal{N}}(\pi)$, the program over $\mathcal{N}$ associated with π.
2. Process each program component $\pi_{\mathcal{N}}^{(i)}$ in accordance with the topological order.
2.1. Substitute the expressions computed in earlier components for the respective variables.
2.2. Type the component by e.g. an algorithm of Milner [Dam82]. If an expression is not typable, approximate it by a $\emptyset$ of an appropriate type. Denote the resulting program by $\pi_{\mathcal{N}}^{(i)'}$.
2.3 Compute an approximation $\vec{F}^{(i)}$ to $I(\pi_{\mathcal{N}}^{(i)'})$ as shown in section 6. By a lemma in 4.3. it is also approximates $I(\pi_{\mathcal{N}}^{(i)})$.
3. Put the results together: After some sorting $\vec{F} = (\vec{F}^{(1)}, \ldots, \vec{F}^{(l)})$ approximates $I(\pi_{\mathcal{N}})$ by the component lemma of 4.3.
4. Compute $E' = [F_1/f_1, \ldots, F_n/f_n]I^{\mathcal{N}}(E)$.
5. Compute a typable expression E'', approximating E'.
6. Compute $N = \xi(E'')$. Then N is an approximation to $[F_1/f_1, \ldots, F_n/f_n]I^{\mathcal{N}}(E)$

7. Let $v_1, \ldots, v_k$ be the free variables in E different from $f_1, \ldots, f_n$.
Represent N as a disjunction of conjunctions of elements of the form $\lambda x_1 \ldots x_l.N'$ with maximal l.
Then by the theorem in 4.3. E is strict in its i-th parameter, respectively in v_i, if $S_i(N) = true$, respectively $S_{v_i}(N) = true$.
Thus output $((v_1, S_{v_1}(N)), \ldots, (v_k, S_{v_k}(N)))$ and $(S_1(N), \ldots, S_l(N))$.

7.2. Example

We now give an example showing how the above algorithm is used to compute strictness information for the functions defined in a program. Some standard operators are written infix and function applications are not curried to improve readability. The example uses the interpretation of constants $I_K^N(+) = I_K^N(-) = I_K^N(=) = \lambda x\, y.\Phi x \cup \Phi y$ and $I_K^N(if) = \lambda b\, t\, e.\Phi b \cup (t \cap e)$. It defines the higher order function *repeat* computing $f^n(a)$. Using *repeat*, *itadd* computes the sum of two elements by successive additions of 1 and *gp* represents a function with $gp(0, a, b) = a + b$, $gp(1, a, b) = a \times b$ and $gp(2, a, b) = a^b$ for $a, b \geq 1$.

$$
(\pi) \quad
\begin{aligned}
repeat &= \lambda f\, n\, a. if\ n = 0\ then\ a\ else\ repeat(f, n-1, f(a)) \\
itadd &= \lambda x\, y. repeat((\lambda z.z+1), x, y) \\
gp &= \lambda st\, a\, b. \\
& \quad if\ st = 0\ then\ a + b \\
& \quad else\ repeat(\lambda x.gp(st-1, x, a), b-1, a)
\end{aligned}
$$

After some simplifications the associated program over need expressions looks like

$$
(\pi_N) \quad
\begin{aligned}
repeat &= \lambda f\, n\, a. \Phi n \cup (a \cap repeat(f, \Phi n, f(a))) \\
itadd &= \lambda x\, y. repeat((\lambda z.\Phi z), x, y) \\
gp &= \lambda st\, a\, b. \\
& \quad \Phi st \cup ((\Phi a \cup \Phi b) \cap repeat(\lambda x.gp(\Phi st, x, a), \Phi b, a))
\end{aligned}
$$

The three program components *repeat*, *itadd* and *gp* can be processed in that order. They are all typable. With the cutting parameter denoted by t, the iteration of section 6 gives as n-th approximation for the *repeat* component $(1 \leq n \leq t)$.

$$
\begin{aligned}
repeat^{(n)} &= \lambda f\, n\, a. \Phi n \cup (a \cap f(a) \cap \cdots \cap f^{n-1}(a)) \\
repeat^{(t+1)} &= \lambda f\, n\, a. \Phi n \cup (a \cap f(a) \cap \cdots \cap f^t(\emptyset)) = repeat^{(t+2)}
\end{aligned}
$$

Thus $repeat^{(t+1)}$ approximates $I(repeat)$. If this result is substituted for *repeat* in the definition of *itadd*, we obtain after some simplifications $itadd = \lambda x\, y.\Phi x$. S_1 reveals then that *itadd* is strict in its first parameter, but it could not be detected that it is also strict in the second one.

As outlined at the end of section 6, the definition of *repeat* can also be approximated such that no infinite depth increase will occur.

$$repeat' = \lambda f\, n\, a. \Phi n \cup (a \cap repeat'(f, \Phi n, f(\emptyset)))$$

can be used for this purpose. Then $repeat'^{(3)} = repeat'^{(2)} = \lambda f\, n\, a.\Phi n \cup (a \cap f(\emptyset))$ approximates $I(repeat')$ and thus $I(repeat)$. It can be used to process component gp. After substitution and simplification the component then takes the form

$$gp = \lambda st\, a\, b.\Phi st \cup \Phi b \cup (\Phi a \cap a \cup gp(\Phi st, \emptyset, a)).$$

The iteration computes $\lambda st\, a\, b.\Phi st \cup \Phi b \cup (\Phi a \cap a)$ as an approximation to $I(gp)$. Then gp can be shown to be strict in its three parameters by means of S_1 through S_3.

8. Discussion

In this paper the possibility was explored to represent strictness information for higher order functions by a version of λ-expressions. This approach came into mind because λ-expressions permit a conceptionally easy representation of the essential operations function application and functional abstraction. Furthermore β-reduction allows to perform function applications. It turned out that one can represent and compute safe strictness information by the introduced need expressions, provided the semantics can by modeled by the denotational semantics defined in 3.1. But an unnatural cutting is necessary to ensure termination. Due to the cutting the information derived by this method may be weaker than that derived by related methods. The algorithm is being implemented by Bernd Bellmann .

The correctness of this approach is based on a quite special denotational semantics, as described in section 3.1. This semantics identifies the constant $\perp$-function with $\perp$. This leads to the identification of the two λ-expressions $\Omega := (\lambda x.xx)(\lambda x.xx)$ and $\lambda y.\Omega$. It may lead to incorrect results if a program computes a function or if functions are passed on strict argument positions, e.g. to *eager cons*. But it is possible to modify section 3 and 5 to avoid this problem.

The approach in this paper is based on work by Mycroft [Myc80]. It extends this work to higher order programs. For first order programs it computes the same information as Mycroft does. This is because Mycroft's programs can trivially be typed and the ·-depth in all intermediate results are bounded by one. The presented approach may need more iterations than Mycroft's does because it distinguishs between e.g. v and Φv which is not necessary for programs of order one.

In 1985 Hudak and Young [Hud85] have published an approach to strictness analysis of higher order functions. They use so called strictness ladders, sequences of functions of increasing arity, to represent strictness information. Programs are required to be polymorphically typed to ensure termination of the usual iteration. Need expressions can be interpreted by means of strictness ladders. They often represent strictness information in a much more compact form. Because the iteration is performed on a purely syntactic level, the cutting operation is necessary beyond typing to ensure termination. This may lead to weaker information.

In these proceedings Burn et al. [Bur85] present a method to compute strictness information for typed programs. The use of typed programs ensures that the abstract domains representing the strictness information are finite, thus ensuring termination of the iteration. Clack and Peyton Jones [Cla85] have found a compact representation for higher order functions over $\mathcal{B}_0$ and developed a sophisticated way to compute these representations during the iteration. Abramsky [Abr85] has generalized the approach of Burn et al. to polymorphically typed programs. Under some circumstances this method computes strictness information for a function several times. Let e.g. $f = \lambda x.x$. To detect that the first occurrence of 1 in $f(1) + f(\lambda x.x)(1)$ is needed, f is interpreted as a function from $\mathcal{B}_0$ to $\mathcal{B}_0$, but as a function from $[\mathcal{B}_0 \rightarrow \mathcal{B}_0]$ to $[\mathcal{B}_0 \rightarrow \mathcal{B}_0]$ to detect that the second occurrence is needed, too. In contrast the approach presented in this paper associates one need expression with each function (and each constant) approximating its strictness properties in all contexts. This may avoid costly recomputations and/or save space. On the other hand information may be less precise because termination must be artificially enforced.

Acknowledgement

I wish to thank R. Wilhelm, A. Lucks, U. Moencke, H.-G. Oberhauser and especially F. Müller for careful reading of the manuscript, helpful discussions and/or pinpointing bugs. Furthermore I thank B. Weisgerber. One of her programs has computed basic data for the application of the Knuth-Bendix algorithm necessary in the proof of the main theorem in section 5.

Bibliography

Abr85 Samson Abramsky, "Strictness Analysis and Polymorphic Invariance", *these proceedings*, 1985.

Apt81 K. Apt and G. Plotkin, "A Cook's Tour of Countable Nondeterminism", *ICALP 81*, p. 479-494, 1981.

Bar81 H.P. Barendregt, "The Lambda Calculus: Its Syntax and Semantics", in *Studies in Logic and the Foundations of Mathematics*, North-Holland, 1981.

Bur85 G. L. Burn, C. L. Hankin and S. Abramsky, "The Theory and Practice of Strictness Analysis for Higher Order Functions", *these proceedings*, 1985.

Bur84 F. Warren Burton, *Controlling Speculative Computation in a Parallel Functional Programming Language*, Feb. 84., unpublished

Cla85 Chris Clack and Simon Peyton Jones, "Strictness Analysis - A Practical Approach", *Proc. Functional Programming Languages and Computer Architecture*, p. 35-49, Sept. 1985.

Dam82 L. Damas and R. Milner, "Principal type schemes for functional programs.", *9th ACM Symp. on Principles of programming languages*, 1982.

Hud85 P. Hudak and J. Young, "A Set-Theoretic Characterization of Function Strictness in the Lambda Calculus", Research Report YALEU/DCS/RR-391, Yale University, Department of Computer Science, Jan. 1985.

Hug85 R.J.M. Hughes, "Why Functional Programming Matters", Internal report, Programming Methodology Group, Chalmers Institute of Technology, Gothenburg, Sweden, 1985.

Ker84 W. H. Kersjes, *A Reduction Strategy for Efficient Parallel Evaluation of Functional Programs Using Program Analysis*, 1984., RWTH Aachen

Mau86 Dieter Maurer, *Strictness Analysis for Higher Order Programs*, 1986., to appear

Myc80 A. Mycroft, "The Theory and Practice of Transforming Call-by-Need into Call-by-Value.", *Proc. 4th Int. Symp. on Prgramming: Lecture Notes in Computer Science, number 83, Paris, pp. 269-281*, 1980.

Sco72 D. S. Scott, "Continous lattices", in *Toposes, Algebraic Geometry and Logic*, ed. F. W. Lawvere, p. 97-136, LNM 274, 1972.

A relational framework for abstract interpretation[1]

Alan Mycroft
Computer Laboratory
Corn Exchange Street
Cambridge CB2 3QG
England

Neil D. Jones
DIKU
Sigurdsgade 41
DK-2200 Copenhagen N
Denmark

Abstract

Abstract interpretation is a very general framework for proving certain properties of programs. This is done by interpreting the symbols of the program, or the symbols of a denotational metalanguage translation, in two different ways (the standard interpretation and the abstract interpretation) and relating them. We set up a new framework for abstract interpretation based on relations (with the intent of inclusive or logical relations). This avoids problems with power domains and enables certain higher-order frameworks to be proved correct. As an example we show how the Hindley/Milner type system can be viewed as a special case of our system and is thus automatically correct.

1 Introduction

This work collects together several ideas from the literature and uses them as a new framework for abstract interpretation including higher types and gives associated examples. The prime importance of this work is this framework and indeed parts of the theory of the examples are well discussed in the literature. Much work remains to be done and we would expect the final shape of these ideas to differ from this preliminary form.

The development uses relations defined inductively on types instead of power domains and adjoined functions of previous works. One argument for using relations instead of functions for abstraction is to consider the example of determining types in a language with a monotyped (Pascal-like) type system. We might want to associate a value (or set of values) with a type by means of a function. However, it is clear by considering the value $\lambda x.x$ that it should be related to the types $(int \rightarrow int)$ and $(bool \rightarrow bool)$, but that these do not have a least upper bound type in this system. Relations naturally encode this many-many property. Another technical reason for using relations is concerned with higher-order objects as discussed in section 3.

In fact, in a sense which we will make more precise later on, the Hindley/Milner polymorphic type discipline is up to a representation function a sublattice of the power set of such types in which $\lambda x.x$ is related by means of a *function* to the set of types of the form $(t \rightarrow t)$ as t ranges over monotypes. This corresponds to the notion of a principal type.

As we might expect from this, many abstraction relations are induced from abstraction functions. We discuss this in section 6.

Finally, we feel that the abstraction functions involved in abstract interpretation and the homomorphisms occurring in universal algebra are special cases of a more general concept — see the discussion in section 3.

[1] A preliminary version of this paper was presented at the Workshop on Abstract Interpretation at Kent University, Canterbury in August 1985.

1.1 What questions do we wish to ask?

One particularly crucial task in program analysis is deciding what questions we wish to have answers to, or more formally, which theorems we wish to prove.

One can separate two cases, the second more general than the first:

- We wish to know the answers to questions pertaining to a form of 'global' correctness – for example that the result of running a program analysed to have a certain type actually yields a value of that type. (Note that correctness here may not have anything to do with termination.) Also, supposing we have a program consisting of a set of recursion equations, we may wish to know certain properties of the individual denotations of the functions (*e.g.* whether they are strict at a certain argument position). Most analyses of functional programs using abstract interpretation have used such a framework – as far as we know the only exception is [7] discussed below.
- We wish to know the answers to questions of 'local' behaviour – for example that only certain variable-value environments may obtain at a given program point (= label). The seminal Cousot paper on abstract interpretation considers such a circumstance, although it is clear that this is not a generalisation of the case above. A recent paper by Jones and Mycroft [7] discusses a framework of abstract interpretation based on 'minimal function graphs' (*mfg*) in which (for the case of first-order recursion equations) we can model the values of arguments the functions are actually called with. Moreover, the standard interpretation is an abstraction of this mfg interpretation and by transitivity so is every 'global' problem as defined above which can be characterised as an abstact interpretation in the 'global' sense above.

One resolution of this dichotomy is to follow Nielson[15] and analyse the *meta*-language of a denotational definition (to be viewed as a translation of object- to meta-language terms). However, Nielson's work has several problems (see chapter 6 in the above reference) the main ones being the absence of any treatment of higher order objects and the hardwired treatment of the least fixpoint operator which seems to preclude the *mfg* analysis above.

For reasons of concreteness (and the clarity of exposition gained in this case) this work deals with constructing a framework (for the special case of the λ-calculus) which may be used to answer questions of the former kind and which deals with higher-order functions. Because of the fixed denotational schema we cannot expect it to be able to express all questions of the latter kind. We would anticipate that it would generalise easily to a framework like Nielson's.

1.2 Related work

The classical paper on abstract interpretation is the Cousots' seminal work[3], which set up a general framework for static program analysis and showed how many apparently *ad hoc* techniques were special cases. Donzeau-Gouge[5] developed the Cousots' framework for denotational semantics parameterising it on certain key domains. Mycroft [13] and later with Nielson [14] extended such techniques for the analysis of functional programs including termination. Unfortunately, the last-mentioned work used a framework using a rather special power-domain construction which only seems to work for the first-order case. Nielson's thesis[15] mentioned above used a similar idea to logical relations (*q.v.*) to relate the standard semantics to the collecting semantics *via* a relation sim_t. However, its most fundamental contribution seems to be the formalisation of the notion of abstract interpretation of a meta-language term.

Recently, Jones and Mycroft [7] developed a theory of abstract interpretation for collecting the arguments with which functions may be called. This included a definition of abstraction as a semi-homomorphic property which lifted in the manner of logical relations to second-order objects. Abramsky[1] has applied (and further developed) the framework described here for strictness analysis of the typed λ-calculus thus simplifying the notation of [2] who gave the first satisfying account of strictness analysis for higher-order functions.

Finally (see also the discussion on the $(\alpha \to \beta)$ relation in section 3) we must mention Dybjer's[6] work on "domain algebras". It is not yet clear as to how relevant this work is to abstract interpretation.

1.3 Organisation

Sections 2 and 3 explain our notation and develop the theory of abstraction relations. Section 4 shows how a language can be given a scheme of denotational meanings parameterised on certain key domains and (function) values. As examples we develop interpretations corresponding to call-by-name, call-by-value, the Hindley/Milner type checking algorithm and strictness analysis. This is followed by section 5 which uses abstraction relations to develop a general theory of relationship between interpretions. This framework can then be used to prove correct analyses based on such related interpretations. As an example the Hindley/Milner type system is proved correct. Section 6 shows how relations can be induced in different ways from a function between interpretations. Section 7 compares this work with the previous framework of power objects and adjoined functions. This is followed by section 8 which gives some category-theoretic thoughts. Finally, we end with some concluding remarks.

2 Notation, definitions

For any *sets* A, B we write $A \to B$ to denote the space of functions from A to B and $A \times B$ to denote their cartesian product. We write $A + B$ for their disjoint union with associated injection functions $in_1 : A \to (A + B)$ and $in_2 : B \to (A + B)$. Similarly, $\mathcal{R}(A, B)$ will denote their set of relations $\{r \subseteq A \times B\}$.

A *cpo* is a partial order with a least element and limits of all directed sets. The word *domain* will be used interchangeably.

We use these same symbols for the corresponding operations on cpo's: $\to$ will then yield the space of continuous functions, $\times$ the cartesian product and $+$ the *separated* sum. The cpo operations will be extended to act on partial orders (*e.g.* a set with equality) provided the result is a cpo. The *set* of relations $\mathcal{R}(A, B)$ between cpo's A, B is just the set of relations on their underlying sets (note that we do not put a domain structure on $\mathcal{R}(A, B)$).

3 Inclusive predicates

In this section we will consider what objects might be used to relate usefully two different meanings of a given program. Similar objects occurring in the literature (although used for different purposes) are:

- *Inclusive predicates* which were independently developed by Milne (see [19] for more details) and Reynolds (*e.g.* [17]) who calls them *directed complete relations*. Both definitions really are that of *admissible predicate* up to the difference between "directed set complete" and "chain complete". However, both Milne and Reynolds then proceed to use these words with the extra understanding that the inclusive predicates or directed complete relations used are actually logically defined in the sense of Plotkin below *and* may also be used on recursive domain definitions. So much so that the words "inclusive predicate" often seem to take the additional meaning of "possibly self-referential" as we see in Mulmulmey's work[11] which discusses these objects and their existence at some length. Gordon[8] uses similar techniques.

- *Logical relations* were introduced by Plotkin [16] to refer to the related concept of relations defined inductively over (non-recursive) type structure, in the manner explained below.

Nielson[15] uses similar ideas in the definition of his sim_t predicate for relating the standard and collecting interpretation but does not explain how his definitions are related to the above.

We turn to summarising the ideas involved. Let A, A', B, B' be sets. Given functions $\alpha : A \to A'$ and $\beta : B \to B'$ it is easy to induce functions $(\alpha + \beta) : (A + B) \to (A' + B')$ and $(\alpha \times \beta) : (A \times B) \to (A' \times B')$ in a natural manner. However, it is not possible in general to induce a function $(\alpha \to \beta) : (A \to B) \to (A' \to B')$ since, considering $(\alpha \to \beta)$ as the natural relation $\in \mathcal{R}(A \to B, A' \to B')$ defined by

$$f(\alpha \to \beta)f' \;\Leftrightarrow\; (\forall a \in A)(f'(\alpha(a)) = \beta(f(a)))$$

turns out not to necessarily be a function.[2] (Consider $A = A' = B = B' = \{0,1\}$ with $\alpha(x) = \beta(x) = 0$ then any two functions f, f' with $f(0) = f'(0) = 0$ are related).

However, Dybjer[6] considers a category of domain algebras in which this relationship *is* functional, but it is unclear whether his work can be applied to abstract interpretation. The exposition and references of his work are also useful.

This motivates Milne and Reynolds' use (and our adoption) of relations since, using Reynolds' notation, given $R \in \mathcal{R}(A, A'), S \in \mathcal{R}(B, B')$ we can define

$$\begin{aligned} R + S &\in \mathcal{R}(A + B, A' + B') \\ R \times S &\in \mathcal{R}(A \times B, A' \times B') \\ R \to S &\in \mathcal{R}(A \to B, A' \to B') \end{aligned}$$

by

$$\begin{aligned} x(R + S)x' &\;\Leftrightarrow\; (x = in_1(a) \wedge x' = in_1(a') \wedge aRa') \vee \\ &\qquad\; (x = in_2(b) \wedge x' = in_2(b') \wedge bSb') \\ (a,b)(R \times S)(a',b') &\;\Leftrightarrow\; aRa' \wedge bSb' \\ x(R \to S)x' &\;\Leftrightarrow\; (\forall a \in A, a' \in A')(aRa' \Rightarrow x(a)Sx'(a')) \end{aligned}$$

One may check that if R and S are relations representing functions then the first two constructions embody the suggested definitions earlier.

Now let us suppose that A, A', B, B' are domains. The definitions of $R \times S$ and $R \to S$ go through unchanged, with pleasant properties such as

$$\begin{aligned} =_A \times =_B \;&=\; =_{A \times B} \qquad & =_A \to =_B \;&=\; =_{A \to B} \\ \sqsubseteq_A \times \sqsubseteq_B \;&=\; \sqsubseteq_{A \times B} \qquad & \sqsubseteq_A \to \sqsubseteq_B \;&=\; \sqsubseteq_{A \to B} \end{aligned}$$

However, for $R + S \in \mathcal{R}(A + B, A' + B')$ there are three distinct natural choices, *viz*

$$\begin{aligned} x(R +^L S)x' &\;\Leftrightarrow\; x = \bot \vee x(R +^X S)x' \\ x(R +^M S)x' &\;\Leftrightarrow\; (x = \bot \wedge x' = \bot) \vee x(R +^X S)x' \\ x(R +^U S)x' &\;\Leftrightarrow\; x' = \bot \vee x(R +^X S)x' \end{aligned}$$

where

$$\begin{aligned} x(R +^X S)x' &\;\Leftrightarrow\; (x = in_1(a) \wedge x' = in_1(a') \wedge aRa') \vee \\ &\qquad\; (x = in_2(b) \wedge x' = in_2(b') \wedge bSb') \end{aligned}$$

---

[2] Universal algebraists note that this is just a special case of an algebra and shows that homomorphisms as we know them do not naturally appear in higher-order algebra.

The second one corresponds to Nielson's sim_t definition, but there are strong reasons for believing that $+^L$ and $+^U$ (read lower and upper) are relevant to dataflow analysis. For example if we are deriving *computable* abstract meanings to the semantics of a program, then given undecidability, we must inevitably confuse certain looping programs with certain halting programs.[3] See section 6.1. The existence of this choice seems to stem from the fact that the separated sum operation is not a domain co-product. The above definitions have the feature that the following equivalences hold, but in general no others hold:

$$\sqsubseteq_A +^L \sqsubseteq_B \;=\; \sqsubseteq_{A+B} \qquad =_A +^M =_B \;=\; =_{A+B} \qquad \sqsupseteq_A +^U \sqsupseteq_B \;=\; \sqsupseteq_{A+B}$$

The next problem to face, and the one with which Milne, Reynolds and Mulmuley above concerned themselves, is the following. Suppose $D = F_A(D)$ is a recursive domain definition of a domain D parameterised on a domain $\mathbf{A}$ and $D' = F_{A'}(D')$ is a similar definition of D'. Now suppose that we have a relation $R \in \mathcal{R}(A, A')$. Can we lift this to a relation in $\mathcal{R}(D, D')$ in a manner similar to the above treatment (and which could immediately be used if $F(D)$ did not depend on D). We consider a special case of this in section 6.1.

Warning: Note that since there is no domain structure on the set of relations it is possible to write recursive 'definitions' of such relations which are plausible only at first sight. Mulmuley[11] discusses this in some detail, including (essentially) the following example: given a domain $D = (D \to D)$ then there is *no* predicate P (in this context the real analogy is a relation $\in \mathcal{R}(D, \{\cdot\})$ for some one point set) such that

$$P(d) \;\Leftrightarrow\; (\forall d' \in D)(P(d') \Rightarrow d(d') = \lambda x.x)$$

In this paper we do not need to insist that all the relations we consider are admissible since we do not consider a fixpoint operator. The use of admissibility is to ensure that relations behave properly at limits implied by the *standard* fixpoint operator.

For our purposes, that of relating two different semantics of a programming language, this notation becomes rather clumsy, and we follow Nielson in adopting a variant of Plotkin's notation for logical relations[16].

Let $\iota_1, \ldots, \iota_n$ be symbols (to be interpreted as A, A' *etc.*) representing base types. The set of *meta-language types* is the closure of $\iota_1, \ldots, \iota_n$ under the binary *syntactic* operations $+, \times, \to$. Given any spaces (sets or domains) $\mathbf{A} = (A_1, \ldots, A_n)$ we can interpret any type σ as a space $[\sigma]\mathbf{A}$ by the definition

$$[\iota_i]\mathbf{A} = A_i \qquad\qquad [\sigma + \tau]\mathbf{A} = [\sigma]\mathbf{A} + [\tau]\mathbf{A}$$
$$[\sigma \times \tau]\mathbf{A} = [\sigma]\mathbf{A} \times [\tau]\mathbf{A} \qquad [\sigma \to \tau]\mathbf{A} = [\sigma]\mathbf{A} \to [\tau]\mathbf{A}$$

Note that here, and below, the left-hand side use of $+, \times, \to$ represents syntax and the right-hand side a function.

Suppose we have two such interpreting spaces $\mathbf{A}, \mathbf{A}'$ and a family of relations indexed by types $R_\sigma \in \mathcal{R}([\sigma]\mathbf{A}, [\sigma]\mathbf{A}')$ then we say that (R_σ) is a *logical relation* if

$$R_{\sigma+\tau} = R_\sigma + R_\tau \qquad R_{\sigma\times\tau} = R_\sigma \times R_\tau \qquad R_{\sigma\to\tau} = R_\sigma \to R_\tau$$

Clearly we can induce a logical relation from its subfamily (R_{ι_i}).

This notation enables us to treat the type as a subscript indicating which relation to choose and this naturally puts the emphasis on the relation rather than its construction from base relations. Moreover, rather than writing (*e.g.*) $R_{\iota_1 \to \iota_2}$ we will often write $R_{A_1 \to A_2}$ to stand for the relation $\in \mathcal{R}(A_1 \to A_2, A'_1 \to A'_2)$ We will further abuse this notation by omitting the subscript entirely when it is clear from context.

From now on no further mention will be made of meta-language types to avoid confusion with the types we give to the language *Exp* in section 4.3.

[3] This implies that computable interpretations are liable to identify certain convex sets of values in the manner of the Egli-Milner ordering, *but* this property is not built into the notion of abstraction as it has been previously.

4 The lambda calculus and its semantics

We give a class of denotational semantics (parameterised on certain domains and operators) to the untyped λ-calculus in the following form (we choose the λ-calculus as being the simplest programming language with higher-order objects). Let x range over a set *Var* of variables, then the class *Exp* of expressions (ranged over by e) conforms to the syntax:

$$e ::= x \mid \lambda x.e \mid e\, e'$$

For this treatment constants are presumed to be pre-bound variables.

Definition

An *interpretation* I is a triple (D_I, lam_I, app_I) where D is a *cpo* and $lam : (D \to D) \to D$ and $app : (D \times D) \to D$ are continuous functions. (We drop the subscripts when the context is clear.) Given an interpretation (D, lam, app) we can define the notion of *environment* (over D) by

$$Env_D = Var \to D$$

We use the letter ρ to range over environments. Such an interpretation, I, naturally defines an *associated semantics*

$$E_I : Exp \to Env_D \to D$$

in the following manner:

$$\begin{aligned} &E[\![x]\!]\rho = \rho(x) \\ &E[\![\lambda x.e]\!]\rho = lam(\lambda d \in D.\ E[\![e]\!]\rho[d/x]) \\ &E[\![e\, e']\!]\rho = app(E[\![e]\!]\rho, E[\![e']\!]\rho) \end{aligned}$$

When considering static program analysis we can consider D as a set of data desciptions, then *lam* encodes the natural view of a lambda term (as a function from input descriptions to output descriptions) in terms of a description itself. *app* reverses this process.

4.1 Example

The *standard interpretation*, *CBN*, of the (call-by-name) untyped λ-calculus with (integer) constants is given by (V, lam, app) where V is the solution of the recursive domain equation

$$V = Z + (V \to V)$$

where Z is the *set* of integers and $+$ denotes the separated sum with associated injection functions

$$in_Z : Z \to V, \quad in_F : (V \to V) \to V$$

lam and *app* are then defined by

$$\begin{aligned} &lam(f) = in_F(f) \\ &app(d, d') = \text{case } d \text{ of } \ \bot \Rightarrow \bot \\ &\qquad\qquad\qquad\qquad\quad in_Z(n) \Rightarrow \bot \\ &\qquad\qquad\qquad\qquad\quad in_F(f) \Rightarrow f(d') \end{aligned}$$

For the purposes of showing the correctness of type checking (more precisely to show that omission of run-time type tags implied by the separated sum above is valid) it is useful to have a related interpretation *CBN** in which type errors lead immediately to an error stop. We define, following Milner, $CBN^* = (V, lam, app)$ where V is now the solution of the recursive domain equation

$$V \;=\; Z + (V \to V) + \{wrong\}$$

and + denotes the ternary separated sum with associated injection functions

$$in_Z : Z \to V, \quad in_F : (V \to V) \to V, \quad in_W : \{wrong\} \to V$$

lam and *app* are similarly defined by

$$\begin{aligned} lam(f) &= in_F(f) \\ app(d, d') &= \text{case } d \text{ of } \; \bot \Rightarrow \bot \\ &\qquad in_W(wrong) \Rightarrow in_W(wrong) \\ &\qquad in_Z(n) \Rightarrow in_W(wrong) \\ &\qquad in_F(f) \Rightarrow f(d') \end{aligned}$$

Note that we could have easily defined call-by-value interpretations *CBV* and CBV^*, the latter by changing $f(d')$ in CBN^* to

$$\begin{aligned} &\text{case } d' \text{ of } \; \bot \Rightarrow \bot \\ &\qquad in_W(wrong) \Rightarrow in_W(wrong) \\ &\qquad in_Z(n') \Rightarrow f(d') \\ &\qquad in_F(f') \Rightarrow f(d') \end{aligned}$$

and similarly for *CBV* from *CBN*.

4.2 Remarks

Given Γ a subset of $\{\alpha, \beta, \eta\}$ we say that an interpretation I is a Γ-*model* of the λ-calculus if, for all $\gamma \in \Gamma$ and for all $e, e' \in Exp$ such that e and e' are 1-step γ-convertible we have that $E_I[\![e]\!] = E_I[\![e']\!]$.

The definition of the semantics in terms of such an interpretation guarantees that all interpretations are α-models. However, as we might expect for the λ-calculus with constants many interpretations such as *CBN* are not η–models. Moreover, interpretations such as *CBV* and *HM* discussed below are not β-models. (The latter corresponds to the difference in type checking rules for $let\ x = e\ in\ e'$ and $(\lambda x.e')e$ in [10].) The interpretations *CBN* and CBN^* are $\alpha\beta$-models.

An interpretation will, in general, preserve β-convertibility only if

$$app(lam(f), x) = f(x)$$

Similarly, η-convertibility will only be preserved in general if

$$lam(\lambda x.app(d, x)) = d$$

[As an aside, if we write $\overline{app}$ for the curried version $\lambda d.\lambda d'.app(d, d')$ of *app* then the above sufficiency conditions reduce to

$$\overline{app} \circ lam = 1_{(D \to D)} \quad \text{and} \quad lam \circ \overline{app} = 1_D,$$

the classical isomorphisms in $D = (D \to D)$. The above conditions are not necessary due at least to the possibility that elements of D which are not used as interpretations of λ-terms cause them to fail.]

4.3 The Hindley/Milner polymorphic interpretation

Hindley[9], for the case of combinatory logic, and Milner[10] (also together with Damas[4]), for a programming language based on the λ-calculus, give a method of ascribing a certain *type scheme* to expressions. (For full details of the usual framework of this work the reader is referred to the above references.) These type schemes are *principal* in that they subsume all other types which may be inferred for a given expression. To make this possible, we have to introduce a set of *type variables* ranged over by $\alpha, \beta, \ldots$ and then introduce a class of types and type schemes (ranged over by τ, σ respectively). These satisfy the syntax:

$$\tau : \mathit{type} ::= \alpha \mid \mathit{int} \mid \tau \to \tau'$$
$$\sigma : \mathit{typescheme} ::= \tau \mid \forall \alpha . \sigma$$

Note that $\to$ above is used as a constructor function (another name for a cartesian product) and not as a function space. For this reason many logic texts use F instead.

We call a type or type scheme *closed* if it contains no free type variables. We often use the conventional wording that a *monotype* is a closed *type*. We say τ is a *(generic) instance of* σ, written $\tau \leq \sigma$, if τ may be obtained from σ by substituting types for quantified type variables subject to the usual rules about name clashes.

A *type environment* or *type assumption* ranged over by η is simply a map *Var* $\to$ *typescheme*. It is *closed* if it maps each variable into a closed type scheme. Inference rules are now given (for atomic statements of the form $\eta \vdash e : \sigma$ meaning under assumptions η we can ascribe type scheme σ to e). In the simple case we consider they may be written:

$$\frac{\eta \vdash e : \sigma}{\eta \vdash e : \tau} \text{ if } \tau \leq \sigma \qquad \text{(type specialisation)}$$

$$\frac{\eta \vdash e : \sigma}{\eta \vdash e : (\forall \alpha . \sigma)} \text{ if } \alpha \text{ is not free in } \eta \qquad \text{(type generalisation)}$$

$$\frac{}{\eta \vdash x : \sigma} \text{ if } \sigma = \eta(x) \qquad \text{(variable)}$$

$$\frac{\eta \vdash e : (\tau' \to \tau) \quad \eta \vdash e' : \tau'}{\eta \vdash (e\, e') : \tau} \qquad \text{(application or } \to \text{ elimination)}$$

$$\frac{\eta[\tau/x] \vdash e : \tau'}{\eta \vdash (\lambda x . e) : (\tau \to \tau')} \qquad (\lambda\text{-abstraction or } \to \text{ introduction})$$

The first two rules merely concern how polymorphic types behave and the last three are defined structurally on λ-terms. We would like to express this type system as an interpretation. In doing this we find that the particular (finitary) representation of type schemes using type variables and quantification tends to get in the way, and we choose an alternative representation using sets of monotypes. This also has the advantage that we could compare the expressiveness of various type systems by representing them both within the same framework.

Let M be the set of monotypes above. Let $S = \mathcal{P}(M)$ be the powerset of the set of monotypes. S is to be ordered by reverse inclusion ($\sqsubseteq = \supseteq$) and as such is a cpo. In our framework members of M play the role of types and members of S play the role of type schemes. Observe that there is a natural injection of the set of closed type schemes into S which maps a type onto its set of closed generic instances. We refer to this map as *Ground*.

We make S into an interpretation by defining functions *lam* and *app* in the following manner:

$$lam(f) = \{(t \to t') \mid t \in M \wedge t' \in f(\{t\})\}$$
$$app(s, s') = \{t \in M \mid (\exists t' \in M)((t' \to t) \in s \wedge t' \in s')\}$$

We use *HM* to refer to this interpretation.

Remarks

The definitions of *lam* and *app* in *HM* are essentially transcribed from the Hindley/Milner inference rules above, with the translation of the type-deduction relation as a map into the powerset S and the use of singleton sets (in *lam*) to represent the special treatment of λ-bound variables as types rather than type schemes (the generic/non-generic distinction).

Further, we really do reconstruct the Hindley/Milner type system: in practice, one only ever uses the above inference rules to deduce $\eta \vdash e : \sigma$ in the situation where η is closed and σ is most general. Now most general types infered from a closed type environment are themselves closed. So, supposing η is a closed type environment and letting σ temporarily range over closed type schemes, then we have

$$E_{HM}[\![e]\!](Ground \circ \eta) = \bigcup\{Ground(\sigma) \mid \eta \vdash e : \sigma\}$$

Proof

It suffices to show that

$$E_{HM}[\![e]\!](Ground \circ \eta) = \{\tau \mid \eta \vdash e : \tau, \tau \text{ a monotype}\}$$

as we can end each deduction of $\eta \vdash e : \sigma$ with the type specialisation rule to yield $\eta \vdash e : \tau$ for any $\tau \in Ground(\sigma)$. This we show by

1. For all $\tau \in E[\![e]\!](Ground \circ \eta)$ we have $\eta \vdash e : \tau$, by structural induction on e.

2. For all deductions $\eta \vdash e : \tau$ we have that $\tau \in E[\![e]\!](Ground \circ \eta)$. This is due to the fact that any derivation of $\eta \vdash e : \tau$ can be transformed into a *ground* derivation (*i.e.* one where every τ' encountered in a consequent $\eta' \vdash e' : \tau'$ is also ground, excepting the variable rule). We now merely show inductively (over the deduction tree) that at each stage $\tau' \in E[\![e']\!](Ground \circ \eta')$.

Corollary

As a rather trivial but illuminating corollary based on the property of most-general types we have that if σ is the most general type for e under η then

$$E_{HM}[\![e]\!](Ground \circ \eta) = Ground(\sigma).$$

4.4 Example: strictness analysis

We can define an interpretation corresponding to strictness analysis for higher-order functions in this scheme by using the domain

$$H = \{\top\} + (H \to H)$$

where + as before is the separated sum with injections in_1, in_2. H can be made into an interpretation $SA = (H, lam, app)$ by defining

$$\begin{aligned} lam(f) &= in_2(f) \\ app(h, h') &= \text{case } h \text{ of } \ \bot \Rightarrow \bot \\ &\qquad\qquad\quad in_1(\top) \Rightarrow in_1(\top) \\ &\qquad\qquad\quad in_2(f) \Rightarrow f(h') \end{aligned}$$

[If we wish to make the natural identification for stictness analysis of $\top$ and $\lambda x.\top$ then it is natural to use the domain $H' = (H' \rightarrow H')_\bot$ instead of H above (and of course modifying *lam*, *app* appropriately).]

5 Abstraction

We say that an interpretation $I' = (D', lam', app')$ is an *ABS*-abstraction[4] of $I = (D, lam, app)$, written $I \triangleright_{ABS} I'$ if the following conditions hold

1. $ABS \in \mathcal{R}(D, D')$. We often write *ABS* as ABS_D.

2. $lam\ ABS_{(D \rightarrow D) \rightarrow D}\ lam'$

3. $app\ ABS_{(D \times D) \rightarrow D}\ app'$

In the following we also assume that *ABS* is extended to the equality relation in $\mathcal{R}(Var, Var)$ and write this as ABS_{Var}.

The essential thing about abstraction is that it is a local property of interpretations which lifts to a property of the induced semantics and hence of all programs that can be written in *Exp*:

Proposition (correctness of abstraction)

$$(\forall e \in Exp)(\forall \rho \in Env_D, \rho' \in Env_{D'})(\rho\ ABS_{Var \rightarrow D}\ \rho' \Rightarrow E_I[\![e]\!]\rho\ ABS_D\ E_{I'}[\![e]\!]\rho')$$

or, more succinctly,

$$(\forall e \in Exp) E_I[\![e]\!]\ ABS_{Env_D \rightarrow D}\ E_{I'}[\![e]\!]$$

Proof

By structural induction on e. The base case of $e = x$ is true *a fortiori* due to the assumption on ρ and ρ'. So inductively assume the proposition is true for all ρ, ρ' (satisfying $\rho ABS \rho'$) and all e subterms. We have $d\ ABS_D\ d' \Rightarrow \rho[d/x]\ ABS_{ENV_D}\ \rho'[d'/x]$ and hence

$$(\lambda d \in D.\ E[\![e]\!]\rho[d/x])\ ABS_{D \rightarrow D}\ (\lambda d' \in D'.\ E[\![e]\!]\rho'[d'/x])$$

Now, by the assumption $lam ABS lam'$ the result holds for $\lambda x.e$. The case for $e\ e'$ is similar.

[4] Compare the notion of "homomorphic image".

Remarks

The proof of this proposition can be better seen as an induction over meta-language terms together with the homomorphic (structural) definition of $E[\![.]\!]$. As such the induction duplicates [16, proposition 1]. A similar theorem occurs within [15, theorem 3.3:14].

Unfortunately, in this framework there seems to be no *a priori* reason why the composition of abstraction relations should itself be one. *I.e.* given $I \rhd_{ABS} I' \rhd_{ABS'} I''$ then in general it is unclear whether there is any systematic manner of obtaining ABS'' such that $I \rhd_{ABS''} I''$. Certainly, there is no reason why $(ABS \circ ABS')_{D\to D}$ should equal $ABS_{D\to D} \circ ABS'_{D\to D}$.

This proposition (in various guises) appears again and again in program analysis. Special cases are the *safety* criterion in dataflow analysis and also the requirement of *semantic soundness* of Milner[10], to which we now turn.

5.1 *HM* abstracts *CBN**

Let us assume that $CBN^* = (V, lam, app)$ and $HM = (S, lam', app')$, and that $S = \mathcal{P}(M)$ as in section 4.3. We define a map (following Milner [10]) $Ideal : M \to \mathcal{P}(V)$, the power *set* of V, by

$$Ideal(int) = \{\bot\} \cup \{in_Z(n) \mid n \in Z\}$$
$$Ideal(t \to t') = \{\bot\} \cup \{in_F(f) \mid f \in (V \to V) \wedge f(Ideal(t)) \subset Ideal(t')\}$$

This now lifts to a map $Ideal : S \to \mathcal{P}(V)$ by defining $Ideal(S) = \bigcap_{M\in S} Ideal(M) = \bigsqcup_{M\in S} Ideal(M)$. Note that if S is empty we accordingly take $Ideal(S) = V$, *i.e.* that an ill-typed program can return any value, including $in_W\{wrong\}$. $Ideal(s)$ is the *ideal* corresponding to type scheme s.

We now can define ABS by

$$v\ ABS\ s \Leftrightarrow v \in Ideal(s)$$

Specialising the "correctness of abstraction" proposition above leads to

$$(\forall e \in Exp)\ (\forall \rho \in (Var \to V), \eta \in (Var \to S))$$
$$(((\forall x \in Var)\rho(x) \in Ideal(\eta(x))) \Rightarrow E_{CBN^*}[\![e]\!]\rho \in Ideal(E_{HM}[\![e]\!]\eta))$$

which is essentially Milner's semantic soundness condition relating type-checking to evaluation.

5.2 Relationship of *CBN* and *CBV*

As in the above we find that *CBN, CBV* are related by $CBN \rhd_{\sqsupseteq} CBV$ where $\sqsupseteq$ is the (inverse) ordering on $D_{CBN} = D_{CBV}$. This result is just the statement that call-by-name (normal order) evaluation yields a more defined result than call-by-value (applicative order) evaluation. It is simply shown by observing that $lam_{CBN} = lam_{CBV}$ and that $app_{CBN} \sqsupseteq app_{CBV}$.

6 Inducing *ABS*-relations from functions

Many abstraction relations, as in the two examples above, are indeed induced from functions. Here we do not mean the "usual" abstraction functions $\in \mathcal{P}(D) \to D'$ but the direct ones $\in D \to D'$. For the relationship with the former kind see section 7. We show there is a choice of ways in which this can be done. Firstly, let us say a relation R is LU-*closed* if $y \sqsubseteq x\ R\ x' \sqsubseteq y' \Rightarrow y\ R\ y'$. Similarly we say it is UL-*closed* if $y \sqsupseteq x\ R\ x' \sqsupseteq y' \Rightarrow y\ R\ y'$. It is convenient to think of LU- and UL-closed relations as generalised orderings.

Suppose that we have a (continuous) function $abs : D \to D'$. We can induce relations $abs^L, abs^M, abs^U \in \mathcal{R}(D, D')$ by defining

$$d\ abs^L\ d' \Leftrightarrow abs(d) \sqsubseteq d' \qquad d\ abs^M\ d' \Leftrightarrow abs(d) = d' \qquad d\ abs^U\ d' \Leftrightarrow abs(d) \sqsupseteq d'$$

Then abs^L is LU-closed and abs^U is UL-closed. Moreover, this process is invertible in that the relations each determine the function. Defining an abstraction relation to be ***principal*** if it is induced as abs^L or abs^U from a function abs then generalises the notion of the principal type (amongst all types) of a value.

For example, given ABS above $\in \mathcal{R}(D_{CBN^*}, D_{HM})$ define $abs : D_{CBN^*} \to D_{HM}$ by $abs(d) = \bigsqcup\{s \mid d\ ABS\ s\}$ then $ABS = abs^L$. Similarly $ABS \in \mathcal{R}(D_{CBN}, D_{CBV})$ of the previous section is r^U induced from the retraction function $r : D_{CBN} \to D_{CBV}$ (note $D_{CBN} = D_{CBV}$) defined by

$$\begin{aligned} r(d) = \text{case } d \text{ of } & \bot \Rightarrow \bot \\ & in_Z(n) \Rightarrow in_Z(n) \\ & in_F(f) \Rightarrow in_F(\lambda d' \in D_{CBV}.d' = \bot \to \bot, r(fd')) \end{aligned}$$

CBN^* can be related to CBN by a similar retraction $unstar : D_{CBN^*} \to D_{CBN}$ given by

$$\begin{aligned} unstar(d) = \text{case } d \text{ of } & \bot \Rightarrow \bot \\ & in_W(wrong) \Rightarrow \bot \\ & in_Z(n) \Rightarrow in_Z(n) \\ & in_F(f) \Rightarrow in_F(\lambda d' \in D_{CBN}.unstar(fd')) \end{aligned}$$

Then $CBN^* \rhd_{unstar^U} CBN$. A similar relationship holds for CBV^* and CBV.

6.1 Inducing relations on recursive domains – strictness analysis

Certain interpretatations, *e.g.* the strictness analysis, SA and call-by-name CBN, CBN^* interpretations presented above, have the property that their underlying domains are closely related. If we have two interpretations $I = (D, lam, app)$ and $I' = (D', lam', app')$ with

$$D = A + (D \to D) \qquad D' = A' + (D' \to D')$$

and an abstraction relation $R \in \mathcal{R}(A, A')$ then we would like to lift R to a relation $R^* \in \mathcal{R}(D, D')$. The question is therefore as to whether there exists such an R^* such that $R^* = R + (R^* \to R^*)$ and, if so, whether it is unique. Formally we should require $R^* = \Phi \circ (R + (R^* \to R^*)) \circ \Phi^{-1}$ where Φ is the relation corresponding the the pair of isomorphisms $\phi : A + (D \to D) \to D$ and $\phi' : A' + (D' \to D') \to D'$. Of course, as we mentioned in section 3, there are three choices for the + symbol in the above. So let us try to find relations

$$R^\sharp = R +^L (R^\sharp \to R^\sharp) \qquad R^\flat = R +^U (R^\flat \to R^\flat)$$

These, if they exist, would correspond to the $\sharp$ and $\flat$ strictness analysis interpretations of [12] (part of [13]) provided merely that R is the universal relation in $\mathcal{R}(Z, \{\top\})$ corresponding to the function $\lambda n.\top$. Note how the difference between the interpretations is determined by the choice of + construction rather than by R.

The natural way to construct $R^\sharp, R^\flat$ is by essentially the inverse limit construction. Let R^* stand for $R^\sharp$ or $R^\flat$ and + for $+^L$ or $+^U$ respectively. Suppose D^n, D'^n are the nth iterates of the above recursive domain equation (with $D^0 = D'^0 = \{\bot\}$). Elements of D can now be considered to be certain members of $\prod_i D^i$. We can lift a relation $R^n \in \mathcal{R}(D^n, D'^n)$ to R^{n+1} by the usual logical relation definition, *i.e.* $R^{n+1} = R^n_{A+(D\to D)}$, with $R^0 = \{(\bot, \bot)\}$. One can now consider R^n

as a restriction of R^{n+1} *via* the retraction (this is a non-trivial lemma to be proved) and take the limit R^* determined by $(d_0,\ldots)R^*(d'_0,\ldots) \Leftrightarrow (\forall i)d_iR^id'_i$. Now we need to show that R^* satisfies the equation for $R^\sharp$ or $R^\flat$ above.

At the time of writing this proof of existence and uniqueness of $R^\sharp, R^\flat$ has not been done.

It seems that the best way to treat this generally would be to generalise Mulmuley's "predicate domains" to "relation domains" (D, D', R) where D, D' are domains and $R \in \mathcal{R}(D, D')$ and then define continuous operations $+^L, +^M, +^U, \times, \rightarrow$ (corresponding to his predictors) on them.

Abramsky[1] considers in much more detail the issue of strictness analysis in the framework of the typed λ-calculus.

7 Comparison with the power object and adjoined function framework

We first consider the conventional framework for abstract interpretation. (In this section most of the definitions are taken from [15] as representing the most up-to-date and most general treatment.)

We have two domains of *standard* values V_1, V_2 and two domains L_1, L_2 of *abstract* values. These domains interpret two sort symbols either as standard or abstract domains. Similarly, we have functions $f : V_1 \rightarrow V_2$ and $g : L_1 \rightarrow L_2$ representing *standard* and *abstract* interpretations of some function symbol. Moreover, we require some form of power object construction $\mathcal{P}(\cdot)$ on V_1 and V_2 together with an associated map $\mathcal{P}(f) : \mathcal{P}(V_1) \rightarrow \mathcal{P}(V_2)$. (This merely says that the power construction is a functor.) The domains $\mathcal{P}(V_i)$ and the function $\mathcal{P}(f)$ are refered to as the *collecting* interpretation although this is at some variance with the Cousots' use of the term.

Additionally, we require that the $\mathcal{P}(V_i)$ and L_i each possess two orders $(\subseteq, \sqsubseteq)$ with respect to which $\mathcal{P}(f)$ and g are monotonic. Typically a power object construction automatically provides $\subseteq$ and $\sqsubseteq$, the latter by the Egli-Milner ordering since the V_i are domains. (We can recover the Cousot-style (termination ignoring) framework by taking $\mathcal{P}(\cdot)$ to be the Hoare power domain in which $\subseteq = \sqsubseteq$ and L to be any complete lattice with $\subseteq$ defined to be $\sqsubseteq$.)

Following [15, p. 258] we require that there are abstraction and concretisation functions

$$abs_i : \mathcal{P}(V_i) \rightarrow L_i, \qquad conc_i : L_i \rightarrow \mathcal{P}(V_i)$$

which are both to be $\sqsubseteq$- and $\subseteq$-monotonic and to further satisfy (for all $s \in \mathcal{P}(V_i), l \in L_i$)

$$(abs_i \circ conc_i)(l) \subseteq l \text{ and } (conc_i \circ abs_i)(s) \supseteq s$$

Now, given the above set up, we say that f is *abstracted* by g if, for all $l \in L_1$, we have $(conc_2 \circ g)(l) \supseteq (\mathcal{P}(f) \circ conc_1)(l)$. This is [15, p. 253] and corresponds to *safety* in dataflow analysis. It is useful because it is preserved by composition and the taking of least fixpoints (modulo some conditions on the behaviour of $\subseteq$ at $\sqsubseteq$-limits).

To show how this idea forms a special case of our framework we define relations $ABS_i \in \mathcal{R}(V_i, L_i)$ by

$$v \; ABS_i \; l \Leftrightarrow v \in conc_i(l)$$

(One should be a little careful with $v \in conc_i(l)$ above — it is really just a shorthand for $\{v\} \subseteq conc_i(l)$.)

The benefit is that the second-order relation "f is abstracted by g" above is now merely equivalent to $f \; ABS_{1\rightarrow 2} \; g$, the natural logically induced relation on functions spaces, defined by

$$f \; ABS_{1\rightarrow 2} \; g \Leftrightarrow (\forall v \in V_1, l \in L_1)(v \; ABS_1 \; l \Rightarrow f(v) \; ABS_2 \; g(l))$$

Proof:

$$\begin{aligned} & (\forall l \in L_1)(conc_2 \circ g)(l) \supseteq (\mathcal{P}(f) \circ conc_1)(l) \\ \Leftrightarrow\ & (\forall l \in L_1)(conc_2 \circ g)(l) \supseteq \{f(v) \mid v \in V_1 \wedge v\ ABS_1\ l\} \\ \Leftrightarrow\ & (\forall l \in L_1)(\forall v \in V_1)(v\ ABS_1\ l \Rightarrow f(v) \in (conc_2 \circ g)(l)) \\ \Leftrightarrow\ & (\forall l \in L_1)(\forall v \in V_1)(v\ ABS_1\ l \Rightarrow f(v)\ ABS_2\ g(l)) \end{aligned}$$

as required.

Note how the relational framework does not require power objects (the problem of defining suitable power objects has so far precluded general use of abstract interpretation when higher order objects are involved). Moreover, the homologue of the collecting interpretation is now the standard interpretation, which is in itself pleasing.

8 The view from Categoria

The fly in the ointment here is that logical relations do not necessarily compose (we are grateful to Samson Abramsky for warning of this particular pitfall). This seems to destroy the intuitive idea from abstract interpretation that abstracting an abstraction yields another abstraction. Perhaps a suitable restriction upon the abstraction relations we consider would recover this property without losing too many interpretations from the general framework.

There seem to be two categorical views which we would otherwise like to put upon all of this. The first is the conventional one that we are dealing with a category whose objects are interpretations and whose arrows are abstractions.

The other view, which probably ought to be investigated further, is that we are dealing with (cartesian closed) categories, certain subcategories of which are interpretations (having sets (with structure) for objects and functions for morphisms) and relating them together using abstraction relations as generalised functors.

9 Conclusions and further work

This work grew out of our increasing dissatisfaction with the complexity and mathematical (foundational) difficulty of the power domain and adjoined function approach to abstract interpretation. This idea was originally developed by one of the authors[13] and further developed with Nielson[14,15]. However, we suspect that this (power domain) development may not endure.

The work presented here is a first attempt to both simplify the theory and to present a plausible theory of abstract interpretation for higher order objects. This is done by the use of relations instead of functions and power objects.

There are still many unanswered questions, such as

- There is a symmetrical treatment of the *ABS* relation. Surely there should be some characterisation as to which of two interpretations is 'more concrete'. Surjectivity appears not to work. Similarly, the problem of composing abstraction relations needs to be tackled.
- The theory needs to be developed into a general framework for relating two different (but of the same 'shape') denotatational semantics of the same programming language possibly along the lines of [15].
- Can the theory presented here be generalised so that it includes classical notions such as (traditional or continuous) algebraic interpretation and homomorphism as a special case?

Acknowledgements

We would like to thank Samson Abramsky and Mike Gordon for their comments on an earlier version of this paper presented at the workshop on *abstract interpretation* at Kent University, Canterbury in August 1985 organised by Samson Abramsky, Chris Hankin and Richard Sykes. Thanks also to Harrald Ganzinger for helping to organise the Copenhagen workshop. Financial support for the two workshops was provided by the British Science and Engineering Research Council and by the Danish Natural Research Council.

References

[1] Abramsky, S. Strictness analysis based on logical relations. Unpublished manuscript, 1985.

[2] Burn, G., Hankin, C. and Abramsky, S. The theory and practice of strictness analysis for higher order functions. Imperial college report DoC 85/6, 1985. To appear in *Science of Computer Programming.*

[3] Cousot, P. and Cousot, R. Abstract interpretation: a unified lattice model for static analysis of programs by construction and approximation of fixpoints. Proc. ACM symp. on Principles of Programming Languages, 1977.

[4] Damas, L. and Milner, R. Principal type schemes for functional programs. Proc. ACM symp. on Principles of Programming Languages, 1980.

[5] Donzeau-Gouge, V. Utilisation de la sémantique dénotationelle pour l'étude d'interprétations non-standard. INRIA rapport 273, 1978.

[6] Dybjer, P. Domain Algebras. Lecture Notes in Computer Science: Proc. 11th ICALP, vol. 172, Springer-Verlag, 1984.

[7] Jones, N.D. and Mycroft, A. Dataflow of applicative programs using minimal function graphs. Proc. ACM symp. on Principles of Programming Languages, 1986.

[8] Gordon, M. Models of pure LISP. Ph.D. thesis, Dept. of Artificial Intelligence, Edinburgh University, 1973.

[9] Hindley, J.R. The principal type scheme of an object in combinatory logic. Transactions of the Amer. Math. Soc., vol 146, pp 29-60, 1969.

[10] Milner, R. A theory of type polymorphism in programming. JCSS 1978.

[11] Mulmuley, K. A mechanisible theory for existence proofs of inclusive predicates. CMU computer science report CMU-CS-85-149, 1985.

[12] Mycroft, A. The theory and practice of transforming call-by-need into call-by-value. Lecture Notes in Computer Science: Proc. 4th intl. symp. on programming, vol. 83, Springer-Verlag, 1980.

[13] Mycroft, A. Abstract Interpretation and Optimising Transformations of Applicative Programs. Ph.D. thesis, Edinburgh University, 1981. Available as computer science report CST-15-81.

[14] Mycroft, A. and Nielson, F. Strong abstract interpretation using power domains. Lecture Notes in Computer Science: Proc. 10th ICALP, vol. 154, Springer-Verlag, 1983.

[15] Nielson, F. Abstract interpretation using domain theory. Ph.D. thesis, Edinburgh University, 1984. Available as computer science report CST-31-84.

[16] Plotkin, G. Lambda definability in the full type hierarchy. In [18].

[17] Reynolds, J.C. Types, abstraction and parametric polymorphism. IFIP 83, (ed) R.E.A. Mason, North-Holland, 1983.

[18] Seldin, J.P., and Hindley, J.R. To H.B. Curry: Essays on combinatory logic, lambda calculus and formalism. Academic Press, 1980.

[19] Stoy, J. Denotational semantics: the Scott-Strachey approach to programming language theory. MIT press, 1977.

EXPECTED FORMS OF DATA FLOW ANALYSES

by

Flemming Nielson
Institute of Electronic Systems
Aalborg University Centre
Strandvejen 19,4
DK-9000 Aalborg C
DENMARK

ABSTRACT

A previous paper developed a general denotational framework for specification of data flow analyses and for proofs of correctness (using abstract interpretation). In particular, the method of "inducing" specifies new data flow analyses that as precisely as possible approximate given data flow analyses.
However, from a practical point of view the induced versions of the functionals are "too precise" and this motivates a study of "expected forms" (or "normal forms"). This paper suggests such forms and shows the correctness of systematically using them.

1. INTRODUCTION

The purpose of data flow analysis is to compute properties about the computations of programs and the major application is in the code optimization phase of a compiler. This means that the data flow information must be

- provably correct, and
- computable within a reasonable time

in order to be useful.

The correctness issue has been addressed by the framework of abstract interpretation [CoCo 77, CoCo 79]. The meaning of a program pro is given by the standard semantics

$\underline{S}[\![\text{pro}]\!] : S \hookrightarrow S$

which is a partial function over a usually countably infinite set S. However, it is convenient to represent the semantics of pro by the collecting semantics

$\underline{C}[\![\text{pro}]\!] : \mathcal{P}(S) \rightarrow \mathcal{P}(S)$

defined by

$\underline{C}[\![\text{pro}]\!] = \lambda Y.\{v \in S \mid \exists u \in Y: \underline{S}[\![\text{pro}]\!](u) = v\}.$

A data flow analysis gives rise to a function (called an approximating semantics)

$\underline{I}[\![\text{pro}]\!] : L \rightarrow L$

where L is a set of data flow properties. The meaning of the data flow properties in L is given by a function

γ: L→P(S).

Correctness of the data flow analysis then amounts to requiring C⟦pro⟧ ($\gamma(\ell)$) to be a subset of γ(I⟦pro⟧ (ℓ)) for all ℓ in L. This is usually written

$$\underline{C}[\![\text{pro}]\!] \cdot \gamma \sqsubseteq \gamma \cdot \underline{I}[\![\text{pro}]\!] \qquad (*)$$

where $\sqsubseteq$ is the pointwise extension (to functions in L→P(S)) of the subset ordering on P(S).

Sets like L must be equipped with a partial ordering $\sqsubseteq$ and it is common to require L to be a complete lattice. The intention with $\sqsubseteq$ is to express when one property can safely be replaced by another property and this corresponds to the subset ordering on P(S). Concerning γ it is generally assumed that there exists a (necessarily unique) function α: P(S)→L such that

$$\alpha(Y) \sqsubseteq \ell \Leftrightarrow Y \subseteq \gamma(\ell).$$

Then (α,γ) is called an adjoined pair, α a lower adjoint and γ an upper adjoint. The intention with α is that it produces the best safe description of its argument. It facilitates reformulating (*) to

$$\alpha \cdot \underline{C}[\![\text{pro}]\!] \cdot \gamma \sqsubseteq \underline{I}[\![\text{pro}]\!] . \qquad (*')$$

It follows that

$$\alpha \cdot \underline{C}[\![\text{pro}]\!] \cdot \gamma: \text{L} \rightarrow \text{L}$$

it not only a safe data flow analysis but in fact the most precise among all safe data flow analyses that use L. It is said to be induced from C⟦pro⟧ .

Example

Take S to be the set of integers and let L be

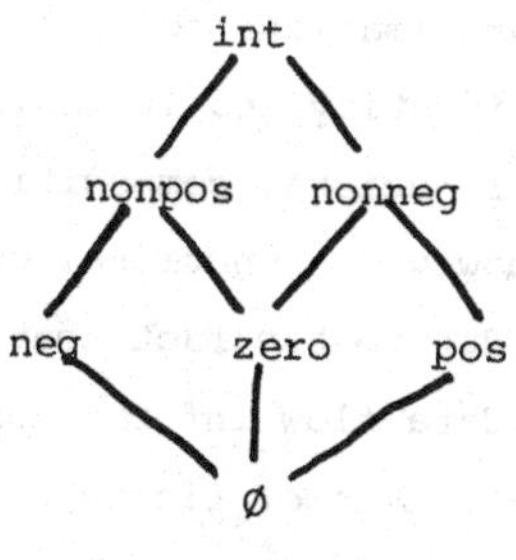

Then γ is specified by γ(neg) = $\{z \mid z<0\}$ etc. This gives an upper adjoint whose lower adjoint α satisfies $\alpha(\{27\})$=pos. (Note that pos is the best description of {27}.) The induced version of the squaring function then sends neg to pos, zero to zero, nonpos to nonneg and int to nonneg. □

The papers referenced above have considered the programming language of flowcharts. In [Nie 84, Nie 85a] the framework of abstract interpretation has been generalised to apply to all programming languages with a denotational definition in terms of a rather general metalanguage. This is done by interpreting a denotational definition in different ways so that all of $\underline{S}[\![\text{pro}]\!]$, $\underline{C}[\![\text{pro}]\!]$, and $\underline{I}[\![\text{pro}]\!]$ can be obtained as meanings of pro. (The details needed for the purposes of this paper are reviewed in section 2.) In particular the notion of inducing generalises to the functionals used to combine meanings of subprograms.

As an example functional consider sequencing. In the collecting semantics

$$\underline{C}[\![\text{pro}_1;\ \text{pro}_2]\!] = \underline{C}[\![\text{pro}_2]\!] \cdot \underline{C}[\![\text{pro}_1]\!]$$

and we shall record this by writing $\underline{C}(\square) = \lambda(g_1,g_2).g_1 \cdot g_2$. Analogously one expects

$$\underline{I}[\![\text{pro}_1;\ \text{pro}_2]\!] = \underline{I}(\square)(\underline{I}[\![\text{pro}_2]\!]\ ,\ \underline{I}[\![\text{pro}_1]\!]\ ).$$

To ensure that the data flow analysis specified by $\underline{I}$ is correct it is natural to require that

$$(\forall i:\ g_i \cdot \gamma \sqsubseteq \gamma \cdot h_i) \Rightarrow \underline{C}(\square)(g_2,g_1) \cdot \gamma \sqsubseteq \gamma \cdot \underline{I}(\square)(h_2,h_1) \qquad (\ddagger)$$

so that the composition of correct data flow analyses gives a correct data flow analysis. This condition plays the counterpart of (*) and by adjoinedness it may be reformulated [Nie 84, Nie 85a] as

$$\lambda(h_2,h_1).\ \alpha \cdot ((\gamma \cdot h_2 \cdot \alpha) \cdot (\gamma \cdot h_1 \cdot \alpha)) \cdot \gamma \sqsubseteq \underline{I}(\square) \qquad (\ddagger')$$

since all h_i, $I(\square)$ and $\underline{C}(\square)$ will be monotonic. As before this shows that the induced functional

$$\lambda(h_2,h_1).\ (\alpha \cdot \gamma) \cdot h_2 \cdot (\alpha \cdot \gamma) \cdot h_1 \cdot (\alpha \cdot \gamma)\ :\ (L \to L)^2 \to (L \to L)$$

is the most precise among all safe approximations to $\underline{C}(\square)$.

We have not assumed $\alpha \cdot \gamma$ to be the identity and it is in fact easy to find examples where the induced version of functional composition is not functional composition. For practical purposes, however, functional composition is preferable to the induced version. This is due to the fact that the functional must be implemented in such a way that the data flow information is computable within a reasonable amount of time. Even though L is of finite height (as usually guarantees computability) it is unclear how to implement the induced operator in a satisfactory manner. Functional composition, on the other hand, is readily implemented. It is then necessary to show that this is a safe solution, i.e. that

$$\lambda(h_2,h_1).\ (\alpha \cdot \gamma) \cdot h_2 \cdot (\alpha \cdot \gamma) \cdot h_1 \cdot (\alpha \cdot \gamma) \sqsubseteq \lambda(h_2,h_1).\ h_2 \cdot h_1.$$

Adjoinedness implies $\alpha \cdot \gamma \sqsubseteq \text{id}$ and that α and γ are monotonic so that when the h_i are also monotonic the condition holds.

It is the purpose of section 4 to consider expected forms for other functionals and to show the correctness of these. This makes use of the structural definition of adjoined pairs that is covered in section 3.

2. THE METALANGUAGE AND APPROXIMATING INTERPRETATIONS

The denotational framework of abstract interpretation [Nie 84, Nie 85a] uses a metalanguage whose types are:

$$ct ::= A_i \mid ct_1+\ldots+ct_k \mid ct_1\times\ldots\times ct_k \mid ct_1\rightarrow ct_2 \mid \text{rec } X.ct \mid X \mid ft$$

$$ft ::= rt_1 \underline{\rightarrow} rt_2$$

$$rt ::= \underline{A}_i \mid rt_1 \underline{+}\ldots\underline{+} rt_k \mid rt_1 \underline{\times}\ldots\underline{\times} rt_k \mid \underline{\text{rec}}\ \underline{X}.rt \mid \underline{X}$$

(for all $k\geq 2$). The types allow to distinguish between run-time domains (given by rt) and compile-time domains (given by ct). This is further motivated in [Nie 85a].

A closed type ct or rt is a type with no free domain variables X or $\underline{X}$. As is usual the semantics of a closed type ct is a cpo. A cpo D = $(D,\sqsubseteq)$ is just a partially ordered set with a least element $\bot=\bot_D$ and a least upper bound $\bigsqcup_n d_n$ of every chain $(d_n)_n$, i.e. of every sequence $d_1\sqsubseteq d_2\sqsubseteq\ldots$ The semantics $[\![A_i]\!]$ of A_i therefore is some fixed cpo, $[\![ct_1+\ldots+ct_k]\!]$ is the coalesced sum of the $[\![ct_i]\!]$, $[\![ct_1\times\ldots\times ct_k]\!]$ is the cartesian product of the $[\![ct_i]\!]$ and $[\![ct_1\rightarrow ct_2]\!]$ is the cpo of continuous functions from $[\![ct_1]\!]$ to $[\![ct_2]\!]$. A continuous function f: D→E is just a total function that satisfies both the monotonicity condition $d\sqsubseteq e \Rightarrow f(d)\sqsubseteq f(e)$ and the condition $f(\bigsqcup_n d_n) = \bigsqcup_n f(d_n)$. For the purposes of this paper it is not necessary to consider rec X.ct and X. Finally, $[\![rt_1 \underline{\rightarrow} rt_2]\!]$ is the cpo of strict and continuous functions from $[\![rt_1]\!]$ to $[\![rt_2]\!]$, i.e. of continuous functions mapping $\bot$ to $\bot$.

The semantics of a closed type rt will also be a cpo but it will vary from one data flow analysis to another. To formalise this a data flow analysis will be represented as a so-called approximating interpretation $\underline{I}$ and the semantics $\underline{I}[\![rt]\!]$ of rt will be relative to this. An approximating interpretation $\underline{I}$ must specify the cpo's denoted by base domains $\underline{A}_i$. It is convenient to restrict the cpo's allowed to the algebraic complete lattices. A cpo D is algebraic if the set

$$B_D = \{\ b\in D \mid \text{for all chains } (d_n)_n:\ b\sqsubseteq \bigsqcup_n d_n \Rightarrow \exists n:\ b\sqsubseteq d_n\ \}$$

of finite elements is countable and satisfies

$$d = \bigsqcup\{\ b\in B_D \mid b\sqsubseteq d\}\ \text{for all d.}$$

A cpo D is a complete lattice if every subset Y of D has a least upper bound. This restriction is quite natural for data flow analyses and includes the collecting semantics. It excludes the standard semantics but this is not a problem because the standard and the collecting semantics are related as sketched in the Introduction [Nie 84, Nie 85a].

To deal with recursive domains (rec X.rt and X) we shall largely follow the approach of [SmPl 82] where a type denotes a functor over a category. So let ACLs be the category [ArMa 75] that has algebraic complete lattices as objects and strict, continuous functions as morphisms. Then $\underline{I}[\![\underline{X}]\!] : \text{ACLs}^N \to \text{ACLs}$ is a projection functor (ignoring the details of [Nie 84] of connecting domain variables with positions) and $\underline{I}[\![\underline{A}_i]\!] : \text{ACLs}^N \to \text{ACLs}$ is the constant functor over the cpo $\underline{I}(\underline{A}_i)$. To handle $\underline{C}[\![rt_1 \underline{\times} \ldots \underline{\times} rt_k]\!]$ we shall need a weaker concept than functor.

Definition

A function f: D→E is totally strict iff $f(d) = \bot \Leftrightarrow d=\bot$ and is additive iff $f(d_1 \sqcup d_2) = f(d_1) \sqcup f(d_2)$. A semifunctor F: $\text{ACLs}^N \to \text{ACLs}$ sends N objects $D_1,\ldots,D_N$ to one object $F(D_1,\ldots,D_N)$ and N morphisms $f_i: D_i \to D_i'$ to one morphism $F(f_1,\ldots,f_N)$. It satisfies

$$F(id,\ldots,id) = id$$

$$F(f_1 \cdot g_1,\ldots,f_N \cdot g_N) \sqsubseteq F(f_1,\ldots,f_N) \cdot F(g_1,\ldots,g_N)$$

$F(f_1,\ldots,f_N)$ is additive and totally strict if all f_i are and then = holds above

A locally continuous semifunctor (abbreviated ℓ.c.semifunctor) is a semifunctor where all $\lambda(f_1,\ldots,f_N).F(f_1,\ldots,f_N)$ are continuous. □

The functors $\underline{I}[\![\underline{X}]\!]$ and $\underline{I}[\![\underline{A}_i]\!]$ are ℓ.c. semifunctors. An approximating interpretation must specify ℓ.c. semifunctors $\underline{I}(\underline{+})$ and $\underline{I}(\underline{\times})$ and then

$$\underline{I}[\![rt_1 \underline{+} \ldots \underline{+} rt_k]\!] = \underline{I}(\underline{+}) \cdot (\underline{I}[\![rt_1]\!], \ldots, \underline{I}[\![rt_k]\!])$$

$$\underline{I}[\![rt_1 \underline{\times} \ldots \underline{\times} rt_k]\!] = \underline{I}(\underline{\times}) \cdot (\underline{I}[\![rt_1]\!], \ldots, \underline{I}[\![rt_k]\!])$$

where · is composition and (...,...,...) is tupling.

To handle $\underline{\text{rec}}\ \underline{X}_{N+1} \cdot rt$ define a semifunctor $\underline{I}(D_1,\ldots,D_N)[\![rt]\!]$ by

$$\underline{I}(D_1,\ldots,D_N)[\![rt]\!](D) = \underline{I}[\![rt]\!](D_1,\ldots,D_N,D)$$

$$\underline{I}(D_1,\ldots,D_N)[\![rt]\!](f) = \underline{I}[\![rt]\!](id_{D_1},\ldots,id_{D_N},f).$$

Let U be a one-element cpo and let an embedding be a lower adjoint e whose upper adjoint e^u is continuous and satisfies $e^u \cdot e = id$. As usual [SmPl 82] we obtain a chain

$$(\underline{I}(D_1,\ldots,D_N)[\![rt]\!]^n(U), \underline{I}(D_1,\ldots,D_N)[\![rt]\!]^n(\bot))$$

in the subcategory ACLe of embeddings. For a specific choice of a limiting cone $(D,r_n) = \text{LIMIT}(rt;D_1,\ldots,D_N)$ we put

$\underline{I}[\![\underline{rec}\ \underline{X}_{N+1}.rt]\!]\ (D_1,\ldots,D_N) = D.$

Next write

$\underline{I}(f_1,\ldots,f_N)[\![rt]\!]\ (f) = \underline{I}[\![rt]\!]\ (f_1,\ldots,f_N,f)$

and define

$\underline{I}[\![\underline{rec}\ \underline{X}_{N+1}.rt]\!]\ (f_1,\ldots,f_N) = \bigsqcup_n r_n' \cdot \underline{I}(f_1,\ldots,f_N)[\![rt]\!]^n(\bot) \cdot r_n^u$

for f_i: $D_i \to D_i'$ and $(D',r_n') = \mathrm{LIMIT}(rt;D_1',\ldots,D_N')$. It is a straightforward structural induction to show that $\underline{I}[\![rt]\!]$: $\underline{\underline{ACLs}}^N \to \underline{\underline{ACLs}}$ is an ℓ.c. semifunctor.

Example

The collecting semantics of types.

To specify the type part of the collecting interpretation we must specify $\underline{C}(\underline{A}_i)$, $\underline{C}(\underline{+})$, and $\underline{C}(\underline{\times})$. A natural choice for $\underline{C}(\underline{A}_i)$ is $\mathcal{P}(S_i)$ for some countable sets S_i. (In [Nie 84, Nie 85a] the relational powerdomains of algebraic and possibly flat cpo's are used instead.) For $\underline{C}(\underline{+})$ we shall use the cartesian product functor × which may easily be shown to be an ℓ.c. semifunctor. As explained in [Nie 85a] this is motivated by the isomorphism between the powerset of a disjoint union and the cartesian product of powersets. Finally, $\underline{C}(\underline{\times})$ will be the tensor product ⊗ [Nie 84, Nie 85b] further described in section 3. It satisfies that $\mathcal{P}(S) \otimes \mathcal{P}(S)$ is isomorphic to $\mathcal{P}(S\times S)$ and the need to consider semifunctors are due to the fact that ⊗ is not a functor over $\underline{\underline{ACLs}}$. □

To complete the presentation of the metalanguage we must consider the expressions. The notation relating to compile-time types is rather standard and does not enter into the consideration of expected forms. The notation relating to run-time types may be defined as follows:

$e ::= f_i$	constants
$\mid e_1 \Box e_2$	composition
$\mid \mathrm{cond}(e_1,e_2,e_3)$	conditional
$\mid \mathrm{case}(e_1,\ldots,e_k) \mid \mathrm{in}_i$	operations upon $\underline{+}$
$\mid \mathrm{tuple}(e_1,\ldots,e_k) \mid \mathrm{take}_i$	operations upon $\underline{\times}$
$\mid$ fold $\mid$ unfold	operations upon $\underline{rec}$

This is subject to certain requirements upon the types, e.g. that the type of e_1 is of the form $rt_2 \underline{\to} rt_3$ and that the type of e_2 is of the form $rt_1 \underline{\to} rt_2$ so that $e_1 \Box e_2$ has type $rt_1 \underline{\to} rt_3$. These requirements will be implicitly stated below in the definition of the expression part of $\underline{I}$.

An approximating interpretation $\underline{I}$ must specify the semantics of all primitive operators. This amounts to

- a family of constants $\underline{I}(f_i) \in \underline{I}[\![ct_i]\!]$ for so-called contravariantly pure types ct_i [Nie 84, Nie 85a], e.g. $ct_i = rt_i \underline{\rightarrow} rt_i'$
- families of functions

  $\underline{I}(in_i) \in \underline{I}[\![rt_i \underline{\rightarrow} rt_1 \underline{+} \ldots \underline{+} rt_k]\!]$

  $\underline{I}(take_i) \in \underline{I}[\![rt_1 \underline{\times} \ldots \underline{\times} rt_k \underline{\rightarrow} rt_i]\!]$

  $\underline{I}(fold) \in \underline{I}[\![rt[\underline{rec}\ \underline{X}.rt/\underline{X}] \underline{\rightarrow}\ \underline{rec}\ \underline{X}.rt]\!]$

  where ...[.../...] is syntactic substitution

  $\underline{I}(unfold) \in \underline{I}[\![\underline{rec}\ \underline{X}.rt \underline{\rightarrow} rt[\underline{rec}\ \underline{X}.rt/\underline{X}]]\!]$

- families of functionals

  $\underline{I}(\square) \in \underline{I}[\![(rt_2 \underline{\rightarrow} rt_3) \times (rt_1 \underline{\rightarrow} rt_2) \rightarrow (rt_1 \underline{\rightarrow} rt_3)]\!]$

  $\underline{I}(cond) \in \underline{I}[\![(rt \underline{\rightarrow} \underline{T}) \times (rt \underline{\rightarrow} rt') \times (rt \underline{\rightarrow} rt') \rightarrow (rt \underline{\rightarrow} rt')]\!]$

  where $\underline{T}$ is some $\underline{A}_i$ intended to model truth-values

  $\underline{I}(case) \in \underline{I}[\![(rt_1 \underline{\rightarrow} rt) \times \ldots \times (rt_k \underline{\rightarrow} rt) \rightarrow (rt_1 \underline{+} \ldots \underline{+} rt_k \underline{\rightarrow} rt)]\!]$

  $\underline{I}(tuple) \in \underline{I}[\![(rt \underline{\rightarrow} rt_1) \times \ldots \times (rt \underline{\rightarrow} rt_k) \rightarrow (rt \underline{\rightarrow} rt_1 \underline{\times} \ldots \underline{\times} rt_k)]\!]$

The definition of $\underline{I}[\![e]\!]$ is then by a straightforward structural induction.

Example

The collecting semantics of expressions.

It should be stressed that the definitions given below are in no way ad hoc but are forced by the close connection between the collecting semantics and a natural standard semantics [Nie 84, Nie 85a]. In the definition we shall take the liberty of assuming that each $\underline{C}[\![rt]\!]$ is a powerdomain although the definitions in the previous example only guarantee isomorphism. We have

$$\underline{C}(\square)(g_1,g_2) = g_1 \cdot g_2$$

$$\underline{C}(cond)(g_1,g_2,g_3) = \lambda Y.\ g_2(\{y \in Y | g_1(\{y\}) \ni true\}) \cup g_3(\{y \in Y | g_1(\{y\}) \ni false\})$$

$$\underline{C}(case)(g_1,\ldots,g_k) = \lambda(Y_1,\ldots,Y_k).g_1(Y_1) \cup \ldots \cup g_k(Y_k)$$

$$\underline{C}(in_i) = \lambda Y.(\emptyset,\ldots,Y,\ldots,\emptyset)$$

$$\underline{C}(tuple)(g_1,\ldots,g_k) = \lambda Y.\bigcup\{g_1(\{y\}) \times \ldots \times g_k(\{y\}) | y \in Y\}$$

$$\underline{C}(take_i) = \lambda Y.\{y_i | (y_1,\ldots,y_k) \in Y\}$$

$$\underline{C}(fold) = \bigcup_n r_{n+1} \cdot \underline{C}[\![rt]\!] (r_n)^u$$

$$\underline{C}(unfold) = \bigcup_n \underline{C}[\![rt]\!] (r_n) \cdot r_{n+1}^u$$

for appropriate embeddings r_n. For a constant f_i of type $rt \underline{\rightarrow} rt'$ we have $\underline{C}(f_i) = \lambda Y.\{v | \exists u \in Y: \phi_i(u) = v\}$ for a function ϕ_i. □

3. RELATIONSHIPS BETWEEN DATA FLOW ANALYSES

In this section it is shown how to relate two data flow analyses that are represented as approximating interpretations $\underline{I}$ and $\underline{J}$. (The collecting interpretation $\underline{C}$ is a natural candidate for $\underline{I}$.) Concerning run-time types the goal is to define pairs

$$(\alpha_{rt}: \underline{I}[\![rt]\!] \to \underline{J}[\![rt]\!] \text{ , } \gamma_{rt}: \underline{J}[\![rt]\!] \to \underline{I}[\![rt]\!])$$

of adjoined functions. The presence of recursive domains means that one cannot restrict attention to closed types. For a type rt with domain variables among $\underline{X}_1,\ldots,\underline{X}_N$ we thus consider

$$A_{rt}(\alpha_1,\ldots,\alpha_N): \underline{I}[\![rt]\!]\,(L_1,\ldots,L_N) \to \underline{J}[\![rt]\!]\,(M_1,\ldots,M_N)$$

$$\Gamma_{rt}(\gamma_1,\ldots,\gamma_N): \underline{J}[\![rt]\!]\,(M_1,\ldots,M_N) \to \underline{I}[\![rt]\!]\,(L_1,\ldots,L_N)$$

where $\alpha_i: L_i \to M_i$ and $\gamma_i: M_i \to L_i$. For a closed type rt one then uses $\alpha_{rt} = A_{rt}(\ )$ and $\gamma_{rt} = \Gamma_{rt}(\ )$.

For technical reasons we shall assume all functions α and γ to be morhpisms of ACLs; it is argued in [Nie 84] that this is not a severe limitation. It is sometimes desirable that a pair (α,γ) is not only adjoined but exactly adjoined which means that $\alpha\cdot\gamma$=id. This is because γ: M→L then is one-one (and α is onto) so that M contains no superfluous elements (as is discussed in [CoCo 79]). Both of these adjoinedness conditions interact well with ℓ.c. semifunctors:

Fact

If F: $\text{ACLs}^N \to$ ACLs is an ℓ.c. semifunctor and each pair (α_i,γ_i) is (exactly) adjoined then so is $(F(\alpha_1,\ldots,\alpha_N),\ F(\gamma_1,\ldots,\gamma_N))$. □

Proof

Adjoinedness of a pair (α,γ) of ACLs morphisms may be reformulated as $\alpha\cdot\gamma \sqsubseteq$ id and $\gamma\cdot\alpha \sqsupseteq$ id. Furthermore, a lower adjoint α is additive and is totally strict (because the upper adjoint γ is strict). Using that F is an ℓ.c. semifunctor the result is then straightforward, e.g.

$$F(\gamma_1,\ldots,\gamma_N)\cdot F(\alpha_1,\ldots,\alpha_N) \sqsupseteq F(\gamma_1\cdot\alpha_1,\ldots,\gamma_N\cdot\alpha_N) \sqsupseteq F(id,\ldots,id) = id$$ □

It follows from this fact that F specialises to a covariant functor over the category ACLsℓ of lower adjoints of ACLs. Likewise for the category ACLsu of upper adjoints.

The structural induction of A_{rt} and Γ_{rt} is similar so we concentrate upon the former. We have

$$A_{\underline{A}_i}(\alpha_1,\ldots,\alpha_N) = \text{some previously specified lower adjoint } \alpha_{\underline{A}_i}$$

$$A_{\underline{X}_i}(\alpha_1,\ldots,\alpha_N) = \alpha_i.$$

For recursive domains the definition models that of $[\![\underline{\text{rec}}\ \underline{X}.rt]\!] (f_1,\dots,f_N)$ so we have

$$A_{\underline{\text{rec}}\ \underline{X}.rt}(\alpha_1,\dots,\alpha_N) = \bigsqcup_n r'_n \cdot (A(\alpha_1,\dots,\alpha_N)_{rt})^n(\bot)\cdot r_n^u$$

where

$$A(\alpha_1,\dots,\alpha_N)_{rt}\ (\alpha_{N+1}) = A_{rt}(\alpha_1,\dots,\alpha_N,\alpha_{N+1})$$

and r'_n and r_n are the appropriate embeddings.

For sums the idea is to first transform each "component" and then transform from $\underline{I}(\underline{+})$ to $\underline{J}(\underline{+})$. This leads to

$$A_{rt_1\underline{+}\dots\underline{+}rt_k}(\alpha_1,\dots,\alpha_N) = A_{\underline{I}(\underline{+})\underline{J}(\underline{+})}(\underline{J}[\![rt_1]\!] (M_1,\dots,M_N),\dots,\underline{J}[\![rt_k]\!] (M_1,\dots,M_N$$
$$\cdot\ \underline{I}(\underline{+})(A_{rt_1}(\alpha_1,\dots,\alpha_N),\dots,A_{rt_k}(\alpha_1,\dots,\alpha_N)).$$

For N = 0 this may be illustrated as the lower path in

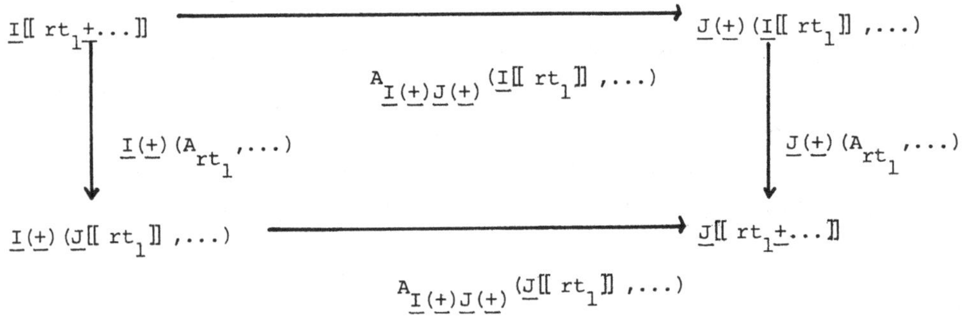

The semifunctor $\underline{I}(\underline{+})$ is a functor upon the lower adjoints and embodies the notion of "componentwise", e.g. when $\underline{I}=\underline{C}$ we have

$$\underline{C}(\underline{+})(A_{rt_1},\dots,A_{rt_k})(\ell_1,\dots,\ell_k) = (A_{rt_1}(\ell_1),\dots,A_{rt_k}(\ell_k)).$$

The function $A_{\underline{I}(\underline{+})\underline{J}(\underline{+})}(\dots)$ transforms from $\underline{I}(\underline{+})$ to $\underline{J}(\underline{+})$. When $\underline{I}(\underline{+}) = \underline{J}(\underline{+})$ we assume it is the identity and an example when $\underline{I}(\underline{+}) \neq \underline{J}(\underline{+})$ is given below. We require A... to be a natural transformation [ArMa 75] from $\underline{I}(\underline{+})$ to $\underline{J}(\underline{+})$, all restricted to ACLs$\ell$, so that the order of transformation is unimportant, i.e. the above diagram commutes. The treatment of product is analogous and thus we obtain the desired pair of adjoined functions:

<u>Lemma</u>

When all (α_i,γ_i) and all $(A_{\underline{I}(\underline{+})\underline{J}(\underline{+})}(\dots),\Gamma_{\underline{I}(\underline{+})\underline{J}(\underline{+})}(\dots)),(A_{\underline{I}(\underline{\times})\underline{J}(\underline{\times})}(\dots),$ $\Gamma_{\underline{I}(\underline{\times})\underline{J}(\underline{\times})}(\dots))$ are (exactly) adjoined then so are all $(\alpha_{rt},\gamma_{rt}) = (A_{rt}(\ ),$ $\Gamma_{rt}(\ ))$. □

Change of method for $\underline{+}$

The collecting interpretation used $\underline{C}(\underline{+})$ because of the isomorphism between the powerset of a disjoint union and the cartesian product of powersets. In general one may consider using $\underline{I}(\underline{+}) = \times$ because intuitively the most precise way of combining properties for summands is to have one property for each summand. For a more approximative way of combining properties one may use a $\underline{J}(\underline{+})$ that behaves like a sum. This corresponds to what is done in [Don 78] and motivates the definition of $\oplus$ below.

The sum $D_1\oplus\ldots\oplus D_k$ is defined to have the elements

$$D_1\oplus\ldots\oplus D_k = \{\bot,\top\} \cup \bigcup_{i=1}^{k}\{i\}\times(D_i-\{\bot\})$$

for new symbols $\bot$ and $\top$. The partial order $\sqsubseteq$ is defined by

$$d\sqsubseteq d' \leftrightarrow (d=\bot) \vee (d'=\top) \vee (d\downarrow 1=d'\downarrow 1 \wedge d\downarrow 2\sqsubseteq d'\downarrow 2).$$

It is straightforward to verify that this is a complete lattice and that it is algebraic when all of the D_i are (because the new $\top$ is a finite element). We may extend $\oplus$ to a functor over ACLs by defining

$$f_1\oplus\ldots\oplus f_k = \lambda d. \begin{cases} \bot & \text{if } d=\bot \text{ or } d=(i,d_i)\wedge f_i(d_i)=\bot \\ (i,f_i(d_i)) & \text{if } d=(i,d_i)\wedge f_i(d_i)\neq\bot \\ \top & \text{if } d=\top \end{cases}$$

as this gives a morphism in ACLs. When the f_i are totally strict and additive also $f_1\oplus\ldots\oplus f_k$ is totally strict and additive and we have:

Lemma

$\oplus$: $\text{ACLs}^k \rightarrow \text{ACLs}$ is a locally continuous semifunctor. □

Assume now that $\underline{I}(\underline{+})=\times$ and $\underline{J}(\underline{+})=\oplus$ and consider how to pass between these semifunctors. Define

$$A_{\times\oplus}(D_1,\ldots,D_k) = \lambda(d_1,\ldots,d_k). \begin{cases} \bot & \text{if } \emptyset=\{j\,|\,d_j\neq\bot\} \\ (i,d_i) & \text{if } \{i\} = \{j\,|\,d_j\neq\bot\} \\ \top & \text{otherwise} \end{cases}$$

and

$$\Gamma_{\times\oplus}(D_1,\ldots,D_k) = \lambda d. \begin{cases} (\bot,\ldots,\bot) & \text{if } d=\bot \\ (\bot,\ldots,d_i,\ldots,\bot) & \text{if } d=(i,d_i) \\ (\top,\ldots,\top) & \text{if } d=\top \end{cases}$$

We then have:

Lemma

$A_{\times\oplus}$ is a natural transformation from $\times$ to $\oplus$ (over ACLsℓ) and $\Gamma_{\times\oplus}$ is a natural transformation from $\oplus$ to $\times$ (over ACLsu) and all $(A_{\times\oplus}(\ldots),\Gamma_{\times\oplus}(\ldots))$ are exactly adjoined. □

Exact adjoinedness is because the least elements of D_i are all identified with the least element in $D_1 \oplus \ldots \oplus D_k$. That $A_{\times\oplus}$ is a natural transformation is because

$$f_1 \oplus \ldots \oplus f_k \cdot A_{\times\oplus}(\ldots) = A_{\times\oplus}(\ldots) \cdot f_1 \times \ldots \times f_k$$

holds for all totally strict functions and because lower adjoints of ACLs are totally strict.

Change of Method for $\times$

There are two well-known methods for combining properties of elements to properties of tuples [JoMu 81]. In the relational method the interdependencies of the components are recorded. An example is the collecting semantics where $\underline{C}(\times)(\mathcal{P}(S_1),\ldots,\mathcal{P}(S_k))$ is isomorphic to $\mathcal{P}(S_1 \times \ldots \times S_k)$. In the independent attribute method the interdependency is not recorded but only the possibilities in each component. In [Nie 85b] it is shown that these methods may be modelled by the tensor product $\circledast$ and the smash product $*$, respectively.

To define the smash product we need the auxiliary function smash defined by

$$\text{smash}(d_1,\ldots,d_k) = \begin{cases} (\bot,\ldots,\bot) & \text{if some } d_i = \bot \\ (d_1,\ldots,d_k) & \text{otherwise} \end{cases}$$

The smash product is then defined by

$$D_1 * \ldots * D_k = \{ \text{smash}(d_1,\ldots,d_k) \mid (d_1,\ldots,d_k) \in D_1 \times \ldots \times D_k \}$$

and it may be extended to a functor over ACLs by defining

$$f_1 * \ldots * f_k = \lambda(d_1,\ldots,d_k).\ \text{smash}(f_1(d_1),\ldots,f_k(d_k))$$

Lemma

$*$: $\text{ACLs}^k \to \text{ACLs}$ is an ℓ.c. semifunctor. □

To define the tensor product call a function f: $D_1 * \ldots * D_k \to D$ separately additive if all

$$\lambda d_i.\ f(\text{smash}(d_1,\ldots,d_i,\ldots,d_k)): D_i \to D$$

are additive.

Definition

A tensor product [ArMa 75] assigns to any k objects $D_1,\ldots,D_k$

- an object $D_1 \circledast \ldots \circledast D_k$
- a separately additive morphism cross: $D_1 * \ldots * D_k \to D_1 \circledast \ldots \circledast D_k$ called the inclusion

such that

for every separately additive morphism $f: D_1 * \ldots * D_k \to D$
there is precisely one additive morphism $f^*: D_1 \circledast \ldots \circledast D_k \to D$
(called the <u>extension</u> of f) such that $f^* \cdot cross = f$. □

In [Nie 84, Nie 85a] it is shown that a tensor product always exists and that defining

$$f_1 \circledast \ldots \circledast f_k = (cross \cdot f_1 * \ldots * f_k)^*$$

gives

<u>Lemma</u>

$\circledast$: $\underline{\underline{ACLs}}^k \to \underline{\underline{ACLs}}$ is an ℓ.c. semifunctor □

The connection with the collecting semantics is given by defining

$$P(S_1) \circledast \ldots \circledast P(S_k) = P(S_1 \times \ldots \times S_k)$$

$$cross = \lambda(Y_1, \ldots, Y_k). Y_1 \times \ldots \times Y_k$$

$$f^* = \lambda Y. \bigcup\{f(\{y_k\}, \ldots, \{y_k\}) \mid (y_1, \ldots, y_k) \in Y\}$$

and showing that this satisfies the definition of a tensor product.

Let now $\underline{I}(\underline{\times}) = \circledast$ and $\underline{J}(\underline{\times}) = *$ and consider how to pass between these semifunctors. Define

$$A_{\circledast *}(D_1, \ldots, D_k) = id^*$$

$$\Gamma_{\circledast *}(D_1, \ldots, D_k) = cross$$

It follows from [Nie 84, Nie 85b] that:

<u>Lemma</u>

$A_{\circledast *}$ is a natural transformation from $\circledast$ to $*$ (over $\underline{\underline{ACLs\ell}}$), $\Gamma_{\circledast *}$ is a natural transformation from $*$ to $\circledast$ (over $\underline{\underline{ACLsu}}$) and all $(A_{\circledast *}(\ldots), \Gamma_{\circledast *}(\ldots))$ are exactly adjoined. □

<u>Compile-time Types</u>

The definitions of pairs$(\alpha_{rt}, \gamma_{rt})$ of adjoined functions suffice for relating $\underline{I}[\![rt]\!]$ and $\underline{J}[\![rt]\!]$. To relate elements of $\underline{I}[\![ct]\!]$ with elements of $\underline{J}[\![ct]\!]$ we define a relation

$$\underline{<}^{\gamma}_{ct}: \underline{I}[\![ct]\!] \times \underline{J}[\![ct]\!] \to \{true, false\}$$

(abbreviated to $\underline{<}_{ct}$ or $\underline{<}$). It is given by

$$g \ \underline{<}^{\gamma}_{rt \underline{\to} rt'} \ h \Leftrightarrow g \cdot \gamma_{rt} \sqsubseteq \gamma_{rt'} \cdot h$$

$$(g_1,\ldots,g_k) \underline{<}^{\gamma}_{ct_1\times\ldots\times ct_k} (h_1,\ldots,h_k) \Leftrightarrow \forall i\colon g_i \underline{<}^{\gamma}_{ct_i} h_i$$

$$G \underline{<}^{\gamma}_{ct\to ct'} H \Leftrightarrow [\forall g,h\colon g \underline{<}^{\gamma}_{ct} h \Rightarrow G(g) \underline{<}^{\gamma}_{ct'} H(h)].$$

In [Nie 85a] this relation is extended to all types ct and to approximating interpretations but this will not be needed here. The intuition behind $u \underline{<} v$ is that v is a safe approximation to u. Hence $\underline{<}$ is the relation to be used when showing the correctness of data flow analyses. (One may check that $\underline{<}_{(\underline{rt\to rt})\times(\underline{rt\to rt})\to(\underline{rt\to rt})}$ is the relation expressed by the equation (‡) in the Introduction.)

The notion of inducing [CoCo 79, Nie 85a] may then be explained as follows. The induced version of u ∈ $\underline{I}$[[ct]] is $\mathrm{induce}^{\gamma}_{ct}(u)$ ∈ $\underline{J}$[[ct]] such that

$$u \underline{<}^{\gamma}_{ct} \mathrm{induce}^{\gamma}_{ct}(u)$$

(so that $\mathrm{induce}^{\gamma}_{ct}(u)$ is a safe approximation to u) and

$$u \underline{<}^{\gamma}_{ct} v \Rightarrow \mathrm{induce}^{\gamma}_{ct}(u) \underline{<}^{id}_{ct} v$$

(so that $\mathrm{induce}^{\gamma}_{ct}(u)$ is as precise as possible). One may check that (*') and (‡') of the Introduction are special cases of this.

4. EXPECTED FORMS

In the Introduction it was argued that the induced versions of functionals need not be desirable from a practical point of view. It was therefore suggested to use so-called "expected forms" (like functional composition for □). This section lists several expected forms and shows the correctness of using these. As a guide towards what is a "reasonable" expected form we shall consider the collecting semantics (where the definitions are "forced").

Conditional

The definition in the collecting semantics may be rephrased as follows:

$$\underline{C}(\mathrm{cond})(g_1,g_2,g_3) = g_2\cdot\underline{C}(\mathrm{filter}_{true})(g_1) \sqcup g_3\cdot\underline{C}(\mathrm{filter}_{false})(g_1)$$

$$\underline{C}(\mathrm{filter}_x)(g) = \lambda Y.\ \bigsqcup\{\{y\}\underline{\subseteq}Y \mid \{x\}\underline{\subseteq}g(\{y\})\ \}.$$

Postponing the issue of an expected form for filter_x it is natural to consider

$$\underline{I}(\mathrm{cond})(g_1,g_2,g_3) = g_2\cdot\underline{I}(\mathrm{filter}_{true})(g_1) \sqcup g_3\cdot\underline{I}(\mathrm{filter}_{false})(g_1)$$

as the expected form of conditional. This expresses the obvious intuition that part of the argument must be propagated along the true branch and part of the argument along the false branch. As in the Introduction the expected form is not preserved by inducing but it is straightforward to verify that it is safe to use the expected form, i.e. that

$$\underline{I}(\mathrm{filter}_x) \underline{<} \underline{J}(\mathrm{filter}_x) \Rightarrow \underline{I}(\mathrm{cond}) \underline{<} \underline{J}(\mathrm{cond})$$

when both $\underline{I}$ and $\underline{J}$ use the expected form.

The expected form for filter_x is less immediate. A simple possibility is to use $\underline{I}(\text{filter}_x)(g) = \lambda\ell.\ell$ corresponding to what is done in many practical data flow analyses. This is unsatisfactory because it does not incorporate the definition of $\underline{C}(\text{filter}_x)$ as a special case. Turning the attention to the formula for $\underline{C}(\text{filter}_x)$ displayed above it is apparent that $\cup$ and $\subseteq$ should be generalised to $\sqcup$ and $\sqsubseteq$ respectively. The remaining problem is to find a generalisation of the notion of a singleton. The idea is that $\{y\}$ is a "primitive" amount of information that is contained in Y and filter_x collects the appropriate "primitives".

One approach to when an element ℓ is "primitive" is that it should not be decomposable into parts. This motivated the requirement in [Nie 84] that ℓ must be irreducible, i.e. $\ell=\ell_1 \sqcup \ell_2 \Rightarrow \ell=\ell_1 \vee \ell=\ell_2$. Here we shall go one step further and require ℓ to be an atom:

$$\forall \ell': \ell \sqsupseteq \ell' \sqsupseteq \bot \Rightarrow \ell' \in \{\ell,\bot\} \wedge \ell \neq \bot.$$

We write A_L for the set of atoms of L and clearly an atom is finite as well as irreducible. The atoms in $P(S)$ are the singletons $\{s\}$ for $s\in S$ (and $\emptyset$ is the only irreducible element that is not an atom). In the complete lattice L from the Introduction the atoms are neg, zero, and pos (and $\emptyset$ is the only irreducible element that is not an atom). The focus on atoms rather than general irreducible elements is motivated by the properties of * [Nie 84]. It is interesting to note that the atoms correspond to the "cases" in the type structures of [ShWa 77].

Let now $I_x \in \underline{I}[\![\, \underline{T}]\!]$ model the truthvalue x and suppose g is an element of $\underline{I}[\![\, rt \underline{\to} \underline{T}]\!]$. Then

$$\underline{I}(\text{filter}_x)(g) = \lambda\ell.\bigsqcup\{\, \ell' \in A_{\underline{I}[\![rt]\!]} \mid \ell' \underline{\sqsubseteq} \ell \wedge I_x \underline{\sqsubseteq} g(\ell') \,\}$$

is the expected form of filter_x. It is convenient to reformulate this to

$$\underline{I}(\text{filter}_x)(g) = \text{lin}(\, \lambda\ell.I_x \underline{\sqsubseteq} g(\ell) \to \ell,\bot)$$

$$\text{lin}(g) = \lambda\ell.\bigsqcup \{\, g(\ell') \mid \ell' \in A_{\underline{I}[\![rt]\!]} \wedge \ell' \underline{\sqsubseteq} \ell \,\}$$

where ...→...,... denotes conditional. As an aid in showing the safeness we note:

Lemma

If $\alpha_{rt}: \underline{I}[\![rt]\!] \to \underline{J}[\![rt]\!]$ sends atoms to atoms then

$$g \leq_{rt \underline{\to} rt'} h \Rightarrow \text{lin}(g) \leq_{rt \underline{\to} rt'} \text{lin}(h) \qquad \square$$

Proof

We have

$$\text{lin}(g)\cdot\gamma_{rt} = \lambda m.\ \bigsqcup\{\, g(\ell') \mid \ell' \in A_{\underline{I}[\![rt]\!]} \wedge \ell' \underline{\sqsubseteq} \gamma_{rt}(m) \,\}$$

$$= \lambda m.\bigcup\{\ g(\ell') \mid \ell' \in A_{\underline{I}[\![rt]\!]} \wedge \alpha_{rt}(\ell') \sqsubseteq m\ \}$$

$$\sqsubseteq \lambda m.\ \bigcup\{\ g(\gamma_{rt}(m')) \mid m' \in A_{\underline{J}[\![rt]\!]} \wedge m' \sqsubseteq m\ \}$$

$$\sqsubseteq \lambda m.\ \bigcup\{\ \gamma_{rt'}(h(m')) \mid m' \in A_{\underline{J}[\![rt]\!]} \wedge m' \sqsubseteq m\ \}$$

$$\sqsubseteq \gamma_{rt'} \cdot \mathrm{lin}(h)$$

□

Assuming that $\alpha_{rt}: A_{\underline{I}[\![rt]\!]} \rightarrow A_{\underline{J}[\![rt]\!]}$ and that $\underline{I}$ and $\underline{J}$ both use the expected forms it is then straightforward that

$$\alpha_{\underline{T}}(I_x) \sqsupseteq \underline{J}_x \Rightarrow \underline{I}(\mathrm{filter}_x) \underline{\leq} \underline{J}(\mathrm{filter}_x).$$

This shows the safeness of the expected form of filter and hence of cond. In practice it is natural to choose $J_x = \alpha_{\underline{T}}(I_x)$.

Preservation of Atoms

Below we shall see that it is not only the safeness of the expected form for cond that relies on the lower adjoints α_{rt} sending atoms to atoms. Due to the structural definition α_{rt} it is natural to consider how this requirement interacts with the definition given in the previous section. Call a semifunctor atomic if it preserves the property of morphisms that atoms are mapped to atoms.

Lemma

If all $\alpha_{\underline{A}_i}$, $A_{\underline{I}(+)\underline{J}(+)}(\ldots)$, $A_{\underline{I}(\times)\underline{J}(\times)}(\ldots)$ send atoms to atoms and if $\underline{I}(+)$ and $\underline{I}(\times)$ are atomic then all α_{rt} send atoms to atoms. □

In practice this lemma means that α_{rt} sends atoms to atoms provided all $\alpha_{\underline{A}_i}$ do. To see this note that the identity function sends atoms to atoms and that this takes care of $A_{\phi\psi}$ when $\phi=\psi$. Next,

Lemma

The semifunctors $\oplus$, $\times$, $*$, and $\circledast$ are atomic and each $A_{\times\oplus}(\ldots)$ and $A_{\circledast *}(\ldots)$ send atoms to atoms. □

Proof

First note that

$$A_{L_1 \oplus \ldots \oplus L_k} = \bigcup_{i=1}^{k} \{i\} \times A_{L_i}$$

$$A_{L_1 \times \ldots \times L_k} = \bigcup_{i=1}^{k} \{\bot\} \times \ldots \times A_{L_i} \times \ldots \times \{\bot\}$$

$$A_{L_1 * \ldots * L_k} = A_{L_1} \times \ldots \times A_{L_k}.$$

It follows from [Nie 85b] that

$$A_{L_1 \circledast \ldots \circledast L_k} = \{\mathrm{cross}(a_1,\ldots,a_k) \mid \forall i:\ a_i \in A_{L_i}\ \}.$$

Given the definitions of $A_{\times\oplus}(\ldots)$ and $A_{\circledast *}(\ldots)$ it is immediate that they map atoms to atoms (since id*·cross = id). That $\oplus$, $\times$, $*$, and $\circledast$ are atomic is straightforward. □

The Constructor $\underline{+}$

The expressions case $(e_1,\ldots,e_k)$ and in_i relate to the domain constructor $\underline{+}$. We have considered two interpretations of $\underline{+}$ and it is only natural that the expected forms for case and in_i depend upon this interpretation. When $\underline{I}(\underline{+}) = \times$ we have

$$\underline{I}(in_i) = \lambda\ell.(\bot,\ldots,\ell,\ldots,\bot)$$

$$\underline{I}(case)(g_1,\ldots,g_k) = \lambda(\ell_1,\ldots,\ell_k).\ g_1(\ell_1) \sqcup \ldots \sqcup g_k(\ell_k)$$

as in the collecting semantics. When $\underline{J}(\underline{+}) = \oplus$ we shall use

$$\underline{J}(in_i) = \lambda\ell.(\ell=\bot) \rightarrow \bot,(i,\ell)$$

$$\underline{J}(case)(h_1,\ldots,h_k) = \lambda\ell. \begin{cases} \bot & \text{if } \ell=\bot \\ h_i(\ell_i) & \text{if } \ell=(i,\ell_i) \\ \top & \text{if } \ell=\top \end{cases}$$

To show the safeness we must consider three cases: whether $(\underline{I}(\underline{+}),\underline{J}(\underline{+}))$ is $(\times,\times)$, $(\times,\oplus)$, or $(\oplus,\oplus)$.

We shall assume that the lower adjoints α_{rt} are as defined in section 3.

Lemma

It is safe to use the expected forms for in_i and take. □

Proof

We only illustrate the proof for the case $\underline{I}(\underline{+}) = \times$ and $\underline{J}(\underline{+}) = \oplus$. Concerning in_i we must show

$$\underline{I}(in_i) \leq^{\gamma}_{rt_i \underline{\rightarrow} rt_1 \underline{+} \ldots \underline{+} rt_k} \underline{J}(in_i).$$

Since

$$\gamma_{rt_1\underline{+}\ldots\underline{+}rt_k} = \gamma_{rt_1} \times\ldots\times \gamma_{rt_k} \cdot \Gamma_{\times\oplus}(\underline{J}[\![rt_1]\!],\ldots,\underline{J}[\![rt_k]\!])$$

this reduces to

$$(\lambda\ell.(\bot,\ldots,\ell,\ldots,\bot)) \cdot \gamma_{rt_i} \sqsubseteq (\gamma_{rt_1} \times\ldots\times \gamma_{rt_k}) \cdot \Gamma_{\times\oplus}(\ldots) \cdot (\lambda\ell.(\ell=\bot) \rightarrow \bot,(i,\ell)).$$

The lefthandside gives

$$\lambda\ell.(\bot,\ldots,\gamma_{rt_i}(\ell),\ldots)$$

and the righthandside gives

$$\lambda\ell.\quad \begin{cases} (\gamma_{rt_1}(\perp),\ldots,\gamma_{rt_k}(\perp)) & \text{if } \ell=\perp \\ (\gamma_{rt_1}(\perp),\ldots,\gamma_{rt_i}(\ell),\ldots,\gamma_{rt_k}(\perp)) & \text{if } \ell\neq\perp \end{cases}$$

Since all γ_{rt_j} are strict the result follows.

Concerning case we must show

$$\underline{I}(\text{case}) \ \underline{\leq}^{\gamma}_{(rt_1\underline{\to}rt)\times\ldots\times(rt_k\underline{\to}rt)\to rt_1\underline{+}\ldots\underline{+}rt_k\underline{\to}rt} \ \underline{J}(\text{case}).$$

So suppose that $g_i\cdot\gamma_{rt_i} \sqsubseteq \gamma_{rt}\cdot h_i$. Then

$$\underline{I}(\text{case})(g_1,\ldots,g_k)\cdot\gamma_{rt_1\underline{+}\ldots\underline{+}rt_k}$$

$$= (\lambda(\ell_1,\ldots,\ell_k).\ g_1(\gamma_{rt_1}(\ell_1)) \sqcup \ldots \sqcup g_k(\gamma_{rt_k}(\ell_k))) \cdot \Gamma_{\times\oplus}(\ldots)$$

$$\sqsubseteq (\lambda(\ell_1,\ldots,\ell_k).\ \gamma_{rt}(h_1(\ell)) \sqcup \ldots \sqcup \gamma_{rt}(h_k(\ell))) \cdot \Gamma_{\times\oplus}(\ldots)$$

$$\sqsubseteq \gamma_{rt} \cdot (\lambda(\ell_1,\ldots,\ell_k).\ h_1(\ell) \sqcup \ldots \sqcup h_k(\ell)) \cdot \Gamma_{\times\oplus}(\ldots)$$

$$= \gamma_{rt} \cdot \lambda\ell.\ \begin{cases} h_1(\perp) \sqcup \ldots \sqcup h_k(\perp) & \text{if } \ell=\perp \\ h_1(\perp) \sqcup \ldots \sqcup h_i(\ell_i) \sqcup \ldots \sqcup h_k(\perp) & \text{if } \ell=(i,\ell_i) \\ h_1(\top) \sqcup \ldots \sqcup h_k(\top) & \text{if } \ell=\top \end{cases}$$

$$\sqsubseteq \gamma_{rt} \cdot \underline{I}(\text{case})(h_1,\ldots,h_k)$$

where the last step is because $h_i \in \underline{J}[\![rt_i\underline{\to}rt]\!]$ is strict. □

<u>The constructor $\underline{\times}$</u>

Analogously to above the expected form for take_i and tuple depend on the interpretation of $\underline{\times}$. When $\underline{J}(\underline{\times}) = *$ we shall use

$$\underline{J}(\text{take}_i) = \lambda(\ell_1,\ldots,\ell_k).\ell_i$$

$$\underline{J}(\text{tuple})(h_1,\ldots,h_k) = \lambda\ell.\ \text{smash}(h_1(\ell),\ldots,h_k(\ell)).$$

When $\underline{I}(\underline{\times}) = \circledast$ we define

$$\underline{I}(\text{take}_i) = \lambda\ell.\ \text{id}^*(\ell){\downarrow}i$$

$$\underline{I}(\text{tuple})(g_1,\ldots,g_k) = \text{lin}(\text{cross}\cdot\text{smash}\cdot\lambda\ell.(g_1(\ell),\ldots,g_k(\ell)))$$

where $(\ell_1,\ldots,\ell_k){\downarrow}i=\ell_i$. The information about tensor products given in section 3 shows that these definitions have those of the collecting semantics as special cases. The equation for tuple is further clarified below.

The use of lin in the equation for tuple corresponds to the special consideration of singletons in the definition of $\underline{C}$(tuple). This is analogous to the definition of conditional and similar to this, atoms are to be the abstract analogue of singletons. As a further motivation of this consider the complete lattice

V = 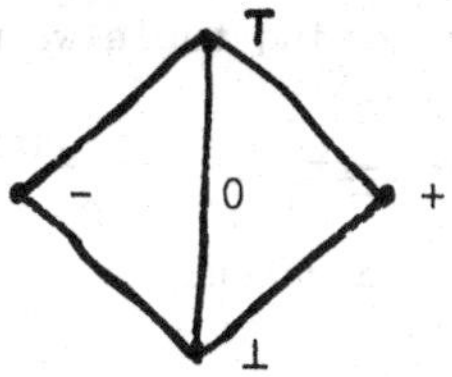

of properties of the integers. The intention is that $\gamma(-)$ is the set of negative integers, $\gamma(0)$ is $\{0\}$ etc. The atoms of V are -, 0 and +. Consider next the pairing function

$$\text{tuple(id,id)}: V \to V \circledast V$$

and its effect upon $\top$. If lin had been removed this would give cross $(\top,\top)$ and it follows from the separate additivity of cross that this equals

$$\text{cross}(-,-) \sqcup \text{cross}(-,0) \sqcup \text{cross}(-,+) \sqcup$$

$$\text{cross}(0,-) \sqcup \text{cross}(0,0) \sqcup \text{cross}(0,+) \sqcup$$

$$\text{cross}(+,-) \sqcup \text{cross}(+,0) \sqcup \text{cross}(+,+).$$

The presence of lin means that

$$\text{cross}(-,-) \sqcup \text{cross}(0,0) \sqcup \text{cross}(+,+)$$

is the result instead. (It follows from [Nie 85b] that these elements are different.) This seems to be the correct result because it does not specify cases like cross(+,-) where the signs of the components differ.

Finally we show

<u>Lemma</u>

It is safe to use the expected forms for take_i and tuple provided all α_{rt} send atoms to atoms. □

<u>Proof</u>

There are three cases to consider: whether $(\underline{I}(\underline{\times}),\underline{J}(\underline{\times}))$ is $(\circledast,\circledast)$, $(\circledast,*)$ or $(*,*)$. We illustrate the proof for $\underline{I}(\underline{\times}) = \circledast$ and $\underline{J}(\underline{\times}) = *$. Concerning take_i we must show

$$\underline{I}(\text{take}_i) \leq^{\gamma}_{rt_1\underline{\times}\ldots\underline{\times}rt_k\underline{\to}rt_i} \underline{J}(\text{take}_i).$$

We conclude

$$\underline{I}(\text{take}_i)\cdot\gamma_{rt_1\underline{\times}\ldots\underline{\times}rt_k}$$

$$= (\lambda\ell.\text{id}^*(\ell)\downarrow i) \cdot \Gamma_{\circledast *}(\ldots) \cdot \gamma_{rt_1}*\ldots*\gamma_{rt_k}$$

$$= (\lambda(\ell_1,\ldots,\ell_k).\ell_i) \cdot \gamma_{rt_1}*\ldots*\gamma_{rt_k}$$

$$= \gamma_{rt_i} \cdot \underline{J}(\text{take}_i)$$

and this establishes the result. Concerning tuple we must show that

$$\underline{I}(\text{tuple}) \leq^{\gamma}_{(rt\underline{\to}rt_1)\times\ldots\times(rt\underline{\to}rt_k)\to rt\underline{\to}rt_1\underline{\times}\ldots\underline{\times}rt_k} \underline{J}(\text{tuple}).$$

So assume that $g_i \cdot \gamma_{rt} \sqsubseteq \gamma_{rt_i} \cdot h_i$ and calculate

$$\underline{I}(\text{tuple})(g_1,\ldots,g_k) \cdot \gamma_{rt}$$
$$= \text{lin}(\text{cross}\cdot\text{smash}\cdot\lambda\ell.(g_1(\ell),\ldots,g_k(\ell)))\cdot\gamma_{rt}$$
$$\sqsubseteq \text{cross}\cdot\text{smash}\cdot(\lambda\ell.\ (g_1(\ell),\ldots,g_k(\ell)))\cdot\gamma_{rt}$$
$$\sqsubseteq \text{cross}\cdot\text{smash}\cdot\gamma_{rt_1}\times\ldots\times\gamma_{rt_k}\cdot\lambda\ell.(h_1(\ell),\ldots,h_k(\ell))$$
$$= \Gamma_{\otimes *}\cdot\gamma_{rt_1}*\ldots*\gamma_{rt_k}\cdot\underline{J}(\text{tuple})(h_1,\ldots,h_k)$$
$$= \gamma_{rt_1\underline{\times}\ldots\underline{\times}rt_k}\cdot\underline{J}(\text{tuple})(h_1,\ldots,h_k)$$

and this establishes the result. □

Recursive Domains

In section 2 the object $\underline{I}[\![\ \underline{rec}\ \underline{X}.rt]\!]$ was obtained as the object D of a limiting cone (D,r_n) for the chain

$$(\underline{I}()[\![\ rt]\!]^n(U),\underline{I}()[\![\ rt]\!]^n(\bot))$$

in the subcategory of embeddings. It is well-known that

$$\theta_I = \bigsqcup_n \underline{I}[\![\ rt]\!]\ (r_n)\cdot r_{n+1}^u$$

defines an isomorphism from D to $\underline{I}[\![\ rt]\!]\ (D) = \underline{I}[\![\ rt[\underline{rec}\ \underline{X}.rt/\underline{X}]\ ]\!]$. It is then natural to use

$$\underline{I}(\text{fold}) = \theta_I^{-1}$$

$$\underline{I}(\text{unfold}) = \theta_I$$

as the expected forms.

The safeness of using these expected forms amounts to showing $\theta_I \underline{<} \theta_J$ and $\theta_I^{-1} \underline{<} \theta_J^{-1}$. We shall show

$$\gamma_{\underline{rec}\ \underline{X}.rt}\cdot\theta_J^{-1} = \theta_I^{-1}\cdot\gamma_{rt[\underline{rec}\ \underline{X}.rt/\underline{X}]}$$

from which $\theta_I^{-1} \underline{<} \theta_J^{-1}$ is immediate and $\theta_I \underline{<} \theta_J$ follows by leftcomposing with θ_I and rightcomposing with θ_J. Induction on rt shows that

$$\gamma_{rt[\underline{rec}\ \underline{X}.rt/\underline{X}]} = \Gamma_{rt}(\gamma_{\underline{rec}\ \underline{X}.rt})$$

so that the desired equation becomes

$$\gamma_{\underline{rec}\ \underline{X}.rt}\cdot\theta_J^{-1} = \theta_I^{-1}\cdot\Gamma_{rt}(\gamma_{\underline{rec}\ \underline{X}.rt}).$$

We refer to [Nie 84, 4.3:4] for a proof of this.

5. CONCLUSION

The use of expected forms for the functionals (□ etc.) is primarily motivated by considerations of how to implement data flow analyses in the form of approximating interpretations. A natural goal is a system that accepts a specification of an approximating interpretation and that computes the result of the data flow analysis upon given programs. The study of expected forms is an aid in making it practical to define an approximating interpretation. Furthermore, we shall claim that the expected forms are natural and we have shown that they are precise in the sense that they incorporate the definitions used in the collecting semantics.

REFERENCES

[ArMa 75] M.A. Arbib, C.G. Manes: Arrows, Structures and Functors: The Categorical Imperative, Academic Press, 1975.

[CoCo 77] P. Cousot, R. Cousot: Abstract Interpretation: a unified lattice model for static analysis of programs by construction or approximation of fixpoints, in: Conf. Record of the 4th ACM Symposium on Principles of Programming Languages, 1977.

[CoCo 79] P. Cousot, R. Cousot: Systematic design of program analysis framework, in: Conf. Record of the 6th ACM Symposium on Principles of Programming Languages, 1979.

[Don 78] V. Donzeau-Gouge: Utilisation de la sémantique dénotationelle pour l'étude d'interprétations non-standard, IRIA report No. 273, France, 1978.

[JoMu 81] N.D. Jones, S.S. Mucknick: Complexity of flow analysis, inductive assertion synthesis and a language due to Dijkstra, in: Program Flow Analysis: Theory and Applications, S.S. Mucknick, N.D. Jones (eds.), Prentice-Hall, 1981.

[Nie 84] F. Nielson: Abstract Interpretation Using Domain Theory, Ph.D. thesis, University of Edinburgh, Scotland, 1984.

[Nie 85a] F. Nielson: Abstract Interpretation of Denotational Definitions, Proceedings STACS 1986, Springer Lecture Notes in Computer Science.

[Nie 85b] F. Nielson: Tensor Products Generalize the Relational Data Flow Analysis Method, 4'th HCSC 1985.

[ShWa 77] A. Shamir, W.W. Wadge: Data Types as Objects, in: Proceedings 4th ICALP, Lecture Notes in Computer Science 52, Springer-Verlag, p.p. 465-479.

[SmPl 82] M.B. Smyth, G.D. Plotkin: The category-theoretic solution of recursive domain equations, SIAM J. Comput., vol. 11 No. 4 (1982), p.p. 761-783.

CODE GENERATION
FROM
TWO-LEVEL DENOTATIONAL META-LANGUAGES

Flemming Nielson
Hanne R. Nielson

Institute of Electronic Systems
Aalborg University Centre
Strandvejen 19, 4
DK-9000 Aalborg C
DENMARK

ABSTRACT

The use of a two-level meta-language in denotational language definitions makes it possible to distinguish between compile-time entities and run-time entities. This is important for language specification and it allows one to formalize Tennents [18] informal distinction between static expressions and expressions. The automatic generation of compilers also benefits from an explicit distinction between run-time and compile-time in the language specification. A theory of abstract interpretation has been developed for the meta-language [8], thereby paving the way for a systematic treatment of data flow analysis and program transformations in the realm of denotational semantics. This paper shows how to generate code from the meta-language by giving an appropriate non-standard interpretation for it.

1. INTRODUCTION

The rigor of denotational language definitions makes it very alluring to use these as basis for automatic generation of compilers. A lot of efforts have been made in this area (see e.g. [1,4,7,14,16,19]). Unfortunately, it has not been possible to generate complete, realistic and reasonably efficient compilers. We believe that the main reason for this is that the traditional distinction between compile-time and run-time has not been fully employed in these approaches.

On the other hand, attribute grammers have been successful in compiler construction [3,5,15] mainly because they can be implemented reasonably efficiently. Attribute grammars can be used for specifying static semantics and code generation, that is, the compile-time actions of a compiler. Paulson's semantic grammars [14] combine the atrribute grammars and the denotational semantics by using the latter for specification of dynamic semantics and thereby the run-time actions of the compiler. The resulting implementations behave like compilers producing code for a λ-calculus machine, the SECD-machine [6].

The code generated by Paulson's system is several orders of magnitude slower than ordinary machine code [14]. Mosses' system SIS [7] has similar drawbacks. Sethi [16] and Jones [4] try to improve the performance by introducing a "smart semantic processor" knowing about semantic concepts such as environments and stores which then can be implemented more efficiently. Wand [19] constructs the abstract machine (to generate code for) from the given denotational definition. Appel [1] suggests to generate code for a register transfer machine thus being closer to the usual intermediate forms of compilers.

In traditional compilers data flow analysis and program transformations are used to improve the generated code. Such approaches have been applied in MUG2, an attribute grammar based system for automatic compiler generation [3]. Recent work [8,9] on abstract interpretation, a framework for specifying data flow analysis and proving it correct, brings these issues into the realm of (two-level) denotational semantics. The aim of this paper is to show how to generate code for such semantic definitions and thereby pave the way for using data flow information in automatic compiler construction from denotational semantics.

The novel aspect of our approach is that we are based on a two-level meta-language allowing us to distinguish between compile-time and run-time, and thereby e.g. formalize Tennent's [18] distinction between static expressions and expressions [13]. Furthermore, the two-level meta-language formalizes the rather undeveloped distinction between binding times in Paulson's semantic grammars mentioned earlier. Various data flow analyses are specified by giving different interpretations of (the run-time level of) the meta-language [8,9,10,11]. Similarly, code generation for various abstract machines can be specified by providing different coding interpretations of the meta-language. In this paper we present one such coding interpretation. Its correctness is proved in [12] and asserts that any language whose semantics is given in the meta-language can correctly be compiled into code for this abstract machine.

2. THE META-LANGUAGE TML_{SC}

A meta-language for denotational semantics usually is given by a typed λ-calculus. The types might realistically be given by the following abstract syntax

$$t ::= A \mid t_1 \times \ldots \times t_k \mid t_1 + \ldots + t_k \mid \text{rec } X.t \mid X \mid t_1 \to t_2$$

In a two-level meta-language we want to distinguish between compile-time entities and run-time entities and this is accomplished by introducing two sorts of types: compile-time types (ct) and run-time types (rt). So imagine a meta-language TML with the following system of types

$$ct ::= A \mid ct_1 \times \ldots \times ct_k \mid ct_1 + \ldots + ct_k \mid \text{rec } X.ct \mid X \mid ct_1 \to ct_2 \mid rt$$

$$rt ::= \underline{A} \mid rt_1 \underline{\times} \ldots \underline{\times} rt_k \mid rt_1 \underline{+} \ldots \underline{+} rt_k \mid \underline{\text{rec } X}.rt \mid \underline{X} \mid rt_1 \underline{\to} rt_2.$$

The syntaxes of the two-levels are rather similar so underlining is used to disambiguate. The interaction between the type levels is somewhat restricted:

at compile-time we can talk about run-time entities but not vice versa. This agrees with the usual practice of compiler writing.

A variant of this meta-language has been used in [8,9] to develop a theory of abstract interpretation. Technical problems preclude run-time function types to be handled in full generality so a restricted meta-language, TML_s, is used instead:

$$ct ::= A \mid ct_1 \times \ldots \times ct_k \mid ct_1 + \ldots + ct_k \mid \text{rec } X.ct \mid X \mid ct_1 \to ct_2 \mid rt_1 \underline{\to} rt_2$$

$$rt ::= \underline{A} \mid rt_1 \underline{\times} \ldots \underline{\times} rt_k \mid rt_1 \underline{+} \ldots \underline{+} rt_l \mid \underline{\text{rec } X}.rt \mid \underline{X}$$

The development could as well have been performed with a variant of TML_s with $ct ::= rt_1 \underline{\to} rt_2$ replaced by $ct ::= rt$ and this might seem more natural given TML as a starting point. However, in the present setting we are allowed much greater leeway since we can interpret $rt_1 \underline{\to} rt_2$ as a domain of code whereas $ct_1 \to ct_2$ is still a domain of functions. We shall assume that the truth values $T(\underline{T})$ are included in the set of (unspecified) basic types.

The expressions of TML_s are given by the following abstract syntax

$$\begin{aligned} e ::= {} & f \mid (e_1, \ldots, e_k) \mid e \downarrow j \mid in_j e \mid is_j e \mid out_j e \\ & \mid \lambda x{:}ct.e \mid e_1(e_2) \mid x \mid \text{mkrec } e \mid \text{unrec } e \\ & \mid e \to e_1, e_2 \mid fix_{ct} e \\ & \mid \underline{tuple}\ (e_1, \ldots, e_k) \mid \underline{take}_j \mid \underline{in}_j \mid \underline{case}\ (e_1, \ldots, e_k) \\ & \mid \underline{mkrec} \mid \underline{unrec} \mid \underline{cond}\ (e, e_1, e_2) \mid e_1 \square e_2 \end{aligned}$$

The first part of this notation is an ordinary typed λ-calculus whose expressions denote elements of type ct. Here f denotes a constant of type ct but not all compile-time types ct are allowed: ct must be contravariantly pure and closed [8]. Intuitively, this means that there must not be run-time function spaces in the domain of a compile-time function space of ct and furthermore, ct must not contain free (type) variables. The second part of the notation is a combinator style notation for elements of type $rt_1 \underline{\to} rt_2$.

The semantics of the meta-language is given by an <u>interpretation</u> $\underline{I}$ consisting of two parts, a type part and an expression part. The type part will define a cpo $\underline{I}[\![ct]\!]$ for each closed type ct [8]. In the case of the standard interpretation $\underline{S}$, the cpo's are obtained in the traditional way by interpreting × as cartesian product, $\underline{\times}$ as smash product, + and $\underline{+}$ as coaleased sum, → as function space and $\underline{\to}$ as strict function space. Recursive domain equations (rec X.ct and $\underline{\text{rec X}}$.rt) are solved up to isomorphism using the categorical approach [17].

The expression part of the interpretation defines a function $\underline{I}[\![e]\!] : \underline{I}[\![ct_1]\!] \times \ldots \times \underline{I}[\![ct_n]\!] \to \underline{I}[\![ct]\!]$ for each well-typed expression e (with free variables of closed types $ct_1, \ldots, ct_n$, resp., and result of type ct). We shall omit the detailed typing conventions (see [8]). The λ-calculus part of the expression language in interpreted as usually; in particular mkrec and unrec are the isomorphisms Θ and Θ^{-1} obtained from solving recursive domain equations. In the standard interpretation $\underline{S}$ the combinator style expressions are interpreted as follows:

$\underline{S}(\underline{\text{tuple}}): \underline{S}[\![rt \underline{\rightarrow} rt_1]\!] \times \ldots \times \underline{S}[\![rt \underline{\rightarrow} rt_k]\!] \rightarrow \underline{S}[\![rt \underline{\rightarrow} rt_1 \underline{\times} \ldots \underline{\times} rt_k]\!]$

$\quad \underline{S}(\underline{\text{tuple}}) = \lambda(E_1,\ldots,E_k).\ \lambda v.\ (E_1 v,\ldots,E_k v)$

$\underline{S}(\underline{\text{take}_j}): \underline{S}[\![rt_1 \underline{\times} \ldots \underline{\times} rt_k \underline{\rightarrow} rt_j]\!]$

$\quad \underline{S}(\underline{\text{take}_j}) = \lambda v.\ v \downarrow j$

$\underline{S}(\underline{\text{in}_j}): \underline{S}[\![rt_j \underline{\rightarrow} rt_1 \underline{+} \ldots \underline{+} rt_k]\!]$

$\quad \underline{S}(\underline{\text{in}_j}) = \lambda v.\ \text{in}_j v$

$\underline{S}(\underline{\text{case}}): \underline{S}[\![rt_1 \underline{\rightarrow} rt]\!] \times \ldots \times \underline{S}[\![rt_k \underline{\rightarrow} rt]\!] \rightarrow \underline{S}[\![rt_1 \underline{+} \ldots \underline{+} rt_k \underline{\rightarrow} rt]\!]$

$\quad \underline{S}(\underline{\text{case}}) = \lambda(E_1,\ldots,E_k).\ \lambda v.\ \text{is}_1 v \rightarrow E_1(\text{out}_1 v),\ldots,$
$\quad\quad \text{is}_k v \rightarrow E_k(\text{out}_k v), \perp$

$\underline{S}(\underline{\text{mkrec}}): \underline{S}[\![rt[\underline{\text{rec}X}.rt/\underline{X}] \underline{\rightarrow} \underline{\text{rec}X}.rt]\!]$

$\quad \underline{S}(\underline{\text{mkrec}}) = \Theta$

$\underline{S}(\underline{\text{unrec}}): \underline{S}[\![\underline{\text{rec}X}.rt \underline{\rightarrow} rt[\underline{\text{rec}X}.rt/\underline{X}]]\!]$

$\quad S(\underline{\text{unrec}}) = \Theta^{-1}$

$\underline{S}(\underline{\text{cond}}): \underline{S}[\![rt \underline{\rightarrow} \underline{T}]\!] \times \underline{S}[\![rt \underline{\rightarrow} rt']\!] \times \underline{S}[\![rt \underline{\rightarrow} rt']\!] \rightarrow S[\![rt \underline{\rightarrow} rt']\!]$

$\quad \underline{S}(\underline{\text{cond}}) = \lambda(E,E_1,E_2).\ \lambda v.\ Ev \rightarrow E_1 v, E_2 v$

$\underline{S}(\underline{\Box}): \underline{S}[\![rt_2 \underline{\rightarrow} rt_3]\!] \times \underline{S}[\![rt_1 \underline{\rightarrow} rt_2]\!] \rightarrow \underline{S}[\![rt_1 \underline{\rightarrow} rt_3]\!]$

$\quad \underline{S}(\underline{\Box}) = \lambda(E_1,E_2).\ \lambda v.\ E_1(E_2 v)$

Code generation will be specified by giving a (non-standard) interpretation of the meta-language. It will be clear in Section 5 that the fixed point operator fix_{ct} of type $(ct \rightarrow ct) \rightarrow ct$ cannot (yet) be handled for all (closed) types ct. This calls for restricting the permissible types by requiring them to be composite: ct is a composite type if and only if

- ct has the form $rt_1 \underline{\rightarrow} rt_2$, or
- ct is pure, that is, contains non run-time types, or
- ct is a cartesian product or discriminated union of composite types.

The meta-language TML_{sc} is the restriction of TML_s where all fix_{ct} occurring in some expression satisfy that ct is composite.

We refer to [13] for a discussion of the pragmatic aspects of how denotational definitions are affected when one uses TML_s or TML_{sc} as meta-language rather than the ordinary (one-level) typed λ-calculus.

3. THE ABSTRACT MACHINE

Since the meta-language TML_{sc} does not allow functions as run-time data objects there is no need to let the abstract machine include instructions for manipulating closures of functions. The machine described below is, none the less, rather close in spirit to Cardelli's abstract machine for ML [2].

The configurations of the machine consist of three components:

- the program counter (PC) points to an instruction in the program (PR) to be executed,
- the value stack (ST) contains the arguments that are passed to functions and contains the results that functions produce,
- the control stack (CS) contains the program counters to be used to restore the program counter when functions are exited.

The stack ST contains values of variable size and type. Typically there will be one cell-type for each basic run-time type (integer, boolean, etc.) in addition to those representing composite values as e.g. tuples. The exact form of these cells is inessential as long as the primitive operations on them have the expected properties. The abstract machine does not assume these cells to contain any information about the type; as we shall see later the correct application of machine instructions is guaranteed since we only consider code for well-typed TML_{sc}-expressions. This is analogue to conventional computers where e.g. the same bit-pattern can be viewed as representing a number as well as a character.

The need for cells of different size can be exemplified by considering the representation of a tuple $(v_1,\ldots,v_k)$ of values. Typically, more bytes will be required for this tuple than for each of its components. A solution of the problem is to represent the composite values by boxed data structures, that is, as sequences of the form $w_1\ldots w_\ell$ where w_1 gives the length (ℓ) of the box and $w_2\ldots w_\ell$ represent the values $v_1\ldots v_k$. In this way values of any type can be kept on a stack with elements of uniform size. Another possibility is to represent composite values on the stack by pointers into a heap; the boxed data structure discussed above can then be used here. This method is used in Cardelli's implementation of ML [2]. The exact choice of representation is not so important here; we shall simply write $[r_1;\ldots;r_n]$ for an n-byte/word representation of a value. In the following let REP be the set of such representations, e.g. REP = BYTE + REP*. We shall assume ST = REP*.

A program (PR) is a finite sequence of instructions of the form

Enter, Switch, Tuple k, Take i, Push i, Branch $\ell_1\ldots\ell_k$, Define ℓ,

Goto ℓ, BranchFalse ℓ, Call ℓ, Return, Opr w

where k and i are natural numbers, $\ell, \ell_1, \ldots, \ell_k$ are labels and w is the name of a primitive operation. Each instruction may cause a change in the current configuration when executed. Representing a configuration by a triple $\langle PC, ST, CS\rangle$ these transitions will be specified by a relation $\rightarrow_{PR}$:

$$\langle PC, ST, CS\rangle \rightarrow_{PR} \langle PC', ST', CS'\rangle.$$

The instruction in PR pointed to by PC is the one being executed and if $\langle PC, ST, CS\rangle$ is the initial configuration then it is replaced by $\langle PC', ST', CS'\rangle$.

The complete set of transitions is given below. The stacks ST and CS are shown with the top to the left and e.g. v::ST' means that v is the top element. We write pc(ℓ) for the (minimal) instruction number in PR defining the label ℓ. The truth values are represented as <u>true</u> and <u>false</u>. Finally, the primitive operations w are implemented by partial functions $\Omega(w)$: REP $\hookrightarrow$ REP.

[Enter]:	$\langle PC, v::ST, CS\rangle \rightarrow_{PR} \langle PC+1, v::v::ST, CS\rangle$
[Switch]:	$\langle PC, v_1::v_2::ST, CS\rangle \rightarrow_{PR} \langle PC+1, v_2::v_1::ST, CS\rangle$
[Tuple k]:	$\langle PC, v_1::\ldots::v_k::ST, CS\rangle \rightarrow_{PR} \langle PC+1, [v_1;\ldots;v_k]::ST, CS\rangle$
[Take i]:	$\langle PC, [v_1;\ldots;v_k]::ST, CS\rangle \rightarrow_{PR} \langle PC+1, v_i::ST, CS\rangle$ $(1\leq i\leq k)$
[Push i]:	$\langle PC, ST, CS\rangle \rightarrow_{PR} \langle PC+1, i::ST, CS\rangle$
[Branch $\ell_1\ldots\ell_k$]:	$\langle PC, i::ST, CS\rangle \rightarrow_{PR} \langle pc(\ell_i), ST, CS\rangle$ $(1\leq i\leq k)$
[Define ℓ]:	$\langle PC, ST, CS\rangle \rightarrow_{PR} \langle PC+1, ST, CS\rangle$
[Goto ℓ]:	$\langle PC, ST, CS\rangle \rightarrow_{PR} \langle pc(\ell), ST, CS\rangle$
[BranchFalse ℓ]:	$\langle PC, \underline{true}::ST, CS\rangle \rightarrow_{PR} \langle PC+1, ST, CS\rangle$
	$\langle PC, \underline{false}::ST, CS\rangle \rightarrow_{PR} \langle pc(\ell), ST, CS\rangle$
[Call ℓ]:	$\langle PC, ST, CS\rangle \rightarrow_{PR} \langle pc(\ell), ST, (PC+1)::CS\rangle$
[Return]:	$\langle PC, ST, PC'::CS\rangle \rightarrow_{PR} \langle PC', ST, CS\rangle$
[Opr w]:	$\langle PC, v::ST, CS\rangle \rightarrow_{PR} \langle PC+1, \Omega(w)v::ST, CS\rangle$ ($\Omega(w)v$ defined)

We shall write $\rightarrow^*_{PR}$ for the reflexive transitive closure of $\rightarrow_{PR}$, that is,

$$\langle PC, ST, CS\rangle \rightarrow^*_{PR} \langle PC', CT', CS'\rangle$$

means that execution of PR from $\langle PC, ST, CS\rangle$ will bring us to $\langle PC', ST', CS'\rangle$ in a finite number of steps. It is easy to see that the machine is deterministic in the sense that $\langle PC, ST, CS\rangle \rightarrow^*_{PR} \langle PC', ST', CS'\rangle$ and $\langle PC, ST, CS\rangle \rightarrow^*_{PR} \langle PC'', ST'', CS''\rangle$ imply that at least one of $\langle PC', ST', CS'\rangle \rightarrow^*_{PR} \langle PC'', ST'', CS''\rangle$ and $\langle PC'', ST'', CS''\rangle \rightarrow^*_{PR} \langle PC', ST', CS'\rangle$ applies. Note that it is possible to reach a configuration $\langle PC, ST, CS\rangle$ from which no next move exists, i.e.

$$\neg\exists \langle PC', ST', CS'\rangle: \langle PC, ST, CS\rangle \rightarrow_{PR} \langle PC', ST', CS'\rangle.$$

This will e.g. be the case when the computation has terminated.

4. REPRESENTATION OF ABSTRACT VALUES

It is not necessary to know how the abstract values are represented in the machine in order to describe the coding interpretation. However, it may prove helpful for the intuitive understanding of the code generation and it will be necessary for the correctness proof [12].

For each run-time type rt we shall specify how the elements are represented in the machine, that is, we shall specify a (strict and injective) function

$$\underline{R}[\![rt]\!] : \underline{S}[\![rt]\!] \rightarrow REP_{\perp}$$

where $\underline{S}[\![rt]\!]$ is the standard interpretation of the type rt. We shall assume that $\underline{S}[\![\underline{A}]\!]$ is a flat cpo for primitive types $\underline{A}$; this means that $\underline{S}[\![rt]\!]$ will be flat for any closed type rt. We shall assume that functions $\underline{R}(\underline{A})$ have been specified for the primitive types $\underline{A}$.

In general rt may contain free type variables, say $\underline{X}_1,\ldots,\underline{X}_N$, so we define a function

$$\underline{R}[\![rt]\!](rep_1,\ldots,rep_N) : \underline{S}[\![rt]\!](D_1,\ldots,D_N) \rightarrow REP_{\perp}$$

where $rep_i : D_i \rightarrow REP_{\perp}$ is a strict function associated with $\underline{X}_i$ (for $1 \leq i \leq N$). We define

$$\underline{R}[\![\underline{A}]\!](rep_1,\ldots,rep_N) = \underline{R}(\underline{A})$$

$$\underline{R}[\![rt_1 \underline{\times} \ldots \underline{\times} rt_k]\!](rep_1,\ldots,rep_N) =$$

$$\text{strict}(\lambda\langle v_1,\ldots,v_k\rangle.[\underline{R}[\![rt_1]\!](rep_1,\ldots,rep_N)(v_1);\ldots; \underline{R}[\![rt_k]\!](rep_1,\ldots,rep_N)(v_k)])$$

$$\underline{R}[\![rt_1 \underline{+} \ldots \underline{+} rt_k]\!](rep_1,\ldots,rep_N) =$$

$$\text{strict}(\lambda\langle j,v\rangle.[j;\ \underline{R}[\![rt_j]\!](rep_1,\ldots,rep_N)(v)])$$

$$\underline{R}[\![X_i]\!](rep_1,\ldots,rep_N) = rep_i$$

Before specifying $\underline{R}[\![\underline{\text{rec}X_{N+1}}.rt]\!](rep_1,\ldots,rep_N)$ it may be worthwhile to have a closer look at $\underline{S}[\![\underline{\text{rec}X_{N+1}}.rt]\!](D_1,\ldots,D_N)$. Let D^o be the one-point cpo and define $D^{i+1} = \underline{S}[\![rt]\!](D_1,\ldots,D_N,D^i)$ for $i \geq 0$. Intuitively, D^i corresponds to the i'th unfolding of the equation. There exist embedding functions $r_i : D^i \rightarrow \underline{S}[\![\underline{\text{rec}X_{N+1}}.rt]\!](D_1,\ldots,D_N)$ with "inverses" r_i^u ($r_i^u \circ r_i$ = id but $r_i \circ r_i^u \sqsubseteq$ id):

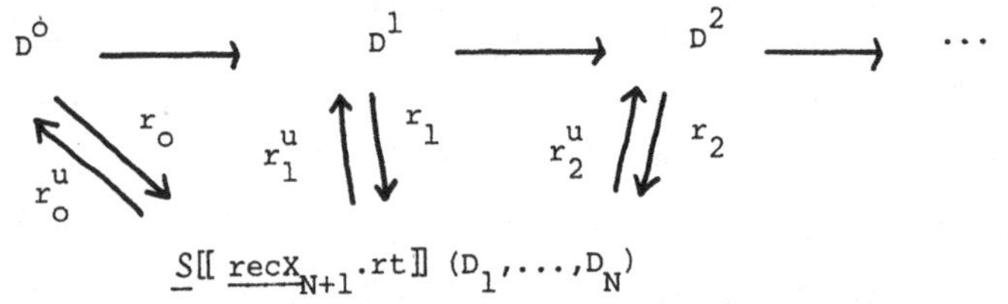

(To be precise this is a limiting cone in an appropriate category of cpo's and embeddings, [8,17]). Let rep^{o} be the (trivial) representation function for D^{o} and define $rep^{i+1}: D^{i+1} \to REP_{\perp}$ by

$$rep^{i+1} = \underline{R}[\![rt]\!] (rep_1, \ldots, rep_N, rep^{i})$$

Then

$$\underline{R}[\![\underline{rec}X_{N+1}.rt]\!] (rep_1, \ldots, rep_N) = \lambda v.\ \bigsqcup_i rep^{i}(r_i^{u} v)$$

that is v is first transformed into one of the approximating domains D^{i} and the appropriate representation function is then applied.

5. THE CODING INTERPRETATION

As mentioned earlier, code generation for TML_{sc} will be defined as a non-standard interpretation. The type part of this interpretation $\underline{K}$ is specified by giving a cpo $\underline{K}(A)$ for each primitive type A and a cpo $\underline{K}(rt_1 \underline{\to} rt_2)$ for each run-time function type $rt_1 \underline{\to} rt_2$. Using the standard interpretation of the type constructors ×, + and → we obtain a cpo $\underline{K}[\![ct]\!]$ for each closed type ct.

Intuitively, an expression of type $rt_1 \underline{\to} rt_2$ specifies a computation performed at run-time so it should give rise to a sequence of abstract machine instructions in the code generation. Since labels must be unique it is not sufficient to define $\underline{K}(rt_1 \underline{\to} rt_2)$ to be the (flat) cpo of finite sequences of instructions. The problem can be solved by introduction of occurrences and a (strict, injective) function

mklab: Occ → Label

where Occ = $(N+\{a,b\})^*_{\perp}$ is the (flat) cpo of occurrences and Label = $N_{\perp}$ that of labels. Now we can define

$$\underline{K}(rt_1 \underline{\to} rt_2) = Occ \to Inst^*_{\perp}$$

where Inst is the set of abstract machine instructions defined in Section 3. This technique of using A → B instead of B is common in modelling situations where A is operationally thought of as a global variable (e.g. the next free label number).

The expression part of $\underline{K}$ is going to define a function of appropriate functionality for each expression e. It is here sufficient to specify the meanings of the primitive functions f and the operators $\underline{tuple}$, $\underline{take}_j$, $\underline{in}_j$, $\underline{case}$, $\underline{mkrec}$, $\underline{unrec}$, $\underline{cond}$, □ (that is the combinator style parts of the expressions) and, finally fix_{ct}. The meaning of the remaining constructs are as in the standard interpretation.

$\underline{K}(\underline{tuple})$: $\underline{K}[\![rt \underline{\to} rt_1]\!] \times \ldots \times \underline{K}[\![rt \underline{\to} rt_k]\!] \to \underline{K}[\![rt \underline{\to} rt_1 \underline{\times} \ldots \underline{\times} rt_k]\!]$

$\underline{K}(\underline{tuple})\ (G_1, \ldots, G_k)\ occ =$

$[Enter]^\wedge G_k(occ^\wedge k)^\wedge\ [Switch]^\wedge \ldots ^\wedge[Enter]^\wedge G_2(occ^\wedge 2)^\wedge$

$[Switch]^\wedge G_1(occ^\wedge 1)^\wedge\ [Tuple\ k]$

$\underline{K}(\underline{take}_j)$: $\underline{K}[\![rt_1 \underline{\times} \ldots \underline{\times} rt_k \underline{\to} rt_j]\!]$

$\underline{K}(\underline{take}_j)\ occ = [Take\ j]$

$\underline{K}(\underline{in}_j)$: $\underline{K}[\![rt_j \underline{\to} rt_1 \underline{+} \ldots \underline{+} rt_k]\!]$

$\underline{K}(\underline{in}_j)\ occ = [Push\ j;\ Tuple\ 2]$

$\underline{K}(\underline{case})$: $\underline{K}[\![rt_1 \underline{\to} rt]\!] \times \ldots \times \underline{K}[\![rt_k \underline{\to} rt]\!] \to \underline{K}[\![rt_1 \underline{+} \ldots \underline{+} rt_k \underline{\to} rt]\!]$

$\underline{K}(\underline{case})\ (G_1, \ldots, G_k)\ occ =$

$[Enter;\ Take\ 2;\ Switch;\ Take\ 1;\ Branch\ \ell_1 \ldots \ell_k]^\wedge$

$[Define\ \ell_1]^\wedge\ G_1(occ^\wedge 1)^\wedge\ [Goto\ \ell_a]^\wedge \ldots ^\wedge[Define\ \ell_{k-1}]^\wedge$

$G_{k-1}(occ^\wedge k\text{-}1)^\wedge\ [Goto\ \ell_a;\ Define\ \ell_k]^\wedge\ G_k(occ^\wedge k)^\wedge$

$[Define\ \ell_a]$

where $\ell_i = mklab\ (occ^\wedge i)$ for $1 \le i \le k$ and $\ell_a = mklab\ (occ^\wedge a)$

$\underline{K}(\underline{mkrec})$: $\underline{K}[\![rt[\underline{recX}.rt/X] \underline{\to}\ \underline{rec\ X}.rt]\!]$

$\underline{K}(\underline{mkrec})\ occ = [\ ]$

$\underline{K}(\underline{unrec})$: $\underline{K}[\![\underline{rec\ X}.rt \underline{\to} rt[\underline{rec\ X}.rt/\underline{X}]\ ]\!]$

$\underline{K}(\underline{unrec})\ occ = [\ ]$

$\underline{K}(\underline{cond})$: $\underline{K}[\![rt \underline{\to} \underline{T}]\!] \times \underline{K}[\![rt \underline{\to} rt']\!] \times \underline{K}[\![rt \underline{\to} rt']\!] \to \underline{K}[\![rt \underline{\to} rt']\!]$

$\underline{K}(\underline{cond})\ (G, G_1, G_2)\ occ =$

$[Enter]^\wedge\ G(occ^\wedge 1)^\wedge\ [BranchFalse\ \ell_a]^\wedge\ G_1(occ^\wedge 2)^\wedge$

$[Goto\ \ell_b;\ Define\ \ell_a]^\wedge\ G_2(occ^\wedge 3)^\wedge\ [Define\ \ell_b]$

where $\ell_\alpha = mklab\ (occ^\wedge \alpha)$ for $\alpha = a,b$.

$\underline{K}(\square)$: $\underline{K}[\![rt_2 \underline{\to} rt_3]\!] \times \underline{K}[\![rt_1 \underline{\to} rt_2]\!] \to \underline{K}[\![rt_1 \underline{\to} rt_3]\!]$

$\underline{K}(\square)\ (G_1, G_2)\ occ = G_2(occ^\wedge 2)^\wedge\ G_1(occ^\wedge 1)$

Note that mkrec and unrec do not give rise to any code because of the way elements of recursively defined domains are represented in the abstract machine (see Section 4).

The definition of $\underline{K}(fix_{ct})$: $(\underline{K}[\![ct]\!] \to \underline{K}[\![ct]\!]) \to \underline{K}[\![ct]\!]$ is more complicated. In the case where ct is pure no run-time types are involved so we define

$\underline{K}(fix_{ct})\ G = LFP(G)$

where LFP(G) denotes the least fixed point of the function G. Thus the fixed point is computed at compile-time. On the other hand, if ct is $rt_1 \underline{\rightarrow} rt_2$ then the fixed point must be computed at run-time so in this case we define

$$\underline{K}(\text{fix}_{ct})\ G\ occ = [\text{Goto } \ell_a;\ \text{Define } \ell_b]^\wedge\ G(g)(occ^\wedge 1)^\wedge$$
$$[\text{Return};\ \text{Define } \ell_a;\ \text{Call } \ell_b]$$

where ℓ_α = mklab $(occ^\wedge\alpha)$ for α = a,b and

$$g = \lambda occ'.[\text{Call } \ell_b]$$

Note that G: $\underline{K}[\![rt_1 \underline{\rightarrow} rt_2]\!] \rightarrow \underline{K}[\![rt_1 \underline{\rightarrow} rt_2]\!]$ and g: $\underline{K}[\![rt_1 \underline{\rightarrow} rt_2]\!]$ so G(g) ensures that the fixpoint recursion in e is replaced by the calls of the label ℓ_b in the code. Intuitively, G is the code for the body of fix_{ct} with holes in it representing the recursive calls.

Assume now that ct is not pure but ct = $ct_1 \times \ldots \times ct_k$. We shall here rely on a k-ary version of Bekic's theorem allowing us to compute a k-ary fixed point by computing k fixed point for appropriate modifications of the projections of the function. In the case k=2 this amounts to

$$\text{LFP}(F) = (H_1, H_2(H_1))$$

where F: $D_1 \times D_2 \rightarrow D_1 \times D_2$, H_1 = LFP(λx: D_1.F(x,H_2(x))$\downarrow$1), and H_2 = λx: D_1.LFP(λy: D_2.F(x,y)$\downarrow$2). Corresponding to this we define

$$\underline{K}(\text{fix}_{ct})\ G = (K_1, K_2(K_1))$$

where

$$K_1 = \underline{K}(\text{fix}_{ct_1})(\lambda x: \underline{K}[\![ct_1]\!] .\ G(x, K_2(x))\downarrow 1)$$
$$K_2 = \lambda x: \underline{K}[\![ct_1]\!] .\ \underline{K}(\text{fix}_{ct_2})(\lambda y: \underline{K}[\![ct_2]\!] .\ G(x,y)\downarrow 2).$$

Without further explanation we shall state the following general definition:

$$\underline{K}(\text{fix}_{ct})\ G = (H_1, H_2(H_1), \ldots, H_k\ (H_1, H_2(H_1), \ldots))$$

where (for $1 \le i \le k$)

$$H_i = \lambda(x_1: \underline{K}[\![ct_1]\!], \ldots, x_{i-1}: \underline{K}[\![ct_{i-1}]\!]).$$
$$\underline{K}(\text{fix}_{ct_i})(\lambda x_i: \underline{K}[\![ct_i]\!] .\ G(x_1, \ldots, x_i,\ H_{i+1}(x_1, \ldots, x_i), \ldots$$
$$H_k(x_1, \ldots, x_i, H_{i+1}\ (\ldots), \ldots, H_{k-1}(\ldots)))).$$

Finally, consider the case where ct = $ct_1 + \ldots + ct_k$ and ct is not pure. Then the value of (or code for) $\underline{K}(\text{fix}_{ct})$ G has to be in one of $\underline{K}[\![ct_1]\!], \ldots, \underline{K}[\![ct_k]\!]$ and because of the way the least fixed point is computed it can be determined which one it actually is by looking at the first approximation G($\perp$) to the solution. So we define

$\underline{K}(\mathrm{fix}_{ct})\ G =$

$$is_1(G(\bot)) \rightarrow in_1(\underline{K}(\mathrm{fix}_{ct_1})(out_1 \circ G \circ in_1)),\ldots$$
$$is_k(G(\bot)) \rightarrow in_k(\underline{K}(\mathrm{fix}_{ct_k})(out_k \circ G \circ in_k)),\bot.$$

This completes the specification of the coding interpretation $\underline{K}$.

Example. Consider the following program computing the factorial function:

$$\mathrm{fix}_{\underline{N \rightarrow N}}\ (\lambda f{:}\underline{N \rightarrow N}.\ \underline{cond}(eq0, con1, times \,\square\, \underline{tuple}(f \,\square\, pred, id))).$$

Here $\underline{N}$ is a primitive type and eq0, con1, times, pred and id are primitive functions with the standard interpretation:

eq0:	$\underline{N \rightarrow T}$	$\underline{S}(eq0) = \lambda x.x=0$
con1:	$\underline{N \rightarrow N}$	$\underline{S}(con1) = \lambda x.1$
times:	$\underline{N \times N \rightarrow N}$	$\underline{S}(times) = \lambda(x,y).x*y$
pred:	$\underline{N \rightarrow N}$	$\underline{S}(pred) = \lambda x.x \neq 0 \rightarrow x-1,\bot$
id:	$\underline{N \rightarrow N}$	$\underline{S}(id) = \lambda x.x$

Assume now that the coding interpretation $\underline{K}$ specifies the following code to be generated for these functions:

$\underline{K}(eq0)$ = [Push 0; Tuple 2; Opr =]

$\underline{K}(con1)$ = [Push 1; Tuple 2; Take 1]

$\underline{K}(times)$ = [Opr *]

$\underline{K}(pred)$ = [Push 1; Switch; Tuple 2; Opr -]

$\underline{K}(id)$ = [ ]

where $\Omega(=) = \lambda[v_1;v_2].[v_1=v_2]$, $\Omega(*) = \lambda[v_1;v_2].[v_1*v_2]$, $\Omega(-) = \lambda[v_1;v_2].(v_1 \geq v_2 \rightarrow [v_1-v_2],\bot)$. Then $\underline{K}$ will generate the following code for the factorial program:

```
Goto ℓa
Define ℓb
Enter
Push 1
Tuple 2
Opr =
BranchFalse ℓ1a
Push 1
Tuple 2
Take 1
Goto ℓ1b
Define ℓ1a
Enter
Switch
Push 1
Switch
Tuple 2
Opr -
Call ℓb
Tuple 2
Opr *
Define ℓ1b
Return
Define ℓa
Call ℓb
```

The larger box contains the code for the body of the fixed point operator, the smaller box is the "hole" corresponding to the recursive call. □

6. CONCLUSION

Given a language defined using two-level meta-language TML_{sc} we can implement it on the abstract machine of Section 3 by simply applying the coding interpretation $\underline{K}$ and, furthermore, the results of [12] shows that the implementation will be correct. The applicability of this approach is of course dependent of how easy it is to specify the semantics of a language using TML_{sc}, but the quality of the generated code is also important.

The pragmatic aspects of writing denotational definitions using two-level meta-languages are discussed in [13]. From the point of view of code generation it is especially interesting to note that transforming a denotational definition written in TML_s into one written in the more restricted TML_{sc} amounts to introducing some notion of activation record, that is, imposing some implementation decisions into the semantic definition. Of course, we would like to avoid this rewriting of denotational definitions, but we have no ideas of how to handle the fix-point operator fix_{ct} in the cases where ct is not composite.

It turns out that the code generated using $\underline{K}$ will be rather inefficient. One reason is the packing of data and this might motivate a study of peep-hole optimizations. However the most severe deficiency is the repetition of code. To illustrate this problem consider an expression fix_{ct} e where ct = $(rt \underline{\rightarrow} rt) \times (rt \underline{\rightarrow} rt)$. Then $\underline{K}[\![fix_{ct} e]\!] = (K_1, K_2(K_1))$ where

$$K_1\ occ = [Goto\ \ell_a;\ Define\ \ell_b]^\wedge$$
$$(\underline{K}[\![e]\!]\ \lambda occ'.[Call\ \ell_b],\ K_2(\lambda occ'.[Call\ \ell_b]))\downarrow 1)(occ^\wedge 1)^\wedge$$
$$[Return;\ Define\ \ell_a;\ Call\ \ell_b],$$

$$K_2\ g\ occ = [Goto\ \ell'_a;\ Define\ \ell'_b]^\wedge$$
$$(\underline{K}[\![e]\!]\ (g,\ \lambda occ'.[Call\ \ell'_b])\downarrow 2)(occ^\wedge 1)^\wedge$$
$$[Return;\ Define\ \ell'_a;\ Call\ \ell'_b]$$

Thus the first component K_1 of $\underline{K}[\![fix_{ct} e]\!]$ will repeat the declaration corresponding to K_2 for each call. The situation for the second component $K_2(K_1)$ is even worse since the code corresponding to K_1 (containing the many repetitions) will be repeated for each call!

In certain cases, including that above, the code generation can be improved such that repetitions of code are avoided. A type ct is called <u>nicely impure</u> if

- ct has the form $rt_1 \underline{\rightarrow} rt_2$, or
- ct is a cartesian product of nicely impure types.

Assume now that $ct = ct_1 \times \ldots \times ct_k$ is nicely impure. To each occurrence of a type of the form $rt_1 \underline{\rightarrow} rt_2$ in ct we associate a sequence $\pi (= \pi_1 \ldots \pi_\ell)$ of numbers being its "address" in ct and if $\tau \in \underline{K}[[ct]]$ we shall write $\tau \downarrow \pi \ (\in \underline{K}[[rt_1 \underline{\rightarrow} rt_2]])$ for $\tau \downarrow \pi_1 \ldots \downarrow \pi_\ell$. The coding interpretation $\underline{K}$ is now modified such that

$$((\underline{K}\,(fix_{ct})\ G)\downarrow\pi)\ occ = [\mathrm{Goto}\ \ell_a]^\wedge\ lin_{ct}(\tau)^\wedge[\mathrm{Define}\ \ell_a;\ \mathrm{Call}\ \ell_{b^\wedge\pi}]$$

where

$$\tau\downarrow\pi = [\mathrm{Define}\ \ell_{b^\wedge\pi}]^\wedge\ (G(g)\downarrow\pi)(occ^\wedge 1^\wedge\pi)^\wedge[\mathrm{Return}],$$

$$g\downarrow\pi = \lambda occ'.\ [\mathrm{Call}\ \ell_{b^\wedge\pi}]$$

$$lin_{rt_1 \underline{\rightarrow} rt_2}\ \tau=\tau,\ lin_{ct_1'\times\ldots\times ct_k'}\ \tau = lin_{ct_1'}\ (\tau\downarrow 1)^\wedge\ldots^\wedge lin_{ct_k'}\ (\tau\downarrow k)$$

and, finally, $\ell_\alpha = mklab\ (occ^\wedge\alpha)$ for $\alpha = a^\wedge\pi, b^\wedge\pi$

For the example considered above the code will be replaced by

$$\underline{K}\ [[\ fix_{ct} e]] = (\lambda occ.K^\wedge[\mathrm{Call}\ \ell_{b1}],\ \lambda occ.K^\wedge[\mathrm{Call}\ \ell_{b2}])$$

where

$$K = [\mathrm{Goto}\ \ell_a;\ \mathrm{Define}\ \ell_{b1}]^\wedge$$
$$(\underline{K}[[\ e]]\ (\lambda occ'.[\mathrm{Call}\ \ell_{b1}],\ \lambda occ'.[\mathrm{Call}\ \ell_{b2}])\downarrow 1)(occ^\wedge 1^\wedge 1)^\wedge$$
$$[\mathrm{Return};\ \mathrm{Define}\ \ell_{b2}]^\wedge$$
$$(\underline{K}[[\ e]]\ (\lambda occ'.[\mathrm{Call}\ \ell_{b1}],\ \lambda occ'.[(\mathrm{Call}\ \ell_{b2}])\downarrow 2)(occ^\wedge 1^\wedge 2)^\wedge$$
$$[\mathrm{Return};\ \mathrm{Define}\ \ell_a].$$

Note that the many repetitions of code are avoided.

ACKNOWLEDGEMENT:

This work is part of the PSI-project supported by the Danish Natural Science Research Council.

REFERENCES

[1] A.W. Appel: Semantics-directed code generation, 12. POPL, 315-324 (1985).

[2] L. Cardelli: The functional abstract machine, Bell Labs 1984.

[3] H. Ganzinger, R. Giegerich, U. Möncke & R. Wilhelm: A truly generative semantics-directed compiler generator, SIGPLAN 82 Symposium on Compiler Construction, 172-184 (1982).

[4] N.D. Jones & H. Christiansen: Control flow treatment in a simple semantics directed compiler generator, in: Formal Descriptions of Programming Concepts II' IFIP TC-2 Working Conference (ed. D. Bjørner), North Holland, Amsterdam (1982).

[5] U. Kastens: The GAG-system - a tool for Compiler Construction, in: Methods and Tools for Compiler Construction (ed. B. Lorho), Cambridge University Press, 162-182 (1984).

[6] P.J. Landin: The mechanical evaluation of expressions, Comput. J. 6, 308-320, 1964.

[7] P. Mosses: SIS-semantics implementation system: Reference manual and user guide, Aarhus University (1979).

[8] F. Nielson: Abstract interpretation using domain theory, Ph.D. thesis, Edinburgh University (1984).

[9] F. Nielson: Abstract interpretation of denotational definitions. Proceedings from STACS, Springer LNCS (1986).

[10] F. Nielson: Tensor products generalize the relational data flow analysis method, 4th Hungarian Conference on Computer Science, 1985.

[11] F. Nielson: Expected forms of data flow analyses, these proceedings.

[12] F. Nielson: Correctness of code generation from a two-level denotational meta-language, (Extended abstract-Preliminary version), Aalborg University Centre (1985).

[13] H.R. Nielson & F. Nielson: Pragmatic aspects of two-level denotational meta-languages, Aalborg University Centre (1985).

[14] L. Paulson: Compiler generation from denotational semantics, in: Methods and Tools for Compiler Construction (ed: B. Lorho), Cambridge University Press, 219-250 (1984).

[15] K.J. Räihä: Attribute grammar design using the compiler writing system HLP, in: Methods and Tools for Compiler Construction (ed: B. Lorho), Cambridge University Press, 183-206 (1984).

[16] R. Sethi: Control flow aspects of semantics directed compiling, ACM TOPLAS 5:4, 554-595 (1983).

[17] M.B. Smyth & G.D. Plotkin: The category-theoretic solution of recursive domain equations, SIAM J. Comput. 11:4, 761-783 (1982).

[18] R.D. Tennent: Principles of Programming Languages, Prentice Hall (1981).

[19] M. Wand: Deriving target code as a representation continuation semantics, ACM TOPLAS 4:3, 496-517 (1982).

MULTILEVEL FUNCTIONS IN MARTIN-LÖF'S TYPE THEORY

Bengt Nordström
Programming Methodology Group
Department of Computer Sciences
University of Göteborg
Chalmers University of Technology
S-412 96 Göteborg, Sweden

Abstract. Multilevel arrays have been used in the VDL and VDM projects for representing abstract syntax trees. In the same way as the function type can be seen as a generalization of the array type, it is possible to generalize multilevel arrays to multilevel functions. They are general trees with finite depth but arbitrary branching. In this paper, a definition of multilevel functions is given in the framework of Martin-Löf's type theory. The formal rules associated with the new data type is given and justified using the semantics of type theory. The paper contains some programs for manipulating the functions and some data types (vectors, natural numbers, lists, binary trees and functions) are seen as special cases of multilevel functions.

1. INTRODUCTION

An array $b_1, \ldots, b_n$ (belonging to the type **array** 1..n **of** B) is similar to a function $b : A \to B$, where the index type A is the interval [1,n] and the range type B is the type of the indexed elements $b_1, \ldots, b_n$. Arrays and functions are computed in different ways: An object in an array-type is completely evaluated when all the indexed elements of the array are computed, the values or canonical objects in **array** 1..n of B are therefore of the form $\mathbf{array}_n(b_1, b_2, \ldots, b_n)$, where $b_1, b_2, \ldots, b_n$ are canonical objects in B, while an object in a function type $A \to B$ is completely evaluated when it is of the form $\lambda x.b$, where $b \in B$ when $x \in A$. Notice that the evaluation strategy for arrays requires that the index type has a decidable equality, otherwise it would be impossible to let the i:th part in $\mathbf{array}_n(b_1, b_2, \ldots, b_n)$ represent the i:th element. Since array-indexing corresponds to function-application and there is no restriction on the index type A in the function type $A \to B$ we can see the function type as a generalization of the array type **array** 1..n **of** B, made possible by a change of the evaluation strategy.

Other generalizations are also possible. One such are the multilevel arrays (also called Vienna objects) used in the VDL project [8] and investigated by Ollongren et al [6,1] and Rosenberg and Thatcher [7]. In such an object the dimensionality of the array (defined to be 0 for types which are not arrays and n+1 if the dimensionality of the range type is n) does not have to be fixed. The multilevel arrays were used in an interpreter to represent the abstract syntax trees as well as the state of a program in execution. In this paper I will generalize multilevel arrays to multilevel functions, a data type which also can be seen as a generalization of the function type. Schematically the following picture can be drawn:

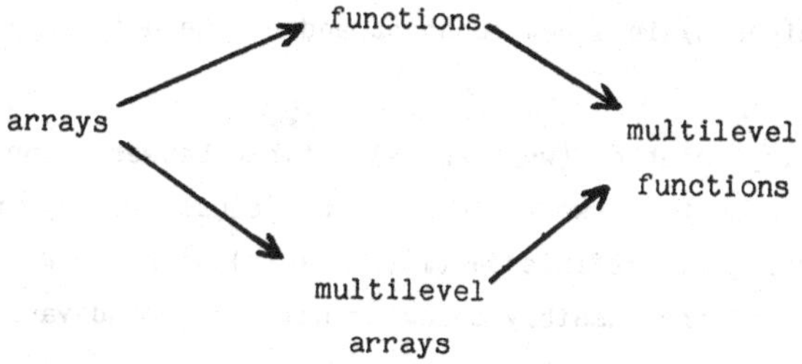

2. INFORMAL DESCRIPTION OF THE TYPE OF MULTILEVEL FUNCTIONS

A multilevel function of type $A \overset{*}{\to} B$ is either a scalar (of type B) or a function whose indexed elements (the index being of type A) are multilevel functions. Intuitively, we want to solve the type equation

$$A \overset{*}{\to} B = B + (A \to (A \overset{*}{\to} B))$$

It is not difficult to get a solution to this equation using Scott's domain theory, interpreting a type as a domain. In this paper I will use a more direct method, relying on the general framework of Martin-Löf's theory of types [2,5,4]. No previous knowledge of this theory is needed for reading the paper.

3. THE SYNTAX AND SEMANTICS OF TYPE THEORY, A SHORT SUMMARY

3.1 The Syntax

The syntax of type theory differs from more traditional languages' in that abstraction is a syntactic concept. From a formal point of view, the syntax of type theory is very similar to typed λ-calculus with one ground type. Expressions in type theory are built up from variables and constants using application and abstraction.

3.1.1 Arities. Each expression has an arity: **0** is the arity of saturated expressions (expressions like 1 or 6+7 which cannot be applied to an expression), if α and β are arities then $\alpha \twoheadrightarrow \beta$ is an arity (the arity of expressions which when applied to an argument of arity α yields an expression af arity β).

Sometimes the arity $\alpha_1 \twoheadrightarrow \alpha_2 \twoheadrightarrow \ldots \twoheadrightarrow \alpha_n$ will be written $(\alpha_1 \times\times \alpha_2 \times\times \ldots \times\times \alpha_{n-1}) \twoheadrightarrow \alpha_n$.

3.1.2 Definitional Equality. It is possible to introduce new constants by abbreviations of the form

a ≡ e

where a (the definiendum) is a new constant and e (the definiens) is an expression (not containing a).

There is an equality relation (written ≡) defined between expressions of a given arity. It is defined such that two expressions are equal if they are syntactically equal after substituting all definienda (macro calls) with their corresponding definiens (macro bodies) and possibly changing names of bound variables. This equality is decidable.

3.1.3 Application. If the arity of f is $\alpha \twoheadrightarrow \beta$ and the arity of a is α, then the arity of the application f(a) is β. The notation f(a,b) will be used instead of f(a)(b). Mathematical conventions like prefix, infix, postfix and mixfix notation will also be used for application; expressions like -3, 3+5, 7! and <a,b> will be used instead of -(3), +(3,5), !(7) and <>(a,b).

3.1.4 Abstraction. If the arity of b is β and the arity of the variable x is α, then the abstraction (x)b has arity $\alpha \twoheadrightarrow \beta$. If, moreover, the arity of a is α, then the following equality holds: ((x)b)(a) ≡ b[a/x] , where b[a/x] is the expression obtained by substituting the expression a for all free occurrences of the variable x. Abstractions will often be written as x.e instead of (x)e and repeated abstraction (x)(y)e will often be written (x,y)e or x.y.e.

3.1.5 Some Examples. The expression (∀x∈A)B is syntactically analyzed as ∀(A,(x)B) and the expression λx.b is analyzed as λ((x)b).

3.2 The Semantics

When defining a programming language one often explains its semantics in terms of mathematical objects like sets and functions. This takes for granted an understanding of these objects. Type theory is intended to be a fundamental conceptual framework for the basic notions (like sets and functions) of constructive mathematics. Therefore, an understanding of type theory cannot depend on an understanding of another mathematical language. Its meaning must be explained in a more direct way.

The semantics is explained starting from the primitive notion of computation; the purely mechanical procedure of finding the value of an expression. An expression which already is computed is called a canonical expression, all other are called non-canonical expressions. Examples of canonical expressions are: λx.s(x), 0, <0,t> and examples of noncanonical ones are: 3+5, fst(apply(λx.y,0)).

The general strategy for evaluating expressions is to evaluate them from without, i.e. normal order or lazy evaluation is used.

The formal system of type theory consists of rules for making judgements of the following forms:

B is a type	abbreviated: B type
B and C are equal types	B = C
b is an object of type B	b ∈ B
b and c are equal objects of type B	b = c ∈ B

A judgement may in general depend on assumptions. I will first explain the meaning of the judgement forms when they depend on no assumptions, then when they depend on one assumption. This can then rather straight forwardly be generalized to an arbitrary number of assumptions.

The first judgement is explained in the following way:

> A type B is defined by prescribing how a canonical object of the type is formed as well as how two equal canonical objects of the type are formed.

The second judgement form is explained as follows:

> Two types, B and C, are equal if a canonical object of type B is also a canonical object of type C and if equal objects of type B also are equal canonical objects of type C and vice versa.

This explanation makes sense since we know how to form the canonical objects of B and C if we already know that B and C are types.

The third judgement form is explained as follows:

> If B is a type then the judgement b ∈ B means that the value of b is a canonical object of type B .

In order to understand a judgement of this form it is necessary to know how expressions are computed. In order to give a rigorous justification of the formal rules of type theory it is sufficient to know the computation rules and the meaning of the different forms of judgements.

Notice that if we know that an expression has a type, then we also know that the computation of it terminates.

The last judgement form is explained as follows:

> If B is a type and $b \in B$ and $c \in B$, then the judgement $b = c \in B$ means that the values of b and c are equal canonical objects in B.

It is now possible to extend the explanations to hypothetical judgements, i.e. judgements depending on assumptions. The simplest assumption is of the form

$$x \in A$$

where x is a variable and A is a type. A hypothetical judgement is a judgement in a <u>context</u>

$$[x_1 \in A_1, x_2 \in A_2, \ldots, x_n \in A_n]$$

where each A_i (which may contain $x_1, \ldots, x_{i-1}$ free) is a type under the assumptions $x_1 \in A_1, x_2 \in A_2, \ldots, x_{i-1} \in A_{i-1}$. In general, assumptions may be hypothetical, i.e. on the form

$$y(x) \in A\ [x \in B]$$

where x is a variable of arity $\mathbf{0}$ and y is variable of arity $\mathbf{0 \twoheadrightarrow 0}$. In this overview of the semantics, I will only deal with assumptions of the simple form $x \in A$.

The meaning of the different forms of judgements when they depend on one assumption is as follows. Notice that the variable x may be free in the expressions b, c, B and C.

The judgement

$$B \text{ type } [x \in A]$$

means that $B[a/x]$ is a type provided $a \in A$. It also means that B is extensional in the sense that if $a = b \in A$ then $B[a/x] = B[b/x]$.

The judgement

$$B = C\ [x \in A]$$

means that $B[a/x]$ and $C[a/x]$ are equal types provided $a \in A$.

The third judgement form

$b \in B\ [x \in A]$

means that $b[a/x] \in B[a/x]$ provided $a \in A$. It also means that $b[a/x] = b[c/x] \in B[a/x]$ provided $a = c \in A$.

Similarly for the last form of judgement:

$b = c \in B\ [x \in A]$

means that $b[a/x] = c[a/x] \in B[a/x]$ provided $a \in A$.

The meaning of a hypothetical judgement with an arbitrary number of assumptions is explained by induction on the length of its context.

4. DEFINITION OF THE TYPE $A \to^* B$

To express the multilevel function type the infix constant $\to^*$ of arity **(0××0)↠0** will be used. If A and B are types then $A \to^* B$ is a type, whose canonical objects are of one of the two forms

leaf(b) $\in A \to^* B$, if $b \in B$.

tree(c) $\in A \to^* B$, if $c(x) \in A \to^* B$ under the assumption that $x \in A$.

So the arity of **leaf** is **0↠0** and the arity of **tree** is **(0↠0)↠0**. Notice that there is no restriction on the types A and B. The different kinds of multilevel functions can be drawn as:

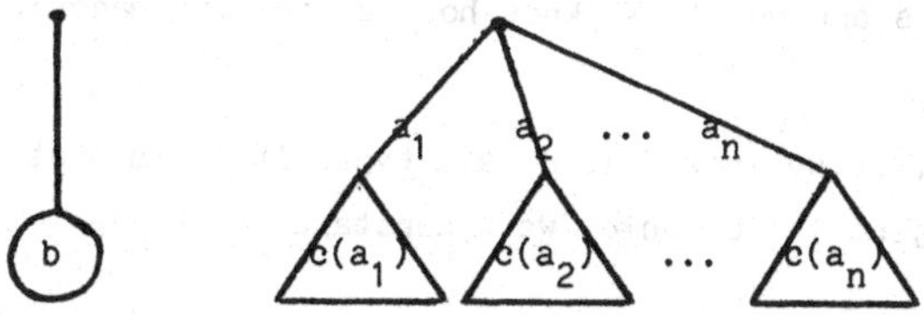

leaf(b) **tree**(c)

In order to define the type $A \to^* B$ it is also necessary to explain how to form two equal canonical objects:

$\mathbf{leaf}(b) = \mathbf{leaf}(b') \in A \to^* B$, if $b = b' \in B$

$\mathbf{tree}(c) = \mathbf{tree}(c') \in A \to^* B$, if $c(x) = c'(x) \in A \to^* B$, for $x \in A$

The selector associated with the type former is **tree-rec** of arity $(\mathbf{0} \times\times (\mathbf{0} \to\to \mathbf{0}) \times\times (((\mathbf{0} \to\to \mathbf{0}) \times\times (\mathbf{0} \to\to \mathbf{0})) \to\to \mathbf{0}) \to\to \mathbf{0}$. The expression

tree-rec(p,e,f)

is computed as follows:

1. Compute the value of p. If $p \in A \to^* B$, the result must be of one of the forms **leaf**(b) or **tree**(c).
2. If the value of p is **leaf**(b), then the value of **tree-rec**(p,e,f) is the value of e(b).
3. If the value of p is **tree**(c), then the value of **tree-rec**(p,e,f) is the value of f(c, (x)**tree-rec**(c(x), e, f))

5. THE FORMAL RULES AND THEIR JUSTIFICATION

The formal rules of the type and their justification can now be given.

$\to^*$-formation 1:

$$\frac{A \text{ type} \qquad B \text{ type}}{A \to^* B \text{ type}}$$

The rule is justified as follows. Assume that A and B are types. To show that $A \to^* B$ is a type, we must know how to form the canonical objects in $A \to^* B$ and know when two canonical objects are equal. We know how to form the canonical objects, since

1. We know what $b \in B$ means, if we know that B is a type. It means that the value of b is a canonical object in B, which we understand if B is a type. Hence we know that

   $\mathbf{leaf}(b) \in A \to^* B$

2. We know what $c(x) \in A \to^* B$ means: For arbitrary $a \in A$, $c(a) \in A \to^* B$. But $c(a) \in A \to^* B$ means that the value of c(a) is either **leaf**(b'), where $b' \in B$, or **tree**(c'), where $c'(x) \in A \to^* B$ for $[x \in A]$, etc., until, eventually, we reach an element of the form **leaf**(d).

Similarly, we know when two canonical objects in $A \to^* B$ are equal.

The next formation rule is justified in a similar way.

$\rightarrow^*$**-formation 2:**

$$\frac{A = A' \qquad B = B'}{A \rightarrow^* B = A' \rightarrow^* B'}$$

The following introduction rules follow immediately from the prescription how to form the canonical objects and how to form equal canonical objects.

$\rightarrow^*$**-introduction 1:**

$$\frac{b \in B}{\textbf{leaf}(b) \in A \rightarrow^* B} \qquad \frac{c(x) \in A \rightarrow^* B \quad [x \in A]}{\textbf{tree}(c) \in A \rightarrow^* B}$$

$\rightarrow^*$**-introduction 2:**

$$\frac{b = b' \in B}{\textbf{leaf}(b) = \textbf{leaf}(b') \in A \rightarrow^* B} \qquad \frac{c(x) = c'(x) \in A \rightarrow^* B \quad [x \in A]}{\textbf{tree}(c) = \textbf{tree}(c') \in A \rightarrow^* B}$$

The elimination rule is:

$\rightarrow^*$**-elimination 1:**

$$\frac{\begin{array}{l} C(x) \ \ \text{type} \ \ [x \in A \rightarrow^* B] \\ p \in A \rightarrow^* B \\ e(x) \in C(\textbf{leaf}(x)) \ \ [x \in B\,] \\ f(y,z) \in C(\textbf{tree}(y)) \ \ [y(x) \in A \rightarrow^* B \ \ [x \in A], \ \ z(x) \in C(y(x)) \ \ [x \in A]] \end{array}}{\textbf{tree-rec}(p,e,f) \in C(p)}$$

Here, the premises have been written on top of each other. In the rest of the paper the rules will not contain premises of the form A type if the conclusion is of the form $a \in A$. This kind of premise is obvious in the sense that the conclusion has no meaning unless the premise holds.

The elimination rule can be justified as follows. Assume the premises to hold. It is necessary to show that the value of **tree-rec**(p,e,f) is a canonical object in C(p). That $p \in A \rightarrow^* B$ means that the value of p is a canonical object in $A \rightarrow^* B$.

<u>Case 1</u>: If the value of p is **leaf**(b), then the value of **tree-rec**(p,e,f) is the value of e(b), which from the meaning of the second premise is a canonical object in C(**leaf**(b)). From the extensionality of C it follows that a canonical object of C(**leaf**(b) is also a canonical object in C(p).

Case 2: If the value of p is **tree**(c), where $c(x) \in A \to^* B$ for $x \in A$, then the value of **tree-rec**(p,e,f) is the value of f(c,(x)**tree-rec**(c(x),e,f)).

It now only remains to show that

tree-rec(c(x),e,f) ∈ C(c(x)) [x ∈ A] (1)

because then

f(c,(x)**tree-rec**(c(x),e,f)) ∈ C(**tree**(c))

by the third premise.

To show (1), let a be an arbitrary element in A. If the value of c(a) is **leaf**(b'), then it follows from the first case that

tree-rec(c(a),e,f) ∈ C(c(a))

Otherwise, continue as in the second case, until we eventually reach a value of the form **leaf**(b). ∎

The induction rule for multilevel functions is obtained by omitting some of the constructions in the elimination-rule:[1]

$\to^*$**-induction:**

$p \in A \to^* B$
C(**leaf**(x)) true [x ∈ B]
C(**tree**(y)) true [$y(x) \in A \to^* B$ [x ∈ A], C(y(x)) true [x ∈ A]]

C(p) true

The rule can be read as follows: If p is a multilevel function of type $A \to^* B$ and if C(x) is a proposition when x is in $A \to^* B$, then an induction proof of that C(p) is true proceed as follows: First prove the base case that C(**leaf**(x)) is true for arbitrary x in B. The induction step is to prove that C(**tree**(y)) is true under the assumptions that $y(x) \in A \to^* B$ and C(y(x)) is true for x ∈ A.

1. A fundamental idea in type theory is that types can be interpreted as propositions, a proposition is vaguely seen as the type of all its proof objects. The type corresponding to a false proposition is then empty and a type corresponding to a true proposition is non-empty. So if we want to make judgements of the form "A true" in type theory we can do so by ignoring the explicit construction a in judgements of the form a ∈ A.

The equality rules, which reflect the way **tree-rec**(p,e,f) is computed, are the following:

$\to^*$**-equality 1:**

$$\frac{\begin{array}{l} b \in B \\ e(x) \in C(\textbf{leaf}(x)) \quad [x \in B] \\ f(y,z) \in C(\textbf{tree}(y)) \quad [y(x) \in A \to^* B \ [x \in A],\ \ z(x) \in C(y(x)) \ \ [x \in A]] \end{array}}{\textbf{tree-rec}(\textbf{leaf}(b),e,f) = e(b) \in C(\textbf{leaf}(b))}$$

$\to^*$**-equality 2:**

$$\frac{\begin{array}{l} c(x) \in A \to^* B \quad [x \in A] \\ e(u) \in C(\textbf{leaf}(u)) \quad [u \in B] \\ f(y,z) \in C(\textbf{tree}(y)) \quad [y(x) \in A \to^* B \ [x \in A],\ \ z(x) \in C(y(x)) \ \ [x \in A]] \end{array}}{\textbf{tree-rec}(\textbf{tree}(c),e,f) = f(c,(x)\textbf{tree-rec}(c(x),e,f)) \in C(\textbf{tree}(c))}$$

6. SOME PROGRAMS AND DATA TYPES DEFINED IN TERMS OF MULTILEVEL FUNCTIONS

In this section, I will define some operations on multilevel functions and also show how to express some data types in terms of multilevel functions.

6.1 Relationship with multilevel arrays

In order to relate multilevel functions to the multilevel arrays used in the VDL-project, the operations selection, updating and the one branch VDL-tree are defined. These can then be used to define the ν-operation, which was extensively used in the VDL-project and related research.

The type **VDL**(A,B) of generalized VDL-trees is defined by the abbreviation:

$$\textbf{VDL}(A,B) \equiv A \to^* \textbf{Lift}(B)$$

where the type **Lift**(A) has one more element than the type A.[2]

2. The canonical elements of **Lift**(A) are elements of the form **up**(a), where a ∈ A, or the element **down**. The control structure or selector associated with the type is **down_or_up**(p,d,e) which is computed by first computing the value of p. If the value of p is **down** then the value of the **down_or_up**-expression is the value of d. If the value of p is **up**(a) then the value of the **down_or_up**-expression is the value of e(a). In a language with pattern-matching, the **down_or_up**-expression above is similar to the expression **cases** p **of down: d, up(x): e(x) end.**

A generalized VDL-tree is either empty, a leaf or a tree, so it will be convenient to make the following abbreviations:

$$\begin{aligned} \mathbf{empty}_{vdl} &\equiv \mathbf{leaf}(\mathbf{down}) \\ \mathbf{leaf}_{vdl}(b) &\equiv \mathbf{leaf}(\mathbf{up}(b)) \\ \mathbf{tree}_{vdl}(c) &\equiv \mathbf{tree}(c) \\ \mathbf{rec}_{vdl}(p,d,e,f) &\equiv \mathbf{tree\text{-}rec}(p,\ x.\mathbf{down\_or\_up}(x,d,e),\ f) \end{aligned}$$

The operation $\mathbf{rec}_{vdl}$ is the natural recursion operator (selector) associated with VDL-trees, it is defined so that the following equalities hold:

$$\begin{cases} \mathbf{rec}_{vdl}(\mathbf{empty}_{vdl}\ ,\ d,\ e,\ f) = d \\ \mathbf{rec}_{vdl}(\mathbf{leaf}_{vdl}(b),\ d,\ e,\ f) = e(b) \\ \mathbf{rec}_{vdl}(\mathbf{tree}_{vdl}(c),\ d,\ e,\ f) = f(c,\ x.\mathbf{rec}_{vdl}(c(x),\ d,\ e,\ f)) \end{cases}$$

The operation can be used to justify an induction principle for VDL-trees:

VDL-induction:

$$\frac{\begin{array}{l} p \in \mathbf{VDL}(A,B) \\ C(\mathbf{empty}_{vdl})\quad \text{true} \\ C(\mathbf{leaf}_{vdl}(u))\ \text{true}\quad [u \in B\ ] \\ C(\mathbf{tree}_{vdl}(y)\quad \text{true}\quad [y(x) \in \mathbf{VDL}(A,B)\ [x \in A],\ C(y(x))\ \text{true}\ [x \in A]] \end{array}}{C(p)\ \text{true}}$$

6.1.1 Selection. The binary infix operator **@** will be used to select a component of a generalized VDL-tree. It is defined as

$$p@i \equiv \mathbf{rec}_{vdl}(p,\ \mathbf{empty}_{vdl},\ x.\mathbf{empty}_{vdl},\ y.z.y(i))$$

so that the following equalities hold:

$$\begin{cases} \mathbf{empty}_{vdl}@i = \mathbf{empty}_{vdl} \\ \mathbf{leaf}_{vdl}(b)@i = \mathbf{empty}_{vdl} \\ \mathbf{tree}_{vdl}(d)@i = d(i) \end{cases}$$

and it is easy to show that indexing is a total operation on VDL-trees, i.e.

$p@i \in \mathbf{VDL}(A,B)$, if $p \in \mathbf{VDL}(A,B)$ and $i \in A$.

6.1.2 Updating. If p,p' ∈ **VDL**(A,B), then the binary infix operator ; will be used to update p with p', The i:th element of the resulting VDL-tree is equal to the i:th element of p' whenever that is nonempty, otherwise it is the i:th element of p. The following equations define the update operator:

$$\begin{cases} p;\mathbf{empty}_{vdl} = p \\ p;\mathbf{leaf}_{vdl}(a) = p \\ p;\mathbf{tree}_{vdl}(b) = \mathbf{tree}_{vdl}(x.\mathbf{if}\ \text{nonempty}\ b(x)\ \mathbf{then}\ b(x)\ \mathbf{else}\ p@x) \end{cases}$$

where $\text{nonempty}(p) \equiv \mathbf{rec}_{vdl}(p,\ \mathbf{false},\ (x)\mathbf{true},\ (y,z)\mathbf{true})$

i.e.

$$p;p' \equiv \mathbf{rec}_{vdl}(p',\ p,\ x.p,\ y.z.\mathbf{tree}_{vdl}(x.\mathbf{if}\ \text{nonempty}\ y(x)\ \mathbf{then}\ y(x)\ \mathbf{else}\ p@x))$$

Theorem:

$$(p;p')@i = \begin{cases} p'@i, & \mathbf{if}\ p'@i \neq \mathbf{empty}_{vdl} \\ p@i, & \mathbf{if}\ p'@i = \mathbf{empty}_{vdl} \end{cases}$$

Proof by induction over p'.
If $p' = \mathbf{empty}_{vdl}$ or $p' = \mathbf{leaf}_{vdl}(a)$, then $p'@i = \mathbf{empty}_{vdl}$ by the definition of @, so it is necessary to show that the second equality holds. But this is immediate since, in these cases, p;p' = p by the definition of ;.

In the third case, if $p' = \mathbf{tree}_{vdl}(b)$, then

$$\begin{aligned}(p;\mathbf{tree}_{vdl}(b))@i &= (\mathbf{tree}_{vdl}(x.\mathbf{if}\ \text{nonempty}\ b(x)\ \mathbf{then}\ b(x)\ \mathbf{else}\ p@x))@i \\ &= \mathbf{if}\ \text{nonempty}\ b(i)\ \mathbf{then}\ b(i)\ \mathbf{else}\ p@i\end{aligned}$$

If $p'@i \neq \mathbf{empty}_{vdl}$, then $b(i) \neq \mathbf{empty}_{vdl}$, so that nonempty b(i) = **true** and $(p;\mathbf{tree}_{vdl}(b))@i = b(i) = p'@i$ as required. In the other case, if $p'@i = \mathbf{empty}_{vdl}$, then $b(i) = \mathbf{empty}_{vdl}$, so nonempty b(i) = **false** and $(p;\mathbf{tree}_{vdl}(b))@i = p@i$.

6.1.3 The one branch VDL-tree. If the index-type A of a multilevel function has a computable equality, i.e. if there is a function eq(x,y) ∈ **Bool** [x,y ∈ A] with the property that eq(x,y) = **true** iff x = y ∈ A then it is possible to define the one branch VDL-tree [i:=q] by

$$[i{:=}q] \equiv \mathbf{tree}_{vdl}(x.\mathbf{if}\ \text{eq}(x,i)\ \mathbf{then}\ q\ \mathbf{else}\ \mathbf{empty}_{vdl})$$

The following equality is immediate:

$$[i{:=}q]@j = \begin{cases} \mathbf{empty}_{vdl}, & \text{if } i \neq j \\ q, & \text{if } i = j \end{cases}$$

and also (from the previous theorem):

$$(p;[i{:=}q])@j = \begin{cases} p@j, & \text{if } i \neq j \\ q, & \text{if } i = j \end{cases}$$

Graphically, the tree corresponding to p;[i:=q] is obtained by replacing the subtree of p rooted at i by the tree q. It corresponds to the operation $\nu(p,i,q)$ in [1]. Notice that the general update-operation ";" is defined for a general VDL-tree $p \in$ **VDL**(A, B), while the ν-operation is only defined when the index-type A has a computable equality. This is one of the reasons of not basing the description of multilevel functions on the ν-operation.

6.2 Finite vectors

A <u>vector</u> $a_1, a_2, \ldots, a_n$ of <u>fixed length</u> n has type

$$\text{Vector}(n,A) \equiv \{x \in \mathbf{VDL}([1..n], A) \mid (\forall i \in [1..n])\text{Is\_a\_leaf}(x,i)\}$$

where [i..j] is the subset of natural numbers between i and j and Is_a_leaf(x,i) is true if and only if the i:th component of x is a leaf, i.e.[3]

$$[i..j] \equiv \{x \in N \mid i \leq x \leq j\}$$
$$\text{Is\_a\_leaf}(x,i) \equiv \mathbf{rec}_{vdl}(x, \bot, y.\bot, z.u.\mathbf{rec}_{vdl}(z(i), \bot, v.\mathbf{T}, w.w'.\bot))$$
$$\mathbf{T} \equiv \{\mathbf{tt}\}$$
$$\bot \equiv \{\}$$

The subset-typeformer of [3] has been used. It is defined by the fact that the canonical objects of $\{x \in A \mid P(x)\}$ are the canonical objects a of A for which P(a) is true.

To construct an object in the vector-type, the following definition can be used:

$$[0{<}i{\leq}n : a] \equiv \mathbf{tree}_{vdl}(i.\ \mathbf{if}\ 0{<}i{\leq}n\ \mathbf{then}\ \mathbf{leaf}_{vdl}(a)\ \mathbf{else}\ \mathbf{empty}_{vdl})$$

where [0<:] is a mixfix constant of arity $\mathbf{0}\times\times(\mathbf{0}\rightarrow\!\!\!\rightarrow\mathbf{0})\rightarrow\!\!\!\rightarrow\mathbf{0}$ and a in general may

3. A person familiar with type theory will notice that the definition of the propositional function Is_a_leaf requires the use of the type of small types (the universe).

depend on i. For instance, the vector containing the first 100 integer squares as elements is [0<i≤100 : i*i].

6.3 **Natural numbers and other inductively generated types**

We get the natural numbers if we let both the index type and the range type of a multilevel function contain only one element. The following abbreviations can be used:

N ≡ **Singleton** $\rightarrow^{*}$ **Singleton**
0 ≡ **leaf**(**tt**)
succ(a) ≡ **tree**(x.a)
rec(p,d,e) ≡ **tree-rec**(p, x.d, u.v.e(u(**tt**), v(**tt**)))
where
Singleton ≡ {**tt**}

To justify these definitions, the rules for the natural numbers have to be proven. The only non-trivial case is N-elimination (mathematical induction):

$$\frac{p \in \mathbf{N} \qquad d \in C(\mathbf{0}) \qquad e(x,y) \in C(\mathbf{succ}(x)) \quad [x \in \mathbf{N},\ y \in C(x)]}{\mathbf{rec}(p,d,e) \in C(p)}$$

The primitive recursion operator **rec** is defined such that **rec**(**0**, d, e) is computed to the value of d and **rec**(**succ**(a), d, e) is computed to the value of e(a, **rec**(a, d, e)) . N-elimination is in type theory justified from the way **rec**(p,d,e) is computed, it is therefore sufficient to show that **rec**(p,d,e) , as defined by the abbreviations above, is computed to a value which is equal to the value which **rec**(p,d,e) , as originally defined, is computed to.

1. The value of **rec**(**0**, d, e) is the value of d, since the value of **tree-rec**(**leaf**(**tt**), x.d, e') is the value of d.

2. The value of **rec**(**succ**(a), d, e) is the value of e(a, **rec**(a, d, e)) since:

   rec(**succ**(a), d, e) ≡
   tree-rec(**tree**(x.a, x.d, u.v.e(u(**tt**),v(**tt**)))=
   (by the computation of **tree-rec**)
   (u.v.e(u(**tt**),v(**tt**)))
   (x.a, y.**tree-rec**(a, x.d, u.v.e(u(**tt**),v(**tt**))))
   = e(a, **tree-rec**(a, x.d, u.v.e(u(**tt**),v(**tt**))))
   ≡ e(a, **rec**(a, d, e)) ■

Other inductively defined data types are easily defined in terms of multilevel functions, for instance the data type **List**$_N$(A), whose canonical objects are **nil**$_N$(a) or **cons**$_N$(a,b) , where a ∈ A and b ∈ **List**$_N$(A):

$$\textbf{List}_N(A) \equiv \textbf{Bool} \overset{*}{\rightarrow} A$$
$$\textbf{nil}_N(a) \equiv \textbf{leaf}(a)$$
$$\textbf{cons}_N(a, b) \equiv \textbf{tree}(x.\textbf{if } x \textbf{ then leaf}(a) \textbf{ else } b))$$
$$\textbf{listrec}_N(p, d, e) \equiv \textbf{tree-rec}(p, d, u.v.e(u(\textbf{true}), u(\textbf{false}), v(\textbf{false}))))$$

The type **BIN**(A) of binary trees (S-expressions) has as canonical objects **atom**(a), where a ∈ A, and **bin**(b,c), where b ∈ **BIN**(A), c ∈ **BIN**(A). It can be defined as:

$$\textbf{BIN}(A) \equiv \textbf{Bool} \overset{*}{\rightarrow} A$$
$$\textbf{atom}(a) \equiv \textbf{leaf}(a)$$
$$\textbf{bin}(b, c) \equiv \textbf{tree}(x.\textbf{if } x \textbf{ then } b \textbf{ else } c))$$
$$\textbf{s-rec}(d, e, f) \equiv \textbf{tree-rec}(d, e, u.v.f(u(\textbf{true}),u(\textbf{false}),v(\textbf{true}),v(\textbf{false})))$$

6.4 Functions

Finally the type A → B of functions from A to B can be defined as:

$$A \rightarrow B \equiv \{f \in A \overset{*}{\rightarrow} B \mid C(f)\}$$
$$\lambda(b) \equiv \textbf{tree}(x.\textbf{leaf}(b(x)))$$
$$\textbf{apply}(p, a) \equiv \textbf{tree-rec}(p, x.a, y.z.\textbf{tree-rec}(y(a), u.u, v.w.a))$$

where

$$C(f) \equiv \textbf{tree-rec}(f, x.\bot, y.z.\forall u\in A.(\text{Is\_leaf}(y(u))))$$
$$\text{Is\_leaf}(g) \equiv \textbf{tree-rec}(g, x.\textbf{T}, y.z.\bot)$$

The following properties hold:

1. If b(x) ∈ B for x ∈ A, then λ(b) ∈ A → B.
2. If f ∈ A → B and a ∈ A then **apply**(f,a) ∈ B.
3. If a ∈ A and b(x) ∈ B for x ∈ A then **apply**(λ(b),a) ∈ B = b(a) ∈ B.

7. DEFINING MULTILEVEL FUNCTIONS WITHIN TYPE THEORY

Instead of defining the type former $A \overset{*}{\rightarrow} B$ by extending the type theory with a new type, it is possible to define the type former as an abbreviation of other types. Martin-Löf showed (private communication) that the type $A \overset{*}{\rightarrow} B$ can be defined using well-orderings. The type of well-orderings is a more general type of trees and more difficult to understand than multilevel functions.

It is also possible to define the type as:

$$A \overset{*}{\rightarrow} B \equiv \Sigma\, x \in \mathbf{N}.(A \overset{x}{\rightarrow} B)$$

where the type $A \overset{x}{\rightarrow} B$ (the type of multilevel functions of depth x) is defined using recursion and universes. The limitation with this definition is that the types A and B have to be coded in a universe.

8. ACKNOWLEDGEMENT

I want to thank Alexander Ollongren who told me about Vienna objects when he visited Göteborg in 1980. I also want to thank Per Martin-Löf, Kent Petersson and Jan Smith for many discussions on type theory.

9. REFERENCES

[1] J. A. Bergstra, H. J. M. Goeman, A. Ollongren, G. A. Terpstra, and Th. P. van der Weide, "Axioms for Multilevel Objects", Annales Societatis Mathematicae Polonae, Series IV: Fundamenta Informaticae, Vol. III.2, pp. 171-180 (1979).

[2] P. Martin-Löf, "Constructive Mathematics and Computer Programming", pp. 153-175 in Logic, Methodology and Philosophy of Science, VI, North-Holland Publishing Company, Amsterdam (1982), Proceedings of the 6th International Congress, Hannover, 1979.

[3] B. Nordström and K. Petersson, "Types and Specifications", pp. 915-920 in Proceedings IFIP '83, Paris, ed. R. E. A. Mason, Elsevier Science Publishers (North-Holland), Amsterdam (1983).

[4] B. Nordström and J. Smith, "Propositions, Types and Specifications of Programs in Martin-Löf's Type Theory", BIT, Vol. 24 no. 3, pp. 288-301 (October 1984).

[5] B. Nordström, K. Petersson, and J. Smith, An Introduction to Type Theory, Programming Methodology Group, Chalmers University of Technology, Göteborg (1985), In preparation.

[6] A. Ollongren, Definition of Programming Languages by Interpreting Automata, Academic Press APIC Series No II (1974).

[7] A. L. Rosenberg and J. W. Thatcher, "What is a multilevel array?", IBM Journal of Research and Development, Vol. 19, pp. 163-169 (1975).

[8] P. Wegner, "The Vienna Definition Language", Computing Surveys, 1972.

An implementation from a direct semantics definition

David A. Schmidt
Computer Science Department
Iowa State University
Ames, Iowa 50011 USA

Implementation techniques for denotational definitions are traditionally tied to the continuation format [3, 10, 11, 13, 31, 32, 33]. A primary advantage of working with continuation-style semantics is that the control facet of an implementation is easy to discern. Further, the continuation operators form an instruction set for a hypothetical machine for the language [32, 33].

On the negative side, the continuation format is low-level, even operational, in nature. The direct semantics format is preferred for defining higher level languages in an abstract, implementation-independent fashion. If we wish to implement a direct semantics definition, we can transform it into continuation form and work from there [10, 19, 26, 31]. Unfortunately, the transformation adds complicating semantic domains and requires a complicated correctness proof. In this paper we construct an implementation for a language directly from its direct semantics definition. We show how operational notions are inferred from a direct semantics definition and hope to encourage others to use direct semantics in their language design and implementation efforts. Unlike the synthesis of an implementation from a continuation definition, which follows a fairly narrow path due to the restrictive nature of continuations, implementation from a direct semantics definition requires more decisions by the implementor. Rather than being a drawback, this freedom of choice regarding data structures and control is an advantage, for it allows the implementor to orient the implementation towards the hardware and software he has available.

The technique will be illustrated by its application to (yet again) a **while**-loop language.

0. Background

A standard strategy for implementing a direct semantics-style denotational definition is to define an evaluator for the definition's semantic notation [11, 14, 15, 16]. A program is mapped to its denotation, which is reduced to a normal form. The leftmost-outermost method suffices for obtaining a normal form [2, 5]. (One exception: a combination $(\underline{\lambda} x.M)N$, that is, a *strict* abstraction and its argument, must be reduced argument-first.)

The evaluator can be an SECD machine [1, 12], a combinator machine [29, 32], or whatever. For simplicity, visualize the evaluator as a tree reduction machine: a denotation is represented in tree form, and the evaluator performs a left-to-right, depth-first traversal of the tree. When a node in the tree is visited, the evaluator determines if the subtree whose root is the visited node is a redex. If it is not, the evaluator visits the next node. If it is, the evaluator replaces the redex by its contractum and then backtracks to visit the parent node of the contractum's (to check for a newly created outermost redex). The method is easy to realize in the various forms of evaluators, but it is inefficient. Our goal is to improve the evaluations by transforming the denotational definition to generate more efficient denotations. The transformations we consider are:

i) Convert those higher order (function space-based) semantic domains in the definition into first order domains, using the closure construction technique described by Reynolds [15] and others [3, 10, 30, 34].

ii) Remove those arguments in the definition that are handled in a sequential parameter passing fashion (are *single-threaded* [28]) and replace them with a global variable, using the method described by Schmidt [21] and Raoult and Sethi [18, 24].

iii) Reduce those expressions that manipulate the global variable. This step is called *control binding* and is presented in this paper.

The transformed definition produces denotations that can be efficiently evaluated by the tree machine or by a more traditional architecture.

The correctness of the transformations are proved with operational criteria. We treat the denotational definition as a syntax directed translation scheme. For each transformation step we fashion a new variant of the evaluator to handle the notation used in the transformed definition and construct a traditional operational simulation proof [35]:

$$\begin{array}{ccc} & \Rightarrow^{*} (\text{in } S) & \\ E & \longrightarrow & E' \\ \alpha \uparrow & & \uparrow \ \alpha \\ F & \longrightarrow & F' \\ & \Rightarrow^{*} (\text{in } T) & \end{array}$$

where S is the original semantic notation, T is the notation resulting from the transformation step, and $\alpha\colon T \to S$ is a recovery map. The proofs of simulation for transformations (i) and (iii) are simple. The proof for (ii) is a bit more involved; see [21, 24].

The example language is presented in figure 1. The domain theory that we use makes use of *predomains* [20, 22], that is, complete partial orders that may lack a least element, $\perp$ (read "bottom"). Call a domain with bottom a *pointed* domain. (If D is a predomain, then $D_{\perp}$ is a pointed domain.) Direct semantics definitions work well with predomains, for sequencing and termination questions are answered succinctly. Predomain theory is also useful to the evaluator, for argument-first evaluation can be used on combinations

Abstract syntax:

C: Command
E: Expression
B: Boolean-expr
I: Identifier
N: Numeral

C ::= C_1;C_2 | I:=E | **if** B **then** C_1 **else** C_2 | **while** B **do** C
E ::= E_1+E_2 | I | N

Semantic algebras:

I. Truth values
Domain $t : Tr = \mathbb{B}$
Operations (the usual ones)

II. Natural numbers
Domain $n : Nat = \mathbb{N}$
Operations (the usual ones)

III. Store
Domain $s : Store =$ Identifier $\rightarrow Nat$
Operations
newstore : *Store*
$newstore = \lambda i.\, zero$

access : Identifier $\rightarrow Store \rightarrow Nat$
$access = \lambda i.\lambda s.\, s(i)$

update : Identifier $\rightarrow Nat \rightarrow Store \rightarrow Store$
$update = \lambda i.\lambda n.\lambda s.\, (\lambda i'.\, i'\ equalid\ i \rightarrow n\ [\!]\ s(i))$

Valuation functions:

C: Command $\rightarrow Store_{\perp} \rightarrow Store_{\perp}$
$\mathbf{C}[\![C_1;C_2]\!] = \underline{\lambda} s.\, \mathbf{C}[\![C_2]\!]\,(\mathbf{C}[\![C_1]\!]s)$
$\mathbf{C}[\![I{:=}E]\!] = \underline{\lambda} s.\, update\,[\![I]\!]\,(\mathbf{E}[\![E]\!]s)\, s$
$\mathbf{C}[\![\mathbf{if}\ B\ \mathbf{then}\ C_1\ \mathbf{else}\ C_2]\!] = \underline{\lambda} s.\, \mathbf{B}[\![B]\!]s \rightarrow \mathbf{C}[\![C_1]\!]s\ [\!]\ \mathbf{C}[\![C_2]\!]s$
$\mathbf{C}[\![\mathbf{while}\ B\ \mathbf{do}\ C]\!] = wh$
where $wh = \underline{\lambda} s.\, \mathbf{B}[\![B]\!]s \rightarrow wh(\mathbf{C}[\![C]\!]s)\ [\!]\ s$

E:Expression $\rightarrow Store \rightarrow Nat$
$\mathbf{E}[\![E_1+E_2]\!] = \lambda s.\, \mathbf{E}[\![E_1]\!]s\ plus\ \mathbf{E}[\![E_2]\!]s$
$\mathbf{E}[\![I]\!] = \lambda s.\, access\,[\![I]\!]\, s$
$\mathbf{E}[\![N]\!] = \lambda s.\, \mathbf{N}[\![N]\!]$

B : Boolean-expr $\rightarrow Store \rightarrow Tr$ (omitted)
N : Numeral $\rightarrow Nat$ (omitted)

Figure 1.

$(\lambda x.M)N$ when N denotes a value from a nonpointed predomain (because argument-first reduction is sufficient for finding normal forms when termination is guaranteed). Since sequential languages (almost) always use strict abstractions on values from pointed domains (one exception: lazy lists), we can use evaluators that apply argument-first reduction.

We now consider the three transformation steps.

1. First order data objects

Those algebras in the denotational definition that define data structures deserve nonfunctional domains. Then the evaluator can create more efficient representations of their values. We convert a function domain $D = A \to B$ to a first order (that is, nonfunctional) domain by representing the members of D as tuples. The conversion is called *defunctionalization* [19]. A D-typed term, an abstraction, is represented by a tuple of the arguments used to create the abstraction. Figure 2 shows the converted form of the *Store* algebra of figure 1. Now operations *newstore* and *update* create labelled tuples. When a store tuple is

---

III′. Store
Domain $s: Store = New + Upd$
where $New = Unit = \{ () \}$
$Upd = Identifier \times Nat \times Store$
Operations

newstore : *Store*
newstore = in*New*()

access : $Identifier \times Store \to Nat$
(*access i s*) = *eval i s*

update : $Identifier \times Nat \times Store \to Store$
(*update i n s*) = in*Upd*(*i*,*n*,*s*)

where
(*eval i s*) = cases *s* of
is*New*() $\to (\lambda i'.\ zero)(i)$
$[]$ is*Upd*$(i', n', s') \to (\lambda i''.\ i''\ equalid\ i' \to n'\ []\ (eval\ i''\ s'))(i)$
end
$= \lambda i.\lambda s.$ cases *s* of
is*New*() $\to zero$
$[]$ is*Upd*$(i', n', s') \to ((i\ equalid\ i') \to n'\ []\ (eval\ i\ s'))$
end

Figure 2.

---

used in an *access*, operation *eval* "restores" the abstraction that the tuple represents and produces the correct result.

The evaluator finds values from defunctionalized domains easier to handle for several reasons. First, a tuple value is physically smaller than the corresponding abstraction that it represents. Second, substitutions of values for free identifiers in *Store* abstractions disappear. (Consider the abstraction that formerly resulted from $(update [\![I_0]\!] n_0 s_0)$. All of $[\![I_0]\!]$, n_0, and s_0 must be bound into the body of the abstraction.) Third, the evaluator is no longer forced to evaluate the body of an abstraction that lacks an argument, for the input and output values of programs are now guaranteed to be first order. Finally, it is straightforward to convert the defunctionalized domain into an even more efficient implementation. For example, the property that $access [\![I]\!] (update [\![I]\!] n\, s)) = n$ implies that a tuple $inUpd([\![I]\!], n, (\cdots inUpd([\![I]\!], m, s') \cdots))$ is operationally equivalent to $inUpd([\![I]\!], n, \cdots s' \cdots)$. An array can be used to represent store values, and the *access* and *update* operations can be array indexing and updating respectively. Paulson comments that ordered binary trees are another useful first order representation for store-like values [15].

A related transformation, *decurrying*, is performed upon the operations of the semantic algebras. An operation $f\colon A_1 \rightarrow A_2 \rightarrow \cdots \rightarrow A_n \rightarrow B$, where all of $A_1, A_2, \cdots, A_n, B$ are first order domains, is (almost) always used in a nested combination $((\cdots ((f E_1) E_2) \cdots) E_n)$. We introduce a new n-ary constructor $(f E_1\, E_2 \cdots E_n)$ for each such f. Now f has arity $A_1 \times A_2 \times \cdots \times A_n \rightarrow B$. Its reduction rule is $(f\, n_1 \cdots n_m) \Rightarrow r$, where $((\cdots (f\, n_1) \cdots) n_m) \Rightarrow^* r$. The obvious advantage of decurrying is that the nested application, which takes several reductions to reach a normal form, is replaced by an application that reduces in one step.

2. Global variables

Our intuitions tell us that the store argument in a sequential language's definition should be treated as a global value. To make this point we replace the *Store* domain in the semantic definition by a store *variable*. The operations in the *Store* algebra no longer require a store argument, for the contents of the store variable will be used instead. Of course, not all semantic definitions can be altered this way. The semantic equations must handle their store arguments in a "sequential" fashion: a store transformation function receives a single store argument, makes changes to it, and passes it on to the next transformation function. This is an operational notion, and we say that an expression is *single-threaded* (in its store argument) if there exists a reduction strategy that can be applied to the expression such that at each stage of the reduction, there exists at most one "active" normal form value of store in the stage [21, 28]. (A value is *active* if it does not appear within the body E of an abstraction $(\lambda x.E)$.)

The reduction strategy that works the best to demonstrate the single-threadedness of an expression is an argument-first one: treat all abstractions in the expression as if they are strict. (This is acceptable if the expression in question contains no abstractions $(\lambda x.E) : A_{\underline{\perp}} \rightarrow B$.)

Figure 3 shows an argument-first reduction. The active normal form values of stores are represented by terms s_i. At each stage of the reduction, there is at most one active normal form value of store. For example, the stage *update* ⟦Y⟧ ((*access* ⟦X⟧ s_1) *plus zero*) s_1 has two occurrences of the one active normal form value s_1. The actions upon the store occur in the same order as they would in a conventional implementation. The multiple copies of the stores could be replaced by a global variable holding a single copy of the store's value. Operations *access* and *update* would use the global variable.

Schmidt [21] has defined criteria which suffice for guaranteeing that the single-threading property holds for a denotation of a program. Sethi has also provided useful guidelines [24]. Lack of space prevents an explanation of the criteria here, but it is the case that the definition of figure 1 satisfies the criteria, that is, the denotations of its programs are single-threaded with respect to argument-first reduction.

The technique for transforming a denotational definition into one which uses a store variable goes as follows:

i) For the *Store* algebra, replace domain $s : Store = D$ by the variable declaration var $s : Store = D$. Destruction operations $f: A_1 \times \cdots \times A_n \times Store \rightarrow B$, $B \neq Store$, defined as $(f\ a_1 \cdots a_n\ s) = e$, become $f: A_1 \times \cdots \times A_n \times Unit \rightarrow B$, $(f\ a_1 \cdots a_n\ ()) = e$,

---

C⟦X:=Z; Y:=X+X⟧(*newstore*)
= $F_2(F_1(newstore))$,
where $F_1 = \underline{\lambda} s.\, update$ ⟦X⟧ (*access* ⟦Z⟧ s) s
$F_2 = \underline{\lambda} s.\, update$ ⟦Y⟧ ((*access* ⟦X⟧ s) *plus* (*access* ⟦X⟧ s)) s
⇒ $F_2(F_1\ s_0)$, where $s_0 =$ in*New*()
⇒ F_2(*update* ⟦X⟧ (*access* ⟦Z⟧ s_0) s_0)
⇒ F_2(*update* ⟦X⟧ *zero* s_0)
⇒ $F_2\ s_1$, where $s_1 =$ in*Upd*(⟦X⟧, *zero*, s_0)
⇒ *update* ⟦Y⟧ ((*access* ⟦X⟧ s_1) *plus* (*access* ⟦X⟧ s_1)) s_1
⇒ *update* ⟦Y⟧ ((*access* ⟦X⟧ s_1) *plus zero*) s_1
⇒ *update* ⟦Y⟧ (*zero plus zero*) s_1
⇒ *update* ⟦Y⟧ *zero* s_1
⇒ s_2, where $s_2 =$ in*Upd*(⟦Y⟧, *zero*, s_1)

Figure 3.

---

and any occurrences of s in e now refer to the variable. (*Unit* is the trivial, one element domain; its only value is ().) Construction operations $g: A_1 \times \cdots \times A_n \times Store \rightarrow Store$, defined as $(g\ a_1 \cdots a_n\ s) = e$, become $g: A_1 \times \cdots \times A_n \times Unit \rightarrow Unit$, $(g\ a_1 \cdots a_n\ ()) = (s := e)$, and the value () results.

ii) For all semantic equations and operations which use occurrences of *Store*-typed identifiers s, replace the occurrences of s by ().

The transformation of the language in figure 1 is presented in figure 4.

A program's denotation is no longer a single expression E, but a pair (E, s), where s is the current value of the store variable. The reduction rules use the expression, store pairs. For example, the new version of the β-rule is $(\cdots (\lambda x.M)N \cdots, s) \Rightarrow (\cdots [N/x]M \cdots, s)$. The reduction rules that manipulate the store are

---

III. Store module
var s: *Store* = *New* + *Upd*
Operations

newstore : *Unit*
newstore = (s := in*New*())

access : *Identifier* × *Unit* → *Unit*
(*access* i ()) = *eval* i s

update : *Identifier* × *Nat* × *Unit* → *Unit*
(*update* i n ()) = (s := in*Upd*(i,n,s))

Valuation functions:

C: Command → *Unit* → *Unit*
$\mathbf{C}[\![C_1;C_2]\!] = \underline{\lambda}().\ \mathbf{C}[\![C_2]\!]\,(\mathbf{C}[\![C_1]\!]())$
$\mathbf{C}[\![\text{if B then } C_1 \text{ else } C_2]\!] = \underline{\lambda}().\ \mathbf{B}[\![B]\!]() \rightarrow \mathbf{C}[\![C_1]\!]()\ [\!]\ \mathbf{C}[\![C_2]\!]()$
$\mathbf{C}[\![\text{while B do C}]\!] = \lambda().\ wh()$
where $wh = \underline{\lambda}().\ \mathbf{B}[\![B]\!]() \rightarrow wh(\mathbf{C}[\![C]\!]())\ [\!]\ ()$
$\mathbf{C}[\![I{:=}E]\!] = \underline{\lambda}().\ update\,[\![I]\!]\ (\mathbf{E}[\![E]\!]())\ ()$

E: Expression → *Unit* → *Nat*
$\mathbf{E}[\![E_1+E_2]\!] = \lambda().\ \mathbf{E}[\![E_1]\!]()\ plus\ \mathbf{E}[\![E_2]\!]()$
$\mathbf{E}[\![I]\!] = \lambda().\ access\,[\![I]\!]\ ()$
$\mathbf{E}[\![N]\!] = \lambda().\ \mathbf{N}[\![N]\!]$

Figure 4.

$$(\cdots(access\ i\,())\cdots, s) \Rightarrow (\cdots n \cdots, s) \quad \text{where } eval\ i\ s = n$$

$$(\cdots(update\ i\ n\,())\cdots, s) \Rightarrow (\cdots()\cdots, \text{in}Upd(i, n, s))$$

The advantage of the new definition over the old is that the cumbersome store argument need not be copied into an expression during reductions. A conventional evaluator would make the store into a fixed machine component and make *access* and *update* into machine instructions.

The () values are "pointers" to the store variable, but more importantly they act as control markers— they give permission to subexpressions to evaluate. For example, the equation for $\mathbf{C}[\![C_1;C_2]\!]$ makes it clear that when control is awarded to the compound command, $[\![C_1]\!]$ immediately gets control. On its completion, control is given to $[\![C_2]\!]$. As another example, the evaluation of the operands of $\mathbf{E}[\![E_1+E_2]\!]$ can be conducted in any order, even in parallel, because the control marker given to the addition expression is simultaneously awarded to both $[\![E_1]\!]$ and $[\![E_2]\!]$.

The global variable transformation has exposed the underlying *store-based control* in the sequential language. We could fashion a machine that mimics with an instruction counter the flow of the control markers through a denotation. When the instruction counter points to (the code of) expression *E*, it represents the combination *E*().

3. Control binding

The definition in figure 4 produces program denotations that contain a large number of combinations of the form $(\lambda().M)()$. These combinations can be optimized out of the denotation before run-time. In fact, they can be optimized out of the semantic equations themselves! Since all the semantic equations for translation function **C** have the form $\mathbf{C}[\![C']\!] = \underline{\lambda}().E'$, any occurrence of $\mathbf{C}[\![C]\!]$ in E' must translate to some $(\underline{\lambda}().E)$. Thus, a combination $\mathbf{C}[\![C]\!]()$ in E' can be simplified where it stands. This technique, called *control binding*, goes as follows:

> For a valuation function **M** such that each equation for **M** has the form $\mathbf{M}[\![M_i]\!] = \lambda().E_i$, rewrite each equation to the form
> $\mathbf{M}'[\![M_i]\!] = [\mathbf{M}'[\![M]\!] / (\lambda().\mathbf{M}'[\![M]\!])()\,][\,(\lambda().\mathbf{M}'[\![M]\!]) / \mathbf{M}[\![M]\!]\,]E_i$,
> that is, replace all occurrences of $\mathbf{M}[\![M]\!]()$ in E_i by $\mathbf{M}'[\![M]\!]$, and replace all occurences of $\mathbf{M}[\![M]\!]$ not in combination with () by $(\lambda().\mathbf{M}'[\![M]\!])$.

An easy structural induction proof shows that for any syntax phrase $[\![M]\!]$, $\mathbf{M}[\![M]\!]()$ is convertible [2, 5] to $\mathbf{M}'[\![M]\!]$, hence reduction properties are preserved.

Figure 5 gives the definition of figure 4 after control binding. All of the **C**, **E**, and **B** translation functions are treated. (We have omitted the primes on the function names.)

The *Store*'s operations are also treated. All trivial bindings of control disappear. The non-trivial ones (in the terminology of [19], these are the "serious" ones) are represented by the combinator ";". Note that a () remains in the equation for the **while**-loop: once a loop completes, control is released for another command to seize.

4. A target machine and compiler

The transformed direct semantics definition generates expressions that are processed reasonably efficiently by the tree evaluator. But we might want an architecture that is nearer to a traditional machine. Recall that the evaluator does a tree traversal, reducing redexes as it proceeds. A standard way of implementing a tree traversal nonrecursively is with a stack that remembers the nodes of the tree that remain to be traversed. Let us call this stack the *control stack*. In addition, we maintain a *temporary value stack* to hold reduced subtrees. Thus, a partially reduced tree is modelled as a $(v\ c)$ configuration, where v is the temporary value stack, that is, the part of the tree that has been traversed, and c is the control stack, that is, the part of the tree that still requires traversal. Finally, the store component needs to be carried along— a machine configuration of the form $(v\,c\,s)$ results, and we have the defined the structure of what we call the *VCS-machine.*

Figure 6 defines the VCS-machine; it is an interpreter of the semantic notation. (Note: the tops of the v and c stacks are on the left, ":" represents stack *cons*, and *nil* is the empty stack.) The reduction rules show that the machine traverses a tree by stacking the subtrees on the control stack in the order of their traversal. It is easy to prove for all program denotations E and stores s_0 that $(E, s_0) \Rightarrow^* ((), s_f)$ iff $(nil\ E\ s_0) \Rightarrow^* (nil\ nil\ s_f)$. (The *wh* function in figure 5 and recursively defined expressions in general are evaluated

---

$$\mathbf{C}[\![C_1;C_2]\!] = \mathbf{C}[\![C_1]\!];\mathbf{C}[\![C_2]\!]$$
$$\mathbf{C}[\![I{:=}E]\!] = \mathit{update}\,[\![I]\!]\ \mathbf{E}[\![E]\!]$$
$$\mathbf{C}[\![\textbf{if } B \textbf{ then } C_1 \textbf{ else } C_2]\!] = \mathbf{B}[\![B]\!] \rightarrow \mathbf{C}[\![C_1]\!] \,\square\, \mathbf{C}[\![C_2]\!]$$
$$\mathbf{C}[\![\textbf{while } B \textbf{ do } C]\!] = \mathit{wh}$$
$$\text{where } \mathit{wh} = \mathbf{B}[\![B]\!] \rightarrow \mathbf{C}[\![C]\!];\mathit{wh} \,\square\, ()$$

$$\mathbf{E}[\![E_1{+}E_2]\!] = \mathbf{E}[\![E_1]\!]\ \mathit{plus}\ \mathbf{E}[\![E_2]\!]$$
$$\mathbf{E}[\![I]\!] = \mathit{access}\,[\![I]\!]$$
$$\mathbf{E}[\![N]\!] = \mathbf{N}[\![N]\!]$$

(note: the expression $E_1;E_2$ abbreviates $(\lambda().E_2)E_1$)

Figure 5.

Machine language:

$E ::= E_1;E_2 \mid (B \rightarrow E_1 \,[\,]\, E_2) \mid cond(E_1, E_2) \mid (update\ i\ E) \mid save\ i \mid (access\ i) \mid$
$\quad E_1\ plus\ E_2 \mid add \mid true \mid false \mid n \mid ()$

Reduction rules:

$v \quad E_1; E_2{:}c \quad s \quad \Rightarrow \quad v \quad E_1{:}E_2{:}c \quad s$

$v \quad (B \rightarrow E_1 \,[\,]\, E_2){:}c \quad s \quad \Rightarrow \quad v \quad B{:}cond(E_1, E_2){:}c \quad s$

$true{:}v \quad cond(E_1, E_2){:}c \quad s \quad \Rightarrow \quad v \quad E_1{:}c \quad s$

$false{:}v \quad cond(E_1, E_2){:}c \quad s \quad \Rightarrow \quad v \quad E_2{:}c \quad s$

$v \quad (update\ i\ E){:}c \quad s \quad \Rightarrow \quad v \quad E{:}save\ i{:}c \quad s$

$a{:}v \quad save\ i{:}c \quad s \quad \Rightarrow \quad v \quad c \quad inUpd(i, a, s)$

$v \quad access\ i{:}c \quad s \quad \Rightarrow \quad a{:}v \quad c \quad s$
$\qquad \text{where } a = (eval\ i\ s)$

$v \quad E_1\ plus\ E_2{:}c \quad s \quad \Rightarrow \quad v \quad E_1{:}E_2{:}add{:}c \quad s$

$a_2{:}a_1{:}v \quad add{:}c \quad s \quad \Rightarrow \quad a{:}v \quad c \quad s$
$\qquad \text{where } a = a_1\ plus\ a_2$

$v \quad n{:}c \quad s \quad \Rightarrow \quad n{:}v \quad c \quad s$

$v \quad (){:}c \quad s \quad \Rightarrow \quad v \quad c \quad s$

Figure 6.

---

by unfolding, e.g., $v \quad wh{:}c \quad s \Rightarrow v \quad (\mathbf{B}[\![B]\!] \rightarrow \mathbf{C}[\![C]\!];wh \,[\,]\, ()){:}c \quad s$.)

Since the VCS-machine is an interpreter, it spends a lot of time decomposing denotations on its control stack. For example, the first two reduction rules in figure 6 are decomposition steps: they lay out the order of traversal of compositions and conditionals respectively. We would like to do the decompositions prior to run-time. That is, a denotation E would be decomposed to some E' such that

i) E' contains no occurrences of the semantic notation but contains only "computational" instructions such as *cond*, *save*, and *add*;

ii) $(nil\ E\ s_0) \Rightarrow^* (nil\ nil\ s_f)$ iff $(nil\ E'\ s_0) \Rightarrow^* (nil\ nil\ s_f)$.

We map E to E' is by systematically mapping the subexpressions of E to their expanded forms. Call the map that does this $\mathbf{T}$: *Denotation* $\rightarrow$ *Machine-language*. The first reduction rule in figure 6 dictates that $\mathbf{T}[\![E_1;E_2]\!] = \mathbf{T}[\![E_1]\!]{:}\mathbf{T}[\![E_2]\!]$. Similarly, the second rule states that $\mathbf{T}[\![B \rightarrow E_1 \,[\,]\, E_2]\!] = \mathbf{T}[\![B]\!]{:}cond(\mathbf{T}[\![E_1]\!], \mathbf{T}[\![E_2]\!])$. However, the reduction rule for (*access* i) does no decomposition but alters the temporary value stack instead. We "decompose" (*access* i) by inventing a new machine operation *fetch* with operational semantics

$v \quad fetch\ i{:}c \quad s \quad \Rightarrow \quad a{:}v\ c \quad s \qquad$ where $a = eval\ i\ s$

(note that *fetch* behaves just like *access*) and then saying that $\mathbf{T}[\![(access\ i)]\!] = fetch\ i$. The remaining constructs translate similarly. Figure 7 shows the new version of the VCS-machine and the code generation map T.

An important characteristic of the new machine is that the control stack is always popped but never pushed. Thus, we can treat *c* as a stored program, for the stack is loaded once, at the initiation of evaluation. Instead of popping the stack, we can use an instruction counter to point to the current instruction in *c* in use. This makes the VCS-machine into a conventional stack machine. One benefit of the instruction counter is that we can replace the instruction $cond(S_1, S_2)$ by the instruction sequence $jumpfalse\ L_1{:}\ S_1{:}\ jump\ L_2{:}\ label\ L_1{:}\ S_2{:}\ label\ L_2$, where the $jump\ L$ instruction is a new machine instruction that moves the instruction counter to the instruction immediately following $label\ L$. ($jumpfalse\ L$ works analogously.)

Machine language:

$S ::= cond(S_1, S_2) \mid fetch\ i \mid save\ i \mid push\ n \mid skip$

Reduction rules:

$true{:}v \quad cond(S_1, S_2){:}c \quad s \quad \Rightarrow \quad v \quad S_1{:}c\ s$

$false{:}c \quad cond(S_1, S_2){:}c \quad s \quad \Rightarrow \quad v \quad S_2{:}c\ s$

$v \quad fetch\ i{:}c\ s \quad \Rightarrow \quad a{:}v \quad c \quad s$

where $a = eval\ i\ s$

$a{:}v \quad save\ i{:}c \quad s \quad \Rightarrow \quad v \quad c \quad \mathrm{in}Upd(i,n,s)$

$v \quad push\ n{:}c\ s \quad \Rightarrow \quad n{:}v \quad c \quad s$

$v \quad skip{:}c \quad s \quad \Rightarrow \quad v \quad c \quad s$

Code generation map:

$\mathbf{T} : Denotation \rightarrow Machine\text{-}language$

$\mathbf{T}[\![E_1; E_2]\!] = \mathbf{T}[\![E_1]\!]{:}\ \mathbf{T}[\![E_2]\!]$

$\mathbf{T}[\![B \rightarrow E_1 \,[\!]\, E_2]\!] = \mathbf{T}[\![B]\!]{:}\ cond(\mathbf{T}[\![E_1]\!], \mathbf{T}[\![E_2]\!])$

$\mathbf{T}[\![update\ i\ E]\!] = \mathbf{T}[\![E]\!]{:}\ save\ i$

$\mathbf{T}[\![E_1\ plus\ E_2]\!] = \mathbf{T}[\![E_1]\!]{:}\ \mathbf{T}[\![E_2]\!]{:}\ add$

$\mathbf{T}[\![access\ i]\!] = fetch\ i$

$\mathbf{T}[\![n]\!] = push\ n$

$\mathbf{T}[\![()]\!] = skip$

Figure 7.

A compiler $G = T \circ C$ results. For example, $G[\![C_1;C_2]\!] = T(C[\![C_1;C_2]\!]) = T(C[\![C_1]\!]; C[\![C_2]\!]) = T(C[\![C_1]\!]): T(C[\![C_2]\!]) = G[\![C_1]\!]: G[\![C_2]\!]$. The other constructs compile similarly. The compilation of the while-loop, however, is a bit puzzling, for $G[\![\text{while } B \text{ do } C]\!] = G[\![wh]\!] = G[\![B]\!]: cond(G[\![C]\!]: G[\![wh]\!], skip)$. If we place the usual partial ordering on the language of denotations [8, 9, 23] (and we admit denotations of infinite length), the least fixed point of $G[\![wh]\!]$ is the infinite sequence

$$G[\![B]\!]: cond(\; G[\![C]\!]: G[\![B]\!]: cond(\; G[\![C]\!]: G[\![B]\!]: cond(\; \ldots \;, skip) \;, skip) \;, skip)$$

An easy simulation proof shows that the reductions taken on the infinite sequence are the same ones as those taken on $G[\![wh]\!]$ when unfolding is used. (This is an example of a "Mezei-Wright property" [8]). Yet another simulation proof shows that the loop code $label\ L: G[\![B]\!]: cond(G[\![C]\!]: jump\ L, skip)$ also has the same reductions as the infinite sequence. Indeed, the loop code is just a finite abbreviation of the infinite sequence. (The abbreviation exists because $G[\![wh]\!]$ is *tail recursive* [27].) We use

$$G[\![\text{while } B \text{ do } C]\!] = label\ L: G[\![B]\!]: cond(G[\![C]\!]: jump\ L, skip)$$

as the translation of the loop.

5. Conclusion

We have developed an implementation from a direct semantics definition, focussing upon the operational properties that arise in the reduction of denotations. Since the structure of a denotation is dictated by the structure of the semantic equations, we were able to tune the equations to produce denotations that are easier to reduce. The target architecture was a consequence of the reduction strategy taken on the denotations.

The transformation steps outlined in this paper are not definitive. The implementation process must be based on common sense and can be directed towards a specific target architecture. It seems disadvantageous to completely automate the process, for there are too many variants that can be profitably exploited by human ingenuity. The direct semantics method of language definition appears useful precisely because it gives the implementor the freedom to choose data structures and evaluation strategies. We hope to study this issue further in a later version of this paper.

Acknowledgement: Mitchell Wand and Neil Jones provided helpful comments on earlier versions of this paper.

6. References

[1] Bauer, F.L., and Wossner, H. *Algorithmic Language and Program Development*. Springer-Verlag, Berlin, 1982.

[2] Berry, G., and Levy, J.-J. A survey of some syntactic results of the lambda-calculus. In *Proc. 8th Symp. on Math. Foundations of Comp. Sci.*, Lecture Notes in Computer Science 74, Springer, Berlin, 1979.

[3] Bjorner, D., and Jones, C.B. *Formal Specification and Software Development*, Prentice-Hall, Englewood Cliffs, N.J., 1982.

[4] Burge, W. *Recursive Programming Techniques*. Addison-Wesley, Reading, Mass., 1976.

[5] Curry, H.B., and Feys, R. *Combinatory Logic, Vol. 1*. North-Holland, Amsterdam, 1958.

[6] Ershov, E.P. On the essence of compilation. In *Formal description of programming concepts*, E.J. Neuhold, ed., North-Holland, Amsterdam, 1978.

[7] Georgeff, M. Transformations and reduction strategies for typed lambda expressions. *ACM TOPLAS* 6 (1984) 603-631.

[8] Goguen, J., Thatcher, J., Wagner, E., and Wright, J. Initial algebra semantics and continuous algebras. *Journal of the ACM* 24(1977) 68-95.

[9] Guessarian, I. *Algebraic Semantics*. Lecture Notes in Computer Science 99, Springer, Berlin, 1981.

[10] Jones, N.D., Muchnick, S.S., and Schmidt, D.A. A universal compiler. Tech. report DAIMI IR-17, Computer science dept., University of Aarhus, Denmark, 1979.

[11] Jones, N.D., and Christiansen, H. Control flow treatment in a simple semantics-directed compiler generator. In *Formal Description of Programming Concepts II*, North-Holland, Amsterdam, 1982, pp. 38-62.

[12] Landin, P.J. The mechanical evaluation of expressions. *Computer Journal* 6 (1964) 308-320.

[13] Milne, R. and Strachey, C. *A Theory of Programming Language Semantics*. Chapman and Hall, London, 1976.

[14] Mosses, P.D. SIS-- reference manual and user's guide. Tech. report DAIMI MD-30, Computer science dept., University of Aarhus, Denmark, 1979.

[15] Paulson, L. A semantics-directed compiler generator. Proc. 9th ACM POPL, Albuquerque, N.M., Jan. 1982, pp. 224-239.

[16] Pleban, U.F. Compiler prototyping using formal semantics. Proc. ACM SIGPLAN 84 Symp. on Compiler Construction, *SIGPLAN Notices* 17-6 (1982) pp. 94-105.

[17] Raskovsky, M. Denotational semantics as a specification of code generators. Proc. ACM SIGPLAN 82 Conf. on Compiler Construction, *SIGPLAN Notices* 17-6 (1982) 230-244.

[18] Raoult, J.-C., and Sethi, R. The global storage needs of a subcomputation. In *Proc. ACM Symp. on Prin. of Prog. Lang.* Salt Lake City, Utah, 1984, pp. 148-157.

[19] Reynolds, J.C. Definitional interpreters for higher order programming languages. In Proceedings, Twenty-fifth ACM National Conference, Boston, 1972, pp. 717-740.

[20] Reynolds, J.C. Semantics of the domain of flow diagrams. *J. ACM* 24 (1977) 484-503.

[21] Schmidt, D.A. Detecting global variables in denotational specifications. *ACM TOPLAS* 7-2 (1985) 299-310.

[22] Schmidt, D.A. *Denotational Semantics: An Introduction.* Allyn and Bacon, Boston, in press.

[23] Scott, D.S. The lattice of flow diagrams. In *Semantics of Algorithmic Languages*, E. Engeler, ed. Lecture Notes Math. 188, Springer, Berlin, 1970, pp. 311-366.

[24] Sethi, R. Pebble games for studying storage sharing. *Theoretical Comp. Sci.* 19-1 (1982) 69-84.

[25] Sethi, R. Control flow aspects of semantics-directed compiling. *ACM TOPLAS* 5-4 (1983) 554-595.

[26] Sethi, R., and Tang, A. Constructing call by value continuation semantics. *Journal of the ACM* 27 (1980) 580-597.

[27] Steele, G.L. RABBIT: A compiler for SCHEME. M.S. Thesis, EECS Dept., MIT, Cambridge, Mass., May, 1977.

[28] Stoy, J. *Denotational Semantics.* MIT Press, Cambridge, Mass., 1977.

[29] Turner, D. A new implementation technique for applicative languages. *Software: Practice and Experience* 9(1979) 31-49.

[30] Wand, M. First order identities as a defining language. *Acta Informatica* 14 (1980) 337-357.

[31] Wand, M. Continuation-based program transformation strategies. *Journal of the ACM* 27 (1980) 164-180.

[32] Wand, M. Semantics-directed computer architecture. In Proceedings, Ninth ACM Symposium on Principles of Programming Languages, Albuquerque, N.M., 1982, pp. 234-241.

[33] Wand, M. Deriving target code as a representation of continuation semantics. *ACM Trans. Prog. Lang. and Systems* 4 (1982) 496-517.

[34] Wand, M. From interpreter to compiler: a representational derivation. This proceedings.

[35] Wegner, P. Programming language semantics. In *Formal Semantics of Programming Languages*, R. Rustin, ed., Prentice-Hall, Englewood Cliffs, N.J., 1972, pp. 149-248.

The Structure of a Self-Applicable Partial Evaluator

Peter Sestoft

DIKU
University of Copenhagen
Universitetsparken 1, DK-2100 Copenhagen Ø, Denmark
November 19th, 1985

Introduction

The present paper describes the ideas behind a simple, self-applicable partial evaluator called Mix as well as its structure. This partial evaluator was developed at DIKU (by Neil D. Jones, Harald Søndergaard, and the author) during 1984 with the explicit goal in mind that it should be self-applicable and thus make possible the automatic construction of compilers from interpreters and even of a compiler generator. This work is already partly documented in the paper (Jones, Sestoft, Søndergaard 85) that gives a broader treatment of partial evaluation and compiling than the present rather technical paper.

Outline

The structure of the present paper is as follows: First, the concept of partial evaluation is defined and various pieces of notation are introduced. Second, the application of partial evaluation to compiling and compiler generation is briefly explained, and the goals of the project are discussed. Third, the solutions to these problems and the resulting structure of Mix are described in the central part of the paper. Finally, we sum up what has and what has not been done, and suggest further work.

1 Partial Evaluation - Concepts and Notation

In this chapter, we give a brief formal definition of partial evaluation and of some concepts related to compiling. These will be used extensively in the following. The definitions are the same as those given in (Jones, Sestoft, Søndergaard 85).

1.1 Programming Languages

Since we use programs as input to other programs and even to themselves, we assume that programs and data will be of the same nature, that is, members of a universal domain D of symbols (e.g. character strings, LISP lists, natural numbers, or the like). Below, D* is the set of finite sequences of elements from D; broken arrow $- \rightarrow$ means partial function; equality "=" means that either both sides are undefined or they are both defined and equal.

Definition A *programming language* L, then, is a "semantics function" $L: D \dashrightarrow D^* \dashrightarrow D$ so that $L\,p$ is the function $L\,p: D^* \dashrightarrow D$ computed by program p, and $L\,p <d_1, ..., d_n>$ is the result of running L-program p on data $<d_1, ..., d_n> \in D^*$. The set of L programs is the subset of D to which L assigns a meaning, i.e. L-programs = domain(L). □

1.2 Partial Evaluation

First, we will introduce the concept of residual program.

Definition Let L be a programming language, $p \in$ L-programs a program. Then $r \in$ L-programs is a *residual program* for p with respect to known input $<x_1, ..., x_m> \in D^*$ iff

$$L\,p <x_1, ..., x_m, y_1, ..., y_n> = L\,r <y_1, ..., y_n>$$

for all sequences of remaining input $<y_1, ..., y_n> \in D^*$. □

That is, the residual program r is the result of "running the original program p on partially known input" or "specializing p to fixed partial input" $x_1, ..., x_m$.

Now, a partial evaluator *mix* is defined as being a program that produces residual programs.

Definition An *L-partial evaluator mix* is an L-program such that for any L-program p, and partially known input $<x_1, ..., x_m> \in D^*$, L *mix* $<p, x_1, ..., x_m>$ is a residual program for p with respect to $<x_1, ..., x_m>$, or in other words,

$$L\,(L\,mix <p, x_1, ..., x_m>) <y_1, ..., y_n> = L\,p <x_1, ..., x_m, y_1, ..., y_n> \quad (1)$$

for all sequences of remaining input $<y_1, ..., y_n> \in D^*$.

The L program p is called a *subject program* and accordingly, L is the *subject language* of the partial evaluator. The data $<x_1, ..., x_m>$ are called the *known input*, and $<y_1, ..., y_n>$ the *unknown* or *residual input*. A partial evaluator defined this way (it is itself written in its own subject language) is called an *autoprojector* by (Ershov 82). □

A partial evaluator is an implementation of the primitive recursive function S from Kleene's S-m-n Theorem of recursive function theory (Kleene 52). By that theorem, partial evaluators exist.

1.3 Interpreters and Compilers

Let L and S be programming languages.

Definition An *interpreter for S (written in L)* is an L-program int so that

$$L\,int <s, d_1, ..., d_n> = S\,s <d_1, ..., d_n> \quad (2)$$

for all S-programs s and input tuples $<d_1, ..., d_n> \in D^*$. □

Definition A *compiler from S to L (written in L)* is an L-program comp so that

$$L\,(L\,comp <s>) <d_1, ..., d_n> = S\,s <d_1, ..., d_n> \quad (3)$$

for any S-program s and all input tuples $<d_1, ..., d_n> \in D^*$. □

2 Applications to Compiling: The Project Goals

2.1 The Applications of Partial Evaluation to Compiling

This is a very brief account of the relations between partial evaluation and compiling. For a fuller treatment, see (Ershov 78, 82), (Futamura 83), (Jones, Sestoft, Søndergaard 85), or (Turchin 80).

In the following, let L be an implementation language, i.e. a language for which we have a processor (compiler, interpreter), so that L-programs, in fact, can be executed. In our case, L is a very small subset of LISP with some syntactic sugar (extensions) which will be described in Section 3.1. Also, let *mix* be an L-partial evaluator (an autoprojector for L), and let S be a programming language. Then, in principle, the following is feasible.

Compiling by running target = L *mix* <int, s> (where int is an S-interpreter and s is an S-program). The result is an L-program target equivalent to the S source program s.

Compiler generation by running comp = L *mix* <*mix*, int> (where int is an S-interpreter). The result is a compiler comp from S to L written in L.

Compiler generator generation by running cocom = L *mix* <*mix*, *mix*>. The result is a compiler generator cocom (for "compiler compiler") capable of transforming interpreters into compilers. (More generally, cocom implements a limited version of the the currying function on the representation of general recursive functions as programs).

The formal justifications for the above claims may be found in (Jones, Sestoft, Søndergaard 85). Compiling and compiler generation along the lines sketched were described for the first time in (Futamura 71), while it seems that (Turchin 79) contains the first reference to the idea of obtaining a compiler generator by partial evaluation (according to Prof. Turchin the idea dates back to 1975).

2.2 Practice Lagging Behind Theory

While the feasibility *in principle* of compiler resp. compiler generator generation has been known for more than a decade, apparently nobody has realized these in practice until fall 1984. Thus, *compiling* using partial evaluation was realized using a variety of formalisms and languages, see for example (Ershov 78), (Emanuelson, Haraldsson 80), (Kahn, Carlsson 84), and (Haraldsson 78). But as far as we know, no one has reported success in producing *compilers* or a *compiler generator* this way.

Inspired by this problem, we (initially Neil D. Jones and Harald Søndergaard) set out to produce a partial evaluator capable of producing compilers as well as a compiler generator. Also, some interest and insight into the problem stemmed from its relationship to the CERES compiler generator project, expounded in (Jones, Tofte 83).

As can be seen above, a partial evaluator has to be *self-applicable* in order to achieve the goal mentioned. Probably, this is the main source of problems, practical as well as theoretical, and the reason why the earlier efforts remained fruitless.

3 The Partial Evaluator Mix

In this chapter a quite detailed account of the algorithms of the partial evaluator Mix will be given. First, the subject language we chose for Mix is presented. Second, the structure of Mix and some of Mix's algorithms are presented together with reasons for their being that way. Third, an extension to Mix called "variable splitting" is described, and some of our experience with producing compilers and a compiler generator using our partial evaluator Mix are described.

The paper (Sestoft 85) gives some directions for using the Mix system implementation (as of spring 1985). This is not attempted here.

3.1 The Subject Language L of Mix

Above, we used L for the subject language of a partial evaluator *mix*. Below we describe our partial evaluator Mix and its *particular* subject language called L. We list some useful characteristics of L and describe a syntactic extension called LETL.

Characteristics of the Language L

We chose L to be a first-order, statically scoped subset of pure applicative LISP without special treatment of numbers. Therefore L has the following characteristics:

- programs are easily represented as data structures (LISP lists), and a program is its own abstract syntax tree; hence, programs are easily analyzed, decomposed and composed, and therefore, easily transformed.
- L is very minimal, having only eight operators **quote, car, cdr, atom, cons, equal, if**, and **call**.
- manipulation of (syntax) trees is naturally expressed by recursion in L.
- L has a very simple and regular syntax (all operators have fixed arities in contrast to "real" LISP where **cond** and **list** violate this requirement) as well as semantics.
- there exist reasonably efficient implementations of L.

The main drawback of this language is that it is very tedious to program in because of all the parentheses needed to express structure and because of the need to use **car/cdr** sequences to select branches in a tree. This problem, however, is alleviated by the extension LETL described below.

Extension LETL of L

LETL extends L with

- **let** and **where** decomposition patterns, e.g. (**let** (op exp1 exp2) = exp **in** ...). This eliminates the need for most **car/cdr** expressions, as well as a lot of parentheses.
- an **if-then-elsf-else** (syntactically sugared McCarthy) conditional
- an infix, right associative **cons** operator "::". (**cons** a (**cons** b c)) = (a :: b :: c)
- logical connectives: **null, not, and, or**
- a **list** builder

We have written a LETL to L compiler automatically transforming the LETL constructs into basic L constructs. The paper (Sestoft 85) describes these languages in more detail.

3.2 Structure of the Partial Evaluator

In this section we will describe the structure of the partial evaluator. First, we give a presentation of the general ideas and an overview of the phase structure of the partial evaluator, then a more detailed discussion is attempted. Section 3.3 below describes the individual phases and the actual algorithms of the partial evaluator.

3.2.1 Ideas Behind and Structure of Mix

An Example of Partial Evaluation

Consider the following LETL-program (in which we have left out some parentheses) with two parameters, an atom x and a linear list y. Output is a list of the same length as the list y, each element of which is the atom x. However, if x is nil, it will be a list of "a"s, preceded by the atom "exception".

```
h(x,y) =    if (null x) then (cons 'exception (call h 'a y))
            else if (null y) then 'nil
            else (cons x (call h x (cdr y)))
```

We would like to partially evaluate this program for y unknown and x known to be nil.

Now we can proceed to evaluate (**call** h 'nil y) symbolically by *unfolding* h, i.e. replacing the call by the function definition. The conditional (**null** x) is known to be true, therefore

```
h( 'nil,y) =  (cons 'exception (call h 'a y))                              (r1)
```

Evaluating (**call** h 'a y) symbolically we get

```
h( 'a,y) =  if (null y) then 'nil else (cons 'a (call h 'a (cdr y)))      (r2)
```

This we could further unfold to

```
h( 'a,y) =  if (null y) then 'nil
            else if (null (cdr y)) then '(a)
            else (cons 'a (cons 'a (call h 'a (cdr (cdr y)))))             (r2')
```

but it would not lead to much improvement, and such further unfolding could never eliminate the need for recursion, since we have no bound on the length of y, and so we stick to the first version (r2) above. Since we cannot do more useful transformations by symbolic evaluation alone, we will make the above equations (r1) and (r2) into a residual program with two functions. The first being the goal function, which is h specialized to x='nil, and the other a variant of h specialized to x='a, thus

$h_{[\text{'nil}]}$ (y) = (**cons** 'exception (**call** $h_{[\text{'a}]}$ y)) (r1)

$h_{[\text{'a}]}$ (y) = **if** (**null** y) **then** 'nil **else** (**cons** 'a (**call** $h_{[\text{'a}]}$ (**cdr** y))) (r2)

Summary: This residual program was constructed by evaluating expressions symbolically, unfolding function definitions, and suspending function calls (deciding *not* to unfold), and finally, by making function variants specialized to certain values of the known parameter. In principle our partial evaluator Mix uses exactly these transformations.

We will introduce a little terminology. Suppose the subject program has goal function

$$f_1\ (x_1, ..., x_m, y_1, ..., y_n) \ = \ exp_1$$

and that the subject program's known input parameters (those available during partial evaluation) are $x_1, ..., x_m$. Then a parameter x_{ij} of some function f_i is said to be *Known* during partial evaluation if the value of x_{ij} can only depend on the values of the parameters $x_1, ..., x_m$ that are available, not on $y_1, ..., y_n$ that are not available. Correspondingly, x_{ij} is said to be *Unknown* if it may depend on $y_1, ..., y_n$.

Mix Principles

a. The residual program corresponding to a subject program and its known input consists of a collection of function definitions, each resulting from *specializing* (the body of) some function definition in the given subject program to known values of some of its parameters. These are called residual functions.

b. Intuitively, partial evaluation proceeds as *symbolic evaluation* of the subject program. Instead of parameters being bound to their actual values, they are bound to L-expressions denoting their possible values. Symbolic evaluation of expressions which do not contain function calls is straightforward reduction/rewriting of the expressions. Evaluating a function call symbolically, we can do one of two things: *Unfold* the call (i.e. replace it with the reduced equivalent of the called function's body) or *suspend* the call (i.e. replace it with a call to a residual variant of the called function).

c. We require the user of the partial evaluator to decide (before applying it) which function calls in the subject program should be *unfolded* (eliminable call) and which should be *suspended* (residual call). This is done by *annotating* the function call with an "r" (for residual, yielding **callr**) if the user wants it to be suspended.

d. The partial evaluation process is *divided into phases.*

First, the (call annotated) subject program is abstractly interpreted over a value domain only distinguishing known and unknown values. This results in information on which parameters of each function will be known at partial evaluation time, and which will possibly be unknown. The information obtained is used in the second phase for annotating the subject program, dividing the parameter list of each function into two: the *eliminable parameters* (known values at partial evaluation time) and the *residual parameters* (values possibly unknown). This is required for the later specialization of each function into its (zero or more) residual variants in the residual program, cf. a above. Also, each *operator* **car**, **cdr**, ... is annotated either as *eliminable* (**care**, **cdre**, ...) or as *residual* (**carr**, **cdrr**, ...), yielding a heavily annotated version of the subject program. The third phase then takes as input the subject program annotated with respect to calls, parameters, and operators, together with the actual values of the subject program's known input. In this phase, the residual program is constructed as a number of variants of the subject program's functions, specialized to various values of their eliminable parameters.

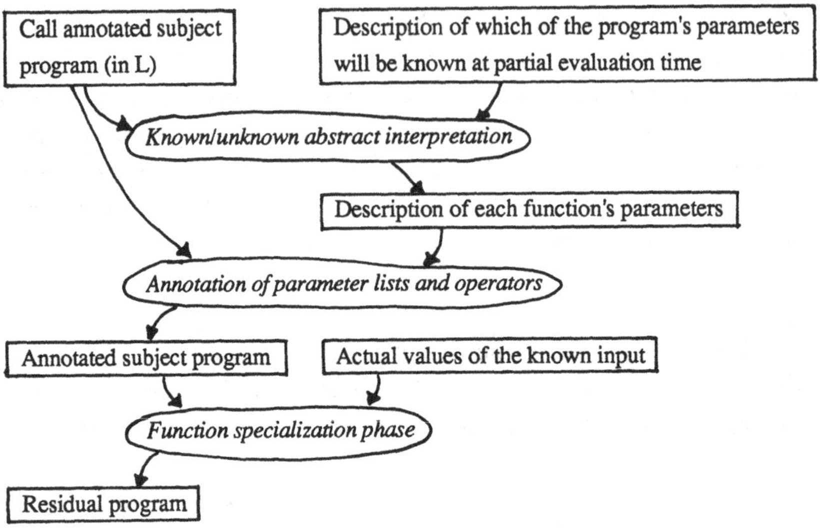

Figure 1: Phase Division of Partial Evaluation

Italics denote phases in the process, whereas plain text denotes objects handled by the phases.

3.2.2 Discussion

Here, a more detailed yet brief treatment of the above is given.

a. **Building the residual program from specializations of the functions** in the subject program is the main principle. In principle, those specializations which have to appear in the residual program are determined as follows: If we consider the space of possible inputs to the subject program with its eliminable parameters restricted to their given, known values $<x_1, ..., x_m>$ we have a subspace $\{<x_1, ..., x_m>\} \times D^n$ of possible inputs, obtained by varying the remaining input $<y_1, ..., y_n>$. Now the residual program has to have a variant $f[<ev_1, ..., ev_i>]$ of a function f specialized to known values $<ev_1, ..., ev_i>$ if in the course of running the subject program on any input from the subspace mentioned, f is called by a residual call with parameter values $<ev_1, ..., ev_i, rv_1, ..., rv_j>$ for some values $<rv_1, ..., rv_j>$ of the residual parameters. The variants in the residual program of a function from the subject program thus make up a kind of *tabulation* of the possible values of that function's eliminable parameters for any computation on the mentioned subspace of inputs. Our partial evaluation technique in this respect thus resembles those described in (Bulyonkov 84) for a simple imperative language, and in (Futamura 83) for an applicative language. Clearly, for partial evaluation to terminate this tabulation has to be finite. For "syntax directed" naturally recursive programs such as interpreters this is usually the case, but for programs handling a recursion stack of known values, for example, this is often not the case. (This might indicate that partial evaluation of imperative programs requires more sophisticated methods than partial evaluation of applicative programs).

b. Symbolic evaluation is the most operational, intuitive conception of partial evaluation. Symbolic evaluation takes place in a "symbolic environment" binding each variable to an expression instead of some concrete value. For each operator **car**, **cdr**, ... we have an evaluation (reduction) procedure that reduces, say, (**car** exp) based on the form of the residual expression exp-r for exp, according to this table:

form of exp-r	(car exp)
(**quote** $(t_1 \ . \ t_2)$)	(**quote** t_1)
(**cons** exp_1-r exp_2-r)	exp_1-r
otherwise	(**car** exp-r)

c. By requiring the user to make the call annotations, we also put much of the responsibility for a reasonable structure of the residual programs on him.

Here we list various anomalous behaviours and explain their relation to call annotations.

1. Partial evaluation may loop infinitely. One reason for this may be too few residual calls, so that it is attempted to unfold a loop whose termination (test) essentially depends on the unknown input. Either, this is an infinite loop that would have occurred in total (usual) evaluation also, or it corresponds to an attempt to build an infinite residual expression, for instance, to try to unfold

f(x) = **if** c(x) **then** e_1(x) **else** (**call** f e_2(x))

(where c(x), e_1(x), and e_2(x) are expressions possibly containing x) to its infinite equivalent

f(x) = **if** c(x) **then** e_1(x)
else if c(e_2(x)) **then** e_1(e_2(x))
else if c(e_2(e_2(x))) **then** ...

(An attempt to produce at partial evaluation time infinitely many specializations of a function is another source of non-termination in partial evaluation, and this is independent of call annotations).

2. Partial evaluation may produce extremely slow residual programs. This can be the consequence of call duplication, that is, in the residual program the same subexpression containing a call is evaluated more than once. In the case that a function calls itself twice on the same substructure of one of its parameters, its run time may well shift from linear to exponential because of call unfolding. Witness the linear time program

f(n) = **if** (**null** n) **then** '1 **else** (**call** g (**call** f (**cdr** n)))
g(y) = (**cons** y y)

(with n unknown) which should not be unfolded to the exponential-time program

f(n) = **if** (**null** n) **then** '1 **else** (**cons** (**call** f (**cdr** n)) (**call** f (**cdr** n)))

Such call duplication usually can be avoided by inserting more residual calls.

3. Partial evaluation may produce extremely large residual programs. This is a "size" counterpart of the above exponential run time anomaly. Consider the program

f(n,x) = **if** (**null** n) **then** x **else** (**call** g (**call** f (**cdr** n) x))

g(y) = (**cons** y y)

with n known, x unknown. When n has length 1, unfolding f('(1) x) yields (**cons** x x), and when n has length 2, unfolding f('(1 1) x) yields (**cons** (**cons** x x) (**cons** x x)). For an n with length 10, the residual expression has $2^{10} = 1024$ x's and 1023 **cons**-operators, and it is equivalent to a program with 12 functions containing a total of 20 **calls** and one **cons**-operator, namely

f_{10}(x) = (**call** g (**call** f_9 x))

...

f_1(x) = (**call** g (**call** f_0 x))

f_0(x) = x

g(y) = (**cons** y y)

None of these problems are contrived; we have experienced all of them, only in more complicated settings. Note that, in general, it may be impossible to make call annotations for a subject program in a way ensuring reasonable residual programs. However, call annotation of syntax directed programs usually is not hard and can be semi-automated (by finding *unsafe* cycles in the call graph of the subject program without a descending known parameter). We have not done that yet, but it is currently being investigated.

d. Dividing the partial evaluation process into phases, a *statically* determined partitioning of each function's parameters into eliminable resp. residual parameters is obtained, as well as a statically determined classification of all operators in the subject program as either (definitely) eliminable or (possibly) residual.

The ideas are that known/unknown abstract interpretation yields *global* information on the subject program's possible run-time behaviour, and that the annotations represent this static information *locally. In principle,* static classification of parameters and operators is not necessary since the classification can be done *dynamically* (during symbolic evaluation/function specialization). That is, it can be determined dynamically whether an operator is doable independently of the unknown input, namely if its operands evaluate (symbolically) to constant expressions (**quote** ...). However, it turns out to be a prerequisite for successful self-application of the partial evaluator (and a distinguishing feature of ours) that the classification *is* made statically based on a description of which of the subject program's input parameters are known. We will try to give an operational explanation of this rather subtle problem.

We attempted to produce a compiler comp (from some S-interpreter int) by running comp = L mix_1<mix_2, int>, with *dynamic* operator classification, i.e. without operator annotations. (Here, $mix_1 = mix_2$ = Mix, the indices are for reference only). This resulted in compilers of monstrous size, far too big to be printed out.

The reason turned out to be this: mix_1 as well as mix_2 contain some procedure for simplifying expressions such as (**car** exp) as much as possible at partial evaluation time. This depends on the residual (reduced) form exp-r of exp, which in turn depends on the form of exp and the values of the subject program int's known input. The operators occurring in mix_2 are of course nicely reduced by mix_1 but consider mix_2 being partially evaluated on int as above. Now focus on the application of mix_2's reduction procedure for **car** on an expression (**car** exp) in int. Let us assume that in int, this **car** expression's operand is int's first parameter (an S source program s). During *compilation* one applies *mix* to int and a source program, target = L *mix* <int,s>. Thus the source program s is present, and the **car** operator of int can be evaluated by *mix*. But during *compiler generation*, running comp = L mix_1<mix_2, int>, the source program s is not available and therefore even the *form* of the residual expression exp-r for exp in int is unknown. Therefore, the reduction procedure (in mix_2) for **car** cannot be executed by mix_1, and the compiler produced (i.e. the residual program for mix_2) will contain the entire reduction procedure for **car** for this single occurrence of **car** in int.

This procedure will be entirely superfluous. Since when running the produced compiler on an S source program, that program will be known, and a single **car** operator could replace the reduction procedure comprising several lines of L text. In fact, the problem is worse yet, because (**car** (**cdr** exp)) in the interpreter int will be "reduced" to the reduction procedure for **car** with the entire reduction procedure for **cdr** instantiated in several places. Thus the size of residual expressions in the compiler depends in an exponential way on the complexity of expressions in the interpreter, and this is clearly not acceptable.

If, on the other hand, operator annotations (static classifications into eliminable resp. residual operators) are used, a **car** operator in int working on int's eliminable input (the S source program) will be annotated eliminable (**care**), and partial evaluation of mix_2 on int will produce a single **car** operator in the compiler instead of a copy of the complicated reduction procedure. Note that it is the annotation of int that matters. Hence, this problem really is one of self-application.

Now, could not mix_1 (dynamically) infer that the operand of the discussed **car** operator in int that mix_2 is about to reduce depends only on int's first parameter, the S source program? Then mix_1 could avoid duplicating the entire reduction procedure for **car** (in mix_2) in the compiler, since it knew that when running the compiler on an S source program, that program would be known, and hence a single **car** would suffice in the compiler. That would require a *global flow analysis* of int at partial evaluation time to determine that the argument of this **car** operator only depends on the first parameter of int, as is done during the first phase, the known/unknown abstract interpretation.

This should suffice to justify the need for dividing the partial evaluator into at least two phases. Notice that the known/unknown abstract interpretation introduces another binding time: The annotation of a subject program not only requires the subject program but also a description of *which* of the subject program's parameters will be known at partial evaluation time, so the subject program is, in fact, annotated for a *particular* use.

This concludes the discussion of the distinguishing principles of our partial evaluator.

3.3 Description of the Phases

In this section, the individual phases of the partial evaluation process and some of the algorithms involved are described in the order they are used.

With reference to the sketch of the structure (Figure 1), the phases are: Known/Unknown abstract interpretation (which will be described in great detail), the process of partitioning parameter lists and annotating operators, and the proper function specialization process.

3.3.1 Known/Unknown Abstract Interpretation

The **purpose** of this phase is to compute for every function in the subject program a safe description of its parameters, whether they are definitely known or possibly unknown at partial evaluation time.

Inputs to this phase are 1) the call annotated subject program, and 2) a description of which of the subject program's (i.e. which of the goal function's) parameters are known and which are unknown at partial evaluation time. That is, this phase does not use the actual values of the known input, just a description telling *which* of the input parameters are known. (Equivalent to providing a value for m in Kleene's S-m-n Theorem).

Output is a *description*, i.e. a mapping that associates with every function a *parameter description*, classifying each of its parameters as Known resp. Unknown at partial evaluation time. Here Known means "definitely known for all possible values of the subject program's known input", and Unknown means "possibly unknown for some (or all) values of the known input".

For the following exposition we will assume this L subject program given

$$((f_1\ (x_{11} \dots x_{1k[1]})\ exp_1)$$
$$\dots$$
$$(f_n\ (x_{n1} \dots x_{nk[n]})\ exp_n)\ )$$

Figure 2: An L Subject Program

consisting of $n \geq 1$ functions f_i each having $k_i \geq 0$ parameters, i=1,...,n. Then the program's input is a k_1-tuple $\in D^{k_1}$, where D is the domain of LISP lists.

Algorithm 3.3.1

The phase works by an abstract interpretation of the subject program over a domain with two values for expressions, **D** = {Known, Unknown}. During this abstract interpretation, for every function a parameter description is maintained, telling for every parameter of the function whether it can be called with an unknown value. (Note that a parameter description may be considered an "abstract environment", associating with every parameter of a function an abstract value). Initially, all parameters except the goal function's are considered Known, and the parameter description for the goal function is the initial description given for the subject program's input parameters.

The abstract interpretation proceeds as follows: The body of the goal function is evaluated (using the parameter description) to see which functions it may call, giving them Unknown parameter values. The parameter descriptions for these functions are modified according to these findings to tell which of their parameters may be Unknown. Then the bodies of these functions are evaluated using the new parameter descriptions to see which functions they in turn may call with Unknown parameter values and so on. Each time a parameter description of a function becomes more unknown than the previous one, its body is re-interpreted using the new parameter description, possibly implying further re-interpretations of other functions. The process stops when no more parameters of any function f_i can become Unknown as a consequence of a call of f_i from some other function. Then the description computed is safe in the sense that any parameter described as Known will have values only depending on the program's known input at partial evaluation time.

More precisely, the abstract interpretation of the body of a function f_i proceeds in this way: For every call (**call** $f_c\ e_1 \ldots e_{k[c]}$) appearing in the body, the actual parameter expressions $e_1, \ldots, e_{k[c]}$ are abstractly interpreted using f_i's current parameter description (as sketched below) yielding an abstract value (Known or Unknown) for every parameter $x_{c1}, \ldots, x_{ck[c]}$ of the called function f_c. If any parameter x_{cj} described as Known in f_c's parameter description becomes Unknown, that parameter description is changed to Unknown for x_{cj}, and the body of the called function f_c is re-interpreted to check if any more parameters of (other) functions become Unknown as a consequence of this.

Abstract interpretation of parameter expressions is straightforward: A variable has the abstract value given in the current parameter description for the function in which it occurs, and any composite expression has value Known if it does not contain any variables described as Unknown. Otherwise, the expression has value Unknown.

A More Formal Description of the Algorithm

In order to describe this process more formally, we put the ordering Known < Unknown on the domain **D**. In the sequel, Known and Unknown will be abbreviated K and U, respectively. A description of the parameters of a function f_i is a tuple in $\mathbf{D}^{k_i}$, and a description of all the parameters in the entire program above is a tuple in $\mathbf{Descr} = \mathbf{D}^{k_1} \times \ldots \times \mathbf{D}^{k_n}$. This domain is partially ordered by using the above ordering "<" componentwise, and it is a complete lattice of finite height, with bottom element $\perp = \langle K^{k_1}, \ldots, K^{k_n} \rangle$, the "most known" description. Notice that the least upper bound $\delta_1 \sqcup \delta_2$ of any two descriptions $\delta_1, \delta_2 \in \mathbf{Descr}$ exists, and is the most known description safely approximating δ_1 as well as δ_2.

Domains and Elements

$\mathbf{D} = \{\text{Known, Unknown}\}$

δ	: $\mathbf{Descr} = \mathbf{D}^{k_1} \times \ldots \times \mathbf{D}^{k_n}$	a description for the entire program.
π	: $\mathbf{D}^*$	a parameter description for a function.

By $\text{only}_i(<v_1, ..., v_{k[i]}>)$ we denote the element δ of **Descr** with

$$\delta[i] = <v_1, ..., v_{k[i]}> \quad \text{and} \quad \delta[j] = <K, ..., K> = K^{k_j} \text{ for } j \neq i$$

i.e. it is K everywhere except at i, where it is $<v_1, ..., v_{k[i]}>$.

Functions

Function **A** : Program → $\mathbf{D}^{k_1}$ → **Descr**

This function returns the final description for the entire subject program, mapping every parameter of every function to either K or U.

$\mathbf{A}[\![((f_1\ (x_{11} \dots x_{1k[1]})\ exp_1) \dots)]\!] <v_1, ..., v_{k[1]}> = h(\text{only}_1(<v_1, ..., v_{k[1]}>))$

<u>whererec</u> $h(\delta) = \delta \sqcup h(\bigsqcup \mathbf{P}[\![exp_i]\!]\ \delta[i] \text{ for } i=1,...,n)$

Function **E** : Expression → **D*** → **D**

This function computes the abstract value (K or U) of an expression in a given abstract environment.

$\mathbf{E}[\![(\mathbf{quote}\ \text{list})]\!]\ \pi = K$

$\mathbf{E}[\![\text{variable } x_{ij}]\!]\ \pi = \pi[j]$

$\mathbf{E}[\![(\mathbf{car}\ \text{exp})]\!]\ \pi = \mathbf{E}[\![\text{exp}]\!]\ \pi$

and similarly for **cdr**, **atom**.

$\mathbf{E}[\![(\mathbf{cons}\ e_1\ e_2)]\!]\ \pi = \mathbf{E}[\![e_1]\!]\ \pi \sqcup \mathbf{E}[\![e_2]\!]\ \pi$

$\mathbf{E}[\![(\mathbf{equal}\ e_1\ e_2)]\!]\ \pi = \mathbf{E}[\![e_1]\!]\ \pi \sqcup \mathbf{E}[\![e_2]\!]\ \pi$

$\mathbf{E}[\![(\mathbf{if}\ e_1\ e_2\ e_3)]\!]\ \pi = \mathbf{E}[\![e_1]\!]\ \pi \sqcup \mathbf{E}[\![e_2]\!]\ \pi \sqcup \mathbf{E}[\![e_3]\!]\ \pi$

$\mathbf{E}[\![(\mathbf{call}\ f_i\ e_1 \dots e_{k[i]})]\!]\pi = (\bigsqcup \mathbf{E}[\![e_j]\!]\ \pi \text{ for } j=1,...,k_i)$

The last rule states that a function having at least one Unknown parameter may return an Unknown value, otherwise only Known values. The rule is the same for **callr**.

Function **P** : Expression → **D*** → **Descr**

This function computes for a given description exp and a given abstract environment a "small" description that tells for the functions that may be called from exp, which of their parameters will be unknown as a consequence of these calls.

$\mathbf{P}[\![(\mathbf{quote}\ \text{list})]\!]\ \pi = \perp$

$\mathbf{P}[\![\text{variable } x_{ij}]\!]\ \pi = \perp$

$\mathbf{P}[\![(\mathbf{car}\ \text{exp})]\!]\ \pi = \mathbf{P}[\![\text{exp}]\!]\ \pi$

and similarly for **cdr**, **atom**.

$\mathbf{P}[\![(\mathbf{cons}\ e_1\ e_2)]\!]\ \pi = \mathbf{P}[\![e_1]\!]\ \pi \sqcup \mathbf{P}[\![e_2]\!]\ \pi$

$\mathbf{P}[\![(\mathbf{equal}\ e_1\ e_2)]\!]\ \pi = \mathbf{P}[\![e_1]\!]\ \pi \sqcup \mathbf{P}[\![e_2]\!]\ \pi$

$\mathbf{P}[\![(\mathbf{if}\ e_1\ e_2\ e_3)]\!]\ \pi = \mathbf{P}[\![e_1]\!]\ \pi \sqcup \mathbf{P}[\![e_2]\!]\ \pi \sqcup \mathbf{P}[\![e_3]\!]\ \pi$

$\mathbf{P}[\![(\mathbf{call}\ f_i\ e_1 \dots e_{k[i]})]\!]\pi = \underline{\text{let}}\ v_j = \mathbf{E}[\![e_j]\!]\ \pi \text{ for } j=1,...,k_i\ \underline{\text{in}}$

$\text{only}_i(<v_1, ..., v_{k[i]}>) \sqcup (\bigsqcup \mathbf{P}[\![e_j]\!]\ \pi \text{ for } j=1,...,k_i)$

same for **callr**

The actual implementation of the algorithm closely resembles this scheme. It has two main data structures; namely, the partially computed description $\delta \in$ **Descr** as above, and a set Pending of pairs of a function name and a parameter description for that function, $(f_i, <v_1, ..., v_{k[i]}>)$. This set represents the function calls whose effects on the final value of **Descr** are not yet computed. A non-deterministic, imperative version of the algorithm is given below (in reality a deterministic, iterative applicative algorithm is used). In one iteration of the algorithm, an element of Pending (i.e. a call description) is chosen and removed from Pending, the effect on δ of this call is computed, and possibly the <u>for</u> statement adds new call descriptions to Pending in case an old description for any function has changed. The algorithm terminates when Pending becomes empty and is guaranteed to terminate (since the lattice **Descr** is of finite height so that the value of δ may only increase a finite number of times). This is a classical way of computing finite fixed points.

Set $<v_1, ..., v_{k[1]}>$:= the description of the subject program's input parameters;
Pending := $\{ (f_1, <v_1, ..., v_{k[1]}>) \}$; $\delta := \bot$;
<u>while</u> Pending $\neq \emptyset$ <u>do</u>
    <u>choose</u> $(f_i, <v_1, ..., v_{k[i]}>) \in$ Pending, and remove it from Pending;
    $\delta' := \delta \sqcup$ **P**$[\![$ exp_i $]\!]$ $<v_1, ..., v_{k[i]}>$;
    <u>for all</u> i=1,...,n <u>do</u>
        <u>if</u> $\delta'[i] > \delta[i]$ <u>then</u> Pending := Pending $\cup \{ (f_i, \delta'[i]) \}$;
    $\delta := \delta'$;
<u>end</u>;

This concludes the description of the Known/Unknown abstract interpretation algorithm.

3.3.2 Annotation of Parameter Lists and Operators

In this phase, the given subject program is transformed, i.e. annotated with respect to parameters and operators for use in the third phase, the function specialization phase.

Inputs to this phase are 1) the call annotated subject program, and 2) the description computed by the above phase, describing every parameter of every function in the program as either Known or Unknown.

Output is the subject program annotated with respect to parameters and operators. That is, the parameter list of each function is divided into a list of eliminable parameters (namely those described as Known) and a list of residual parameters (those described as Unknown). Of course, the argument list of every call to a function f_i is divided into two lists in exactly the same way as the formal parameters of f_i. Also, every operator **car, cdr, cons,** ... is annotated either as eliminable or as residual, becoming **care, cdre, conse,** ... or **carr, cdrr, consr,** ... respectively. An operator being eliminable implies that it is doable during the function specialization phase to follow, or in other words, its result depends only on the values of the known input supplied to the subject program at partial evaluation time, not the unknown. This is not quite true for the **if** operator, since its being eliminable means that the value of its conditional expression depends only on the known input, but then the **if** expression can be reduced to one of its branches during the function specialization phase.

Algorithm 3.3.2

This phase works like a recursive descent compiler, building the annotated subject program one function at a time as it goes through the given subject program. A parameter list (in a function definition) or an argument list (in a function call) is divided into two lists using the description (computed in the previous phase) in a straightforward way. Operators are annotated on the basis of an abstract interpretation of their argument expressions using the function **E** from subsection 3.3.1, associating with every expression an abstract value in {Known, Unknown}.

An annotated version of the subject program in Figure 2 may look like

$$((f_1 \ (ex_{11} \ ... \ ex_{1k[11]}) \ (rx_{11} \ ... \ rx_{1k[12]}) \ exp_1^{ann})$$
$$...$$
$$(f_n \ (ex_{n1} \ ... \ ex_{nk[n1]}) \ (rx_{n1} \ ... \ rx_{nk[n2]}) \ exp_n^{ann}) \ )$$

Figure 3: An Annotated Subject Program

where $ex_{i1}, ..., ex_{ik[i1]}$ are the eliminable parameters, $rx_{i1}, ..., rx_{ik[i2]}$ the residual parameters of function f_i, and together they form a permutation of the original parameter list $x_{i1}, ..., x_{ik[i]}$, so $k_{i1} + k_{i2} = k_i$, and exp_i^{ann} is the annotated version of exp_i. This annotated subject program will be used for reference below.

3.3.3 Function Specialization

This phase constructs the residual program by making a number of specialized variants of the annotated subject program's functions.

Inputs are 1) the annotated subject program produced by the previous (annotation) phase, and 2) the known input to the subject program, i.e. actual values for those of the goal function's parameters described as Known.

Output is the residual program that is constructed from variants of the annotated subject program's functions. They are specialized to various actual values of their eliminable parameters. The goal function of the residual program is the variant of the subject program's goal function that is specialized to the actual values for its eliminable parameters, i.e. the known input to the subject program. The (formal) parameters of a residual function corresponding to the original function f_i are the residual parameters $rx_{i1}, ..., rx_{ik[i2]}$, cf. Figure 3. The residual function's name will be (the composite) $f_i[<v_1, ..., v_{k[i]}>]$ when the function is called by a residual call with values $<v_1, ..., v_{k[i]}>$ for the eliminable parameters $ex_{i1}, ..., ex_{ik[i1]}$.

Algorithm 3.3.3

The construction of the residual program has two aspects: 1) Deciding which residual functions are needed for the given values of the known input (cf. subsection 3.2.2, first paragraph), and 2) Producing these residual functions. In principle, this can be done in separate stages, but in our partial evaluator and in the algorithm sketched here, these phases are intermixed. It is not clear whether this really is advantageous or whether it just obscures the algorithm. First, the algorithm will be described in words then a more formal algorithm like that of subsection 3.3.1 will be given. The reader is invited to keep the annotated subject program shown in Figure 3 in mind while reading this section.

Informal Description of the Algorithm

The algorithm resembles the fixed point computation of the Known/Unknown abstract interpretation (subsection 3.3.1) to a great extent. In fact, it can formally be considered an abstract interpretation over some suitable domain also, see (Jones, Mycroft 86) on "minimal function graphs", but here a less rigorous treatment is given. At any time the algorithm keeps a set Pending of function specializations which still have to be produced, and a list Out which contains the residual functions produced so far. The elements of Pending are pairs (f_i,<v_1, ..., $v_{k[i1]}$>) of a function name f_i and a tuple of values <v_1, ..., $v_{k[i1]}$> for f_i's eliminable parameters. A pair (f_i,<v_1, ..., $v_{k[i1]}$>) being in Pending indicates that a variant of f_i specialized to <v_1, ..., $v_{k[i1]}$> is required, but it may already be among the residual functions in Out.

Initially Out is the empty list, and Pending contains one element, namely the pair (f_1,<v_1, ..., $v_{k[11]}$>) consisting of the goal function's name and the known input to the subject program. Hence, there will always be a residual variant of the subject program's goal function, specialized to the subject program's known input, and this becomes the goal function of the residual program.

Now the algorithm works as follows:

1. If Pending is empty, the process is complete and Out is the residual program. Otherwise, choose some pair (f_i,<v_1, ..., $v_{k[i1]}$>) in Pending. If the corresponding residual function already is in Out, repeat this step.

2. Otherwise, produce a residual variant of f_i, called f_i[<v_1, ..., $v_{k[i1]}$>], with parameters rx_{i1}, ..., $rx_{ik[i2]}$ (the residual parameters of f_i), and a body exp_i-r, which is the result of evaluating the body exp_i^{ann} of f_i symbolically.

3. Collect the set of residual functions needed by the residual function just produced, i.e. those which it can call. This is represented as a set of pairs (f_j, <v_1, ...,$v_{k[j1]}$>) of a function name f_j and values for its eliminable parameters, and corresponds to the set of residual calls that are encountered when evaluating exp_i symbolically. Add this set to Pending and continue with step 1.

Now we sketch the two main procedures: The procedure constructing the residual equivalent of an expression by symbolic evaluation, and the procedure collecting the residual functions called by the residual expression.

Symbolic Evaluation takes place in a "symbolic environment" binding the parameters of a function to expressions rather than values. Here, of course, the eliminable variables are bound to constant expressions (**quote** ...), and residual variables are bound to arbitrary expressions. Symbolic evaluation is quite straightforward. For instance, a variable evaluates to the expression to which it is bound, and symbolic evaluation of expressions which do not contain calls works by reduction. Symbolic evaluation *of calls* is the most interesting case.

An eliminable call (**call** f_i (e_1 ... $e_{k[i1]}$) (r_1 ... $r_{k[i2]}$)) is evaluated symbolically by evaluating the body exp_i of f_i symbolically in a symbolic environment constructed like this: The parameter expressions are evaluated symbolically, yielding residual expressions $ev_{i1}, ..., ev_{ik[i1]}$ resp. $rv_{i1}, ..., rv_{ik[i2]}$ for the eliminable resp. the residual parameter expressions. Now the eliminable parameters $ex_{i1}, ..., ex_{ik[i1]}$ of the called function are bound to $ev_{i1}, ..., ev_{ik[i1]}$, and the same is the case for the residual parameters. Thus symbolic evaluation of an eliminable call is usual call-by-value evaluation, except that the value domain consists of expressions. Note that non-termination is possible here (as in usual evaluation) if a function calls itself recursively by an eliminable call.

A residual call (**callr** f_i (e_1 ... $e_{k[i1]}$) (r_1 ... $r_{k[i2]}$)) has to appear in the residual program, and thus the result of symbolic evaluation is a call (**call** $f_i[<ev_{i1}, ..., ev_{ik[i1]}>]$ rv_{i1} ... $rv_{ik[i2]}$) to a function with the composite name $f_i[<ev_{i1}, ..., ev_{ik[i1]}>]$ and residual argument expressions $rv_{i1}, ..., rv_{ik[i2]}$. Here, as above, $ev_{i1}, ..., ev_{ik[i1]}$ and $rv_{i1}, ..., rv_{ik[i2]}$ are the residual equivalents of the parameter expressions in the call that was symbolically evaluated.

Collecting the Residual Functions Needed for an expression exp to be evaluated symbolically in a certain "symbolic environment" resembles symbolic evaluation a great deal except that the value of an expression is a set of pairs, each representing a necessary residual function. This takes place in an environment where only the eliminable parameters are bound to (constant) expressions. In constant expressions, in variables, and in eliminable expressions **care, cdre**, ... (except **ife**), no (new) residual calls can appear. The residual calls of an eliminable **ife** expression are the residual calls of one of its branches; which branch is decided by the value of the conditional expression in the given symbolic environment. The set of residual calls of any expression other than a call is the union of the sets of residual calls of its subexpressions. The set of residual calls of an eliminable call (**call** f_i (e_1 ... $e_{k[i1]}$) (r_1 ... $r_{k[i2]}$)) is the union of those appearing in the expressions $r_1, ..., r_{k[i2]}$ for the residual parameters with those in the body exp_i of f_i. Similarly, the set of residual calls of a residual call (**callr** f_i (e_1 ... $e_{k[i1]}$) (r_1 ... $r_{k[i2]}$)) is the union of those appearing in the residual parameter expressions with the singleton $\{(f_i, <ev_1, ...,ev_{k[i1]}>)\}$, representing the call itself, where ev_j is the residual equivalent of eliminable parameter expression e_j, $j=1,...,k_{i1}$.

3.4 Variable Splitting

Below we describe an extension to Mix allowing the generation of better residual programs.

A Problem with Generality

As can be inferred from subsection 3.3.3 on function specialization, any residual variant of a function f_i has at most the same number of parameters as f_i, since the parameters of the variant are the residual parameters of f_i, i.e. a subset of f_i's parameters. This can sometimes be unfortunate.

Consider an S-interpreter int for a functional language. This interpreter may contain a parameter (say, "vnames") holding parameter *names* for a function in the source program of this interpreter, and another (say, "vvalues") holding *values* for these parameters.

When partially evaluating int with respect to some S source program, "vnames" is known and disappears during partial evaluation, whereas "vvalues" is unknown and is found in the target program. In the target program, this *one* variable holds the values of *all* the parameters in the source program's function's parameter list. This results in much packing and unpacking of values when the target program is run and is quite wasteful.

In the interpreter, this generality is necessary: We *have* to represent the parameter values as a list of values packed into one variable, since we do not know in advance the length of the parameter list in the S source program to be interpreted. But in the target program, this length is known and fixed, and thus the list could be replaced by a number of variables each corresponding to one parameter from the S source program (or by an array, if our language allowed this). The problem is not contrived; the compiler generator cocom generated by an earlier version of Mix spent approximately 75% of its run time doing garbage collection.

A Solution: Variable Splitting

We would like that for a function of a specific S source program s for which the parameter names are vnames = (z_1 z_2 ... z_k), there should be k variables representing the source program's k parameters in the target program produced. To obtain this, we have extended the function specialization phase of Mix and introduced a new kind of annotation. Using the annotations one can express, for example, that the value of residual parameter "vvalues" will always be a list of the same form as the value of eliminable parameter "vnames". Then in the residual (target) program, the simple variable "vvalues" is replaced by as many variables as there are elements in "vnames". In the above case, where vnames = (z_1 z_2 ... z_k) at compile time, the target program will contain k variables called "z_1", "z_2", ..., "z_k" instead of the single residual variable "vvalues". This improvement of Mix works well in practice, generating more efficient and more readable residual programs.

4 Experience with Using Mix

4.1 Compilers Generated by Self-Application of Mix

A compiler generated by self-application of Mix is a residual program for the function specialization phase of Mix (here called Mix3), and it may therefore inherit some of Mix3's structure and components.

In general the characteristics of a Mix-generated compiler are these.

a. Its main recursion structure is that of Mix3 for generating a set of residual functions.

b. It contains the reduction procedures for operators **carr**, **cdrr**, ..., working as optimizing code generation functions (inherited from Mix3).

c. It contains a number of compiling functions (and auxiliary functions) obtained by transforming interpreting functions (and auxiliary functions) from the interpreter int.

All in all, a Mix generated compiler usually has a reasonable structure. This structure resembles that of a recursive descent compiler, except that Mix carries out constant folding and some symbolic reduction while constructing the target program, not in a separate pass.

The size (in lines) of a compiler depends highly on reasonable call annotations in the interpreter (and in Mix3). It may therefore require some experimentation to get a compiler of a reasonable size.

Two compilers generated by Mix shall be mentioned: A compiler made from a 105 line interpreter int (for a very small imperative language MP with a list data type) comprised 381 lines ("pretty-printed" LISP text). It compiles a 30 line MP source program in 0.16 second, which is 20 times as fast as compiling by partially evaluating the interpreter. Also, surprisingly, compile time *plus* target program run time is almost 6 times smaller than interpreted source program run time.

As a more complex example of a compiler, we may take the compiler generator cocom (produced from the "interpreter" Mix3). Whereas Mix3 comprises 591 lines, cocom is 1736 lines and generates the compiler mentioned above in less than 5 seconds run time (VAX11/785), 16 times as fast as doing compiler generation by partially evaluating Mix with respect to the interpreter (Section 2.1).

This indicates that the compilers have usable size and run time (in fact, not much larger than for equivalent hand-written compilers), although they often contain code that is obviously superfluous.

4.2. Partially Evaluating a Self-Interpreter

Another interesting experiment is partial evaluation of a (self-) interpreter for L written in L. Call such a program "sint" for self-interpreter. It has the property

$$\text{L sint} \langle p, d_1, \ldots, d_n \rangle = \text{L p} \langle d_1, \ldots, d_n \rangle$$

for any L-program p and input $\langle d_1, \ldots, d_n \rangle$ in D*. Now by equation (1), for any L-program p and input $\langle d_1, \ldots, d_n \rangle$,

$$\text{L (L Mix} \langle \text{sint}, p \rangle) \langle d_1, \ldots, d_n \rangle = \text{L sint} \langle p, d_1, \ldots, d_n \rangle = \text{L p} \langle d_1, \ldots, d_n \rangle$$

so L Mix $\langle \text{sint}, p \rangle$ is an L-program equivalent to p. Furthermore, with

$$\text{transf} = \text{L Mix} \langle \text{Mix}, \text{sint} \rangle$$

the program "transf" is an equivalence preserving L program transformer, i.e.

$$\text{L(L transf} \langle p \rangle) \langle d_1, \ldots, d_n \rangle = \text{L p} \langle d_1, \ldots, d_n \rangle .$$

Since the transformed program L transf $\langle p \rangle$ = L Mix$\langle \text{sint}, p \rangle$ will have some of the properties of the self-interpreter, we may obtain different kinds of transformations. For a "natural" self-interpreter the transformed program produced is not only semantically equivalent to the original program, but also textually equivalent (modulo renaming of functions). Although this might not seem interesting, it establishes a kind of non-triviality of our partial evaluator, since the most trivial partial evaluator would not be able to reproduce a program verbatim by partial evaluation of a self-interpreter. (A trivial partial evaluator is one that does no reduction or optimization, see (Jones, Sestoft, Søndergaard 85)).

4.3 Other Experiments

Other experiments with Mix concern parser generation and parser generator generation from a general parsing algorithm (taking as inputs a grammar and a subject string to be parsed). A series of such experiments is rather completely documented in (Dybkjær 85), reporting on successes, problems and pitfalls in applying a version of Mix to this. Although reasonable parser generators etc. could be generated, this required some experimentation and a certain programming style.

5 Summary

We have described an experimental, self-applicable partial evaluator Mix capable of generating compilers and a compiler generator of reasonable size and efficiency. To our knowledge this is not done before. The partial evaluator has a multiphase structure which seems to be a prerequisite for successful self-application and which has not been used for partial evaluators before.

One of the main deficiencies of our partial evaluator is that the decision whether to unfold or suspend a function call is not automated. We require the user of the partial evaluator to make this decision in advance. Also, the partial evaluator is not a powerful general purpose tool: The goal of the project was to construct a self-applicable partial evaluator, and here modesty seems essential.

Future Work

Much work remains to be done before compilers and compiler generators produced by partial evaluation can be used in practice. Partial evaluation of imperative languages requires more sophisticated techniques than the ones described here and deserves investigation.

The most promising next step (in a practical direction) probably would be to build a more powerful partial evaluator along the lines drawn here for some other language having the same characteristics, e.g. a Prolog subset or a higher order functional language.

Also, there is a pressing need for a more well-founded "theory of partial evaluation". For example, it might be possible to prove (or disprove) that the *static* classification of variables described in this paper is essential for self-application of a partial evaluator.

Acknowledgements

All of this is joint work with Neil D. Jones and Harald Søndergaard (at DIKU). I would like to thank them for a most fruitful collaboration without which this paper would not have been.

References

(Bulyonkov 84)
Bulyonkov, M. A. Polyvariant mixed computation for analyzer programs. *Acta Informatica 21*, (1984), pp. 473-484.

(Dybkjær 85)
Dybkjær, Hans. Parsers and partial evaluation: An experiment. DIKU Student Report 85-7-15 (July 1985). 128 pp.

(Emanuelson, Haraldsson 80)
Emanuelson, Pär & Anders Haraldsson. On compiling embedded languages in LISP. In *Conf. Rec. of the 1980 LISP Conference, Stanford, California*, pp. 208-215.

(Ershov 78) Ershov, Andrei P. On the essence of compilation. In Neuhold, E. J. (ed.): *Formal Description of Programming Concepts*, North-Holland, 1978, pp. 391-420.

(Ershov 82) Ershov, Andrei P. Mixed computation: Potential applications and problems for study. *Theoretical Computer Science 18* (1982), pp. 41-67.

(Futamura 71)
Futamura, Yoshihiko. Partial evaluation of computation process - an approach to a compiler-compiler. *Systems, Computers, Controls 2*, no. 5 (1971), pp. 45-50.

(Futamura 83)
Futamura, Yoshihiko. Partial computation of programs. *Proc. RIMS Symp. Software Science and Engineering, Kyoto, Japan, 1982. Springer LNCS 147* (1983), pp. 1-35.

(Haraldsson 78)
Haraldsson, Anders. A partial evaluator and its use for compiling iterative statements in LISP. In *Conf. Rec. of the 5th ACM POPL, Tucson, Arizona, 1978*, pp.195-203.

(Jones, Mycroft 86)
Jones, Neil D. & Alan Mycroft. Data flow analysis using minimal function graphs. In *Conf. Rec. of the 13th ACM POPL, St. Petersburg, Florida, 1986*. (To appear).

(Jones, Sestoft, Søndergaard 85)
Jones, Neil D., Peter Sestoft & Harald Søndergaard. An experiment in partial evaluation: The generation of a compiler generator. In *Proc. 1st Intl. Conf. on Rewriting Techniques and Applications, Dijon, France, 1985. Springer LNCS 202* (1985), pp. 124-140. (A preliminary version appeared as DIKU Report 85/1, January 1985).

(Jones, Tofte 83)
Jones, Neil D. & Mads Tofte. Some principles and notations for the construction of compiler generators. Unpublished working paper, DIKU, July 29, 1983. 15 pp.

(Kahn, Carlsson 84)
Kahn, Kenneth M. & Mats Carlsson. The compilation of Prolog programs without the use of a Prolog compiler. In *Proc. of the International Conference on Fifth Generation Computer Systems, Tokyo, Japan, 1984*, ICOT, 1984, pp. 348-355.

(Kleene 52) Kleene, S. C. *Introduction to Metamathematics*. Van Nostrand, 1952.

(Sestoft 85) [Sestoft, Peter]. The Mix system: User manual and short description. DIKU, April 26th, 1985. 14 pp.

(Turchin 79) Turchin, Valentin F. A supercompiler system based on the language REFAL. *SIGPLAN Notices 14*, no. 2 (February 1979), pp. 46-54.

(Turchin 80) Turchin, Valentin F. Semantic definitions in REFAL and the automatic construction of compilers. In Jones, Neil D. (ed.): *Semantics Directed Compiler Generation. Springer LNCS 94*, (1980), pp. 441-474.

PROGRAM TRANSFORMATION BY SUPERCOMPILATION

Valentin F. Turchin
The City College of New York
New York, N.Y. 10031

1. Introduction

A *supercompiler* is a program transformer of a certain type. The usual way of thinking about program transformation is in terms of some set of rules which preserve the functional meaning of the program, and a step by step application of these rules to the initial program. This concept is suggested by axiomatic mathematics. A rule of transformation is seen as an axiom, and the journal of a transformation process as the demonstration of equivalency. The concept of a supercompiler is a product of cybernetic thinking. A program is seen as a machine. To make sense of it, one must observe its operation. So a supercompiler does not transform the program by steps; it controls and observes (SUPERvises) the machine, let us call it M_1, which is represented by the program. In observing the operation of M_1, the supercompiler COMPILES a program which describes the activities of M_1, but it makes shortcuts and whatever clever tricks it knows, in order to produce the same effect as M_1, but faster. The goal of the supercompiler is to make the definition of this program (machine) M_2, self-sufficient. When this is achieved, it outputs M_2, and simply throws away the (unchanged) machine M_1.

The supercompiler concept comes closest to the way humans think and make science. We do not think in terms of rules of formal logic. We create mental and linguistic *models* of the reality we observe. How do we do that? We observe phenomena, generalize observations, and try to construct a self-sufficient model in terms of these generalizations. This is also what the supercompiler is doing. Generalization is the crucial aspect of supercompilation. A supercompiler would run M_1 in a general form, with unknown values of variables, and create a graph of states and transitions between possible configurations of the computing system. This process (called *driving*), however, can usually go on infinitely. To make it finite, the supercompiler performs the operation of *generalization* on the systems configurations in such a manner that it finally comes to a set of generalized configurations, called *basic* , in terms of which the behaviour of the system can be expressed. Thus the new program becomes a self-sufficient model of the old one.

In many applications of supercompilation, the function call for which an optimized program must be constructed has partially defined arguments.The procedure of going through a program and computing whatever can be computed is known as *partial evaluation.*The idea to systematically use partial evaluation as a programming tool goes back to [Lombardi 1967], and was further developed in [Futamura 1971], [Beckman et al. 1974], [Ershov 1977, 1982]; there is a review paper [Futamura 1983]. Important work on partial evaluation in the context of programming systems is being done by

N.Jones and co-workers in Denmark (see [JonTof 1983], [Jones et al. 1985]). In the strategy of supercompilation we use, there are close parallels to the concept of delayed rules in [Vuillemin 1974], lazy evaluation of Lisp programs in [HenMor 1976], the use of suspensions by [FriWis 1967].

Although supercompilation includes partial evaluation, it cannot be reduced to it. This is a distinct concept. It exploits the concept of a configuration (generalized state) of the computing system, and a strategy of looping back by generalizing one configuration to another. Supercompilation can improve a program even if all the actual parameters in the function calls are variables; we shall give examples below. The supercompilation process aimes at the reduction of redundancy in the original problem, but this redundancy is not necessarily coming from fixed values of variables; it can result from nested loops, repeated variables, etc.

The work on the supercompiler project was started by the author in Moscow in the early 1970's. From its very inception, the project has been tied to a specific programming language, or rather metalanguage, Refal, which will be defined in Section 2. The philosophy behind the design of Refal has been to have a language which would facilitate the formalization of *metasystem transitions*, i.e. transitions from a system to a metasystem, which is to be performed in the computer and repeated asutomatically as many time as necessary. The idea of a supercimpiler was an outgrowth of that philosophy.

The equivalence transformations necessary for supercompilation were defined in [Turchin 1972]. An important aspect of the philosophy of metasystem transition is the requirement that the algorithms of supercompilation are written in the same language in which the programs to be transformed are written. If this condition is met, then having only a supercompiler we can automatically produce compilers for newly defined programming languages; we have only to define the semantics of the new language in Refal through the process of program interpretation. That interpreters can be automatically converted to compilers by partial evaluation was first discovered by Futamura [1971]. Several years later the author rediscovered this independently in the Refal context; we also noticed that a compiler compiler can be automatically produced in this way (see [REFAL 1977], [Turchin 1980a, b]). In the English language, the supercompiler project was first described in [Turchin 1979]. A systematic exposition of the project, including the definition of Refal and some programming techniques, can be found in [Turchin 1980a].

We shall now proceed with more precise definitions of the basic concepts. Our formalism is based on the concept of a computing system. Whenever speaking of functions, we shall have in mind computable partial functions. A function in this approach is simply a process in the computing system dependent on some initial (input) parameters.

Suppose we have a computing system (machine) which is finite at every moment but capable of potentially infinite expansion. It can be in different states, and we assume that there is a language to describe these states. We call this languages *the basic description language*. We assume further that the elements (words) of this language are strings of letters in a certain alphabet, which includes, among others, two distinguished characters, the left and the right parentheses "(" and ")", and that only those words are permissible in which the parentheses are properly paired. Accordingly, we shall call the words of the description language *expressions* . The use of expressions instead of strings makes it easier to represent complex, structured objects (states of the computing system). Subsystems of a computing systems can be naturally represented by subexpressions of the overall expression. For instance, the state of a computer might be described by the expression (C)M, where C is (represents the state of) the controlling device, and M is the memory. The subexpression C might have the form $(R_1)(R_2) \dots (R_n)$, where R_i for i= 1,2, ... n, are binary words representing the state of the registers.

When we work with strings, each time that want to represent a finite sequence of strings $S_1, S_2, \dots, S_n$ as a string we must extend the alphabet to include special separators, or use a still less appealing device like the Goedel enumeration. With expressions, the sequence $(S_1)(S_2) \dots (S_n)$ is uniquely broken down into its constituents. An expression is, essentially, a tree with a potentially infinite number of ordered branches at each node.

The process of computing is a sequence of states of the computing machine, which are referred to as the *stages* of the process. A process may be deterministic or non-deterministic, finite or infinite. We shall distinguish *passive* and *active* states. A state is passive if, by the nature of the system, it cannot change in time. A passive state is an object, an unchangeable detail of the computing machine. An active state is capable, at least potentially, of changing in time. It stands for a process, not an object. If some stage of a process becomes passive, the process is finite, and this stage is its last stage. We can say that time stops for a process when it reaches a passive stage. While the stage is active, the process continues (even though it may infinitely repeat itself). Expressions representing passive or active states are, respectively, *passive* or *active.*

Each next stage in a process is the result of one *step* of the computing machine. If the machine is deterministic the next stage is uniquely defined by the step function, which is a mapping from the set of active states S^a to the set of all states S. If it is non-deterministic, its operation is defined by the step relation, which is a subset of $S^a \times S$. When we add a definition of the step function or relation to the basic descriptive language, we have an equivalent of what is known as an *applicative* language. Our passive expressions correspond to constants, active to applications.

Supercompilation is based on the analysis of computation histories in a generalized form. To be able to do it, we must extend our basic language to include means to describe generalized states of the computing system, i.e. certain sets of precise states. So, the extended descriptive language will include expressions that represent *configurations* of the system. This is an important concept of the theory. A configuration is a set of precise states of the computing system or its subsystem. Not any set of states, however, but only a set that can be represented by an expression in the extended descriptive language we have chosen.The concept of a configuration is language-dependent. Consider, e.g., a subsystem D represented by one decimal digit. Its possible precise states are 0,1, ... ,9. Probably, we would want to have variables whose possible values are exactly digits. Let d be such a variable, and assume that variables are allowed as structural components in the extended descriptive language. Then the set of exact states 0,1, ... ,9 of D is a configuration, because it can be represented by the expression d . Consider the generalized state of D which includes the states 0 and 5 only. If we have a variable in the language that has <0,5> as its domain, then it is a configuration; if we have no such variable, it is not. We have to treat it as a union of the configurations 0 and 5 .

The expressions of the basic descriptive language describing precise states of the machine will be referred to as *ground* expressions; the expressions of the extended language, representing sets of precise states, will be called *non-ground* . Passive ground expressions will be referred to as *object* expressions.

Supercompilation can be defined in the context of an arbitrary applicative language, but as we go into detail, this becomes progressively more awkward; and there always is the need of examples. Thus, from the next section we start using a specific applicative language, Refal. There is only one more feature we want to discuss first in a general form.

Supercompilation includes a metasystem transition: we have a computer system, and create a metasystem for which the original system is an object of study. Moreover, we want the metasystem to be the same computing system as the object system -- i.e. an identical copy of it. Non-ground and active expressions representing configurations of the object system must become objects for the metasystem. Hence we need a mapping from the set of general (including active and non-ground) expressions to the set of object expressions. We call such a mapping, M, a *metacode* , provided that it satisfies these two requirements:

(1) M is homomorphic with respect to concatenation: $M(E_1E_2) = M(E_1)M(E_2)$.

(2) M is injective: $E_1 \neq E_2 \rightarrow M(E_1) \neq M(E_2)$.

The metacode of E will be denoted as μE. Because of (2), metacoding has an inverse operation, *demetacoding* , denoted $\mu^{-}E$.

It would be ideal if the metacode, while transforming non-ground and active expressions into object expressions, did not change object expressions at all. Unfortunately, this is impossible, because of the following simple theorem: there is no metacode which transforms all object expressions into themselves. To prove it, suppose that we have such a metacode μ. Let E represent a non-ground expression. Then μE is an object expression, and $\mu\mu E = \mu E$. Hence, E and μE, which are unequal, have the same image; this violates (2). So, any metacode, though introduced to transform general expressions into object expressions, will have the (undesirable) effect of transforming object expressions also. The only thing we can do is to minimize the effect of metacoding on object expressions.

2.. The language Refal

In the present paper we define and use Refal in a mathematical style syntax; the actual format required by the existing implementations is of no concern here.

The elementary syntax units of Refal are of two kinds: special signs and object symbols (or just *symbols*). The special signs include:

- structure brackets "(" and ")";
- activation brackets "<" and ">";
- free variables, which are represented by subscripted "s" (a symbol variable) or "e" (an expression

variable), e.g., s_1, s_x, e_5.

The object symbols used in Refal are supposed to belong to a finite alphabet, which may, however, vary from one use of Refal to another. We use as object signs: characters distinct from the special signs, subscripted and superscripted capital letters, Algol identifiers (sometimes underlined to stand out). In computer implementation we also allow the use of whole numbers as object signs (in which case, of course, the alphabet of object signs becomes infinite).

We use capital italic letters $A, B, \ldots E, E_1, \ldots$ etc. as metasymbols to denote Refal objects. We agree that the subscripts i, j, k of variables, as in e_i, may mean *some* subscripts, when this is clear from the context.

A Refal *expression* is one of the following:

- the empty string, which we may represent just by nothing, or by the metasymbol empty;
- a symbol (i.e. an object symbol, not a special sign);
- a variable;
- $E_1 E_2$, or (E_1), or $<E_1>$, where E_1 and E_2 are expressions.

An expression that is either a symbol, or a variable, or (E_1), or $<E_1>$, is referred to as a *term*. An expression is *passive* if it includes no activation brackets; it is *active* otherwise. An expression without free variables is a *ground* expressions; otherwise it is a *non-ground* expression. A pattern is a passive, and generally non-ground, expression. A passive ground expression is an *object* expression.

An *L-expression* is a pattern which (a) contains no more than one occurrence of every expression variable (we say e-variable for short), and (b) contains no more than one e-variable on the top level in every subexpression, i.e no its subexpression can be represented as $E_1\, e_i\, E_2\, e_j\, E_3$, where E_1, E_2, E_3 are some expressions. Examples of L-expressions:

$$Ae_1,\ BC(DE),\ e_1 + (e_2)(e_3),\ s_1 e_x s_1,\ (e_x)ABCe_y.$$

Examples of pattern expressions which are not L-expressions:

$$(e_x)ABCe_x,\ e_1 + e_2,\ e_1 s_2((e_1 + e_3)).$$

A Refal sentence has the form $<L> = R$, where L is a pattern, and R is an arbitrary general expression. The equality sign is just a symbol (not a special sign) used for visual convenience. The right side R can include only those variables which appear in the left side $<L>$. The pattern L starts usually with a symbol which is referred to as the function symbol. A Refal program is a list (ordered) of sentences.

Given an object expression E and an L-expression L, the *matching* operation $E : L$ is defined as finding such a substitution S for the variables in L, that applying S to L yields E. The values assigned to s-variables in substitutions must be single symbols, while e-variables can take any expressions as their values. If there is such a substitution, we say that the matching succeeds, and E is recognized as (a special case of) L . If there is no such substitution, the matching fails.

Let E be an object expresion, and L an L-expression. The following algorithm performs the matching operation $E : L$, and shows that if there is a substitution transforming L into E, it is unique (this holds as long as L is an L-expression, but may not hold for other patterns). We refer to E as the *target* and L as the *pattern* in matching.The pair E : L itself is referred to as a *clash* . Substitutions for the variables in L are *assignments*; they are written in the form A <– V, where V is a variable, and A an object expression. A list of assignments is a *partial environment*, PENV; if the list includes assignments for all the variables in L , it is a *total* environment.

The matching algorithm

begin

Set PENV empty; set STACK-OF-CLASHES to include one member E : L .

NEXT-CLASH:

Take CLASH from STACK-OF-CLASHES.

CLASH-LOOP: Use the rule for any of the applicable cases.

case 1. CLASH is empty : empty . Go to END-CLASH.

case 2. CLASH is E : e_i . Add E <– e_i to PENV. Go to END-CLASH.

case 3. CLASH is SE : SL , or ES : LS, where S is a symbol; put CLASH = E : L; go to CLASH-LOOP.

case 4a. CLASH is SE : s_iL , or ES : Ls_i , and there is no assignment for s_i in PENV. Add S <– s_i to PENV; put CLASH = E : L; go to CLASH-LOOP.

case 4b. CLASH is SE : s_iL , or ES : Ls_i , and there is the assignment S <– s_i in PENV. Put CLASH = E : L; go to CLASH-LOOP.

case 5. CLASH is (E_2)E_1 : (L_2)L_1 or E_1(E_2) : L_1(L_2). Add (E_2 : L_2) to STACK-OF-CLASHES; put CLASH = E_1: L_1; go to CLASH-LOOP.

case 6. If none of the above is applicable, the matching fails (recognition impossible).

END-CLASH: If STACK-OF-CLASHES is empty, the matching succeeds, and PENV is the full environment. Otherwise go to NEXT-CLASH.

end of the matching algorithm.

The semantics of Refal is defined operationally by the *Refal machine* which executes algorithms written in Refal. The Refal machine has two potentially infinite information storages: the *program-field* and the *view-field*. The program field contains a Refal program, which is loaded into the machine before the run and does not change during the run. The view-field contains a ground expression which changes in time as the machine works; this expression will often be referred to simply as the view-field.

The Refal machine works by *steps* . Each step is executed as follows. If the expression in the view-field is passive, the Refal machine comes to a normal stop. Otherwise it picks up one of the pairs of activation brackets in the view-field, and declares the term it delimits the *leading* active term. Then it compares the leading term, let it be <*E*>, with the consecutive sentences in the program field, starting with the first one, in search of an *applicable* sentence. A sentence is applicable if E can be recognized as the pattern L in its left side, i.e. the matching $E:L$ is successful. On finding the first applicable sentence, the Refal machine copies its right side and applies to it the substitution resulting from the matching $E:L$ .The ground expression thus formed is then substituted for the leading active term in the view-field. This ends the execution of the current step, and the machine proceeds to execute the next step. If there is no applicable sentence, the Refal machine comes to an abnormal stop.

The definition of the leading active term may vary, so that we can have several variants of the Refal machine. Originally, the Refal machine was defined as evaluating subexpressions according to the rule "inside-out, from left to right" (known as applicative order). Then the leading active term is defined as the leftmost active term $<E>$ with a passive E. This is also the way it works in the existing implementations.

However, an outside-in left-to-right Refal machine can also be used (the normal evaluation order). It will start by trying to apply the program sentences to the outermost activation brackets, first on the left. Then the expression E in the leading active term $<E>$ is not, generally, an object expression, but may include some activation brackets. The matching process $E:L$ must then be generalized as follows. We say that the active subexpression $<E_1>$ of E *does not prevent* the matching $E:L$, if the substitution of any expression for $<E_1>$ has no effect on the success or failure of the matching; otherwise $<E_1>$ ***prevents*** the matching. If the current matching is not prevented by some active subexpression, the outside-in Refal machine goes on and may complete a step with some values in the substitution resulting from the successful matching being active. If it finds that some subexpression prevents the matching, this subexpression becomes the next attempted leading active term.

We can also construct a Refal machine with many step-executing processors.Such a machine will attach one processor to every activation brackets pair in the view-field. Parallel activations as in $(<E_1>)\ <E_2>$, will be executed in parallel. As for nested activations, in the situation of prevention, the outer activation will wait until the preventing configuration is – partially or competely – computed.

If the inside-out evaluation process is finite, the outside-in process will also be finite and will yield exactly the same result. It may happen, however, that the inside-out evaluation never stops, while the outside-in evaluation results in a finite process (this situation is well-known from the lambda-calculus). The order of parallel activations does not effect the results. So we take as the basic Refal machine the inside-out left-to-right kind. This will be referred to simply as the Refal machine. If a computation process is finite with this machine, all other kinds will produce the same result. But we can also write a Refal program meant specifically for outside-in execution.

A function is defined by specifying: (a) a general Refal expression F called the *format* of the function, and (b) a Refal program which is its *definition* . Substituting some values for the variables in F , we put it in the view-field of the Refal machine which is loaded with some definition. If after a finite number of steps the Refal machine comes to a normal stop, the resulting object expression in the view-field is the value of the function.

Consider some examples. In the unary number system, zero is represented by 0, one by 01, two by 011, etc. We want to define the function of addition for these numbers. Let the format be $<+(e_x)e_y>$. Then the definition is:

$$<+(e_x)\ 0> \ = \ e_x$$
$$<+(e_x)\ e_y 1> \ = \ <+(e_x)\ e_y>\ 1$$

With the input values 01 for e_x and 011 for e_y, the Refal machine will exhibit the following computation process:

$$<+(01)\ 011>$$
$$<+(01)\ 01>\ 1$$
$$<+(01)\ 0>\ \ 11$$
$$0111$$

We could have chosen a different format, e.g. $<+(e_1)(e_2)>$, or $<\text{add } e_x,e_y>$, etc.

The function reversing a string of symbols can be defined as:

$$<\text{reverse } s_1\ e_2> \ = \ <\text{reverse } e_2>\ s_1$$
$$<\text{reverse } > \ =$$

As an example of the use of nested activation brackets in the right side, we define the adding machine for binary numbers:

$$<\text{addb } (e_x\ 0)\ e_y\ s_1> \ = \ <\text{addb } (e_x)\ e_y>\ s_1$$
$$<\text{addb } (e_x\ 1)\ e_y\ 0> \ = \ <\text{addb } (e_x)\ e_y>\ 1$$
$$<\text{addb } (e_x\ 1)\ e_y\ 1> \ = \ <\text{addb } (<\text{addb } (e_x)\ 1>)\ e_y>\ 0$$
$$<\text{addb } (e_x\ )\ e_y\ > \ = \ e_x\ e_y$$

The format is $<\text{addb } (e_1)\ e_2>$. Note that the variables we choose for formats have nothing to do with the variables used in programs. Also, the variables in different sentences are in no way related (though we usually keep the same variables as a matter of convenience). The last sentence of the program for addb may not be understood immediately. It will work correctly because it will be used only in the situation where at least one of the two arguments e_x and e_y is empty. The program would be more readable if instead of that sentence we used these two:

$$<\text{addb } (e_x)\ > \ = \ e_x$$
$$<\text{addb } ()\ e_y> \ = \ e_y$$

The language we defined above is referred to as the *strict* Refal. It is the basis for equivalent transformation and automatic generation of programs. For conveniency of programming, however, we introduce some natural extensions of the strict language. The interpretive implementation of Refal allows the extensions, but the supercompiler requires strict Refal on the input. A special Refal program translates programs written in extended Refal into strict Refal.

The first step to extend strict Refal is to remove the restriction on the left sides of sentences. This version of the language is referred to as the *basic* Refal. It allows any pattern expressions in the left sides of sentences, not just L-expressions. When the pattern P in the matching $E : P$ is not an L-expression, there may be more than one substitution transforming P to E. So a rule is necessary that would tell us which of the substitutions must be used. Our rule corresponds to matching from left to right: of all substitutions the one is chosen that assignes the least (with respect to the number of constituent terms) value to the leftmost e-variable; if this does not eliminate ambiguity, the same selection is made for the second e-variable from the left, etc.

Using arbitrary patterns, we can define the function chpm that changes every "+" into "-" in a string as follows:

<chpm e_1+ e_2> = e_1 - <chpm e_2>
<chpm e_1> = e_1

When the argument E is successfuly matched against e_1+ e_2, the character "+" in the pattern is associated with the first "+" from the left in E. So we can take e_1 out of the activation brackets and apply chpm recursively to e_2. To define this function in strict Refal, we need three sentences:

<chpm + e_1> = - <chpm e_1>
<chpm s_2 e_1> = s_2 <chpm e_1>
<chpm > =

The metacode transformation we use in Refal singles out one symbol, let it be the asterisk "*", to build up the images of variables and activation brackets. The metacodes of s_i and e_i are *Si and *Ei, respectively. The pair of activation brackets <> becomes *(). Any symbol distinct from * remains itself, while * becomes *V . For instance, the active non-ground expression <F e_1(<G s_x>)> becomes, when metacoded, the object expression *(F *E1(*(G *SX))) .

3. Graph of states and transitions

Refal is a substitutional language. The operation of the Refal machine can conveniently be described in terms of elementary operations that are, essentially, certain types of substitutions. We introduce two kinds of substitutional operations: *assignments* and *contractions*.

An assignment is represented as E <– V, where E is an expression, and V is a variable. (Here and in the following it should be clear from the context whether a letter is used as a metasymbol for a Refal expression, or just as a Refal symbol). The execution of this assignment results in the association of the value E with the variable V. To apply an assignment as a substitution to an expression, it must be put on the left side: (E <– V)E_1 ; this stands for the result of replacing every occurrence of V in E_1 by E.

A contraction is represented as $V \to L$, where V is a variable, and L is an L-expression. If the current value of V is an object expression E^o, then the execution of the contraction is the matching E^o: L. If this matching fails, we say that the contraction cannot be applied to V. If it succeeds, the resulting total environment contains an assignment for every variable in L, and we interpret these assignments as giving the new values of these variables. After the execution of the assignment, the contracted variable V becomes undefined, unless it appears also in the right side of the contraction L. So,the contraction can be read as "break down the value of V according to the pattern L". For instance, if the current value of e_1 is AB(X+Y)A , then the execution of the contraction $e_1 \to s_x e_1 s_x$ will succeed and result in the value A for s_x, and the new value B(X+Y) for e_1. To apply a contraction as a substitution, we put it on the right of the expression, so $E_1(V \to E) = (E \leftarrow V)E_1$.

Our notation, though unusual, is, however, quite consistent and natural. It implements the following two principles: (a) when the thing is seen as a substitution, the arrow is directed from the variable to its replacement, and the variable stands close to the transformed expression; (b) when it is seen as an operation in an environment, the old variables, the value of which are defined, are on the left, while the new variables being defined are on the right.

As is well known, the effect of simultaneous substitutions is, generally, different from that of their sequential execution. Let $V_1, \dots, V_n$ be the free variables of a configuration C. Then $(V_1) \dots (V_n)$ will be referred to as the *varlist* of C, and denoted as <u>var</u> C. When we deal with simultaneous contractions or assignments, it is convenient to deal with one object, the varlist, instead of speaking all the time of sets of variables. Suppose we have a set of simultaneous contractions $(v_1 \to L_1) \dots (v_k \to L_k)$, where v_1 to v_k are some variables from C. Take <u>var</u> C and apply all the contractions to it. The result, L, may be not an L-expression only if some of the L_i's in the contractions had used the same e-variable. In that case we will rename the variables in the L_i's to avoid conflicts. So we assume that L is an L-expression. It gives a full account of the contractions applied, as well as of what variables were *not* affected by the contractions. If, e.g., the varlist is $(e_1)(s_2)(e_3)$, and the contractions are $(s_2 \to A)(e_3 \to Be_3)$, then L is $(e_1)(A)(Be_3)$, which reminds us that there is also the variable e_1 in the varilst that was not affected by contractions. Such *list contractions* will be represented as $V \to L$. In our example:

$$(e_1)(s_2)(e_3) \to (e_1)(A)(Be_3)$$

We shall also write assignments in the full form: $E \leftarrow V$, e.g.

$$(e_1)(B)(e_2+ABCe_1) \leftarrow (e_1)(s_2)(e_3).$$

We often treat varlists as unordered sets. We write $V_1 \le V_2$ to mean that every variable from V_1 is also in V_2. If $V_1 \le V_2$ and $V_2 \le V_1$, we say that V_1 and V_2 are equal as sets. At the same time one must remember that a varlist is a definite Refal expression, and when taken in isolation its terms cannot be reordered.

When only one variable from the full varlist , say e_1, is affected by a contraction, we may represent it by a single contraction term $(e_1 \rightarrow L_1)$. We can then find that we want a composition of several such terms. In fact, this is exactly how the generalized matching algorithm, to be discussed shortly, works. One should keep in mind, however, that the meaning of an individual contraction may depend on the full list of variables. Take, e.g., the contraction $e_1 \rightarrow s_x e_1$. If s_x is not in the varlist, then this contraction succeeds whenever the value of e_1 starts with any symbol; s_x takes on this symbol as its value. If s_x is in the varlist, then our individual contraction is actually a part of the contraction $(e_1)(s_x) \rightarrow (s_x e_1)(s_x)$. For it to succeed, the value of e_1 must start with the symbol which is the current value of s_x, not just any symbol.

In full contractions we can rename the variables in the right side in any (consistent) way; the meaning of the operation will not be changed. For examle, instead of the contraction above we could write $(e_1)(s_x) \rightarrow (s_y e_1)(s_y)$. The only difference would be that what we called s_x before is now called s_y. When we have an individual contraction, we must make it clear, with respect to every variable in the right side, whether the variable is *old*, i.e. belongs to the current varlist, or *new*, i.e. was not used before. Repeated e-variables are not allowed in L-expressions. So we agree, in order to avoid unnecessary renamings, that an e-variable with a subscript already used in the varlist can be used in the right side of contractions only in the contraction for itself (and only once, of course). Since in such a use the variable is redefined and not compared with another value, we do not call it an old variable: e-variables cannot be old. It is only s-variables that must be categorized in individual contractions as new or old.

The rule for the composition (*folding*) of full contractions follows from our definitions:

$$\text{If } V_2 \leq \underline{var}\, L_1 \text{ then } (V_1 \rightarrow L_1)(V_2 \rightarrow L_2) = (V_1 \rightarrow L_1(V_2 \rightarrow L_2))$$

If we have a contraction $V \rightarrow L$, the variables in L are said to be the *derivatives* of the variables in V. The way we use contractions, it will never happen that a contraction appears for a variable that is not a derivative of the preceding varlist; such a situation would have no sense.

The rule for folding assignments is:

$$\text{If } V_2 \leq \underline{var}\, E_1 \text{ then } (E_2 \leftarrow V_2)(E_1 \leftarrow V_1) = ((E_2 \leftarrow V_2)E_1 \leftarrow V_1)$$

Now consider the sequence $(E \leftarrow V)(V \rightarrow L)$. It represents a situation when the varlist V is assigned the value E, after which we ask to restructure it according to the pattern L. The assignment *clashes* with the contraction. To resolve the clash we must match E : L. In fact, the matching operation is the only operation we use; contractions and assignments, for individual variables and for varlists, are only special cases.

If the target E in the clash E : L is an object expression, its resolution is given by the matching algorithm which is part of the definition of the Refal machine. Now we are interested in a situation where E may be a non-ground, although still passive, expression. Thus both operands in the clash represent sets of groung (object) expressions. A ground expression E^g is an element of the set represented by E , iff the matching E^g: E succeeds. The union of non-ground expressions E_1 and E_2

considered as sets will be represented as the sum $E_1 + E_2$; their intersection as $E_1 * E_2$. For the matching of two non-ground expressions the following formula holds:

(1) $$E : L \;=\; \Sigma_k\, (\underline{var}\, E \;\text{->}\; L^k)\, (E^k \;\text{<-}\; \underline{var}\, L), \qquad 1 \le k \le N$$

where the left side is a clash, and the right side its *resolution*. For every additive term in the resolution, $\underline{var}\, E^k$ is equal (as a set) to $\underline{var}\, L^k$, and

(2) $$E\, (\underline{var}\, E \;\text{->}\; L^k) \;=\; (E^k \;\text{<-}\; \underline{var}\, L) L, \qquad 1 \le k \le N$$

is a subset of the intersection E*L. These subsets are disjoint, and their sum in (1) is the full intersection E*L. Following is the algorithm to resolve a given clash.

The generalized matching algorithm, GMA

Let the clash be E:L. Let $W_e = \underline{var}\, E$, and $W_l = \underline{var}\, L$. In the following, E and L will be used as variables, but W_e and W_l are fixed, referring to the initial values of E and L.

A *partial resolution term*, PRT, is a list contraction followed by assignments for a subset W_l' of W_l. A CPRT (current Clash and PRT) is a clash and a PRT. The GMA is operating on a sum of CPRTs, to be referred to as STATE. Every term in STATE is processed independently. In the processing, a term may be eliminated, or give rise to more than one term. A term can be *closed*, which means that the clash in it disappears (being resolved), and the partial resolution becomes complete. In the end, the closed CPRTs (which become PRTs after closing) make up the sum in (1). If no terms are left, (k = 0), E*L is empty. We denote this result of the resolution as Z. It is the unity of the summing operation: X+ Z = X.

The *update* of the CPRT $(E{:}L)(W_e \;\text{->}\; L^k)(E^k \;\text{<-}\; W_l')$ by the PRT $(\underline{var}\, L^k \;\text{->}\; L^i)(E^i \;\text{<-}\; W_l'')$ is the result of the following transformation of the CPRT:

1. Replace E by $E(\underline{var}\, L^k \;\text{->}\; L^i)$;
2. Replace E^k by $E^k\, (\underline{var}\, L^k \;\text{->}\; L^i)$;
3. Replace L^k by $L^k\, (\underline{var}\, L^k \;\text{->}\; L^i)$;
4. Add $(E^i \;\text{<-}\; W_l'')$ to $(E^k \;\text{<-}\; W_l')$.

To update a CPRT by a sum of PRTs, we take one copy of the CPRT for each PRT, update it, and sum the results.

An *internal s-clash* is a clash S:S', where S and S' are either specific symbols, or s-variabes from the same varlist $\underline{var}\, L^k$ of a CPRT. It is resolved according to these rules, where id is the identity contraction, and A is an arbitrary symbol:

1. $S : S \;=\; \underline{id}$
2. $s_i : S \;=\; (s_i \;\text{->}\; S)$
3. $A : s_i \;=\; (s_i \;\text{->}\; A)$
4. If none of the above, Z.

The main procedure follows:

begin

Put STATE = (E : L) id.

Until all terms in STATE are closed, do:

begin Pick any of the CPRTs in STATE. Let C be the clash in CPRT, and PRT the partial resolution term. Use any applicable rule of the follows:

case 1. C is empty : empty . Close CPRT (by eliminating C).

case 2. C is E : e_i . Update CPRT by E <– e_i and close it.

case 3. C is S'E : SL , or ES' : LS. Here and in the following S is either a symbol or a symbol variable, and so is S'. If S is a variable for which there is no assignment in CPRT, put CPRT equal to (E:L) PRT and update it by S' <– S . If S is a symbol, say A, or a variable whose assignment value in PRT is A, resolve the internal clash S': A, let the resolution be R, put CPRT = (E : L) PRT, and update it by R.

case 4. C is $(E_1)E_2 : (L_1)L_2$ or $E_2(E_1) : L_2(L_1)$. Using the GMA recursively, resolve the clash $E_1: L_1$ starting with STATE = $(E_1: L_1)$ PRT, and let the result be R. Put CPRT = $(E_2: L_2)$ PRT and update it by R.

case 5L. C is e_jE : SL. Update CPRT by (e_j –>) + (e_j –> $s_{j'}e_j$). Here and in the following, j' stands for a *new* variable index, i.e. one that was not yet used in var E or its derivatives.

case 5R. C is Ee_j: LS. Update CPRT by (e_j –>) + (e_j –> $e_js_{j'}$).

case 6L. C is e_jE : (L_1)L. Update CPRT by (e_j –>) + (e_j –> $(e_{j'})e_j$).

case 6R. C is Ee_j: $L(L_1)$. Update CPRT by (e_j –>) + (e_j –> $e_j(e_{j'})$).

case 7. If none of the above is applicable, the current CPRT is eliminated.

end processing terms.

Collect all closed resolution terms as the output. If none, output Z (matching impossible).

end of the algorithm.

It is easy to prove that the contractions var E –> L^k in (1) are pairwise incompatible, i.e. the intersection $L^k*L^{k'}$ for k not equal k' is empty. The idea: all the branchings in cases 5L to 6R are such that one branch produces object expressions which have at least one term more than those produced by the other branch in comparable subexpressions.

The GMA is a generalization of the well-known concept of *unification* in term-rewriting systems. The data structure in Refal is more general than the structure of terms formed by constructors. When we limit Refal expressions to that subset, the GMA is reduced to unification.

Consider a ground (i.e. without free variables) configuration C_1. Put it in the view-field of the Refal machine. Suppose C_1 is active. The definition of the Refal machine uniquely determines the next state of the system, which is another ground configuration C_2. If it is active again, the next stage follows, and so on. Thus to every precise state a sequence of states C_1, C_2, ... etc. corresponds. If one of these is passive, we take it as the result of the computation, and the history of computation becomes finite. Otherwise it is infinite, and there is no result.

Now suppose that the configuration C_1 includes free variables. Then it defines a generalized state of our computing system. We want to construct the generalized history of computation which starts with

C_1. It will not be, in the general case, linear, as for a precise configuration, but will be represented by a graph, normally infinite. To construct this graph, we use *driving*.

The idea of driving is to execute one or more steps of the Refal machine in the situation where the contents of the view-field is not completely defined, but is described by a non-ground configuration which includes unknown subexpressions represented by free variables. The Refal machine is not meant to deal with free variables in the view-field; we "drive" free variables forcefully through the sentences of the program.

Let the leading active subexpression in C_1 be <F E>. Let the sentences for F in the program field be:

$$<F\ L_1> \ = \ R_1$$

.....

$$<F\ L_n> \ = \ R_n$$

For those values of the free variables in E with which E matches L_1, the Refal machine will use the first sentence. To find this subset, we resolve the clash:

$$E : L_1 \ = \ \Sigma_k\ (\underline{var}\ E \rightarrow L_1{}^k)(E_1{}^k \leftarrow \underline{var}\ L_1)\ , \qquad 1 \leq k \leq N_1$$

Under each contraction in the sum, the Refal machine will take the first sentence and replace the expression under concretization by $(E_1{}^k \leftarrow \underline{var}\ L_1)R_1$, because the assignment part of the resolution gives us the values to be taken by the variables in L_1 in the process of matching. It is only the variables from L_1 that are allowed to be used in R_1, hence after the substitution we have an expression which depends only on the variables in E and its derivatives.

Thus the first part of the graph of states for C_1, corresponding to the first sentence in the definition of F will consist of N_1 branches:

$$(\underline{var}\ E \rightarrow L_1{}^k)\ C_2{}^k\ , \qquad 1 \leq k \leq N_1$$

where at the end of each branch we have the new configuration

$$C_2{}^k \ = \ (E_1{}^k \leftarrow \underline{var}\ L_1)R_1{}^k$$

For those members of the initial configuration C_1 which do not belong to any of the subclasses we separated, the first sentence will be found unapplicable. The Refal machine will then try to apply the second sentence, which we should take into account by separating another group of subclasses of E and adding it to the first group. Repeating this procedure for each sentence in the definition of F, and renumbering the contractions throughout the whole set, we come to the graph of states which can be represented by the expression:

$$C_1 \, (\, (\underline{var}\; E \to L^1) \, C_2{}^1$$
$$+(\underline{var}\; E \to L^2) \, C_2{}^2$$
$$\ldots$$
$$+(\underline{var}\; E \to L^N) \, C_2{}^N \,)$$

where $N = N_1+N_2+ \ldots +N_n$. The parenthesized sum of branches following C_1 will be referred to as the *development* of the configuration C_1, and denoted as <u>dev</u> C_1. There is an obvious optimization which can be applied to the construction of the graph of states. If, for the i-th sentence, the argument E is found to match L_i without contractions, which means that E is a subset of L_i, then the branches originating from all the sentences starting from the i+1-th can be omitted, because they will be never used.

The graph of states has a double significance. Firstly, it is a history of computation, and we can use it in this role for analysis of algorithms and equivalent transformation of functions. Secondly, since it is a *generalized* history, it is a ready program to execute one or more steps of the algorithmic processes described by the initial configuration of the graph. Indeed, let the values of the variables in C_1 be given. Then we can apply the contractions on the branches to these values, and use the first applicable branch to make the step from C_1 to C_2. If we have the graph of states for C_2, we can make one more step, and so on. The ordering of the arcs in the graph of states is important. The groups of branches originated from different sentences must be ordered in the same way as the sentences in the original definitions. The ordering of branches within groups, though, is immaterial, because the corresponding contractions are, as we know, incompatible.

If the initial configuration C_1 is $\langle F\, e_1 \rangle$, the resulting graph will have exactly one branch, $(e_i \to L_i)\, R_i$, for each sentence, where L_i is the left, and R_i the right side of the sentence. Thus, the Refal program is nothing else but the collection of the transition graphs for the configurations of the form $\langle F\, e_1 \rangle$, where F runs over all the functions used. We can combine all these graphs into one graph, which we shall denote by G_{tot}, by introducing the special variable e_0 which stands for the contents of the view-field. So, the contraction $e_0 \to \langle F^m e_1 \rangle$ should be read: "if the configuration $\langle F^m e_1 \rangle$ is in the view-field, then". The total graph is:

$$G_{tot} = \quad (\, (e_0 \to \langle F^1\, e_1 \rangle) \, \underline{dev} \; \langle F^1\, e_1 \rangle$$
$$+ \, (e_0 \to \langle F^2\, e_1 \rangle) \, \underline{dev} \; \langle F^2\, e_1 \rangle$$
$$\ldots$$
$$+ \, (e_0 \to \langle F^n\, e_1 \rangle) \, \underline{dev} \; \langle F^n\, e_1 \rangle \,)$$

It is also convenient to end each branch with assigning the resulting configuration to e_0, which is read: "put C_2 into the view-field". Now every branch in the total graph, as well as in configuration developments, consists only of contractions and assignmnents. It starts with a contraction for e_0, which specifies the configuration we put in the view-field, and ends with the assignment to e_0 which specifies what will appear in the view-field as the result. The development of a configuration C is different in that its branches start with contractions for the variables of C. The total graph may be viewed as dev e_0.

In the development of C_1, we can apply driving to every active configuration $C_2{}^k$, replacing it with its development. We shall have then the history of two steps of computation starting with C_1. Now we can drive all active configurations in the developments of all $C_2{}^k$, and so on. At every stage of this process we have a tree where the walks represent generalized computation histories. Every walk ends either with a passive expression (terminated walk), or with a call of some configuration.

If we use the breadth-first principle and drive indefinitely long, we construct an infinite tree without active configurations, which includes all possible computation histories. Some walks in this tree may terminate, while others may be infinite. A walk that terminates in n steps has the form:

$$(\underline{var}\ C_1 \rightarrow L^1)\ (\underline{var}\ L^1 \rightarrow L^2) \ldots\ (\underline{var}\ L^{n-1} \rightarrow L^n)\ (E^n \leftarrow e_0)$$

where E^n is a passive expression which can include only the free variables from L^n. We can fold all n contractions into one, ($\underline{var}\ C_1 \rightarrow L$). Recalling that we deal with the development of C_1, we can write the formula of a terminated walk as:

$$(e_0 \rightarrow C_1)\ (\underline{var}\ C_1 \rightarrow L)\ (E^n \leftarrow e_0)$$

This is, essentially, a formula for one step of the Refal machine. A configuration can be seen as a function of its free variables. Each terminated walk in the infinite driving of C_1 gives us a subset of the domain of C_1, and the algorithm of computing C_1 on this subset by one Refal step, i.e. by simply restructuring C_1 into E^n. We shall call these subdomains *the ultimate neighborhoods* in the computation of C_1. Infinite driving breaks down the domain of the initial configuration into ultimate neighborhoods. It is analogous to the enumeration of the pairs argument-value in the theory of recursive functions. In our case, each pair consists of $C_1(\underline{var}\ C_1 \rightarrow L)$ and E^n, i.e. a pair of sets of expressions, not individual expressions; the rule of transforming the argument into the value goes with the pair.

4. Supercompilation

Infinite driving graphs are useful in many ways, but to use a graph as an executable program it must be finite. Also from the viewpoint of history analysis, the infinite graph as defined above is not very convenient, because each new configuration produces new sets of contractions in the development, so it is hard to see where are those basic, repeating elements in terms of which one could do analysis. To convert a potentially infinite graph resulting from driving into a finite graph is the purpose of *supercompilation.*

The supercompilation process, by one way or another, leads to the definition of a finite set of configurations referred to as the *basis* of the graph. The members of this set, known as basic configurations, and only they, are allowed to stay in the final graph. The initial configuration is included in the basis by definition. As for other configurations, they may either be included into the basis at the outset, by the programmer's will, or be deduced and declared as basic in the process of supercompilation; we do not go into specifics, at present. The supercompilation starts as driving. In the course of driving, if the current configuration to be driven, C_i, can be recognized as a specialization of one of the basic configurations C_b, i.e. the result of applying some substitution $(E \leftarrow \underline{var}\ C_b)$ to C_b, then it is not driven but replaced by $(E \leftarrow \underline{var}\ C_b)C_b$. Thereby we reduce C_i to C_b, and instead of tracing further C_i as an independent configuration, assign the necessary values to the variables of C_b, and call C_b. A set of configurations is valid as a basis only if for each basic configuration a development can be constructed by driving, in which every end configuration is either passive or reduced to one of the basic configurations.

It is easy to convert a graph resulting from supercompilation into a standard Refal program. To every basic configuration C_i a function is put in correspondence with the format $<C_i\ \underline{var}\ C_i>$. The walks in the graph have one of the two forms:

passive end: $(\underline{var}\ C_i \rightarrow L^1)\ (\underline{var} L^1 \rightarrow L^2) \ldots (\underline{var}\ L^{n-1} \rightarrow L^n)\ (E^n \leftarrow e_0)$

active end: $(\underline{var}\ C_i \rightarrow L^1)\ (\underline{var} L^1 \rightarrow L^2) \ldots (\underline{var}\ L^{n-1} \rightarrow L^n)\ (E^n \leftarrow \underline{var}\ C_j)(C_j \leftarrow e_0)$

In each walk we fold the contractions; let the result be $(\underline{var}\ C_i \rightarrow L)$. Then we form the sentence:

$$<C_i\ L> \ = \ E^n$$

in the case of a passive walk-end, and the sentence:

$$<C_i\ L> \ = \ <C_j\ E^n>$$

if the walk-end is active. Taking all sentences in their order, we have the definition of the function C_i. Taking the definitions for all basic configurations we have the complete Refal program equivalent to the original program as far as the computation of the initial configuration C_1 is concerned.

Let us consider a very simple example of supercompilation. Take the following definitions:

$$<F^a\ A\ e_1> \ = \ B\ <F^a\ e_1>$$
$$<F^a\ s_2\ e_1> \ = \ s_2\ <F^a\ e_1>$$
$$<F^a> \ =$$
$$<F^b\ B\ e_1> \ = \ C\ <F^b\ e_1>$$
$$<F^b\ s_2\ e_1> \ = \ s_2\ <F^b\ e_1>$$
$$<F^b> \ =$$
$$<F\ e_1> \ = \ <F^b\ <F^a\ e_1>>$$

Let the initial configuration C_1 be $<F\ e_1>$. After the first step of driving it becomes, without any branchings and contractions, $<F^b <F^a\ e_1>>$. We call such configurations as $<F\ e_1>$ *transient* .There is no need to keep them in the memory of the supercompiler. We simply redefine C_1 as $<F^b <F^a\ e_1>>$. According to the inside-out semantics of the standard Refal machine, the evaluation of these nested function calls requires two passes of the argument e_1. However, there is nothing to prevent us from using the outside-in principle during the driving, as an optimization technique. Whereas on the programming level we can choose the inside-out semantics for its simplicity, or the outside-in semantics for its sophistication, the supercompiler should always use the outside-in evaluation in order to implement a more efficient algorithm. The only risk we run is that the domain of the function will be extended, but this is hardly a risk at all. (In this specific case, though, even this does not happen). So we start from the outside trying to drive the call of F^b. We immediately find, however, that the driving is prevented by the inner call of F^a. So we go inside and drive this call. This results in the graph:

$$
\begin{array}{ll}
(1) & (e_0 -> C_1)\ (\ (e_1 -> A e_1)\ <F^b\ B <F^a\ e_1>> \ <- e_0 \\
 & \quad + (e_1 -> s_2 e_1)\ <F^b\ s_2 <F^a\ e_1>> \ <- e_0 \\
 & \quad + (e_1 -> \underline{empty})\ \ \underline{empty} <- e_0\ )
\end{array}
$$

What shall we do further? At every step of supercompilation we must decide whether each active configuration found in the current development should be driven further, or declared basic. The algorithm of decision taking of this kind is referred to as the *strategy* of supercompilation. We cannot discuss here details of possible strategies of supercompilation. Even though the supercompiler we have at the present time will make the required choices automatically, we have to present it here without explanations. So, we decide to go on with the first active configuration we see in (1), i.e. $<F^b\ B <F^a\ e_1>>$. We again start from the outside, but this time we find that the inner active expression does not prevent us from successful matching and driving. The development is a very simple graph:

$$
(2) \qquad\qquad C\ <F^b <F^a\ e_1>> \ <- e_0
$$

The active configuration here is identical to C_1, which is basic by definition, so we do not drive it further.

The driving of the second active configuration in (1), $<F^b\ s_2 <F^a\ e_1>>$, yields:

$$
\begin{array}{ll}
(3) & (s_2 -> B)\ \ C <F^b <F^a\ e_1>> \ <- e_0 \\
 & + \ s_2 <F^b <F^a\ e_1>> \ <- e_0
\end{array}
$$

Again, the end configurations are all identical to C_1. Substituting (2) and (3) in (1), and reducing the end configurations to C_1 (which in this case is trivial), we have the final graph:

```
(e0 ->C1) ( (e1->Ae1)  C <C1(e1)> <- e0
          +(e1->s2e1) ( (s2-> B)  C<C1(e1)> <- e0
                       + s2 <C1(e1)> <- e0 )
          +(e1-> empty )   empty <-e0 )
```

Thus the only function in the basis is C_1. Folding contractions in this graph, we have the Refal program:

```
<C1(A e1)>  =  C <C1(e1)>
<C1(B e1)>  =  C <C1(e1)>
<C1(s2 e1)>  =  s2 <C1(e1)>
<C1( )>  =
```

If the outside-in execution of a Refal program results in exactly the same steps as the inside-out execution, the program will be called *bidirectional.* The program for $<C_1(e_1)>$ is bidirectional, because there always is only one active term in the view-field.The original program for $<F\ e_1>$ is not bidirectional. Its inside-out execution requires 2n loops if the length of the input string is n. The outside-in (lazy) evaluation involves only n loops. It is well-known, however, that lazy evaluation entails certain overheads, because of the necessity to analyze, at every step, which of the activation brackets must be developed first. The use of the supercompiler gives the best solution of the problem. It implements the same efficient algorithm as the lazy evaluator, but executes the overhead operations at the compile time. This results in a bidirectional program that reflects the semantics of the outside-in evaluation but can be directly executed on the simple inside-out machine. The supercompiler transformed a two-pass algorithm into a one-pass.

It is not always the case, though, that the outside-in evaluation is algorithmically better than the inside-out evaluation. Consider the initial configuration

(4) $<rep3\ <F^a\ e_1>>$

where the function rep3 (repeat three times) is defined as:

$$<rep3\ e_x> \ = \ (e_x)(e_x)(e_x)$$

With the inside-out rule, we compute F^a, then make two copies of the result and form a list of the three identical subexpressions. With the outside-in strategy, we find that the step execution for the function rep3 is not prevented, so we make the step, which results in the configuration:

$$(<F^a\ e_1>)\ (<F^a\ e_1>)\ (<F^a\ e_1>)$$

When this configuration is evaluated, the function call $<F^a\ e_1>$ is evaluated three times: an obvious waste.

The outside-in evaluation strategy can be modified so as to bar this effect. In Refal it is easy to keep track of the copying of the values of variables. We call a variable *duplicated* if in the right side of the sentence there are more occurrences of this variable than in the left side. Duplicated variables can be marked in the left sides of program's sentences by way of preprocessing. Now, when the supercompiler (or a direct outside-in evaluator) establishes that a Refal step is not prevented by any of the inner active terms, it makes the additional step of checking that none of the duplicated variables (note that they have already been assigned definite values at this moment) has active subexpressions. If it is not the case, the step execution must be delayed, and the active subexpressions of the duplicated variables developed first, in some order.

It does not always happen that every active configuration called in the graph of states is either to be further driven, or can be recognized as one of the configurations already declared basic. Take this example. Redefine the function F^a above as follows:

$$
\begin{array}{l}
<F^a\, e_1> \;=\; <F^1(\,)e_1> \\
<F^1\,(e_1)\, A\, e_2> \;=\; <F^1\,(e_1 B)\, e_2> \\
<F^1\,(e_1)\, s_x\, e_2> \;=\; <F^1\,(e_1 s_x)\, e_2> \\
<F^1\,(e_1)\,> \;=\; e_1
\end{array}
$$

Let the initial configuration be $<F\, e_1>$ again. After the obvious two steps we have $<F^b <F^1()e_1>>$ as the new C_1. Driving from the outside, we find that we cannot make a step in F^b, therefore we make a step in F^1:

$$
\begin{array}{lll}
(5) & (e_0 \text{->}\, C_1) & (\,(e_1 \text{->}\, A\, e_1)\; <F^b <F^1(B)\, e_1>> \;\text{<-}e_0 \\
 & & +\, (e_1 \text{->}\, s_2\, e_1)\; <F^b <F^1(s_2)\, e_1>> \;\text{<-}e_0 \\
 & & +\, (e_1 \text{->}\, \underline{\text{empty}})\; <F^b> \;\text{<-}e_0\;)
\end{array}
$$

Neither of the two active configurations here coincides with, or is a special case of, C_1. Try to drive on. We can see that the F^b call will not be ready for development, again, and will never be ready as long as F^1 is called recursively, because F^1 puts each new symbol in its own "pouch", and not outside, as F^a does. Since the recursive calls reproduce themselves at each step, the driving could go on infinitely. This is the situation when a new configuration C_2 is "dangerously close" to the old C_1 (the same function F^1 is being developed), so that we cannot simply drive it on, yet we cannot reduce C_2 to C_1. We have to construct a generalization of C_1 and C_2, i.e. a configuration C_g such that both C_1:C_g, and C_2:C_g succeed. Then we reduce the old configuration C_1 to C_g, declare C_g basic, and develop it in a hope that this time we will be able to close the graph.

The possible algorithms of generalization turn out to be rather complex in the full Refal. If we limit ourselves to constructor-formed trees, generalization simplifies. We cannot go into detail here, but in our example the simple technique known as left-to-right L-generalization leads to success. Going from left to right in both configurations, we factor out those structural components of the matching process which are the same, and when they are not the same, we replace by an e-variable the whole remaining subexpression. So, the generalization of <u>empty</u> with any non-empty expression is an e-variable; different symbols generalize to a symbol variable, etc.

In supercompilation we use the depth-first principle as the basic way. The generalization of the first new configuration $<F^b <F^1(B)\, e_1>>$ with the old one $<F^b <F^1()e_1>>$ yields $<F^b <F^1(e_2)e_1>$. Taking this configuration as the new basic $<C_2(e_1)(e_2)>$, and redriving it from the moment of generalization, we transform (5) as follows:

$$
\begin{array}{lll}
(6) & (e_0 \to C_1) & (\underline{empty} \leftarrow e_2)\ <C_2(e_1)(e_2)>\ \leftarrow e_0 \\
 & & \\
 & (e_0 \to C_2) & (\ (e_1 \to A\, e_1)\ <F^b <F^1(e_2\, B)\, e_1>>\ \leftarrow e_0 \\
 & & +\ (e_1 \to s_3\, e_1)\ <F^b <F^1(e_2\, s_3)\, e_1>>\ \leftarrow e_0 \\
 & & +\ (e_1 \to \underline{empty})\ \ <F^b\, e_2>\ \leftarrow e_0\ )
\end{array}
$$

Now the first two active configurations in the development of C_2 can be recognized as C_2. The third one will be found basic, and the program for it will be identical, except for format differences , to that for F^b.In the end we have the program:

$$
\begin{array}{lll}
<C_1(e_1)> & = & <C_2()(e_1)> \\
<C_2(A\, e_1)(e_2)> & = & <C_2(e_1)(e_2 B)> \\
<C_2(s_3\, e_1)(e_2)> & = & <C_2(e_1)(e_2\, e_3)> \\
<C_2()(e_2)> & = & <C_3(e_2)> \\
<C_3(Be_1)> & = & C <C_3(e_1)> \\
<C_3(s_2\, e_1)> & = & s_2 <C_3(e_1)> \\
<C_3()> & = &
\end{array}
$$

It differs from the original program in that there are no nested calls in the right sides. This is the result of changing the *basis* of the program to include a nested configuration of the original functions. It does not make the new program significantly more efficient, though, if only a bit easier to implement.

In the preceding we have tacitly assumed that there are no nested configurations in the graph resulting from supercompilation. This is not always the case, however; instead of taking the combination $<F^b <F^1(e_2)e_1>$ as a basic configuration, we could *decompose* it as:

$$
(<F^1(e_2)e_1>\ \leftarrow h_1)\ \ <F^b\, h_1>\ \leftarrow e_0
$$

The variable h_1 stands here for the "hole" effected by the removal of a subexpression. It is, basically, the same as an e-variable, because the removed subexpression may evaluate to anything. But it is convenient to have holes syntactically different. Both the inner configuration, $<F^1(e_2)e_1>$ in this case, and the remaining outer configuration (with holes replaced by e-variables) are declared basic in decomposition.

In the preceding example we could, in the very beginning, decompose:

$$C_1 = \ <F^b <F^1()e_1>> \ = \ (<F^1()e_1> \ <\!-\, h_1) <F^b\, h_1> \ <\!-\, e_0$$

Then, after a generalization, $<F^1(e_2)\, e_1>$ and $<F^b\, e_1>$ would be declared basic, and the transformed program would reproduce the original one. While in this case we could decompose or not, in other cases decomposition can be necessary to construct a finite graph. Take the recursive definition of the factorial in the unary system:

$$<\text{fact } 01> \ = \ 01$$
$$<\text{fact } e_n 1> \ = \ <\text{mult } (e_n) <\text{fact } e_n>>$$

After the first step of driving we have, for $C_1 = \ <\text{fact } e_n>$, the graph:

$$(e_0 \text{-->}\, C_1) \quad ((e_n \text{-->}\, 01)\, 01 \ <\!-\, e_0$$
$$+(e_n \text{-->}\, e_n 1) \ <\text{mult } (e_n) <\text{fact } e_n>> \ <\!-\, e_0 \ )$$

We must recognize here that the leading active subexpression in the second branch is a match to C_1, i.e. basic, and take it out by decomposition. This leads to declaring $<\text{mult } (e_n)\, e_1>$ basic too. If we do not do that, but simply drive on, we face an infinite sequence of nested calls:

$$<\text{mult } (e_n) <\text{fact } e_n>>$$
$$<\text{mult } (e_n 1)<\text{mult } (e_n) <\text{fact } e_n>>>$$
$$<\text{mult } (e_n 11) <\text{mult } (e_n 1)<\text{mult } (e_n) <\text{fact } e_n>>>> \ \ldots \text{ etc.}$$

Another reason why decomposition may be necessary is the use of built-in (and not defined in Refal) functions. Such function calls must be either immediately computed, if it happens that they have all their arguments known, or treated as basic configurations otherwise. Using the host computer's numbers we can define the factorial as follows:

$$<\text{fact } 1> \ = \ 1$$
$$<\text{fact } e_n> \ = \ <\text{mult } (e_n) <\text{fact } <\text{prec } e_n>>>$$

where the functions <u>mult</u> and <u>prec</u> are built-in. When the nested call appears in the graph and is developed, the call of $<\text{prec } e_n>$ must be taken out. Then <u>fact</u> is taken out as basic, which results in a complete decomposition.

To conclude, consider an example which shows how a supercompiler can deal with another type of redundancy, the occurence of the same variables more than once in the initial expression. The problem we want to solve can be formulated as a theorem, namely: If *S = S*, where S is a string of symbols, then S consists of asterisks * only. In algorithmic terms we define the function of equality:

#E1 $\quad <=(s_1e_2)(s_1e_3)> \; = \; <=(e_2)(e_3)>$

#E2 $\quad <=(\,)(\,)> \; = \; T$

#E3 $\quad <= e_z> \; = \; F$

and want to transform the program for the configuration $C_1 = \; <=(*\, e_s)(e_s*)>$ into a program that simply checks that all the symbols in e_s are asterisks.

So we start with driving the equality call in C_1. Since it is not quite trivial, let us trace the use of the GMA. We match C_1 to the left side of #E1. First we have Case 4, i.e. two subproblems: $*e_s$: s_1e_2 , and e_s*: s_1e_3. The first one is resolved easily and results in one PRT, which is $(* <\!\!-s_1)(e_s <\!\!-e_2)$. Resolving the second, we face Case 6L, which produces a pair of contractions $(e_s\!-\!>)$ and $(e_s\!-\!> s_4e_s)$. (Note that we could use s_1 instead of s_4, because the variabe $s_{j'}$ in the rule must be *new* only with regard to the varlist it belongs to, and the actual implementation of the supercompiler will do so in this situation. However, for the convenience of the reader we pick up an entirely new variable). Applying the contractions, we have two CPRTs: $*$: s_1e_3, and s_4e_s* : s_1e_3. Since s_1 has taken the value $*$, we have Case 3 with internal clashes in both CPRTs. The clash $*$: $*$ is resolved trivially in the first one, while in the second we have $s_4\!-\!> *$. In both terms, the matching succeeds then. The result of matching with the left side of #E1 is two contractions, $e_s\!-\!>$ <u>empty</u> and $e_s\!-\!> *e_s$. Thus the driving through #E1 produces two branches:

(B1) $\quad (e_s\!-\!>) \; <=(*)(*)> \; <\!\!-e_0$

(B2) $\quad +(e_s\!-\!> *e_s) \; <=(**e_s)(*e_s*)> \; <\!\!-e_0$

The second sentence, #E2, is not applicable; driving through #E3 results in the third branch:

(B3) $\quad F <\!\!- e_0$

The end configurations in (B1) and (B2) are transient. In one more step of driving we come to the graph:

$(e_0\!-\!> C_1) \quad (\,(e_s\!-\!>) \; T <\!\!-e_0$
$\qquad\qquad +(e_s\!-\!> *e_s) \; <=(*e_s)(e_s*)> \; <\!\!-e_0$
$\qquad\qquad + \; F <\!\!-e_0 \,)$

The only active configuration here is reduced (identical) to C_1, and we come to the program:

$<C_1()> \; = \; T$
$<C_1(*\, e_s)> \; = \; <C_1(e_s)>$
$<C_1(e_s)> \; = \; F$

which is exactly what we wanted.

5. Conclusions

A supercompiler is a program which constructs the tree of states and transitions for a given initial configuration of the computing system and makes it finite by generalizing intermediate configurations to certain configurations called *basic*. Partial evaluation occurs naturally as an aspect of this procedure, but the supercompiler is also capable of eliminating other types of redundancy.

The language we find most conductive for the task of supercompilation is Refal. We have given a formal definition of Refal, and illustrated the work of a Refal supercompiler by simple examples. We introduced the concept of *driving*, which allows us to construct generalized histories of computation over any number of Refal steps. We defined the algorithm of generalized matching which is the core of the driving procedure and a generalization of unification.

More examples of the work of the supercompiler created at the CCNY can be found in [TurNirTur 1982]. They illustrate the following applications of supercompilation: program specialization, program optimization, the use of interpretive definitions of programming languages to produce efficient compiled programs, problem solving of different kinds, and theorem proving.

The author expresses his appreciation and gratitude to the members of the group working on the supercompiler: Robert Nirenberg, James Picarello, and Dimitri Turchin. We have made some changes to the syntax of Refal following the suggestions made by John Backus, which we highly appreciate, as well as a discussion of supercompiler.Special thanks are due to Neil D.Jones for suggestions on the semantics of Refal and many fruitful discussions.

REFERENCES

[Beckman et al. 1974] L.Beckman,A.Haraldson,O.Oskarson, O.Sandewall. A partial evaluator and its use as a programming tool. *Artificial Intelligence* 7, 319-357.

[Ershov 1977] A.P.Ershov. On the essence of translation, in Neuhold E.J., ed. *Formal Description of Programming Concepts*, North-Holland, 391-418.

[Ershov 1982] A.P.Ershov. Mixed computation: potentilal applications and problems for future studies. *Theoretical Computer Science,* 18, North-Holland, 41-67.

[Futamura 1971] Y.Futamura. Partial evaluation of computation process - an approach to compiler-compiler. *Systems, Computers, Control*, 2(5), 45-50.

[Futamura 1983] Y.Futamura. Partial computation of programs, *Proc RIMS Symp. Software Science and Engineering,* Springer-Verlag, LNCS 147, 1-35.

[FriWis 1967] D.P.Fridman and D.S.Wise, CONS should not evaluate its arguments, in *Automata, Languages and Programming*, Michaelson and Millner ed-s, Edinburgh Univ. Press, 257-284.

[HenMor 1976] P.Henderson and J.H.Morris Jr. A lazy evaluator. *Proc. 3rd Symp. on POPL*, 95-103.

[JonSch 1980] N.Jones and D.Schmidt. Compiler generation from denotational semantics, in Jones N. ed.,*Semantics-Driven Compiler Generation*, Springer-Verlag, LNCS 94, 70-93.

[Jones et al.1985] N.D.Jones,P.Sestoft, H.Søndergaard. An experiment in partial evaluation: the generation of a compiler generator, *International Conference on Rewriting Techniques and Applications*, 1985 Springer-Verlag (to be published).

[JonTof 1983] N.Jones and M.Tofte, Some principles and notation for the construction of compiler generators, DIKU, Univ. of Copenhagen, Internal report.

[Lombardi 1967] L.A.Lombardi. Incremental computation, *Advances in Computers*, 8 Academic Press.

[REFAL 1977] *Basic Refal and its Implementation on Computers* (in Russian), GOSSTROI SSSR, TsNIPIASS, Moscow 1977 (The authors are not indicated in the book. In fact they are: V.F.Khoroshevski, And.V.Klimov, Ark.V.Klimov, A.G.Krasovski, S.A.Romanenko, I.B.Shchenkov, V.F.Turchin.)

[Turchin 1972] V.F.Turchin, Equivalent transformation of recursive functions defined in Refal (in Russian), in *Trudy Vsesoyuzn. Simpos. "Teoria Yazykov i metody progr"*. Alushta-Kiev. pp. 31-42

[Turchin 1979] V.F.Turchin. A supercompiler system based on the language Refal, SIGPLAN Notices, 14, 46-54.

[Turchin 1980a] V.F.Turchin. *The Language Refal, the Theory of Compilation, and Metasystem Analysis, Courant Institute Report* #20, New York.

[Turchin 1980b] Semantics definitions in Refal and automatic production of compilers, in Jones N. ed.,*Semantics-Driven Compiler Generation* , Springer-Verlag, LNCS 94, 443-474.

[TurNirTur 1982] V.F.Turchin, R.N.Nirenberg, D.V.Turchin. Experiments with a supercompiler, in *ACM Symposium on LISP and Functional Programming*, 47-55.

[Vuillemin 1974] J.Vuillemin. Correct and optimal implementation of resursion in a simple programming language. *J. of Computer and System Studies* 9, #3, Dec. 1974.

Listlessness is Better than Laziness II:
Composing Listless Functions

Philip Wadler
Programming Research Group, Oxford University
11 Keble Road, Oxford, OX1 3QD

1. Introduction

This paper is a successor to "Listlessness is Better than Laziness" [Wadler 84a,b]. That work described a method that can automatically transform a program to improve its efficiency, by eliminating all intermediate lists.

The listless transformer applies only to programs from which all intermediate lists can be removed. In [Wadler 84b] this is made precise by defining the class of programs that are subject to bounded evaluation (b.e. programs), that is, programs that can be lazily evaluated in constant bounded space. Unfortunately, the listless transformer only acts as a semi-decision procedure for determining whether a given program is b.e.: it will succeed if the given program is b.e., but may enter an infinite loop if the program is not b.e.

Clearly, it would be desirable to have a simple way of structuring programs which guarantees that they are listless. An obvious rule that comes to mind is *composition*. That is, one would like to be able to say: if `f` and `g` are functions computed by listless programs, then so is `(f ∘ g)`. (As usual, `(f ∘ g) x = f (g x)`.) Unfortunately, this is not true; a counterexample will be given in section 2. However, there is a simple restriction of listless programs, namely *preorder listless programs*, for which this property does hold. Thus, if `f` and `g` are functions computed by preorder listless programs, then so is `(f ∘ g)`.

Further, this paper will present an algorithm that given the preorder listless programs that compute `f` and `g` will return a preorder listless program that computes `(f ∘ g)`. This means that one can transform an expression of the form `(f ∘ g)` in a modular way: first transform `f` and `g`, and then combine the results. This is in contrast to the previous listless transformer, which would need to transform `(f ∘ g)` in a single (possibly large) operation. The advantages of performing the transformation in this way are similar to the advantages of independent compilation as opposed to a single monolithic compilation.

Of course, not all programs are listless. For example, there is no listless program to sort or reverse a list, since in these cases the entire input list must be read (and saved) before the first element of the output list can be written. On the other hand, the function to merge two sorted lists is listless.

In general, few useful programs are listless as a whole, although most programs contain large sections which are listless. This suggests that listlessness will be useful in practice only if one can find a way to combine listless programs with other programs that are not listless. This paper discusses a method for combining general programs evaluated by a reduction machine with listless programs evaluated by a listless machine. With this method, the use of listlessness in an optimizing compiler appears to be a practical possibility.

A method similar to that described in this paper is discussed in [Ganzinger and Giegrich 85], which deals with the composition of attribute grammars.

This paper is organized as follows. Section 2 explains the difference between listless programs and preorder listless programs. Section 3 demonstrates that the composition of two preorder listless programs is a preorder listless program. Section 4 gives a formal description of listless programs. Section 5 describes an algorithm that composes two preorder listless programs to obtain a new listless program. Sections 6 and 7 extend this algorithm to more general forms of composition and to listless programs that include primitives. Section 8 discusses schemas to provide listless programs for library functions. Sections 9 and 10 discuss how listless programs can be interfaced to a general graph reducer. Section 11 discusses a detail related to strong correctness and gives a semantic characterization of preorder traversal. Section 12 presents conclusions. Appendix 1 describes some standard functions used in this paper, and appendix 2 gives definitions of these functions.

2. The importance of being preorder

This section presents a counterexample, to show that the composition of two listless programs is not necessarily listless. Consider the following two function definitions:

```
join (pair xs ys)  =  append xs ys
copy zs            =  pair zs zs
```

Here `pair` is a constructor of arity two (different from the constructor `cons`) and `append` concatenates two lists. Both `join` and `copy` are listless, that is, can be computed by listless programs. Informally, `join` is computed by first traversing the list `xs`, copying each element to the output, and next traversing `ys`, copying each element to the output; and `copy` is computed by traversing `zs`, copying each element to both lists in the output pair.

The composition of these two functions is

```
(join ∘ copy) zs   =  append zs zs
```

But appending a list to itself is not listless, that is, cannot be computed by a listless program. The only way to compute `append zs zs` without using intermediate lists requires traversing `zs` twice, and this violates the definition of listless program, which requires that each input list is traversed only once.

The problem with composing `join` and `copy` is that `copy` produces its output in a different order from that in which `join` traverses its input. That is, `copy` first creates a pair node; it then provides the first element of both lists in the pair, then the second element, and so on. On the other hand, `join` first examines the input pair node; it then completely traverses the first list in the pair before examining the second list.

This problem arises because the definition of listless program says nothing about the order in which the input or output data structures are traversed. This motivates the concept of preorder listless program. In a preorder listless program, the input and output data structures must each be traversed in preorder from left to right. For example, `copy` is not preorder listless because it produces the two result lists together, rather than completely producing the first result list from left to right, and then producing the second result list. On the other hand, `join` is preorder listless because it traverses the first input list from left to right, and then traverses the second input list; and the output list is also produced from left to right.

Most useful listless programs are in fact preorder. For example, the term

```
sum (map square (upto 1 n))
```

finds the sum of the squares of the numbers from 1 to `n`, and `sum`, `map square`, and `upto` are all preorder listless. (See the appendix for definitions of `sum`, `map`, and `upto`.) Indeed, the idea that inputs and outputs should be traversed in order is so natural that many people on encountering listless programs make the (mistaken) assumption that they are the same as preorder listless programs.

There is one useful class of functions that are listless but not preorder listless. These are the functions, such as `copy`, that return more than one list. In this case each output list is traversed in order, but the lists must be bundled into a structure, such as the `pair` in `copy`, which is not traversed in order. Another example of such a function is:

```
split p xs   =  pair (filter p xs) (filter (not ∘ p) xs)
```

which given a predicate `p` and a list `xs` returns a pair of lists, one containing elements in `xs` with property `p` and the other containing elements in `xs` not satisfying `p`. Although each instance of `filter` is preorder listless, the combination of the two into a `pair` is not. This paper will not deal with such functions, but extending the work described here to handle such cases is an obvious area for future research. It seems clear that such an extension is possible.

3. Composing preorder listless functions

The composition of two preorder listless functions is also preorder listless. This may be intuitively obvious, but the proof can be made more explicit as follows. Consider the preorder listless programs that compute `f` and `g`. To compute `f ∘ g` one simply runs the program for `f` (possibly producing some output) until it requests some input; one then runs the program for `g` (possibly traversing some input) until it produces some output. Since f traverses its input in preorder, and g produces its output in preorder, the input required by f must be the same as the output produced by g, so one may now continue running f. This process is repeated until f and g finish execution.

In other words, f and g can be run as coroutines. No "buffering" is needed between f and g, because f requests input in the same order that output is produced by g. Thus, if f and g can be computed in space bounded by the constants C and C′ respectively, then f ∘ g can be computed in space bounded by C + C′. Or, to put it another way, if the programs for f and g have N and N′ different states respectively, then f ∘ g can be computed by a program with N × N′ different states. (In general, if a listless program has N different states, then its space is bounded by a constant C proportional to log N.)

This shows that f ∘ g is listless. Further, since f produces its output in preorder and g consumes its input in preorder, it follows that f ∘ g is also preorder listless.

An example of the composition of preorder listless functions will be given in the next section.

4. Listless programs

This section re-introduces listless programs, with some changes in notation from the previous work. The syntax of listless programs is as follows:

listless program	q	::=	done	termination
		|	v ← p ; q	output step
		|	case v of {pi ⇒ qi}	input step
pattern	p	::=	c v1 ... vk	(where c has arity k)

Here c is a constructor and v is an input or output variable. The notation (case v of {pi ⇒ qi}) is a shorthand for:

```
case v of
    p1 ⇒ q1
    ...
    pn ⇒ qn
```

Listless programs are graphs, but the above notation treats them as if they were (possibly infinite) trees. In practice, listless programs can be represented in the computer by cyclic structures, which represent the graph directly in the computer memory.

For example, here are the definitions of three functions:

```
nots        =  map not
every       =  rightreduce and true
everynot    =  every ∘ nots
```

The function nots takes a list of booleans, and returns a list with each element in the input replaced by its complement. The function every takes a list of booleans, and returns true if every element in the input list is true. (The functions map, rightreduce, not, and and are defined in the appendix.) The functions nots and every are preorder listless, and hence everynot is also preorder listless.

The three listless programs corresponding to the above definitions are given in figure 1. Here x, xs, z, zs are input variables; y, ys, a are output variables; true, false, nil are constructors of arity zero; and cons is a constructor of arity two. Labels such as NOTS are used to indicate cycles in the listless programs. This is just a notational convenience; as mentioned, the programs can be represented in the computer directly by cyclic structures.

The programs in figure 1 can, of course, be derived by applying the listless transformer. In addition, the program for everynot can also be derived by applying the method of composition, described in section 5, to the programs for nots and every.

Incidentally, if we define

```
some        =  rightreduce or false
notsome     =  not ∘ some
```

and then generate the listless program corresponding to notsome (either directly or by the composition method), then this program will be identical to the program for everynot given in figure 1. This amounts to an automatic proof of a generalized version of DeMorgan's law.

A description of the listless transformer is beyond the scope of this paper; it can be found in [Wadler 84b]. It is easy to modify the transformer described there so that it is restricted to traverse the input and output in preorder. Further, as a result of this restriction, there is only one possible candidate for the input variable at each input step. This means that the expensive breadth-first search of input variables discussed in [Wadler 84b] is not required for this version of the listless transformer.

As mentioned in the introduction, one can define a concept of bounded evaluation (b.e.) that corresponds to a program that can be evaluated in bounded space, not counting space occupied by its input or output. In [Wadler 84b] it is shown that the listless transformer succeeds in converting a functional program to an equivalent listless program if and only if the functional program is b.e. Similarly, one can define a concept of preorder bounded evaluation (p.b.e.) that corresponds to a program that can be evaluated in bounded space, not counting space occupied by its input or output, and traverses its input and output in preorder. One can show that the modified listless transformer succeeds in converting a functional program to an equivalent preorder listless program if and only if the functional program is p.b.e. The precise definition of p.b.e. and the proof are straightforward modifications of the work in [Wadler 84b].

Figure 1: *Listless programs for* `nots`, `every`, *and* `everynot`.

```
{ys ← nots xs}

   NOTS:        case xs of
                   nil          ⇒  ys ← nil;  done
                   cons x xs    ⇒
                       ys ← cons y ys;
                       case x of
                           true    ⇒  y ← false;  NOTS
                           false   ⇒  y ← true;   NOTS


{a ← every zs}

   EVERY:       case zs of
                   nil          ⇒  a ← true;  done
                   cons z zs    ⇒
                       case z of
                           true    ⇒  EVERY
                           false   ⇒  a ← false;  done


{a ← everynot xs}

   EVERYNOT:    case xs of
                   nil          ⇒  a ← true;  done
                   cons x xs    ⇒
                       case x of
                           true    ⇒  a ← false;  done
                           false   ⇒  EVERYNOT
```

5. The composition algorithm

Section 3 showed how two listless programs might be composed by executing them as coroutines. This section will show how two listless programs can be combined directly into a single program. The advantage of doing this, as opposed to simply running the two programs as coroutines, is that the overhead associated with the coroutine linkage is eliminated.

If q and q′ are two listless programs corresponding to g and f, we write q >> q′ for the listless program corresponding to f ∘ g. That is, q >> q′ is the program that results from connecting the output of q to the input of q′. For example, the program EVERYNOT in figure 1 can be derived by computing NOTS >> EVERY.

Algorithm 1: *Simple Listless Composition.* Given q and q′ one may derive a listless program to compute q >> q′ by applying the following rules.

If q′ is done, then so is q >> q′:

(1) q >> done = done

If q′ is about to perform an output step, then so should q >> q′:

(2) q >> (v′ ← p′ ; q′) = v′ ← p′ ; (q >> q′)

If q is about to perform an input step, then so should q >> q′:

(3) (case v of {pi ⇒ qi}) >> q′ = case v of {pi ⇒ (qi >> q′)}

If q is about to perform an output step and q′ is about to perform an input step, then the output from q may be used to select which path is taken in q′:

(4) (v ← p; q) >> (case v′ of {pi′ ⇒ qi′}) = q >> qj′

where p has the same constructor as pj′

In rule (4) one knows that the output variable v of q must correspond to the input variable v′ of q′, because outputs of q and inputs of q′ happen in the same order. □

These rules must be applied in the order given; e.g., if both rule (1) and rule (3) apply then rule (1) should be chosen. This corresponds to the use of lazy evaluation: the only actions of q that should be performed are those that are needed by q′.

The above description says nothing explicitly about loops in the listless program. This is handled implicitly by "memoizing" the corresponding (functional) program that combines the structures representing two listless programs. That is, in order to compute q >> q′ we maintain a table containing entries of the form ((q, q′), q >> q′). To compute q >> q′ we first check the table. If there is an appropriate entry it is returned. Otherwise, q >> q′ is computed using rules (1) -- (4) above, and then a new entry is made in the table. If lazy evaluation is used then computation of q >> q′ can be guaranteed to terminate, and the structure returned will contain appropriate cycles. For a further discussion of memoization see [Hughes 85a]. A similar technique is also used in [Mont-Reynaud 76].

Algorithm 1, together with algorithms 2 and 3 below, has been implemented as a (non-listless) functional program. The programming language used was Orwell [Wadler 85a], augmented with lazy memo functions [Hughes 85a]. It is pleasing to see that the implemented program looks almost identical to rules (1) -- (4) above. The resemblance is particularly close because Orwell allows the user to define new infix symbols (such as >>, ←, and ;).

6. Generalised composition

Section 3 presented an argument to show that if f and g are preorder listless functions then so is f ∘ g. The same argument can be modified to show a more general result, namely, if f and g are preorder listless functions of arity m and n respectively, then h is an preorder listless function of arity m+n−1, where

```
(*)       h x1 ... x(i-1) y1 ... yn x(i+1) ... xm
                  = f x1 ... x(i-1) (g y1 ... yn) x(i+1)... xm
```

and x1, ..., xm, y1, ..., yn are all distinct variable names. The argument is essentially the same as before: run the listless programs for f and g as coroutines. The program for f is run until it requires an input. If the input is some xj with i ≠ j then the input occurs directly and the program continues. If the input is xi then the program for g is run until it produces an output. This works because the input variables are all distinct, and therefore do not interact with each other.

For example, consider the function

```
appendnots xs ys  =  append xs (nots ys)
```

Since append and nots are preorder listless functions of arity two and one respectively, it follows from the above result that appendnots is also preorder listless.

It is not hard to modify the algorithm of section 5 to handle this more general version of function composition. The >> notation must be modified to include some extra bookkeeping, as follows. Let q and q′ be two preorder listless programs, each with an arbitrary number of input and output variables. If necessary, rename the variables of q so they are distinct from the variables of q′. Let V be a set of pairs of the form (v, v′) where v is an output variable of q and v′ is an input variable of q′. Then q >>(V) q′ denotes the listless program that results from connecting each output v of q to the corresponding input v′ of q′ for each (v, v′) in V. The inputs of this program are the inputs of q plus the inputs of q′ not in V, and the outputs of this program are the outputs of q′. (Initially, V contains a single pair, but it may contain more than one pair during execution of the algorithm below.)

For example, consider the listless programs APPEND and NOTS with the following specifications:

```
APPEND     =  {xs ← append xs1 xs2}
NOTS       =  {ys ← nots ys1}
```

Let V = {(ys, xs2)}. Then NOTS >>(V) APPEND is equivalent to the listless program

```
APPENDNOTS  =  {xs ← append xs1 (nots ys1)}
```

More generally, let F and G be listless programs with the following specifications:

```
F  =  {x ← f x1 ... xm}
G  =  {y ← g y1 ... ym}
```

Then the function h defined in (*) above is computed by the listless program G >>(V) F, where V = {(y, xi)}. This program can be computed by the following algorithm.

Algorithm 2: *Generalized Listless Composition.* Given q, q′, and V as above, where q and q′ have no names in common, the listless program that computes q >>(V) q′ can be derived by the following rules. As with algorithm 1, the rules should be applied in order, and memoization (on (q, q′, V)) should be used to handle loops in the listless programs.

If q′ is done, then so is q >>(V) q′:

```
(1)    q >>(V) done    =    done
```

If q′ is about to perform an output step, then so should q >>(V) q′:

```
(2a)   q >>(V) (v′ ← p′ ; q′)    =    v′ ← p′ ; (q >>(V) q′)
```

If q′ is about to perform an input step on a variable not in V, then so should q >>(V) q′:

```
(2b)   q >>(V) (case v′ of {pi′ ⇒ qi′})
                     =    case v′ of {pi′ ⇒ (q >>(V) qi′)}

                if (v, v′) ∉ V  for any v
```

If q is about to perform an input step, then so should q >>(V) q′:

```
(3a)   (case v of {pi ⇒ qi}) >>(V) q′    =    case v of {pi ⇒ (qi >>(V) q′)}
```

If q is about to perform an output step and q′ is about to perform an input step on the corresponding variable in V, then the output from q may be used to select which path is taken in q′:

(4a) (v ← p; q) >>(V) (case v′ of {pi′ ⇒ qi′}) = q >>(V′) qj′

if (v, v′) ∈ V
where p has the same constructor as pj′
and c v1 ... vk = p
and c v1′ ... vk′ = pj′
and V′ = V − {(v, v′)} ∪ {(v1, v1′), ..., (vk, vk′)}

(For example, if q performs the output step (xs ← cons x xs; qq) and q′ performs the input step (case ys of ... cons y ys ⇒ qq′) and V is {(xs, ys)} then q >>(V) q′ is equivalent to qq >>(V′) qq′ where V′ is {(x, y), (xs, ys)}.) This rule is valid because all output and input variables are traversed in pre-order, so the output steps on v1, ..., vk in q will take place in that order, as will the input steps on v1′, ..., vk′ in q′. □

7. Primitive operations

In order to be practical, listless programs must be extended to include operations on primitive data, such as integers. This section briefly describes such an extension, and presents corresponding extensions to algorithm 2.

Listless machines are extended to include a new class of variables, primitive variables, in addition to input and output variables. Four new kinds of step are added to listless programs, as follows:

listless program	q ::=	...	
		| u ← v ; q	primitive input
		| u ← t ; q	primitive operation step
		| v ← u ; q	primitive output step
		| case u of {pi ⇒ qi}	primitive case step
primitive term	t ::=	u | f t1 ... tk	(where f has arity k)

Here f is a primitive function and u is a primitive variable. A primitive input step copies data from an input variable to a primitive variable, and a primitive output step copies data from a primitive variable to an output variable. A primitive operation step performs some computation on primitive variables (for example, adding two variables together) and puts the result back into a primitive variable. A primitive case step branches on the contents of a primitive variable; in the primitive case step, each pi must be a constructor ci of arity zero (for example, true and false).

For example, consider the function:

```
sumsq n  =  sum (map square (upto 1 n))
```

which finds the sum of the squares of the numbers from 1 to `n`. Figure 2 gives listless programs to compute `sum`, `map square`, `upto`, and `sumsq`. Algorithm 2 is extended to handle primitive steps in algorithm 3 below. The program `SUMSQ` in figure 2 can be derived by calculating

```
UPTO >>({(ws,xs)}) SQUARES >>({(ys,zs)}) SUM
```

using two applications of algorithm 3.

To define algorithm 3, it is convenient to treat several kinds of steps together. Input steps and primitive case steps are together called case steps, and are written in the form `case w of {pi ⇒ qi}`, where `w` is `v` or `u`. Similarly, the remaining kinds of steps (except `done`) are called assignment steps and written in the form `w ← r`, where `w` is `v` or `u`, and `r` is `p`, `u`, or `t`.

Algorithm 3: *Generalized Listless Composition with Primitives.* To find `q >>(V) q'`, where `q` and `q'` may contain primitive steps, algorithm 2 may be modified as follows. Rules `(1)` and `(4a)` are left unchanged. Rules `(2a)`, `(2b)`, and `(3a)` are generalized to case steps and assignment steps by replacing `v` by `w`, and `p` by `r`, where appropriate. Finally, the following two rules are added.

If `q` is about to perform an assignment step on a variable not in `V`, then so should `q >>(V) q'`:

```
(3b)  (w ← r ; q) >>(V) q'   =   w ← r ; (q >>(V) q')

              if  (w,v') ∉ V  for any v'
```

If `q` is about to perform a primitive output step and `q'` is about to perform a primitive input step on the corresponding variable in `V`, then the output value of `q` should be copied to `q'` (by a trivial primitive computation step):

```
(4b)  (v ← u ; q) >>(V) (u' ← v' ; q')   =   u' ← u ; (q >>(V') q')

              if  (v,v') ∈ V
              where  V' = V - {(v,u')}
```

As a further optimization, the trivial assignment `u ← u'` can be eliminated by renaming all instances of `u'` in `q'` to `u`. (If this optimization is not performed, then the last line of `SUMSQ` in figure 2 should be: `u3 ← u0; u4 ← u3 × u3; u6 ← u4; u5 ← u5 + u6; u0 ← u0 + 1; SUMSQ'`.) □

Figure 2: *Listless programs for* upto, map square, sum, *and* sumsq.

```
{ws <- upto 1 n}

    UPTO:       u0 ← 1;  u1 ← n;  UPTO'
    UPTO':      u2 ← (u0 ≤ u1);
                case u2 of
                    false  ⇒  ws ← nil;  done
                    true   ⇒  ws ← cons w ws;
                              w ← u0;  u0 ← u0 + 1;  UPTO'

{ys <- map square xs}

    SQUARES:    case xs of
                    nil         ⇒  ys ← nil;  done
                    cons x xs   ⇒  ys ← cons y ys;
                                   u3 ← x;  u4 ← u3 × u3;
                                   y ← u4;  SQUARES

{a <- sum zs}

    SUM:        u5 ← 0;  SUM'
    SUM':       case zs of
                    nil         ⇒  a ← u5;  done
                    cons z zs   ⇒  u6 ← z;  u5 ← u5 + u6;  SUM'

{a <- sumsq n}

    SUMSQ:      u0 ← 1;  u1 ← n;  u5 ← 0;  SUMSQ'
    SUMSQ':     u2 ← (u0 ≤ u1);
                case u2 of
                    false  ⇒  a ← u5;  done
                    true   ⇒  u4 ← u0 × u0;  u5 ← u5 + u4;
                              u0 ← u0 + 1;  SUMSQ'
```

8. Listless schemas

The preceding sections have developed a method for combining two listless programs to produce another listless program. But where do the initial listless programs come from?

Of course, they could be derived by applying the listless transformer to functions that the user declares to be listless. This will be useful in general for user-defined functions. In practice, however, this generality will often not be needed, because most of the listless functions in a program will be standard library functions, or instances of them.

For example, one would expect to find the functions `every` and `some` from section 4 in a standard library, and the library could also store the corresponding listless programs. Another listless library program is `merge`, which merges two sorted lists of numbers into a single list. (A listless program for `every` is given in figure 1, and a listless program for `merge` is discussed in [Wadler 84b].)

Of more general utility is the fact that many higher-order library functions have instances that are listless. For example, if `f` has a listless program, then so does `map f`. Moreover, the listless program for `map f` can be derived from the listless program for `f`, using the following schema:

(map schema)
if {y ← f x} has a listless program,
then {ys ← map f xs} has the listless program:

```
MAPF:      case xs of
               nil        ⇒  ys ← nil;  done
               cons x xs  ⇒  ys ← cons y ys;  y ← f x;  MAPF
```

This schema should be applied as follows. Let `F` be a listless program for `f` with input variable `x` and output variable `y`. Then the listless program for `map f` is as given above, where the portion of the program that reads `y ← f x; MAPF` is replaced by `F`, with `MAPF` substituted for every instance of `done` in `F`.

For example, `not` can be computed by the listless program:

```
NOT:      case x of
              true   ⇒  y ← false;  done
              false  ⇒  y ← true;  done
```

Applying the map schema to `NOT` gives the listless program `NOTS` shown in figure 1.

Figure 3 gives several other schemas, for the functions `leftreduce`, `filter`, `while`, and `repeat`; these functions are defined in the appendix. These schemas are not quite so general as the map schema, in that they require that their argument functions are primitives (such as + or ⩽). (However, a way of relaxing this restriction is discussed in section 10.)

Figure 3: *Listless schemas.*

(leftreduce schema)

if f is a primitive function,
then {y ← leftreduce f a xs} has the listless program:

```
REDUCEF:   u ← a;
REDUCEF':  case xs of
              nil        ⇒  y ← u;  done
              cons x xs  ⇒  u ← f u x;  REDUCEF'
```

(filter schema)

if f is a primitive function,
then {ys ← filter f x} has the listless program:

```
FILTERF:   case xs of
              nil        ⇒  ys ← nil;  done
              cons x xs  ⇒
                 u ← f x;
                 case u of
                    true  ⇒  ys ← cons y ys;  y ← x;  FILTERF
                    false ⇒  FILTERF
```

(while schema)

if f is a primitive function,
then {ys ← while f x} has the listless program:

```
WHILEF:    case xs of
              nil        ⇒  ys ← nil;  done
              cons x xs  ⇒
                 u ← f x;
                 case u of
                    true  ⇒  ys ← cons y ys;  y ← x;  WHILEF
                    false ⇒  ys ← nil;  done
```

(repeat schema)

if f is a primitive function,
then {ys ← repeat f a} has the listless program:

```
REPEATF:   u ← a;
REPEATF':  ys ← cons y ys;  y ← u;  u ← f u;  REPEATF'
```

As an application of these schemas, note that the functions sum and upto can be defined by

```
sum       =  leftreduce (+) 0
upto m n  =  while (≤ n) (repeat (+ 1) m)
```

(Here (+ 1) is the function that adds one to its argument, and (≤ n) is the function that returns true if its argument is less than or equal to n.) The programs for SUM and UPTO given in figure 2 can be derived by applying the schemas in figure 3 and using the composition algorithm. For example, SUM is derived by applying the leftreduce schema where f is +, and composing this with the (trivial) listless program for {a ← 0}.

Another example of a listless library function is append. The function append differs from, say, merge, in that append is listless only when its type is known. That is, there exists a listless program to append two lists of numbers, and there also exists a listless program to append two lists of lists of numbers; but these are different programs. If one is using a typed functional language (say, Miranda [Turner 85] or Orwell [Wadler 85a]) then the transformation system can detect when the type of the arguments to append is known, and replace append by the appropriate listless program. (Again, a way of relaxing this restriction is discussed in section 10.)

The same technique used for append may also be used for

```
reduceappend  =  rightreduce append nil
```

which appends together a list of lists (where each list is itself a list of numbers, or a list of lists of numbers, or so on).

9. Interfacing listless programs with graph reducers

Of course, not all programs are listless. Indeed, very few useful programs are listless as a whole. The main attraction of the listless transformer is that most programs contain significant portions which are listless. This means that if the listless transformer is to be usable in practice, then it is essential that it be possible to combine listless programs with other programs that are not listless. This section explains one method for combining general programs evaluated by a reduction machine with listless programs evaluated by a listless machine. Roughly speaking, the method is to run the reduction machine and the listless machine as coroutines.

It is assumed that the reduction machine behaves as follows. Initially, it is given a pointer to a node representing an expression to be evaluated. There will be various types of nodes, e.g., application nodes, constructor nodes, and so on. The evaluator examines the node to determine its type, and then performs the appropriate action. This action will overwrite the node with a new and equivalent node. This cycle is repeated on the new node, until the node is in an appropriate normal form. For example, a node representing square 3 will be overwritten by a node representing 3 × 3 and this in turn will be overwritten by a node representing 9, which is in normal form. (See [Peyton Jones 86] for a more detailed description of graph reduction.)

To interface a listless program with a reduction machine one simply defines a new kind of node, called an interface node, that corresponds to a value computed by a listless program. The interface node contains a pointer to the corresponding listless machine, which is represented by a vector (say) containing each of its input and output variables and the current state of the listless program. The action taken to reduce an interface node is simply to run the corresponding listless machine until it produces the desired output. While running, the listless machine may perform some input steps. Each input step will cause a recursive call of the reduction machine to evaluate the node pointed at by the input variable.

Recall from [Wadler 84a] that each output variable of the listless machine points at the location where the output is to be placed. This location itself initially contains the interface node that points at the listless machine. Thus, the interface node and the listless machine each point at the other (similar to the way in which two coroutines point to each other). When the listless machine performs an output step to the location, the interface node is overwritten with a constructor node. The fields of the new constructor node (e.g., the head and tail of a `cons` node) will themselves be interface nodes, containing pointers to the listless machine and pointed at by its output variables.

Using this method one can evaluate, for example, any term of the form `f (g (h s))` where `f` and `h` are general functions to be evaluated by a reduction machine, `g` is a function to be evaluated by the corresponding listless program `G`, and `s` is a structure. The initial state of the corresponding graph is shown in figure 4.

For a second example, consider the Hamming problem: find a list sorted in ascending order such that the list contains the number 1; and the numbers 2 × i, 3 × i, and 5 × i whenever i is in the list; and no other numbers. This problem is a popular example in papers on functional programming, because it has a nice functional solution:

```
ham  =  cons 1
             (merge (map (× 2) ham)
                    (merge (map (× 3) ham)
                           (map (× 5) ham)))
```

The definition of `ham` is not, of itself, listless. However, it is easy to see that it can be rewritten in the form:

```
ham  =  cons 1 (f ham ham ham)
f xs ys zs  =  merge (map (× 2) xs)
                     (merge (map (× 3) ys)
                            (map (× 5) zs)))
```

where `f` can be seen to be listless by repeated application of the composition rule. Indeed, one could imagine a compiler performing this transformation automatically. The initial graph to be evaluated by the graph reducer is shown in figure 5.

Figure 4: *Initial configuration to evaluate* f (g (h s)), *where* g *has listless program* G.

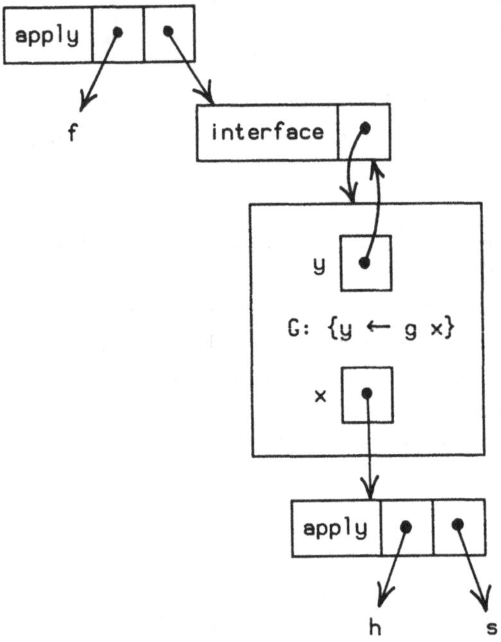

Figure 5: *Initial configuration for the Hamming problem.*

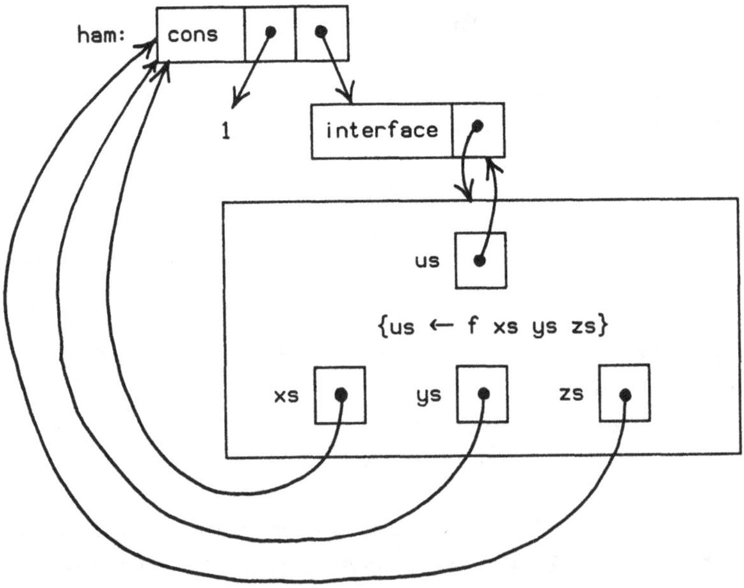

It should be possible to implement this method efficiently. For example, Johnsson and Augustsson's work on the G-machine [Johnsson 84] shows one efficient way of implementing a reduction machine on a conventional architecture, and it appears to be straightforward to extend the G-machine to include interface nodes as described above.

10. Almost listless programs and algebraic rules

The method described so far allows one to embed listless programs inside general graph reduction programs. It is also possible to do the reverse, that is, to embed general graph reduction program inside listless programs. This is done by adapting the listless schemas from section 8.

For example, the map schema shows how to convert a listless program for `f` into a listless program for `map f`. Now consider the case that `f` is a general function to be evaluated by the graph reducer. Then one can treat the program `MAPF` as an "almost listless" program to compute `map f` by simply re-interpreting the step `y ← f x`. This step is now taken as a variation of a primitive step. However, instead of applying `f` to the value of `x` and storing the result in `y`, it just constructs an unevaluated node representing the application `f n`, where `n` is the node pointed at by `x`, and stores a pointer to this node in `y`. Eventually the value of the node `f n` may be demanded by the graph reducer, and this will cause `f n` to be replaced by its value.

All of the schemas given in figure 3 can be re-interpreted in the same way. One can now also have a general almost listless program for `append`:

```
{ws ← append xs ys}

    APPEND:     case xs of
                    nil          ⇒  APPEND'
                    cons x xs    ⇒  ws ← cons w ws;  w ← x;  APPEND

    APPEND':    case ys of
                    nil          ⇒  ws ← nil;  done
                    cons y ys    ⇒  ws ← cons w ws;  w ← y;  APPEND'
```

Here the steps `w ← x` and `w ← y` are interpreted as copying the input node to the output node without yet forcing it to be evaluated. This schema should be used only when the type-checker cannot give more specific information about the type of some instance of `append`.

The composition algorithm for listless programs with primitives is still valid under this new interpretation of primitive steps. For example, consider a program containing the term `map f ∘ map g` where `f` and `g` are to be evaluated by the graph reducer. Let `MAPF` and `MAPG` be the almost listless programs for `map f` and `map g`, respectively. One can derive the composition `MAPG >> MAPF` using algorithm 3. The resulting almost listless program produces an output list containing elements of the form `f (g n)` where `n` is the node that is the corresponding element of the input list. In other words, in this case the composition algorithm achieves the same effect as the algebraic rule `map f ∘ map g = map (f ∘ g)`. In fact, the composition rule is more efficient, since it returns elements in the form `f (g n)` instead of in the form `(f ∘ g) n`.

The composition algorithm can achieve the effect of other algebraic rules as well. For example, [Wadler 81] presents four rules for composing the functions `map`, `leftreduce`, and `generate`; one of these is the rule for `map f ∘ map g` given above. All four of these rules, and many others beside, are subsumed by the listless schemas in section 8 combined with the composition algorithm. Further, in [Wadler 81] the function `generate` has to be treated as a single entity, but using the approach described here it can be defined in terms of simpler functions:

```
generate f g h  =  map f ∘ while g ∘ repeat h
```

In addition, the composition algorithm handles many cases that cannot be handled easily by algebraic rules. For example, there are no simple algebraic rules to simplify terms of the form `while f ∘ map g` or `append xs (map f ys)`, because there are no simple, standard functions that correspond to these compositions. But the composition algorithm, or course, does apply to these terms. (See [Bellegarde 85] for other examples of algebraic rules.)

These results might be summarised by the motto: "listless composition reaches the parts algebraic rules cannot reach". On the other hand, algebraic rules also reach some parts that listless composition cannot reach. For example, `reverse ∘ reverse = identity` is a useful algebraic law for finite lists. The listless composition algorithm cannot achieve the effect of this law, since the function `reverse` is not listless.

11. Strong correctness

This section explains a small detail important to strong correctness, which has been ignored so far in this paper. In doing so, it also provides a semantic characterization of preorder traversal.

As usual, let ⊥ denote an undefined value (e.g., the result of executing an infinite loop). When a listless machine is interfaced to a graph reduction machine, as described in sections 9 and 10, it is possible that the input to the machine may contain ⊥. In this case, the output of the listless machine may be less defined than the output of the corresponding functional program.

For example, consider the listless program `NOTS`, defined in figure 1, which corresponds to the functional program `map not`. If `map not` is applied to the input list `[false, ⊥, true]` it will return the output list `[true, ⊥, false]`. On the other hand, if `NOTS` is applied to the same input list it will construct the output list `(cons true (cons y ys))`, where `y` and `ys` are output variables still to be bound, before it examines the ⊥ in the input. Replacing the unbound variables by ⊥, we have that

```
cons true (cons ⊥ ⊥)  ⊑  [true, ⊥, false]
```

that is, the output returned by `NOTS` is less defined then the output returned by `map not`.

The difference between the lists returned by `NOTS` and `map not` will only be apparent if the general graph reducer examines, say, the third element before the second element. No problem can arise so long as all outputs and inputs to listless programs are traversed in preorder. In order to guarantee preorder traversal we define a new function `pre` that is equivalent to the identity function but forces its argument to be traversed in preorder.

First, we require a precise definition of structure. A structure `s` is either ⊥ or has the form `c s1 ... sk` where `c` is a constructor of arity `k` and `s1, ..., sk` are structures. Here are three examples of structures:

```
cons true (cons false nil)
cons true (cons ⊥ (cons false nil))
cons (cons ⊥ nil) nil
```

(here `cons` is a constructor of arity 2, and `nil`, `true`, and `false` are constructors of arity 0). The first structure does not contain ⊥, and the second two do.

Preorder traversal of `c s1 ... sk` requires that `s1` is traversed in preorder, then `s2` is traversed in preorder, and so on up to `sk`. If ever the value ⊥ is encountered, then the traversal stops. So if `si` contains ⊥ then preorder traversal cannot distinguish between the two structures `c s1 ... si s(i+1) ... sk` and `c s1 ... si ⊥ ... ⊥`.

This motivates the following definition of `pre`. The function `pre` is defined such that for any constructor `c` of arity `k`,

```
pre (c s1 ... sk)  =  c s1' ... sk'
```

where `si'` is ⊥ if there is any `j < i` such that `sj` contains ⊥, and `si'` is `(pre si)` otherwise. Here are three examples:

```
pre (cons true (cons false nil))       =  cons true (cons false nil)
pre (cons true (cons ⊥ (cons false nil)))  =  cons true (cons ⊥ ⊥)
pre (cons (cons ⊥ nil) nil)            =  cons (cons ⊥ ⊥) ⊥
```

It is easy to see that `pre s ⊑ s`, and that `pre s = s` if `s` does not contain ⊥. Further, the preceding discussion shows that preorder traversal cannot distinguish between `s` and `pre s` for any structure `s`. Indeed, `pre s` is the largest structure (under the ⊑ ordering) that is indistinguishable from `s` using preorder traversal.

It is easy to see that the listless machine `NOTS` is strongly equivalent to `(pre ∘ map not ∘ pre)`, and in general that the listless machine `MAPF` is strongly equivalent to `(pre ∘ map f ∘ pre)`, where `MAPF` and `f` are as in the `(map schema)` in section 8. More generally, strong equivalence with the listless machine can always be guaranteed by applying `pre` to the input and output of the corresponding function.

In many cases, strong correctness is guaranteed even without the use of `pre`. For example, let `f` be a primitive function (so `f x` returns ⊥ whenever `x` contains ⊥, that is, `f` is hyper-strict). Then the function `(filter f)` is guaranteed to traverse its input and output in preorder, or more formally,

```
filter f  =  pre ∘ filter f ∘ pre
```

Similarly, `(leftreduce f a)`, `(while f)`, and `(repeat f a)` are also guaranteed to be preorder whenever `f` is primitive; and `some`, `every`, and `merge` also preorder. Further, if `f` is primitive then

```
pre ∘ map f  =  map f ∘ pre  =  pre ∘ map f ∘ pre
```

This means that many compositions of `map f` with other listless functions may automatically be deduced to be preorder. The functions `append` and `reduceappend` have a similar property.

In the remaining cases where functions cannot be guaranteed preorder, two other methods may be used. One is to use functions which are preorder by definition, such as `map'`, where

```
map' f  =  pre ∘ map f ∘ pre
```

and to only replace instances of `map'`, not `map`, by listless programs. A second method is to apply strictness analysis ([Hughes 85b, Wadler 85b]) to determine cases where preorder traversal is guaranteed. For example, if an instance of `map` takes as input and produces as output a list that is strict in the head, then preorder traversal is guaranteed.

12. Conclusions

One of the pervading principles of computer science is modularity: the ability to decompose a problem into parts which can be solved seperately. Indeed, one of the fundamental advantages of functional programming is that it provides modular ways of creating programs, such as function composition. (See [Hughes 85c] for a further discussion of modularity in functional programs.)

Therefore, it was disquieting that the listless transformer, as originally described in [Wadler 84a,b], could only deal with programs in a monolithic rather than a modular fashion. The major advance of this work is to introduce methods that allows one to construct and transform listless programs in a modular way. This paper has discussed two different kinds of modularity: the ability to compose two listless programs into a single listless program, and the ability to combine listless programs with general graph reduction programs.

Of course, modularity is desirable not just because it is elegant in theory, but because it is essential to practice. It is precisely because they support modularity that the techniques introduced in this paper bring listlessness much closer to practical use.

Acknowledgements

Richard Bird, Geoff Barrett, and John Hughes made useful comments on earlier versions of this paper. This work was performed while on a research fellowship funded by ICL.

Appendix 1. Standard functions

The call (map f xs) applies f to every element of the list xs.

```
map square [1, 2, 3]            =  [1, 4, 9]
```

The calls (rightreduce f a xs) and (leftreduce f a xs) combine elements of the list xs using the binary function f, using a as the value for the empty list; they associate to the right and left respectively.

```
rightreduce (+) 0 [1, 2, 3]     =  1 + (2 + (3 + 0))
leftreduce  (+) 0 [1, 2, 3]     =  ((0 + 1) + 2) + 3
```

The call (filter p xs) returns all elements of xs that satisfy p, and the call (while p xs) returns the initial segment of xs that satisfies p.

```
filter odd [3, 1, 4, 5, 2]      =  [3, 1, 5]
while odd  [3, 1, 4, 5, 2]      =  [3, 1]
```

The call (repeat f a) returns the infinite list [a, (f a), (f (f a)), ...].

```
repeat (+ 1) 0                  =  [0, 1, 2, 3, ...]
```

The call (upto m n) returns the list of numbers from m up to n.

```
upto 1 3                        =  [1, 2, 3]
```

The function append appends two lists, the function merge merges two sorted lists into a single sorted list, and the function reduceappend appends together a list of lists:

```
append [1, 2, 3] [4, 5, 6]      =  [1, 2, 3, 4, 5, 6]
merge [1, 3, 4] [2, 5, 6]       =  [1, 2, 3, 4, 5, 6]
```

Appendix 2. Function definitions

```
map f nil                      =  nil
map f (cons x xs)              =  cons (f x) (map f xs)

rightreduce f a nil            =  a
rightreduce f a (cons x xs)    =  f x (rightreduce f a xs)

leftreduce f a nil             =  a
leftreduce f a (cons x xs)     =  leftreduce f (f a x) xs

filter p nil                   =  nil
filter p (cons x xs)           =  cons x (filter p xs)      IF p x
                                  filter p xs               OTHERWISE

while p nil                    =  nil
while p (cons x xs)            =  cons x (while p xs)       IF p x
                                  nil                       OTHERWISE

repeat f a                     =  cons a (repeat f (f a))

merge nil ys                   =  ys
merge (cons x xs) nil          =  cons x xs
merge (cons x xs) (cons y ys)  =  cons x (merge xs (cons y ys))  IF x < y
                                  cons y (merge (cons x xs) ys)  OTHERWISE

not true                       =  false
not false                      =  true

and true  x                    =  x
and false x                    =  false

or  true  x                    =  true
or  false x                    =  x

every                          =  rightreduce and true
some                           =  rightreduce or false
```

References

[Bellegarde 85] Bellegarde, F. Convergent term rewriting systems can be used for program transformation. This volume.

[Ganzinger and Giegrich 84] Ganzinger, H. and Giegrich, R. Attribute coupled grammars. *Proceedings of the ACM SIGPLAN Symposium on Compiler Construction. SIGPLAN Notices*, 19(6). June, 1984.

[Hughes 85a] Hughes, R.J.M. Lazy memo functions. *Conference on Functional Programming Languages and Computer Architecture*, Nancy, France. September, 1985.

[Hughes 85b] Hughes, R.J.M. Strictness detection on non-flat domains. This volume.

[Hughes 85c] Hughes, R.J.M. Why functional programming matters. Internal report, Programming Methodology Group, Chalmers Institute of Technology, Gothenburg, Sweden. 1985.

[Johnsson 84] Johnsson, T. Efficient compilation of lazy evaluation. *Proceedings of the ACM SIGPLAN Symposium on Compiler Construction. SIGPLAN Notices*, 19(6). June, 1984.

[Mont-Reynaud 76] Mont-Reynaud, B. Removing trivial assignments from programs. Stanford University, Dept. of Computer Science technical report STAN-CS-76-544. March, 1976.

[Peyton Jones 86] Peyton Jones, S. *Implementing Functional Languages by Graph Reduction*. To appear.

[Turner 85] Turner, D. Miranda: a lazy functional language with polymorphic types. *Conference on Functional Programming Languages and Computer Architecture*, Nancy, France. September, 1985.

[Wadler 81] Wadler, P.L. Applicative style programming, program transformation, and list operators. *Conference on Functional Programming Languages and Computer Architecture*, Portsmouth, New Hampshire. October, 1981.

[Wadler 84a] Wadler, P.L. Listlessness is better than laziness: lazy evaluation and garbage collection at compile-time. *ACM Symposium on Lisp and Functional Programming*, Austin, Texas. August, 1984.

[Wadler 84b] Wadler, P.L. Listlessness is Better than Laziness. Ph.D. Dissertation, Carnegie-Mellon University. August, 1984.

[Wadler 85a] Wadler, P.L. An introduction to Orwell. Internal report, Programming Research Group, Oxford University. 1985.

[Wadler 85b] Wadler, P.L. Strictness analysis on non-flat domains (by abstract interpretation over finite domains). To appear.

From Interpreter to Compiler: A Representational Derivation

Mitchell Wand
College of Computer Science
Northeastern University
360 Huntington Avenue 161 CN
Boston, MA 02115 USA

This material is based on work suppported by the National Science Foundation under grant number MCS 8303325. Part of this work was done while the author was at Brandeis University, Waltham, MA.

Author's address: College of Computer Science, Northeastern University, 360 Huntington Avenue, Boston, MA 02115 USA

Introduction

In a series of papers [Wand 82a,82b,83], we introduced the idea of *combinator-based compiling*. In this paradigm, we considered representations for the algebra of functions generated by the semantics of a programming language. The semantics induced a map from the language to the language of representations (the so-called "concrete semantics"). We showed that for a suitable representation language, one could always take the concrete semantics of a program and transform it (via equality-preserving transformations) into a representation which was formally equivalent to machine code for a relatively standard machine architecture. Although we and our students have been able to derive suitable combinators for most standard languages, this work has been criticized on the grounds that it requires excessive cleverness to design the combinators.

In this paper, we describe another approach to the design of semantic algebras. While it lies in the same class of techniques as our original combinator techniques, we believe it is more "user-friendly" and accessible than our previous work on the subject. We show how this technique can be used to derive an abstract machine architecture and a compiler for a simple applicative language which resembles Scheme. We show two versions of this development, one which is very straightforward and one in which some optimization has been done. The second version is very similar to an existing family of Scheme compilers [Clinger 84].

1. Discussion

For our purposes, we consider a compiler as consisting of a front end, which converts concrete syntax to abstract syntax, a middle end, which translates abstract syntax to code for some idealized machine, and a back end, which maps the registers of the idealized machine onto the resources of the target machine and generates real machine code. Our work is concerned entirely with the middle end of the compiler.

The key to the new technique is the representation of functions as data structures [Reynolds 72, Wand 80]. Reynolds represented only the continuation and environment functions, and thereby obtained an interpreter. On the other hand, by currying a standard interpreter, we obtain a large number of functions. If we represent *all* of these in a fairly straightforward way, we obtain a compact representation of the meaning of the original program which closely resembles the target code of a conventional compiler. The algorithm for interpreting these representations winds up looking like a register-transfer specification of a machine. The representations are far more intuitive than those used in our earlier papers. The use of continuations makes the resulting machine simpler, but otherwise is immaterial to the derivation.

We begin with the semantics for a simple applicative language which resembles Scheme. This semantics is of the form:

```
(define meaning
  (lambda (exp)
    (if (atom? exp)
        (lambda (env k) ...)
        ...)))
```

We then propose representations for the various functions (lambda (env k) ...) that arise. The primary cleverness in the representation is the introduction of a single operator (called *jsr) to represent sequencing in the interpreter. This replaces the infinite set of sequencing combinators D in our earlier work, and also eliminates the need (at least for this architecture) for the associative and distributive laws we used earlier.

Having decided on a set of representations, we can write a function meaning-rep, which produces the representations instead of the functions, and a function interpret-code, which interprets the representations. The former becomes the compiler and the second becomes the virtual machine.

The virtual machine is tail-recursive and uses only data structures, rather than functions, so it is at the same level as a conventional virtual machine definition. One can implement it using standard techniques: either as a byte-code interpreter in a more conventional programming language, such as Pascal or assembly language, or by translating the virtual machine code to native code on a specific target machine.

We have chosen to present the development in terms of a Scheme-based metalanguage, rather than in terms of "Oxford-style" denotational semantics. We have done so to emphasize the intuition behind the method. The foundation remains the same as in our previous work: by Currying and transforming the interpreter, we obtain some combinators; the virtual machine then simulates the reduction sequences of terms built from the combinators.

We will show two different versions of this development. Our first version is a naive compiler and machine. In the second version, we optimize the representations to eliminate superfluous stack manipulation across simple operations.

2. Choosing Representations for the Meaning of an Expression

The language we wish to compile is given by the following abstract syntax:

⟨exp⟩ ::= (&identifier ⟨identifier⟩) |
(&lambda (⟨identifier⟩*) ⟨exp⟩) |
(&application ⟨exp⟩ ⟨exp⟩*)

Thus, an expression consists of an identifier, an abstraction (possibly of more than one argument), or an application (of a function to a sequence of arguments), and the abstract syntax is represented as a variant record structure. We express the semantics of expressions as a function of one argument (the expression), which branches on the variant record and returns a function of the appropriate type. That is, the meaning of an expression is now itself a function of two arguments: an environment env and a continuation k. We express the branching in terms of a Scheme construct record-case, which branches on the tag of the variant record and binds the values of the other fields, in a way which we hope is apparent. We can now write down the semantics:

```
(define meaning
  (lambda (exp)
    (record-case exp
      [&identifier (ident)
        (lambda (env k) (k (env:lookup ident env)))]
      [&lambda (formals body)
         (lambda (env k)
           (k (lambda (actuals k1)
                ((meaning body)
                 (env:extend env formals actuals)
                 k1))))]
      [&application (fn-exp arg-exps)
        (meaning-of-application fn-exp arg-exps)])))
```

```
(define meaning-of-application
  (lambda (fn-exp arg-exps)
    (letrec
        ([loop
           (lambda (l)
             (if (null? l)
                 (lambda (env k ev)
                   ((meaning (fn-exp))
                    env
                    (lambda (fn) (fnrep:apply fn ev k))))
                 (lambda (env k ev)
                   ((meaning (car l))
                    env
                    (lambda (v)
                      ((loop (cdr l))
                       env
                       k
                       (cons v ev)))))))])
      (lambda (env k)
        ((loop (reverse arg-exps)) env k nil)))))

(define fnrep:apply (lambda (fn args k) (fn args k)))
```

This version of `meaning-of-application` is somewhat tricky. We have followed the practice of several Scheme compilers by evaluating the arguments from right to left instead of left to right, with the function position evaluated last. We could have evaluated left-to-right, but the resulting machine would be somewhat more complicated. The second trick in `meaning-of-application` is the curried `loop` with the ev-variable. Here the inner loop accumulates the results of the argument evaluations using the variable `ev`. The relation between this version and a more straightforward formulation of right-to-left evaluation can be proved easily by structural induction (in a manner analogous to that in [Wand 80]), but is omitted here for lack of space. The introduction of the ev variable in meaning-of-application leads to a simpler presentation and eventual architecture of our virtual machine than if we had stuck to the meaning-of-all approach we used in our earlier interpreters. See [Wand 82ab] for how this derivation proceeds without the ev-variable.

Our next step is to introduce representations for all of the inner lambda expressions in meaning and meaning-of-application. By doing this, we begin to build up a machine language for our virtual machine. We will need to represent two kinds of functions. The first kind of function is of the form (lambda (env k) ...). We call a representation of this kind a *code*. The second kind of function is of the form (lambda (env k ev) ...), which is the result of calling loop in meaning-of-application. We call a representation of this kind of function a *sequence*, short for *instruction sequence*. The aptness of this name will become apparent later.

In designing our representations, we will take advantage of the fact that our interpreter is syntax-directed by eliminating any expression of the form (meaning *exp*) in favor of its representation. Thus our representations will be self-contained and will not have arbitrary pieces of source code hidden in them.

From meaning we get:

```
(*fetch ident) = (lambda (env k)
                   (k (env:lookup ident env)))

(*close formals code) =
        (lambda (env k)
          (k
            (lambda (actuals k1)
              (code
                (env:extend env formals actuals)
                k1))))
```

Notice in the definition of *close how we replaced the call to (meaning body) by a code, as we suggested.

From the body of meaning-of-application we get:

```
(*clear-ev seq) = (lambda (env k) (seq env k nil))
```

It remains to choose a representation for the functions of three arguments which appear in the inner loop of meaning-of-application. Rather than represent these as variant records, we will represent them by lists of items, which we call *instructions*. We shall see how these items eventually correspond to traditional machine instructions. We represent instructions in the conventional variant-record style. For the moment, there are exactly two such functions to be represented:

```
((*evfn code))
```

```
    = (lambda (env k ev)
        (code env
          (lambda (fn)
            (fnrep:apply fn ev k))))

((*jsr code) . seq) = (lambda (env k ev)
                        (code env
                          (lambda (v)
                            (seq env k (cons v ev)))))
```

We shall see a bit later why we called the second instruction `jsr`. But we immediately notice that these two functions are suspiciously similar. Can they be unified? They can, if we introduce the sequence

```
((*ap)) = (lambda (env k ev) (fnrep:apply (car ev) (cdr ev) k))
```

Then we can show that `((*evfn code))` represents the same function as `((*jsr code) (*ap))`. To see this, we calculate:

```
((*jsr code) (*ap)) = (lambda (env k ev)
                        (code env (lambda (v) (((*ap)) env k (cons v ev)))))

                    = (lambda (env k ev)
                        (code env (lambda (v) (fnrep:apply v ev k))))

                    = ((*evfn code))
```

Given this fact, we will eliminate `*evfn`, and use `((*jsr code) (*ap))` as our representation of the base case in the inner loop.

Next we introduce representations for functions in the defined language. We proceed as we did in Chapter 4. The first representation replaces the inner `lambda` expression in `*close`; it provides a representation of closures. The second represents the meaning of a primitive function; we assume we already have some representation of the primitive functions.

```
(*closure code env formals)
    = (lambda (actuals k1)
        (code
          (env:extend env formals actuals)
          k1))

(*primop primop-rep)
```

```
    = (lambda (actuals k1)
          (apply-primop-rep primop-rep actuals k1))
```

To finish the job, we introduce representations for the continuations that arise. The first is a the initial continuation that only appears as the last frame in a *krep*, a continuation representation.

```
(*initk) = (lambda (v) v)

(*frame seq env ev k)
       = (lambda (v) (seq env k (cons v ev))))
```

To facilitate the building of frames, we use the function

```
(define make-frame
   (lambda (seq env ev k)
      (make-record '*frame seq env ev k)))
```

Now we can write a translator from expressions to the representations of their meanings. The result is essentially a compiler.

```
(define meaning-rep
   (lambda (exp)
      (record-case exp
         [&identifier (ident)
            (make-record '*fetch ident)]
         [&lambda (formals body)
            (make-record '*close formals (meaning-rep body))]
         [&application (fn-exp arg-exps)
            (application-rep fn-exp arg-exps)])))
```

```
(define application-rep
   (lambda (fn-exp arg-exps)
      (letrec
          ([loop
              (lambda (l)
                 (if (null? l)
                     (cons
                        (make-record '*jsr (meaning-rep fn-exp))
```

```
                    '((*ap)))
                  (cons
                    (make-record '*jsr (meaning-rep (car l)))
                    (loop (cdr l))))))])
          (make-record '*clear-ev
            (loop (reverse arg-exps))))))
```

Notice how the loop unwinds the meaning of the arguments into a sequence of *jsr's. We next observe that the two branches in the loop can be unified using the help function make-jsr, as follows:

```
(define make-jsr
  (lambda (exp seq)
    (cons
      (make-record '*jsr (meaning-rep exp))
      seq)))
```

This makes application-rep look like this:

```
(define application-rep
  (lambda (fn-exp arg-exps)
    (letrec
      ([loop
         (lambda (l)
           (if (null? l)
               (make-jsr fn-exp '((*ap)))
               (make-jsr (car l) (loop (cdr l)))))])
      (make-record '*clear-ev
        (loop (reverse arg-exps))))))
```

We now recognize loop as a familiar recursion on linear lists, which we can write with the list-recursion operator list-recur:

```
(define list-recur
  (lambda (seed fn)
    (lambda (l)
      (if (null? l)
          seed
          ((list-recur seed fn) (cdr l))))))
```

```
(define application-rep
  (lambda (fn-exp arg-exps)
     (make-record '*clear-ev
        ((list-recur
            (make-jsr fn-exp '((*ap)))
            make-jsr)
          (reverse arg-exps)))))
```

Before proceeding, let us look at some output from this compiler. The translation of (+ x y) is

```
(*clear-ev
   ((*jsr (*fetch y))
    (*jsr (*fetch x))
    (*jsr (*fetch +))
    (*ap)))
```

A more elaborate application, (cons (+ x y) z), becomes

```
(*clear-ev
 ((*jsr (*fetch z))
  (*jsr
   (*clear-ev
      ((*jsr (*fetch y))
       (*jsr (*fetch x))
       (*jsr (*fetch +))
       (*ap))))
  (*jsr (*fetch cons))
  (*ap)))
```

This code is somewhat cumbersome, but we shall see in Section 4 how we can modify the architecture in order to improve it.

3. Building the Virtual Machine.

In the combinator-based compiling paradigm, the job of the compiler was to produce a combinatory term which represented the semantics of the source code. The job of the machine was to simulate the reduction sequence of that code. These responsibilities remain unchanged. If we have a representations of some functions from A to B, then the job of the machine is to take a representation and an element of A and produce the correct element of B, namely, the result of applying the function which the representation represents. Since there are four kinds of representations—codes, sequences, kreps, and fnreps—we will have four functions, one to interpret each kind of representation. Since the underlying meaning function was tail-recursive, the interpretation functions will be tail-recursive also, and will therefore look like a virtual machine.

The operation of the machine is obtained directly from the meanings of each representation, and not from any other consideration. For example, let us consider the interpretation of codes. A code represents a function `(lambda (env k) ...)`, and a code is a variant record. Hence `interpret-code` will look like:

```
(define interpret-code
   (lambda (code env k)
      (record-case code
         ...
         )))
```

We decided that the code `(*fetch` *id*`)` represented

```
(lambda (env k) (krep:apply k (env:lookup id env)))
```

Hence `interpret-code` will have a branch

```
        [*fetch (id) (krep:apply k (env:lookup id env))]
```

and so on. We can now write the interpreter for our target code:

```
(define interpret-code
   (lambda (code env k)
      (record-case code
         [*fetch (id)
            (krep:apply k (env:lookup id env))]
         [*close (formals body)
            (krep:apply k
             (make-record '*closure body env formals))]
         [*clear-ev (seq)
          (interpret-seq seq env k nil)])))
```

```
(define interpret-seq
   (lambda (seq env k ev)
      (let ([ir (car seq)]
```

```
          [seq (cdr seq)])
    (record-case ir
       [*ap ()
        (fnrep:apply (car ev) (cdr ev) k)]
       [*jsr (code)
        (interpret-code code env
           (make-frame seq env ev k))]))))
```

```
(define fnrep:apply
   (lambda (fnrep actuals k1)
      (record-case fnrep
         [*closure (body env formals)
          (interpret-code body
             (env:extend env formals actuals)
             k1)]
         [*primop (primop-rep)
          (primop:apply primop-rep actuals k1)])))
```

```
(define krep:apply
   (lambda (krep v)
      (record-case krep
         [*initk () v]
         [*frame (seq env ev k)
          (interpret-seq seq env k (cons v ev))])))
```

We think of a sequence as a list of instructions. Hence, when we take the car of **seq** in **interpret-seq**, we call it the **ir** by analogy to the instruction register in a conventional machine.

We have a machine which is tail-recursive, uses data structures, and processes virtual machine code. We can turn this machine into a "real" machine in at least three different ways:

First, we can interpret the machine code, using some suitable language. If we already have a Scheme system, we can just use **interpret-code**. If we use a language like Pascal, or an implementation of Lisp which does not do tail recursion properly, we will have to do the tail-recursive-to-imperative transformation [McCarthy 62]. Furthermore, with Pascal we must build a storage manager to do **cons** and garbage collection.

Second, we can translate the virtual machine code to the machine language for another target machine. To do this, we decide how to represent each of our registers (**exp**, **env**, **k**, **ev**, and **v**) using the registers and memory of the target machine. For each virtual machine instruction, we then emit appropriate target-machine code to do the appropriate operations on these registers. This code can either be assembled in-line, or be threaded.

Third, we can build the virtual machine in hardware. It has essentially a conventional von Neumann architecture with some registers controlled by a finite-state controller. Since the memory is list-structured, rather than linear, we must build a more complicated memory controller than is customary.

4. Optimizing The Architecture

The machine we developed in the last section does more pushing and popping of the control stack than is necessary. In particular, when we do a `*jsr` before a `*fetch` or `*close`, we push the registers on the stack, we look up the identifier (or build the closure), and then we immediately do a `krep:apply` to pop the stack. We can get improved performance by combining these common sequences of actions into a single instruction. To do this, we first take a closer look at the instruction `*jsr` :

```
((*jsr code) . seq) =

        (lambda (env k ev)
           (code env
              (lambda (v)
                 (seq env k (cons v ev)))))
```

Considering the possibilities for `code`, we do an analysis for each of the `*fetch` and `*close` representations.

```
((*jsr (*fetch exp)) . seq)

     = ((*jsr (lambda (env k)
                   (k (env:lookup exp env))))
        . seq)

     = (lambda (env k ev)
          ((lambda (env k)
              (k (env:lookup exp env)))
           env
           (lambda (v) (seq env k (cons v ev)))))

     = (lambda (env k ev)
          ((lambda (v) (seq env k (cons v ev)))
           (env:lookup exp env))

     = (lambda (env k ev)
             (seq env k (cons (env:lookup exp env) ev)))
```

We represent this case by `((*push exp) . seq)`.

Similarly, for `*close` codes, we introduce

```
((*pushcl formals code) . seq)

        = ((*jsr (*close formals code)) . seq)

        = ((*jsr (lambda (env k)
                      (k (*closure code env formals))))
            . seq)

        = (lambda (env k ev)
             ((lambda (env v)
                 (k (*closure code env formals)))
              env
              (lambda (v) (seq env k (cons v ev)))))

        = (lambda (env k ev)
             ((lambda (v) (seq env k (cons v ev)))
              (*closure code env formals)))

        = (lambda (env k ev)
             (seq env k
                (cons
                   (*closure code env formals) ev)))
```

We now have *push and *pushcl as new machine instructions. To take advantage of them, we first rewrite make-jsr by doing a case analysis on the three kinds of code representations.

```
(define make-jsr
   (lambda (exp seq)
      (record-case exp
         [&identifier (ident)
            (cons
               (make-record '*jsr
                  (make-record '*fetch ident))
               seq)]
         [&lambda (formals body)
            (cons
               (make-record '*jsr
                  (make-record '*close formals (meaning-rep body)))
               seq)]
         [&application (fn-exp arg-exps)
            (cons
               (make-record '*jsr
                  (application-rep fn-exp arg-exps))
               seq)])))
```

We then replace the *jsr-*fetch and *jsr-*close sequences by *push and *pushcl:

```
(define make-jsr
   (lambda (exp seq)
      (record-case exp
         [&identifier (ident)
            (cons (make-record '*push ident)
                  seq)]
         [&lambda (formals body)
            (cons
               (make-record *pushcl
                  formals
                  (meaning-rep body))
               seq)]
         [&application (fn-exp arg-exps)
            (cons
               (make-record '*jsr
                  (application-rep fn-exp arg-exps))
               seq)])))
```

We now have two flavors of push and push-closure instructions in our machine. This might be acceptable in some circumstances, but one of our goals is to build a small machine, with as simple an architecture as possible. To do this, we seek to eliminate *fetch and *close by some code sequences involving *push and *pushcl.

To do this, we consider the following code fragment:

```
(*clear-ev ((*jsr code) (*restore)))
```

where (*restore) is defined as

```
(lambda (env k ev) (k (car ev))).
```

Then we have:

```
(*clear-ev ((*jsr code) (*restore))

      = (lambda (env k)
            (((*jsr code) (*restore)) env k nil))

      = (lambda (env k)
            ((lambda (env k ev)
                (code env
                   (lambda (v)
                      ((*restore) env k (cons v ev)))))
             env
             k
             nil))
```

```
= (lambda (env k)
    (code env
       (lambda (v)
          ((*restore) env k (cons v nil)))))

= (lambda (env k)
    (code env
       (lambda (v)
          ((lambda (env k ev) (k (car ev)))
           env
           k
           (cons v nil)))))

= (lambda (env k)
    (code env
       (lambda (v) (k v))))

= (lambda (env k) (code env k))

= code
```

We can now use this identity in the function `meaning-rep`, observing that:

```
(*fetch exp)

      = (*clear-ev ((*jsr (*fetch exp)) (*restore)))

      = (*clear-ev ((*push exp) (*restore)))
```

and

```
(*close formals code)

      = (*clear-ev ((*jsr (*close formals code))
                    (*restore)))

      = (*clear-ev ((*pushcl formals code) (*restore)))
```

We can therefore replace `(*fetch` *exp*`)` by `(*clear-ev ((*push` *exp*`) (*restore)))`, and similarly replace `(*close` *formals code*`)` by `(*clear-ev ((*pushcl` *formals code*`) (*restore)))`. This yields the following version of `meaning-rep`

```
(define meaning-rep
```

```
(lambda (exp)
   (record-case exp
      [&identifier (ident)
         (make-record '*clear-ev
            (cons (make-record '*push ident)
                  '(*restore)))]
      [&lambda (formals body)
         (make-record '*clear-ev
            (cons
               (make-record '*pushcl formals (meaning-rep body))
               '(*restore)))]
      [&application (fn-exp arg-exps)
         (application-rep fn-exp arg-exps)])))
```

Now we no longer need `*fetch` and `*close` at all!

Recapitulating, we have the following grammar for ⟨seq⟩'s:

⟨seq⟩ ::= (⟨instruction⟩ ...)
⟨instruction⟩ ::= (*ap) |
(*restore) |
(*push ⟨ident⟩) |
(*pushcl ⟨formals⟩ ⟨code⟩) |
(*jsr ⟨code⟩)
⟨code⟩ ::= (*clear-ev ⟨seq⟩)

Since there is only one production for ⟨code⟩, we need not represent the tag `*clear-ev` explicitly. Therefore we will continue our development using the concrete syntax

⟨code⟩ ::= ⟨seq⟩

This gives us a new version of the compiler, derived from the preceding one by eliminating `*clear-ev` from the representation:

```
(define meaning-rep
   (lambda (exp)
      (record-case exp
         [&identifier (ident)
            (cons (make-record '*push ident)
                  '(*restore))]
         [&lambda (formals body)
            (cons
               (make-record '*pushcl formals (meaning-rep body))
               '(*restore))]
```

```
      [&application (fn-exp arg-exps)
         (application-rep fn-exp arg-exps)])))
```

```
(define application-rep
   (lambda (fn-exp arg-exps)
      ((list-recur
          (make-jsr fn-exp '((*ap)))
          make-jsr)
       (reverse arg-exps))))
```

We can now show the code produced by our new compiler for the same examples we used before. For (+ x y), we get

```
((*push y) (*push x) (*push +) (*ap))
```

while for (cons (+ x y) z), we get

```
((*push z)
 (*jsr ((*push y)
        (*push x)
        (*push +)
        (*ap)))
 (*push cons)
 (*ap))
```

This is far better-looking code. In the conclusion we will discuss how this code can be improved even further.

We perform the same transformation on the machine itself. Since there is only one kind of code, the function interpret-code becomes:

```
(define interpret-code
   (lambda (code env k)
      (interpret-seq code env k nil)))
```

The function interpret-seq now contains lines for the new kinds of seq's: *restore, *push, and *pushcl. Since seq points at a list of instructions, we think of it as an abstract program counter, and interpret-seq takes its first element, the "current instruction", and dispatches on the "opcode". This is analogous to the fetch-execute cycle of a conventional machine. To reinforce it, we use ir as the name for the first element of the sequence, and pc as the name for the rest, just as a conventional machine is often said to advance the program counter before executing the instruction in the instruction register.

Nonetheless, the action it takes is determined just by taking the function which that opcode represents, as before. Since the representation of functions and continuations is unchanged, so are the functions `fnrep:apply` and `krep:apply`.

```
(define interpret-seq
   (lambda (seq env k ev)
      (let ([ir (car seq)]
            [pc (cdr seq)])
           (record-case ir
              [*ap ()
                   (fnrep:apply (car ev) (cdr ev) k)]
              [*restore ()
                 (krep:apply k (car ev))]
              [*push (id)
                     (interpret-seq pc env k
                        (cons (env:lookup id env) ev))]
              [*pushcl (formals code)
                 (interpret-seq pc env k
                    (cons
                       (make-record '*closure
                          formals code)
                       ev))]
              [*jsr (code)
                    (interpret-code code env
                       (make-frame pc env ev k))]
              ))))
```

```
(define fnrep:apply
   (lambda (fnrep actuals k)
      (record-case fnrep
         [*closure (code env formals)
          (interpret-code code
             (env:extend env formals actuals)
             k)]
         [*primop (primop-rep)
            (primop:apply primop-rep actuals k1)])))
```

```
(define krep:apply
   (lambda (krep v)
      (record-case krep
         [*initk () v]
```

```
          [*frame (seq env ev k)
           (interpret-seq seq env k (cons v ev))])))
```

Since we have observed that the krep (`*initk`) can only appear as the last frame in the k register. Thus, we can represent continuations as

$$\langle \text{krep} \rangle ::= () \mid (\langle \text{seq} \rangle\ \langle \text{env} \rangle\ \langle \text{ev} \rangle\ .\ \langle \text{krep} \rangle)$$

With this change, we rewrite `make-frame` and `krep:apply` as

```
(define make-frame
   (lambda (seq env ev k)
      (cons seq (cons env (cons ev k)))
```

```
(define krep:apply
   (lambda (krep v)
      (if (null? krep)
           v
           (match krep
              [((seq env ev) . k)
                (interpret-seq seq env k (cons v ev))]))))
```

or, unwinding the `match`, as

```
(define krep:apply
   (lambda (k v)
      (if (null? krep)
           v
           (let ([seq (car krep)]
                 [env (cadr krep)]
                 [ev (caddr krep)]
                 [k (cdddr krep)])
                (interpret-seq seq env k (cons v ev))))))
```

This completes the derivation of the machine. This machine resembles a conventional architecture far more than our earlier one did. It has a conventional fetch-execute architecture, with a single main dispatch state for decoding opcodes (`interpret-seq`). It has four main registers: `seq`, `env`, `k`, and `ev`.

5. Conclusions

We have presented a derivation of two combinator-based compilers in a new style, which uses far more "programming intuition" than our earlier presentations. We find this new style easier for our own use as well: we have been able to go farther in the derivation of architectures than we have before. In this new style we have been able to derive the replacement of lexical identifiers by (*chain-position, offset*) pairs (similar to what we did in [Wand 82b], but far simpler) and a treatment of stack discipline, including threading the static chain in the stack and using rewriteable locations in the stack. We hope to report on these elsewhere.

References

[Clinger 84]
Clinger, W. "The Scheme 311 Compiler: An Exercise in Denotational Semantics," *Conf. Rec. 1984 ACM Symposium on Lisp and Functional Programming* (August, 1984), 356–364.

[Reynolds 72]
Reynolds, J.C. "Definitional Interpreters for Higher-Order Programming Languages," *Proc. ACM Nat'l. Conf.* (1972), 717–740.

[McCarthy 62]
McCarthy, J. "Towards a Mathematical Science of Computation," *Information Processing 62* (Popplewell, ed.) Amsterdam:North Holland, 1962, 21–28.

[Wand 80]
Wand, M. "Continuation-Based Program Transformation Strategies," *J. ACM 27* (1980), 164–180.

[Wand 82a]
Wand, M. "Semantics-Directed Machine Architecture" *Conf. Rec. 9th ACM Symp. on Principles of Prog. Lang.* (1982), 234–241.

[Wand 82b]
Wand, M. "Deriving Target Code as a Representation of Continuation Semantics" *ACM Trans. on Prog. Lang. and Systems 4*, 3 (July, 1982) 496–517.

[Wand 83]
Wand, M. "Loops in Combinator-Based Compilers," *Conf. Rec. 10th ACM Symposium on Principles of Programming Languages* (1983), 190–196.

Vol. 167: International Symposium on Programming. Proceedings, 1984. Edited by C. Girault and M. Paul. VI, 262 pages. 1984.

Vol. 168: Methods and Tools for Computer Integrated Manufacturing. Edited by R. Dillmann and U. Rembold. XVI, 528 pages. 1984.

Vol. 169: Ch. Ronse, Feedback Shift Registers. II, 1–2, 145 pages. 1984.

Vol. 170: Seventh International Conference on Automated Deduction. Edited by R.E. Shostak. IV, 508 pages. 1984.

Vol. 171: Logic and Machines: Decision Problems and Complexity. Proceedings, 1983. Edited by E. Börger, G. Hasenjaeger and D. Rödding. VI, 456 pages. 1984.

Vol. 172: Automata, Languages and Programming. Proceedings, 1984. Edited by J. Paredaens. VIII, 527 pages. 1984.

Vol. 173: Semantics of Data Types. Proceedings, 1984. Edited by G. Kahn, D.B. MacQueen and G. Plotkin. VI, 391 pages. 1984.

Vol. 174: EUROSAM 84. Proceedings, 1984. Edited by J. Fitch. XI, 396 pages. 1984.

Vol. 175: A. Thayse, P-Functions and Boolean Matrix Factorization, VII, 248 pages. 1984.

Vol. 176: Mathematical Foundations of Computer Science 1984. Proceedings, 1984. Edited by M.P. Chytil and V. Koubek. XI, 581 pages. 1984.

Vol. 177: Programming Languages and Their Definition. Edited by C.B. Jones. XXXII, 254 pages. 1984.

Vol. 178: Readings on Cognitive Ergonomics – Mind and Computers. Proceedings, 1984. Edited by G.C. van der Veer, M.J. Tauber, T.R.G. Green and P. Gorny. VI, 269 pages. 1984.

Vol. 179: V. Pan, How to Multiply Matrices Faster. XI, 212 pages. 1984.

Vol. 180: Ada Software Tools Interfaces. Proceedings, 1983. Edited by P.J.L. Wallis. III, 164 pages. 1984.

Vol. 181: Foundations of Software Technology and Theoretical Computer Science. Proceedings, 1984. Edited by M. Joseph and R. Shyamasundar. VIII, 468 pages. 1984.

Vol. 182: STACS 85. 2nd Annual Symposium on Theoretical Aspects of Computer Science. Proceedings, 1985. Edited by K. Mehlhorn. VII, 374 pages. 1985.

Vol. 183: The Munich Project CIP. Volume I: The Wide Spectrum Language CIP-L. By the CIP Language Group. XI, 275 pages. 1985.

Vol. 184: Local Area Networks: An Advanced Course. Proceedings, 1983. Edited by D. Hutchison, J. Mariani and D. Shepherd. VIII, 497 pages. 1985.

Vol. 185: Mathematical Foundations of Software Development. Proceedings, 1985. Volume 1: Colloquium on Trees in Algebra and Programming (CAAP'85). Edited by H. Ehrig, C. Floyd, M. Nivat and J. Thatcher. XIV, 418 pages. 1985.

Vol. 186: Formal Methods and Software Development. Proceedings, 1985. Volume 2: Colloquium on Software Engineering (CSE). Edited by H. Ehrig, C. Floyd, M. Nivat and J. Thatcher. XIV, 455 pages. 1985.

Vol. 187: F.S. Chaghaghi, Time Series Package (TSPACK). III, 305 pages. 1985.

Vol. 188: Advances in Petri Nets 1984. Edited by G. Rozenberg with the cooperation of H. Genrich and G. Roucairol. VII, 467 pages. 1985.

Vol. 189: M.S. Sherman, Paragon. XI, 376 pages. 1985.

Vol. 190: M.W. Alford, J.P. Ansart, G. Hommel, L. Lamport, B. Liskov, G.P. Mullery and F.B. Schneider, Distributed Systems. Edited by M. Paul and H.J. Siegert. VI, 573 pages. 1985.

Vol. 191: H. Barringer, A Survey of Verification Techniques for Parallel Programs. VI, 115 pages. 1985.

Vol. 192: Automata on Infinite Words. Proceedings, 1984. Edited by M. Nivat and D. Perrin. V, 216 pages.1985.

Vol. 193: Logics of Programs. Proceedings, 1985. Edited by R. Parikh. VI, 424 pages. 1985.

Vol. 194: Automata, Languages and Programming. Proceedings, 1985. Edited by W. Brauer. IX, 520 pages. 1985.

Vol. 195: H.J. Stüttgen, A Hierarchical Associative Processing System. XII, 273 pages. 1985.

Vol. 196: Advances in Cryptology: Proceedings 1984. Edited by G. R. Blakley and D. Chaum. IX, 491 pages. 1985.

Vol. 197: Seminar on Concurrency. Proceedings, 1984. Edited by S.D. Brookes, A. W. Roscoe and G. Winskel. X, 523 pages. 1985.

Vol. 198: A. Businger, PORTAL Language Description. VIII, 186 pages. 1985.

Vol. 199: Fundamentals of Computation Theory. Proceedings, 1985. Edited by L. Budach. XII, 533 pages. 1985.

Vol. 200: J.L.A. van de Snepscheut, Trace Theory and VLSI Design. VI, 0–140 pages. 1985.

Vol. 201: Functional Programming Languages and Computer Architecture. Proceedings, 1985. Edited by J.-P. Jouannaud. VI, 413 pages. 1985.

Vol. 202: Rewriting Techniques and Applications. Edited by J.-P. Jouannaud. VI, 441 pages. 1985.

Vol. 203: EUROCAL '85. Proceedings Vol. 1, 1985. Edited by B. Buchberger. V, 233 pages. 1985.

Vol. 204: EUROCAL '85. Proceedings Vol. 2, 1985. Edited by B. F. Caviness. XVI, 650 pages. 1985.

Vol. 205: P. Klint, A Study in String Processing Languages. VIII, 165 pages. 1985.

Vol. 206: Foundations of Software Technology and Theoretical Computer Science. Proceedings, 1985. Edited by S.N. Maheshwari. IX, 522 pages. 1985.

Vol. 207: The Analysis of Concurrent Systems. Proceedings, 1983. Edited by B.T. Denvir, W.T. Harwood, M.I. Jackson and M.J. Wray. VII, 398 pages. 1985.

Vol. 208: Computation Theory. Proceedings, 1984. Edited by A. Skowron. VII, 397 pages. 1985.

Vol. 209: Advances in Cryptology. Proceedings, 1984. Edited by T. Beth, N. Cot and I. Ingemarsson. VII, 491 pages. 1985.

Vol. 210: STACS 86. Proceedings, 1986. Edited by B. Monien and G. Vidal-Naquet. IX, 368 pages. 1986.

Vol. 211: U. Schöning, Complexity and Structure. V, 99 pages. 1986.

Vol. 212: Interval Mathematics 1985. Proceedings, 1985. Edited by K. Nickel. VI, 227 pages. 1986.

Vol. 213: ESOP 86. Proceedings, 1986. Edited by B. Robinet and R. Wilhelm. VI, 374 pages. 1986.

Vol. 214: CAAP '86. 11th Colloquium on Trees in Algebra and Programming. Proceedings, 1986. Edited by P. Franchi-Zannettacci. VI, 306 pages. 1986.

Vol. 215: Mathematical Methods of Specification and Synthesis of Software Systems '85. Proceedings, 1985. Approx. 240 pages. 1986.

Vol. 216: Ch. Fernstrom, I. Kruzela, B. Svensson, LUCAS Associative Array Processor: Design, Programming and Application Studies. XII, 323 pages. 1986.

Vol. 217: Programs as Data Objects. Proceedings, 1985. Edited by H. Ganzinger and N.D. Jones. X, 324 pages. 1986.